"Peter Nye blends decades of research and interviews with more than a thousand cyclists into a fast-paced and engaging narrative that puts the 'story' into the history of American bicycle racing. The 'herstory' is here, too, with impressive coverage of women's racing throughout."

—Roger Gilles, author of *Women on the Move: The Forgotten Era of Women's Bicycle Racing*

"*Hearts of Lions* is not just a title but a perfect description of the determination and passion pulsating from these pages. Our love of bicycle racing is rooted in this lifetime labor of love from Peter Nye. Reading the first edition of this more than a quarter-century ago launched me into a life of cycling. This new version is like a tailwind pushing me home."

—Daniel Lee, author of *The Belgian Hammer: Forging Young Americans into Professional Cyclists*

"How can we know where we are going without knowing where we have been? This book tells it all and should be required reading for everyone in the sport."

—Connie Carpenter Phinney, 1984 Olympic gold medalist

"A sumptuously detailed account of American bicycle racing. . . . A loving tribute to those athletes who race bicycles for a living."

—*New York Times*

"With this book, cycling aficionados everywhere have been given back something that was lost."

—*Outside*

"Highly readable, even gripping. . . . Nye has brought back the long-forgotten heyday with its host of marvelous characters, and done it in a manner that will fascinate enthusiasts and beginners alike."

—*Toronto Globe and Mail*

"A significant contribution to American sports history."

—*Publishers Weekly*

"It is what any wonderful history book should be. Factual about its subject. Poetic about its heroes. And visual when it comes to the great battles that took place. Nye obviously loved writing it, and I loved reading it."

—Steve Tesich, Academy Award winner for Best Original Screenplay for *Breaking Away*

"A rousing, rollicking history. . . . A labor of love told with as fast a pace as a speeding cyclist."

—*Kirkus Review*

HEARTS of LIONS

HEARTS *of* LIONS

The **History** *of* **American Bicycle Racing**

SECOND EDITION

PETER JOFFRE NYE

Foreword by **ERIC HEIDEN**

University of Nebraska Press
LINCOLN

First edition published by W. W. Norton in 1988.

Library of Congress Cataloging-in-Publication Data
Names: Nye, Peter, 1947– author. |
University of Nebraska Press.
Title: Hearts of lions: the history of American bicycle racing /
Peter Joffre Nye; foreword by Eric Heiden.
Other titles: History of American bicycle racing
Description: Second Edition. | Lincoln: University of
Nebraska Press, 2020. | "First edition published 1988"—T.p.
verso. | Includes bibliographical references and index.
Identifiers: LCCN 2019032794
ISBN 9781496219312 (hardback)
ISBN 9781496221346 (mobi)
ISBN 9781496221339 (epub)
ISBN 9781496221353 (pdf)
Subjects: LCSH: Bicycle racing—United States. |
Cycling—United States.
Classification: LCC GV1049 .N84 2020
DDC 796.60973—dc23
LC record available at https://lccn.loc.gov/2019032794

Set in Minion Pro by Laura Buis.
Designed by R. Buchholz.

For Valerie—my first reader, first in my heart

If history were taught in the form of stories,
it would never be forgotten.

—RUDYARD KIPLING

The past is an inheritance, a gift and a burden. It can't be shirked. You carry it everywhere. There's nothing for it but to get to know it.

—JILL LEPORE, *These Truths*

CONTENTS

FOREWORD

ERIC HEIDEN

During the cycling season, racers are bombarded with all kinds of questions, from both the press and the public. The gamut of questions is infinite, but there are a couple that regularly pop up as people try to understand the character that makes a bicycle racer: Why did you become a cyclist rather than some other type of athlete? What's the motivating factor behind your athletic career?

The variety of responses to these types of questions is broad, but a common thread runs through each, and a person can gain much insight into the mind-set of a bicycle racer by understanding this common desire.

You see, bicycle racers—men and women—love living on the edge. They need to know the extremes of their physical limitations and often enjoy living beyond them.

How else could you explain the thrill a racer experiences flying down a narrow mountain road sandwiched within a pack of other racers? Racers constantly strive to go faster, to feel more wind on their faces. Occasionally on a descent a racer will see a friend miscalculate a corner and disappear into a cloud of dust. Never in any racer's mind are thoughts of what the consequences would be to have an accident at speeds of more than 60 mph. A racer *knows* there will be no mistake, no crash.

How else can you explain the excitement sensed by a racer sprinting for the finish line elbow-to-elbow with a worthy rival? Both racers feint and dart from one side of the street to the other while in a full-out sprint. They may touch wheels, but neither will hesitate or back off. Each believes that there is no one faster.

If there weren't this need to find the limits of personal physical ability, racers would never have any desire to compete in cycling's greatest race—the Tour de France. Even though the Tour is three weeks long, covering more than two thousand miles, a racer cannot wait for the chance. Every racer dreams of one day competing in the Tour de France and winning, because all racers believe—they *know*—that they have the ability.

To reach the top, an athlete must push in every training workout. In a sport that is considered one of the most physically demanding, a racer knows there are no shortcuts to success. A racer must live the dedicated life of a monk, or a nun, devoting most every waking hour of every day to the sport. Rain or shine, training and racing must go on. When I have something big to do, like a demanding training program, I set aside the time I need and get into a regular rhythm, day after day. So does my sister, Beth, who has won world championships in cycling and speed skating. This devotion and physical suffering binds cyclists together.

On their bicycles, racers love to push themselves to the limit. At times, they may go too far and have to pay the consequences, yet they will be greatly satisfied in having gained a greater understanding of their limitations. It is this go-for-broke attitude that many racers also live by off their bicycles.

Their escapades are often their legacies. Occasionally, cyclists will live as if there is no tomorrow, and this is how many of their stories begin. The tales of many of these characters become stranger than fiction over time. As the stories are passed from one generation to the next, from father to son, to daughter, to grandchildren, their subjects become larger than life.

It has long been assumed that bicycle racing originated in Europe, but in fact it is one of America's oldest spectator sports—older, even, than basketball. Racers like Greg LeMond and myself owe an enormous debt to the racers who came before us, because without their courage and determination the sport would have disappeared decades ago.

Hearts of Lions describes this country's remarkably rich cycling past. There were years when bicycle racing was such a popular spectator sport that it was rivaled only by baseball and horseracing. A black bicycle racer, Major Taylor, won the world professional championship in 1899 and may be considered the first black athlete to cross the color barrier in professional sports. Women cyclists have made important contributions, especially since the 1960s when they began leading American men in capturing medals at international competitions. Without these earlier bicycle racers who kept the sport going, sometimes through very lean years of poor financial support and failing public enthusiasm, the sport in the United States would probably not exist today.

Bicycle racing is reemerging as a popular spectator sport in this country. Stars like Greg LeMond received a good deal of media attention and, by virtue of their celebrity status, helped to restore glory to the racers who came before them. *Hearts of Lions* tells the history of the sport through the lives of the leading racers and promoters since the late nineteenth century. This book will help resurrect lost legends, rescue neglected championships, and revive the rich lore of American bicycle racing.

HEARTS of LIONS

ONE

The Golden Years

1

To the White House

Sic transit gloria mundi
(Thus passes away the glory of this world).

On a sun-splashed August morning in 1986 I was waiting on the White House grounds for the arrival of Greg LeMond. He was on his way for a private meeting with President Ronald Reagan. I was there to cover it for a magazine.

LeMond, from Carson City, Nevada, had just become the first non-European to win the world's grandest annual sporting event, the three-week Tour de France bicycle race, held since 1903. Every July this combined sports extravaganza and media lollapalooza sweeps more than two thousand miles around the country of France, approximately the size of Texas, with occasional jaunts into neighboring countries—it's as if the Super Bowl were to hit the road from one city or town to another for three weeks straight. His dramatic victory catapulted him to international stardom. The *Washington Post* rarely covered cycling yet suggested in a gracious editorial that LeMond was possibly "America's finest athlete."

President Reagan wanted to give his personal congratulations. Aides had been trying for a week to arrange a visit. The twenty-five-year-old cyclist's schedule was too busy and he canceled a July 30 appointment. At 5 p.m. on July 31, a White House press assistant told me that nothing was scheduled. At 9 a.m. the next day, a get-together was suddenly on for 10:45 a.m.

As I waited on the White House grounds, I thought back to an older man who had told me years earlier about two six-day bike racers, Fred Spencer and Bobby Walthour Jr., so popular that President Calvin Coolidge invited them to the White House to meet them. That older man was James Armando of Hartford, Connecticut, a member of the U.S. cycling team in the 1924 Paris Olympics. I was a teenager in the early 1960s when he approached me one steamy summer afternoon at a race program in Connecticut.

"Don't you *ever* go swimming," he admonished, stern as a drill sergeant to a feckless recruit, as though he had reached me barely in time to avert a disaster. "That water will make your muscles soft."

I immediately imagined my quadriceps turning to pulp in water. The prospect was terrifying.

Armando, in his sixties, stood scarcely five feet tall. He had a head of wavy iron-gray hair, a leathery face tanned to mahogany and shadowed by stubble. He pedaled a vintage three-speed bicycle, the frame's enamel faded and motley with scratches and chips, to watch races. He was a mason by trade, a union man. Years of heavy lifting on construction sites built up his back and shoulders. He had a disfigured right forearm, the result of a fall from his bicycle; he was outrageously self-reliant and strong enough to set the fractured bone with his other hand. He proudly said he spoke Esperanto, an auxiliary international language, which never acquired widespread acceptance. No matter how hot the summer sun burned, he wore a grubby long-sleeved shirt, sometimes a second one over the first, buttoned to the neck, collar turned up. He walked around gripping an orange as if he was afraid of dropping it while sucking, juice staining his chin.

After the pack of racers in the men's division whipped past in vibrant-colored jerseys like a comet on wheels, he loudly complained: "Riders today don't know what it is to really race. They're loafing. *Loafing!*"

My event, the prelim for boys sixteen and under, had already taken place. I watched the men's race with keen interest, seeing my heroes zoom by in a tight pack—backs curved low, legs pumping, tires hissing over the pavement. I was offended when Armando accused them of loafing.

After a while I started to tell my coach, Joe Tosi, what I thought of Armando. Tosi had a son and daughter a few years older than I was.

He served as the volunteer Connecticut state cycling representative granting amateur licenses and offering advice on training, equipment, and diet when people asked. In the Nutmeg State, his name was synonymous with bicycle racing.

"This Armando guy—" I began, but Tosi cut me short, his deep-set, dark eyes serious.

"It's *Mister* Armando to you, young man, and you listen to what he says. He was the best in his time. James Armando made the Olympic cycling team."

"But he says the riders today don't know what racing is," I argued. "He says they're loafing. Why, he's so crazy he told me not to go swimming because the water will make my muscles soft."

A smile crept over Tosi's lined face. "The business about the water and softening muscles is something they used to say when he was your age. They believed it then. That was when riders like Bobby Walthour Sr., Major Taylor, and Frank Kramer used to beat all the best competition in this country, when American riders were the best. Then they got on a boat and went to Europe to beat whoever was left over. They made big money in those days."

"What do you mean, *left over*?" I asked, incredulous at the prospect. "The best riders used to live here? I thought the best riders were in Europe—Italy, France, Belgium."

"That's right," Tosi said. "In James Armando's younger days the best riders in the world used to knock one another over the head to get to Newark to race. They came from all around the world. Newark was known as the home of cycling. If you were any good, you went to Newark to prove it."

"Newark, New Jersey?" My mind, nurtured on the irreverence of *Mad Magazine* and familiar only with that state's sooty industrial corridor, read satire into the license-plate motto: Garden State.

Tosi grinned and nodded, amused at my reaction.

"What happened?" I demanded. "Where did it all go?"

"Ah!" Tosi gasped, frowning and gesturing as though trying to grasp something elusive. "What happened? A lot happened! Like the Depression. A world war. But if you want to know more about riders like Bobby Walthour Sr., Major Taylor, and Frank Kramer, you ask James

Armando. He will tell you about how those guys got to be world champions. He knows all about them."

Weeks passed before I met up again with Mr. Armando at another weekend race. I asked about Walthour, Taylor, and Kramer. His coal-black eyes brightened. He talked nonstop of another era, of steeply banked wooden cycling tracks called velodromes, how cycling flourished in this country as a moneymaking spectator sport. With uncharacteristic animation, he told of round-the-clock six-day bicycle races—grueling endurance grinds with more than a dozen teams of two riders each, one teammate spinning around the oval while the other rested in a berth on the infield—in Madison Square Garden, the Circus Maximus of entertainment. Its annual sixes drew such high attendance that you could toss a penny from the balcony and the coin would never hit the floor.

When I asked him about Newark, he said it hosted the world championships (in 1912). Cycling was so popular that when the Newark Velodrome sold out of tickets, the overflow went to Wiedenmayer's Park to watch the Class A Newark Bears, a New York Yankees farm team, play baseball. Armando was letting me in on an open secret.

I went back to Tosi and told him what Armando had said. "Is there any truth to it?"

"Any truth?" Tosi repeated impatiently. "When James Armando talks to you about cycling history, everything he says is true."

"What about swimming and water making my muscles soft?"

"I said history, not hygiene," Tosi retorted playfully. "When I was young, I used to train with him. James Armando was the best in his day and I learned from him. He came into the sport a little late in life for an athlete, but he went straight to the top. He was past his prime when I trained with him in the late thirties and after I got out of the army at the end of World War II. He could push me to new, higher limits. In 1938 he'd pedaled back and forth across the country. On the way he set a national record for riding up Pikes Peak in Colorado. He beat the truck carrying a cameraman filming the ride.

"Training with James Armando made me a better rider. He taught me the most important thing a racer must have. He used to say that it's not special new equipment that just came in off the boat from France or Italy. And not some fancy training program that you can do in ten minutes a day."

Tosi thumped his chest with a fist. "The real equipment is *here*. If you're going to race, you've got to have the heart of a lion. That is what makes one racer different from another, what distinguishes a winner from all the others."

I left New England for college. The last time I visited Tosi, in 1973, he was a grandfather. He said Armando, the old Olympian, died and left his estate—including more than $200,000 cash stuffed into shoe boxes, crammed into clothes drawers, stored under his mattress—to fund bicycle races in Connecticut. Armando never married. His surviving brother and sister contested the will. Most of the money went to lawyers before his will was upheld.

Tosi was run over by a truck in July 1980 on a training ride and killed. I learned of his death weeks later from a friend who sent a *Hartford Courant* clipping to me, when I was living in Washington DC. The article reported that five thousand cyclists rode behind his hearse. That, too, seemed like an incredible story that Armando could have told. Yet I knew Tosi and was aware that people would turn out on short notice to make one last ride with him.

Armando was still fondly remembered in Washington DC by cycling's old guard. In the 1940s he used to pedal there from Hartford. The 350 miles between the cities took him a few days—often over dirt country roads. He'd parlayed his Olympian status and muscular build into paying gigs posing for sculptors at the Corcoran School of the Arts & Design in a Beaux Arts limestone building a few blocks from the White House. He roomed in a boarding house or, during shorter stays, slept in one of the stuffed chairs in the lounge of the Roger Smith Hotel at Eighteenth Street and Pennsylvania Avenue, near the Corcoran and one block from the White House. The old guard noted his aversion to water. They said his lips never touched water—only wine, although Tosi told me that after some rides together Armando walked into his kitchen, scooped up the cat's milk dish from the floor, and chug-a-lugged. Some bronze statuary enshrining men of history, swanning around on the banks of the Potomac, may have torsos modeled after his.

Stories Armando had told me came to mind as I strolled to the tall black gate next to the paper-white sentry hut of the White House, styled after southern plantation manses, at 1600 Pennsylvania Avenue. LeMond walked up with wife, Kathy, holding son Geoffrey, age two and a half, in her arms.

After I filed my story, I decided to find out how popular cycling was in America, why it faded, and how a U.S. rider could take over cycling's race of races.

2

The Fastest Things on Wheels

Gather ye rose-buds while ye may,
Old time is still a-flying:
And the same flower that smiles today,
Tomorrow will be dying.

—ROBERT HERRICK, *To the Virgins, to Make Much of Time*

When electricity, light bulbs, telephones, typewriters, and elevators were forever transforming how people lived, socialized, and worked in the late nineteenth century, bicycle riders were the fastest things on wheels. Charles M. Murphy proved it in an audacious way that rang wire-service bells in newsrooms from coast to coast announcing major news.

Murphy had first made his name racing in the 1890s on the Grand Circuit. This bike-racing circuit started in northeastern cities in May, migrated south down the Eastern Seaboard to Miami, then swung west to venues including Cleveland, Toledo, Chicago, Peoria, Indianapolis, Council Bluffs, Ottumwa, Des Moines, St. Louis, Cape Giradeau, Lincoln, Salt Lake City, and Denver before concluding around October in San Jose, San Francisco, and Los Angeles. Murphy joined other pros competing almost every day except Sunday or when rain bucketed down.

Sites varied—one day everyone raced on a dirt horse track, the next day around a concrete oval, the day after leaning through sloping turns on a wooden velodrome. Murphy traveled this national circuit on passenger trains rumbling over steel rails up to 40 mph to reach the next city, the next race. He beat the best talents of his generation to the line while negotiating different surfaces—the way tennis players today switch from playing on clay to asphalt to grass courts.

Short distances were his specialty, and he won national titles from one to five miles. Period accounts describe him as having sandy-colored hair, standing five feet seven, and weighing 140 pounds. He came from Brooklyn and his fame spread across the Atlantic. Paris promoters invited him with a hefty contract to board a ship and come for the 1896 season, and he could keep his winnings. By 1899, he had set seven world records and seventeen national marks.

Under a clear azure sky in mid-June 1899, he crouched on his bicycle and pedaled behind a train car over a smooth board surface carpenters had constructed between the tracks on a two-mile stretch of the Long Island Rail Road. In five attempts, he kept snug to the rear of the car pulled by a steam-powered locomotive going all-out to reach 60 mph. A collection of fifty timers, officials, and newspaper reporters—the penny press then constituting the media—witnessed the scene from the back platform or from inside the passenger car pacing Murphy. After his sixth attempt, covering one mile in just over sixty-four seconds, 55 mph, it was apparent he needed a more powerful locomotive.

America's seventy-five million population was less than one-quarter of today's and Murphy was one of some six hundred pro cyclists—more than triple the number registered today with USA Cycling and nearly the same total of contemporary Major League Baseball rosters during the regular season. Racers were so popular that tobacco companies inserted four-color souvenir cards of cyclists in cigarette packs for collecting, similar to youngsters today amassing baseball cards.

Murphy became fixed on the idea of cracking the mystical breakthrough of a mile a minute in 1894. He had been working out on a home trainer, a stationary treadmill similar to what cyclists and triathletes still use indoors during foul weather or outdoors to warm up before a big competition somewhere convenient to the start line. His home trainer had a cylindrical wooden roller holding the rear wheel of the bicycle and connecting to a device that measured the equivalent of the distance he would have traveled on a road. On his home trainer, he pedaled a mile in thirty-seven seconds, equivalent to 97 mph.

To a generation that relied on horses, such speed seemed astonishing. If a city had a speed limit, it was 10 mph, in deference to the horse-drawn vehicles that ruled the roads, as equines had for millennia. Racing cyclists like Murphy had noticed that riding behind another rider reduced wind resistance—common knowledge today but then not universally accepted. The cycling community accepted the benefit of riding in another person's slipstream. The most frequent cause of arguments after races came from competitors reprimanded for sitting back rather than going to the front. Yet nobody could explain the science.

Surely, Murphy liked to tell anyone who would listen, he could draft behind a train car pulled by a locomotive and keep up—even a mile a minute. "I immediately became the laughingstock of the world," he later recalled in a self-published monograph, *A Story of the Railroad and a Bicycle: When "A Mile a Minute" Was Born.*

Sixty miles an hour represented the same sort of irresistible challenge that the speed of sound later became to aviators. No automobile had yet driven a mile that fast. Car engines were low powered, tires were unreliable, and most roads were dirt and too bumpy with ruts and holes at even modest tempos. Murphy figured he needed a locomotive pulling a train car to pace behind to prove his theory of wind resistance and pedal a mile a minute. In attempting to sell his bold dream, he unsuccessfully petitioned one railroad company after another, which only increased his determination.

Finally, an official for the Long Island Rail Road saw the public relations value and agreed to provide Murphy what he needed. On a flat stretch of the Central Branch, a siding between Farmingdale and Babylon, a fleet of carpenters sawed and hammered a seamless 2.3-mile pine track laid down between the rails for Murphy to ride on, and fitted a hood over the back of the passenger car he was to draft behind as a wind shield. Skeptics scoffed that the speeding locomotive would create a suction that would pull him along. That theory was easily disproved: handkerchiefs, pieces of paper, even kites promptly fell when tossed behind speeding trains in test runs.

Murphy proved his point about being able to keep up with the locomotive when he completed his sixth ride and the steam engine was declared inadequate. Another date was set in nine days for a new attempt, behind a faster engine.

On June 30, the same gathering of officials assembled. Murphy, twenty-eight, never gave a thought to donning a helmet or gloves. He wore robin's egg–blue woolen tights covering his legs and a matching long-sleeved jersey, the colors of his sponsor's Tribune bicycle, made in Erie, Pennsylvania. His only safety measure to protect him from swirling dirt was to pull on goggles and a dust mask fashioned from cotton with a rubber respirator, which a journalist suggested made him look like a man from Mars. The passenger car Murphy paced behind had a protective crossbar covered in rubber and set high enough to let the front wheel pass under but low enough to block the head of the bicycle frame. He intended to keep his front wheel close to a three-inch-wide strip of white wood set at the back of the train car for him to follow like a compass.

At 5 p.m. he swung a leg over the top tube of his Tribune and commenced his historic ride. The bicycle used a gear of 104 inches, equivalent to wheels more than eight feet in diameter so that every turn of his pedals carried him much farther than normal.

Unlike his previous attempt, Murphy encountered an abrasive cloud of dirt and dust scratching his face and stinging his eyes. The head of his bike frame kept bumping against the rubber crossbar; he later complained he felt as if the boards were flying up from underneath and rapping against his wheels. He ignored these distractions and charged through the first quarter-mile, designated by an American flag on a pole mounted beside the track, in 15.2 seconds. Exuberant cheers from officials and news hounds gave him encouragement.

Just as Murphy got his pace under control, the ride was jeopardized. A well-meaning official at the rear of the train car yelled through a megaphone if anything was wrong. Murphy raised his head from the bent aero position he rode in, but before he could reply he slowed slightly and instantly dropped behind by fifty feet. He renewed his effort and began to regain the lost ground.

"It was a hot, fast, serious, life or death contract on my hands," he recounted. He spun past the half-mile marker in 29.4 seconds. The judges' earlier feelings of despair and frustration gave way to confidence.

At three-quarters of a mile, Murphy clocked 43.8 seconds. When he hurtled like a blue streak past the American flag beside the track, designating the finish, timing officials jammed their thumbs on stopwatches: 57.8 seconds.

He proved his theory of wind resistance. Before he could relax, the train engineer abruptly shut off the locomotive's steam, causing the train to slow sharply. Murphy smacked the bumper behind the car and slammed headfirst into the rear of the coach. Officials gathered there reached out nervously and pulled him aboard—bicycle and all. Seconds later, the train dashed over the end of the carpet of boards he had been riding on; he would have hit the railroad ties and suffered disaster.

Murphy's feat caused tremendous publicity. Newspapers around the country heralded his exploit. Men and women were said to have fainted upon hearing the news. The *New York Times* proclaimed that he "drove a bicycle a mile faster than any human being ever drove any kind of machine and proved that human muscle can, for a short distance at least, excel the best power of steam and steel and iron."

Headline coverage catapulted Murphy to a national hero. A theater promoter signed him to perform on the national vaudeville circuit to ride his Tribune against riders, all on home trainers set up on theater stages featuring an oversized dial and big arrows to inform the audience how far each cyclist was pedaling. The following year, he retired from sports to join the New York City Police Department. For the rest of his life, he was called Mile-a-Minute Murphy.

• • •

In Murphy's prime, cycling set off America's first national fad. The draw was that on a bicycle any man or woman without athletic ability whatsoever could pedal 10 mph or quicker—considerably faster and easier than they could walk. Prices ranged from forty to one hundred dollars, hardly an extravagant purchase for general urban consumers otherwise unable to afford owning and stabling a horse or dream of buying a pricey new-fangled "horseless carriage."

Men and women of all social classes took to the roads in ever-growing numbers as a bicycle-touring wave gripped the country. To meet the surging demand to improve the quality of roads threading through America's thirty-eight states, to promote cycling, and to establish guidelines for races, enthusiasts of the wheel sport incorporated the League of American Wheelmen on the weekend of Decoration Day (now called Memorial Day) of 1880. The place was Newport, Rhode Island, the Atlantic seaside Shangri-La of railroad barons, merchant tycoons, and heiresses.

The LAW inaugurated a national championship program on Decoration Day, creating a tradition before eleven territories—including North and South Dakota, Montana, Washington, and Arizona—gained statehood. By 1898 LAW membership topped one hundred thousand.

LAW members included oil industry magnate John D. Rockefeller and painter-sculptor Frederic Remington. Perhaps the most flamboyant wheelman was portly New York bon vivant and financier James "Diamond Jim" Brady. Brady caused a sensation when he gave the admired singer and actress Lillian Russell a gold-plated bicycle, its handlebars inlaid with mother-of-pearl, and with rubies, diamonds, and sapphires in the spokes and hubs. His gift came in a plush-lined leather case.

One of the biggest international boosters of cycling was Arthur Conan Doyle, the British medical doctor best remembered as author of the Sherlock Holmes stories. In the January 18, 1896, issue of *Scientific American* he prescribed, "When the spirits are low, when the day appears dark, when work becomes monotonous, when hope hardly seems worth having, just mount a bicycle and go out for a spin down the road, without thought on anything but the ride you are taking." His advice was heeded by vast numbers of people in this country, Great Britain, across Europe, and Australia.

Some of the sharpest mechanical minds were involved in the booming young industry. Charles and Frank Duryea were among more than three hundred U.S. bicycle manufacturers before they created America's first gas-powered automobile. So did Alexander Winton, builder of the country's first eight-cylinder engine. Albert Champion of Paris came to America to race under contract for a Boston bicycle manufacturer in the 1900 season. He invested his prize money to become a dashing tycoon in the wild new auto industry, leaving his initials in the General Motors division ACDelco and his name on a separate business, Champion Spark Plugs. In 2015 a bronze statute of him was unveiled in downtown Flint, Michigan, next to fellow European pro-cyclist-turned-auto-maker Louis Chevrolet.

Orville and Wilbur Wright operated a bike shop in Dayton, Ohio, and made their own bicycles before they invented the airplane. Glenn Curtiss raced bicycles he crafted and soon challenged the Wright brothers as aviation pioneers. Today their names are yoked in the Curtiss-Wright Corporation.

If the Duryeas, Winton, Champion, Chevrolet, the Wrights, and Curtiss shared any traits beyond simple mechanical talent, it might be that working with bicycles early in their careers taught them how to construct light and rigid frames as well as how to vary gear ratios to get maximum benefit from a particular level of power.

U.S. Census data indicates that America at the start of the twentieth century had 10 million bicycles, compared with 18 million horses and mules, and some 8,000 motorcars. One of the largest bicycle-making centers was a neighborhood in Chicago called Cycle Row. For nearly two miles along Jackson Boulevard, Cycle Row was lined with cycling-related stores and shops, most turning out bicycles with ready-made parts and fittings for shipment around the country.

It may be hard to realize today, but bicycle racing is one of the country's oldest sports. The first recorded competition took place in Boston's Beacon Park on May 24, 1878—two years after the National League of Professional Baseball Clubs was formed, three years after the first running of the Kentucky Derby, and thirteen years before basketball was invented. That first U.S. race, held over three miles on high wheelers, was won by Harvard University student C. A. Parker. Bicycle racing's approval escalated. By the mid-1890s, America boasted more than a hundred cities offering dirt, concrete, and wooden tracks.

The heroism of Charles Murphy reflected the public fascination with speed counting among the foremost factors drawing enormous crowds. It was not unusual for cycling programs, like the one in Springfield, Massachusetts, from Tuesdays to Thursdays to involve more than five hundred novices, open amateurs (age seventeen and older), and pros in events from the quarter-mile to twenty-five miles. Businesses closed so employees could take off the afternoon and go watch. Springfield's population in the 1880s and '90s was 35,000; attendance at the annual Diamond Jubilee sometimes topped 38,000. The dirt-and-clay track featured a grandstand for 4,000 with sixty private boxes, each seating eight spectators, on the eighty-feet-wide home stretch, and bleacher seats elsewhere.

Most cities supported cycling tracks. Indianapolis had two, including the Newby Oval, a quarter-miler built from matched and dressed white pine. It featured a telegraph office for sending race results worldwide and natural-gas lights for racing programs after dark. Up to 20,000 spectators passed through the fifteen turnstile entrances leading to the grandstand amphitheaters and bleachers. This account from the July 5, 1898, *Indianapolis News* indicates fans watched the races with gusto: "Nearly every man, as well as a few of the women, who took to the oval in the afternoon took a revolver and about a hundred rounds of blank cartridges. As each heat or final was finished, the riders, as they approached the tape, were greeted with a discharge of ammunition which resembled a volley of musketry."

• • •

About a hundred years earlier, a tinkerer in Germany discovered that two wheels joined by a board frame enabled a pedestrian to travel faster than on foot. In the 1860s, in Paris, French artisans fitted pedals to cranks attached to the front wheel for better transmission. And a decade later the English added an oversized front wheel to their "boneshaker" for greater speed. The big wheel, awkward looking today, was based on the leg inseam of the vehicle's owner; a considerably smaller rear wheel, about the size of a dinner plate, was added for balance. These two-wheelers were dubbed Penny Farthings, after the size contrasts of England's penny coin, which filled the palm of a hand, and the much smaller and lesser-valued farthing.

The front wheel functioned as the machine's only gear. Cyclists mounted the heavy steel frame from the rear and sat on a leather saddle set at shoulder height. These bicycles were not easily maneuvered. Worse, when the front wheel struck a hole, a rock, or a fallen branch, it would pitch the rider over the handlebars—a fall, called a "header"—often causing dislocated or broken collarbones.

High-wheel riders set impressive times, promising new possibilities. In 1886, George M. Hendee rode his machine on solid-rubber tires (preceding pneumatics) over a half-mile dirt track to a new world record for the mile in 2 minutes, 27.4 seconds. Hendee had been thrust into prominence in 1882 at age sixteen when he won the League of American Wheelmen national championship, the mile, that October in Boston as part of LAW's annual convention. For the next five years, Hendee, a gentleman amateur, dominated in all the popular distances up to twenty miles. He captured five consecutive national titles.

All this helped make Hendee a star in his hometown of Springfield, Massachusetts. In late summer when the city held its Diamond Jubilee, shop owners tacked up placards on door panels and shutters bearing the announcement "Gone to see Hendee ride." He grew up in an upper-middle-class Connecticut family whose modest fortune came from the silk trade. Hendee was bound for Yale until 1882 when he discovered the wheel sport and devoted himself full time to racing and traveling to meets. He became a public favorite: there were Hendee hats, Hendee suits, and Hendee cigars. Two weeks before the 1887 national championships, however, he fell while riding and broke his collarbone. He retired from the sport and went into business making bicycles, which he marketed under the name, Indian.

The 1890s brought more technical improvements and enabled faster speeds. Early in the decade pneumatic tires from Dublin, Ireland, invented by the Scottish veterinarian John Boyd Dunlop—another name linking early bicycling with today's automobiles—were imported. About the same time, high wheelers were supplanted by the modern safety bicycle, with a chain transmission, a diamond frame, and both wheels the same size. These cycles appealed to women and allowed riders to prevent falls by simply putting their feet to the ground. Wooden tracks with banked turns were introduced. Hendee's records disappeared as a new generation took over.

In the year Murphy shattered the one-minute barrier for the mile,

Henry Ford was an obscure mechanic in a small group that formed the Detroit Automobile Company. Ford soon left the enterprise to build racing cars. In early 1902, he received financial backing from Tom Cooper, a retired national professional cycling champion. Cooper was as intrigued with speed as Ford. They formed a partnership, the Cooper-Ford Racing Team: Cooper provided the capital and Ford designed a pair of racing cars in a shop in Detroit.

Cooper was part of the wave of pro cyclists who won substantial sums from races in this country and in France—where he also competed. He had quit a promising career as a registered pharmacist in Detroit to race the Grand Circuit. Bicycle manufacturers, as well as companies that manufactured saddles and tires, paid stars like him to ride their equipment and added lucrative bonuses for victories and setting new national records. A contract of $1,000 a year—double the average annual wage of a workingman—was not unusual for a top rider like Cooper. He rode Monarch Bicycles, made in Chicago; the name Monarch was inscribed across his jersey front and back.

In the late 1890s, Cooper emerged as a top rider renowned for his chain-lightning finishing kick against Eddie Bald, whose sprint was so fast he was called "the Cannon." Bald, a former bicycle messenger in Buffalo, became the first to win three national professional titles in a row, starting in 1895. A duel between Bald and Cooper delighted crowds eager to see who would win.

Cooper stood six feet, considered tall for the period, with handsome features that appealed to women. He was twenty-seven when the *New York Times* wrote in July 1901 that he was "arguably the richest racing cyclist in the world today. Not only has the Detroit representative some $30,000 worth of stock in the Detroit Telephone Company, but his cement business and various other enterprises, if sold, would probably net him $60,000, most of which has been won with the aid of his strong legs." Allowing for inflation, Cooper's portfolio today would be worth almost $3 million.

He admired Ford's mechanical ability. They built a racing car they dubbed 999 after a famous locomotive, which set so many records its name became a buzzword for speed. The Cooper-Ford 999 was cumbersome, with a ten-foot wheelbase, and it tipped the scale at three thousand pounds. Instead of a steering wheel, it was turned by a straight steel bar like bicycle handlebars with turned-up handgrips at each end. (Today the 999, a one-off prototype, sits on display in the Henry Ford museum complex in Dearborn, Michigan.)

Cooper's pal was Barney Oldfield, a fellow pro cyclist. Oldfield, born on a farm outside Toledo, Ohio, was five years Cooper's junior. They were the same height, but Oldfield had bigger bones, more muscle. Oldfield liked to say he lived for speed. He became an ardent booster of Cooper. They traveled together on trains jostling over the rails to cities around the Grand Circuit. After Cooper and Ford had made the 999, Cooper brought in Oldfield as chief mechanic.

Cooper, Oldfield, and Bald were part of a migration from bicycles to motor vehicles. Bald hung up his bicycle wheels in the early 1900s and jumped into car racing; afterward he opened one of the first auto dealerships in Pittsburgh. Arthur Newby quit his Newby Oval to cofound the Indianapolis Motor Speedway, America's first track dedicated to automobile racing and home to the Indianapolis 500. Former bicycle manufacturers who became synonymous with fast cars included brothers Fred and August Duesenberg—autos bearing their name won three Indy 500s and dozens of other major car races in the 1920s Jazz Age. George M. Hendee switched from producing bicycles to found the Indian Motocycle Company; for the first half-century, his motorcycles rivaled Harley-Davidsons in races and records.

The Cooper-Ford team's chief opponent was former Cleveland bicycle maker Alexander Winton. His Winton Motor Carriage Company was the first to sell regularly produced cars in the United States (the business subsequently became part of General Motors). He thought his racing car was so fast he dubbed it the Bullet. His Bullet lived up to its label and once was considered invincible.

Early automakers proved their quality in races. Winton's victories helped him capture the major market share of car sales. Not surprisingly, Cooper and Ford were eager to have their 999 beat Winton's Bullet in a five-mile race on October 25, 1902, at the mile-long Grosse Pointe Racetrack near Detroit, on the western shore of Lake St. Clair.

Cooper felt intimidated after driving the 999 around the track. The car had four massive cylinders, each the size of a small powder keg;

their combustion matched the deafening roar of Niagara Falls. Oldfield had never driven a car, but he knew how to compete. On race day, he pressed the accelerator to the floor from the start and kept his 999 running full throttle to beat Winton's Bullet and the two other cars. Ford took credit for designing the winning car.

Ford and Cooper had a falling out, resulting in Ford selling his interest in the 999 to Cooper. The next year Henry Ford formed the Ford Motor Company, which was to make cars available at prices the workingman could afford ($750 each in 1904) and thus have a profound effect on America and the world.

Oldfield and Cooper took the 999 by train to Indianapolis. On June 15, 1903, Oldfield revved up the 999's engine, combusting like cannons, on the Indianapolis State Fairgrounds horse track. He hunched over the car's steel handlebars and roared into automobile history when he zoomed through the mile in 59.6 seconds—making Oldfield the fastest driver in America around an elliptical track.

In August, he set another speed record in Indianapolis when he steered his 999 to a mile in 55.8 seconds, improving upon his national record and generating publicity that turned him into a national icon.

• • •

The year 1903 ushered in a new era of flight, and cyclists led the way. While Oldfield was setting speed records and winning car races, Orville and Wilbur Wright in Dayton, Ohio, manufactured bicycles in their shop under the brands of Van Cleve and St. Claire. The brothers invented a rear-wheel hub and coaster brake, which let the cyclist brake by pedaling backward.

The Wright Brothers became obsessed with the possibility of flying—the ultimate challenge. In their bike shop they created a wooden wind tunnel, six feet long and sixteen inches square, with a gas-combustion engine at one end to blow air through. They studied how to use air to keep a heavy machine aloft. Borrowing their sister's sewing machine, they stitched muslin together and stretched it over hickory sticks they glued together with Arnstein's Bicycle Cement. Their homemade apparatus had two pairs of wings and was powered by a twelve-horsepower gas-combustion engine that turned a propeller.

They transported their prototype aeroplane most of the way east by train and the final miles on a horse-drawn carriage to a remote area near Kitty Hawk, on the Outer Banks of North Carolina next to the Atlantic Ocean. On a chilly December 17, Orville crawled between the wings, laid prone, opened the throttle of the engine, and took off. For twelve seconds he was airborne and covered 120 feet over sand dunes. Hours later, Wilbur went up and covered 852 feet while staying aloft for fifty-nine seconds.

The Wrights became the fathers of aviation. They established more aviation records: the first to turn in an airplane (previous flights had been in a straight line), the first to fly a figure eight, and the first flight over a half hour.

Glenn Curtiss in upstate New York's Hammondsport followed their lead. He had progressed from producing bicycles named after the valiant Greek hero Hercules to making engines he built with hand tools for Hercules motorcycles. Encouraged by Alexander Graham Bell, inventor of the telephone, Curtiss customized an engine for an aeroplane he designed. On July 4, 1908, Curtiss won the *Scientific American* trophy as the first to fly one kilometer (five-eighths of a mile) in public before judges, reporters, and photographers.

He subsequently introduced five hundred inventions for aircraft design, particularly ailerons, or wing flaps, which strengthened wings and allowed the plane to turn. Curtiss built the first seaplane, taught navy officers to fly, and is celebrated today as the father of naval aviation.

Barney Oldfield turned into what the *New York Times* called "one of the greatest of the dusty daredevils of automobile racing." In March 1910 he drove a Blitzen Benz that thundered along a straight line on the flat, hard-packed sand of Daytona Beach to a new world speed record of 131.724 mph. He was depicted in newspapers and magazines clenching a cigar between his teeth—not to smoke it during the race but to use the rolled tobacco as a mouth guard while the car he was driving bounced and thumped over rough roads while he gripped the steering wheel. He felt like a beaten-up old man when he quit racing at age forty in 1918.

Oldfield cashed in on his fame by acting in plays and movies and earned a celebrity's income promoting auto safety. The *New York Times* said, "He was described as the greatest automobile driver that the world ever saw and the side of many a youngster's scooter was inscribed with the names of his famous cars."

An unending cascade of technology advancements caused dramatic changes in the way people lived, worked, and entertained. The effects of wind resistance became common knowledge after Murphy proved his theory behind a speeding train. Subsequent generations of cyclists may not have heard of Murphy, Cooper, or Oldfield, but they shared the same excitement of youth, wealth of talent, and hearts of lions.

3

Gentlemen Amateurs Turn Professional

A. A. Zimmerman . . . Holder of World's Title
Had Won More than 1,400 Races.
—*New York Times*, October 22, 1936

New stars like August Zimmerman, George Banker, and Major Taylor gained international fame. In 1893 Zimmerman won the first world cycling championship, in the track sprint, open only to amateurs. His turning pro inspired Banker to follow and become America's first professional world champion in the same discipline five years later. Taylor, an African American, won the world pro sprint championship in 1899 to become the first black athlete to capture a major title in pro sports—nine years before Jack Johnson defeated Tommy Burns for the world boxing heavyweight title, fifteen years before heavyweight champion Joe Louis was born, and nearly fifty years before Jackie Robinson integrated Major League Baseball.

Zimmerman traveled across not only the Atlantic but also the Pacific on steamships to become America's first international superstar. Part of his box office appeal came from the graceful way he pedaled to such high speeds. When Paris journalist Victor Breyer, a founding member of the sport's international governing body, the Union Cycliste Internationale, reminisced about his more than seventy-five years of observations, he cited Zimmerman as "the greatest pedaler of all time," regardless of nationality, specialty, or era.

Breyer quoted a French spectator who described Zimmerman's style in the heat of blasting for the finish "as if the man was mounted on rails, so complete is the absence of wobbling and the semblance of effort."

Zimmerman was trim, a well-proportioned five feet eleven. A native of Camden, New Jersey, he attended a military school where he won county running meets in the high jump, long jump, and the triptych hop, skip, and jump. He discovered cycling at the age of seventeen. "I liked it so well that I jumped in the game with all the spirit that was in me," he said.

He took up cycling in the mid-1880s on a high wheeler and turned into a top rider with a reputation for cool composure in fierce races. When the modern chain-drive bicycles were introduced after 1890, Zimmerman resisted parting with his high wheeler. But he realized he had to give in to advanced technology and switched machines to claim the 1891 half-mile LAW national championship, setting a world record of 29.5 seconds in the last quarter mile.

Early modern bicycles had longer wheelbases than today's descendants, and the steel handlebars fit straight into the head of the steel frame. Riders of his era sat upright, which favored Zimmerman. His sharp acceleration from a seated position came from spinning relatively small gears with fast cadence, up to 200 revolutions per minute—compared with the 70 to 110 rpm of cyclists in today's Tour de France. Reporters in his Garden State compared him to fleet-flying mosquitos, dubbing him the Jersey Skeeter.

He was reputed to have won forty-seven races in one week, probably including heats, from the quarter mile to twenty-five miles, and finished several seasons with a hundred or more victories—feats comparable to the 267 strikeouts in one season, or the four seasons with thirty or more victories each, pitched by the legendary Christy Mathewson of the New York Giants.

In 1912, Zimmerman lived in Asbury Park, New Jersey, and gave a *Newark Evening News* interviewer a glimpse of what the race schedule was like from 1887 to 1893. "The racing in those days extended over a greater part of the country. Nearly every state and county fair had bicycle racing as an attraction."

Most often, he continued, cyclists "rode principally on dirt tracks—trotting tracks—and we made a regular circuit, going from one city or town to another and riding practically every day. It was often the case that the riders after spending several hours on a train would be obliged to go immediately to the track where they were billed to appear, and without any warming up go out and ride. This happened day after day."

Men and women packed the grandstands and bleachers to cheer nail-biting finishes. Racers competed as fervently for collar buttons and cuff links as they did for pianos, deeds to houses, and parcels of land. The Springfield Diamond Jubilee in Massachusetts awarded diamond tiepins.

At the age of twenty-three, Zimmerman was approaching the height of his prowess. His father, known as T. A. Zimmerman, was a successful New Jersey realtor and a member of the New York Athletic Club, dedicated to amateur sports. The son rode for the NYAC and wore its trademark white winged foot on the front of his black jersey. Through the NYAC, he received an invitation from the British governing body of cycling to race in England for the 1892 season, with residence provided near the Herne Hill track in southeast London.

The request represented a high honor, as Great Britain prevailed as an international sports power. George Hendee and other U.S. riders had already ventured to England, but none had captured one of Britain's national titles.

Zimmerman complained that he disliked like the gray, damp English climate, yet he said he enjoyed the company of the English riders, and Herne Hill's red shale track with banked turns suited his talents. In July he defeated all-comers to claim Britain's national titles at one, five, and twenty-five miles.

The only event remaining in the program was the fifty-miler. Zimmerman caused a hullabaloo among spectators and officials when he announced he would enter it. He had no experience racing that far; the defending English distance star Frank Shorland was the overwhelming favorite. Nobody gave the American much of a chance. Zimmerman's victories thus far had scored few records. His preferred tactic was to tag along at the back of the pack of competitors and gauge his sprint late in the game to beat the competition—rather than the clock. He often spoke of how an athlete needed courage to match fitness as a prerequisite for racing. London's press corps observed that unlike many cyclists inclined to take rest days, the American diligently trained daily, often twice. His attitude toward clothing was casual, like riding with baggy shorts and socks collapsed around his ankles. He enjoyed cigars and whiskey with the guys, even on the night before a big meet.

During the fifty-mile title event, the brisk tempo set by Shorland and his rivals left dozens of challengers drifting behind, gasping and grimacing. Zimmerman bided his time and moved up in places until, after more than two hours of exertion, only he and Shorland remained in contention. They rode close together for the final miles. Around the last turn, Zimmerman uncorked his sprint to surge ahead—and complete his incredible sweep of British cycling titles.

Zimmerman's triumphs brought benefits that were both alluring and threatening to his career. The Raleigh Bicycle Company in Nottingham gave him two bicycles—and likely under-the-table money. The company distributed large posters depicting Zimmerman riding a Raleigh. A Leicester publisher asked him to write a book, *Points for Cyclists with Training*, one of the first on bicycle racing and training. The English press corps called him the Flying Yankee.

News dispatches of Zimmerman's success were cabled to America. Soon after capturing the British titles, he boarded a steamship and headed back to New Jersey. His arrival was eagerly awaited. When watchers in his hometown of Asbury Park sighted his ship cresting the horizon, cannons boomed from the shore, flags around the town were waved, and a horde of people came out to honor him. As he stepped ashore, he was seized by jubilant well-wishers. A procession formed to escort the cyclist to Ocean House, a large civic hall, where he was feted as guest of honor at a dinner.

Later that summer in Massachusetts, when basketball was played for the first time across town at Springfield College, Zimmerman capped his season by winning the Diamond Jubilee's big event, the mile. The *New York Times* reported his winnings included "twenty-nine bicycles, several horses and carriages, half a dozen pianos, a house and a lot, household furniture of all descriptions, and enough silver plates, medals and jewelry to stock a jewelry store."

• • •

By 1893 bicycling had turned into a craze sweeping the world as people sought affordable individual transportation. National governing bodies like the League of American Wheelmen flourished in Europe, Australia, and Canada. That spring, leaders of the various governing bodies formed the International Cycling Association (predecessor to today's Union Cycliste Internationale) to regulate the sport, particularly headliners like Zimmerman.

Officials in American and British cycling alike regarded money as vulgar for corrupting a gentlemanly pursuit of sport. Pros were barred from competing against amateurs—which comes from the Latin *amator*, meaning "love," as in playing without remuneration. Pros and amateurs were the water and oil of athletes.

Formation of the International Cycling Association coincided with the World's Columbian Exposition in Chicago, which opened that year, ostensibly to mark the four hundredth anniversary of Columbus's discovery of the New World, although that celebration took place the previous year. Nicknamed White City for the spectacular display of new electric lights sprawling over 690 acres in Jackson Park, the great fair introduced alternating current (AC) for electricity, the first zipper as a nifty gadget to replace buttons on clothes, and a huge Ferris wheel, designed after a bicycle wheel, which sat two thousand people. The exposition drew more than twenty-seven million people from forty-six countries.

Leaders of the International Cycling Association organized the first world cycling championships for member nations to send their best to battle on the track. Chicago was a natural choice. August was the month.

Zimmerman launched his season that spring by shipping back to England to defend his titles and tune up for the world championships. Traveling with him was Walter Sanger, a six-foot-three, two-hundred-pounder from Milwaukee. Sanger's brute strength occasionally beat Zimmerman in short races.

In England, the Flying Yankee was enthusiastically greeted by the public as a star. But British cycling officials accused him of violating amateur rules for accepting payment to author his training book and for being featured in the Raleigh advertisements. Officials forbade him from racing there.

Race organizers in Ireland and France cabled the American with invitations. Sanger was free to stay in England and compete but he accompanied his compatriot out of the country. Races in which the Flying Yankee appeared drew up to thirty thousand spectators. Both he and Sanger racked up victories.

Denunciations that British officials heaped on Zimmerman to justify their ban had no effect in the United States. Zimmerman, known for unaffected modesty, attracted a huge following among LAW officers. He remained eligible to compete in the inaugural world championships, open to amateur men, at distances of 1 mile, 10 miles, and 62.5 miles (100 kilometers). What few pros the sport had were dismissed as outliers by the LAW; some pros entered the championships to game the system and compete as amateurs.

The inaugural worlds took place August 7 to 12 on a dirt track built by the Chicago Pirates baseball club at its South Side Park. The club took one-third of the gross receipts. The revenue helped make up for a deep drop in attendance at games during the Depression of 1893, which saw more than fifteen thousand companies fail, almost six hundred banks fold, and the nation's unemployment hit 18 percent.

Zimmerman outclassed opponents, among them world champion speed skater and accomplished pro cyclist Johnny S. Johnson of Red Wing, Minnesota, whom he edged to take the one-mile sprint title. After a brief rest, Zimmerman captured the 10-kilometer (6.2-mile) world championship. He passed up the 100-kilometer (62.5-mile) championship, won by twenty-five-year-old Laurens Meintjes, lionized ever since in the Republic of South Africa as its first world champion in any sport.

• • •

The 1894 season opened with a group of pros passionate about abolishing two taboos permeating a range of American sports—one prohibiting Sunday competitions, the other forbidding cash prizes. Dozens of bicycle makers ignored the latter and hired riders anyway. One prominent manufacturer was Arthur Goodwill Spalding, a former Major

League Baseball player and cofounder of the National League. His A. G. Spalding & Brothers company made bicycles and hired Walter Sanger and two teammates. They climbed aboard trains snaking around the country to cities on the racing circuit. They appeared in stores selling his goods, and they wore jerseys with Spalding stitched large across the front.

Zimmerman couldn't resist turning pro with an offer from a theater agent in Paris promising an appearance fee of $10,000—worth $300,000 today—paid in gold, plus 30 percent of the gate, and any prizes he won. The agent created twenty-five major meets, each serving up $5,000 purses, including $1,000 to the winner. Raleigh had a distributorship in Paris and paid him at least $1,000 to ride their brand. Other promoters in Italy and Belgium created syndicates. Altogether Zimmerman could realize up to $30,000—worth nearly $1 million today.

A rough crossing of the Atlantic in March followed by foul weather in Paris put him off to an uncharacteristically slow start. In his first races, in Florence and Brussels, he lost to lesser riders. "Then the champion suddenly found his legs," Breyer wrote in his 1947 reminiscence, "and a campaign started which may well be termed as one of fireworks."

Most of his races were in Paris on the famous Vélodrome Buffalo, a 333-meter (365-yard) concrete oval built on the site where William "Buffalo Bill" Cody had entertained Parisians with his techniques for fighting Indians in the Plains States. Men and women dressed in their finest filled the grandstand on the finishing straight and the benches the rest of the way around.

In a legendary 1,000-meter (five-eighths of a mile) match race on the Buffalo track, the best of three races, Scottish rider R. A. Vogt and two Frenchmen, named André and Hermet (first names were not used in media of the day), promised to beat the Flying Yankee. To their chagrin, Zimmerman won the first match decisively. His opponents loudly vowed they would trounce him in the next match. Zimmerman, never prone to overstatement, reportedly told the announcer simply, "After the bell."

His opponents began the second race with an aggressive pace intended to take the snap out of his legs. Zimmerman seemed content to bring up the rear of the line they formed for two blistering laps. When the cowbell rang to announce the last lap, Vogt sprinted with a vengeance. Gaps opened between riders. Zimmerman bided his time at the back. As they rounded the final turn, his position looked hopeless. Then his legs spun faster. He went wide through the turn to take advantage of the banking as he accelerated, then sped up more, swooped down off the turn, and flew along the final straight like a homing pigeon. He flashed past the two Frenchmen and near the line overtook Vogt, the Scot, to claim two consecutive matches, much to the crowd's delight.

At another meet at the Vélodrome Buffalo, the promoter pitted Zimmerman in a legendary mile handicap against twenty-five of Europe's best. Zimmerman started behind everybody, on scratch. After the crack of the starter's pistol, he began catching competitors one by one until down the final backstretch he had passed half of them. Twenty thousand spectators leaped to their feet as he whipped off the final turn, his back bent low over his bicycle, and overtook the remaining dozen riders hammering their pedals for the finish.

"The deed created a formidable impression," Breyer said. "Even today, it is cited with admiration by those who lived long enough to bear witness to that stupendous exploit."

• • •

Zimmerman had gone to Paris accompanied by a cohort of adventurous compatriots looking to see the sights and compete for cash, including George Banker of Pittsburgh. The French governing body took a laissez-faire attitude toward awarding money, unlike the LAW and its counterpart in Britain disparaging money for corrupting the sport.

Banker and fellow Americans discovered the French theatrical approach to track races. On the Buffalo track, each race concluded with the winner being awarded a bouquet of flowers in a ceremony on the infield near the band performing for the audience. Winners clutched their bouquet on their victory lap and waved to the applauding audience.

George August Banker was born in Wooster, Ohio, and grew up in a middle-class household, the son of a carriage-maker father who moved the family to Pittsburgh when George, the youngest of six children, was eighteen in 1891. The elder Banker, William, quit making carriages to open a bike shop in Pittsburgh's East End. Young George began cycling with his brothers, Arthur and Alfred. They competed for the Pittsburgh Athletic Club. George was six feet tall, with long legs and became the fastest in the family. In 1893 he traveled twenty thousand miles on trains to twenty-five cities to compete up and down the East Coast and in the upper Midwest. The *Pittsburgh Press* reported that he won forty-seven races that year. He and brother Arthur pedaled a tandem in Augusta, Georgia, to pace Arthur Zimmerman to victory in the half-mile race in which "Zim" set a new national record. George's prizes included fifteen bicycles, ten solid-gold watches, and eight diamond rings.

He was still twenty years old in the spring of 1894 when he joined Zimmerman and six others on a ship to France. Sprinters dominated cycling as aristocrats on tracks filled with spectators eager to watch tactical savvy and athletes endowed with daring and speed. He and Zimmerman battled through heats against international sprinters to reach the final of one of the season's major contests on the Buffalo track, the Grand Prix de l'Union Vélocipédique de France. Before an audience that filled the grandstand to standing room only, the Americans scored a remarkable one-two finish, with Zimmerman triumphing.

The season concluded with the introduction of the Grand Prix de Paris, exclusively for pros, at the Vélodrome de l'Est. Banker had turned twenty-one in August. He wore his jersey with the Pittsburgh Athletic Club triangle on his chest and tied an American flag around his waist. He joined some forty top-speed merchants from around the Continent. A crowd of fifteen thousand spectators watched in the rain as Banker advanced through three-rider match qualifiers to reach the final against France's premier sprinters: Julien Delansorne and Paul Baras. Banker scored an upset victory, eclipsing Delansorne, ahead of Baras, later a famous pioneer racecar driver. Banker's Grand Prix de Paris triumph boosted him to star status, what the French called a *vedette*. He was hailed as the toast of Paris.

In the summer of 1895, Banker finished third in the Grand Prix de Paris. A week later he got revenge by winning the prestigious Grand Prix de l'Union Vélocipédique de France against the same two sprinters who defeated him the previous week. He boarded a train to Germany and competed on its track circuit. Banker went to the medieval city of Cologne for the worlds, which added a new category for professional sprinters.

The four-day Cologne program, organized by the International Cycling Association, took place in mid-August. It drew about a hundred amateurs and pros from a dozen nations, culminating in the pro sprint championship. Banker raced through knockout heats to reach the final. He faced Robert Protin, three-time national champion of Belgium, and the new Belgian champion, Émile Huet.

Protin, sporting a neat mustache, took the pole position, where his trainer held him up next to the official starter. Along Protin's flank, Banker and Huet were supported by their trainers. The starter, nervous with his responsibility, held the German flag on a stick. He raised the flag overhead. Silence descended on the stadium. The atmosphere grew tense, the air hot in the sun. The anxious official brought the start flag down in a chopping motion and accidentally poked the end of the stick in Protin's left eye.

Banker and Huet, looking straight ahead, missed what happened to Protin and fought a duel around the track, won by Banker. The American was ready to begin his victory lap when Protin, rubbing his teary eye, strenuously protested. Judges and trainers huddled to figure out what to do. Thousands in the stadium watched. Ultimately, the judges demanded that the riders run the race again. Angry, Banker refused. He felt he'd won fairly. Winning the worlds entitled him to higher appearance fees.

The judges scolded Banker and said he was not the world champion. That ignited a thunderous exchange back and forth between Protin, rubbing his smarting eye, his trainer loudly defending him, the fuming Banker and his trainer, and the gaggle of judges in their black morning coats and silk hats ganging up like angry crows against the American. The fracas resulted in the championship race being rerun in Paris four weeks later. Protin unleashed his frustration to beat a disheartened Banker, ahead of Huet. Banker yielded, however reluctantly, to accept second place. He vowed to stay in Europe and win the worlds.

Late that season Banker was racing in the South of France when he took ill with typhoid fever. News dispatches flashed around the Continent and reached the United States that he died in Nice. The reports proved erroneous as he recovered and resumed racing. He finished the season credited with winning sixty-one races, with sixteen second-places, and five thirds.

Over the next three years Banker traveled by trains and boats to race in eighty programs each season in cities across France, Italy, Germany, Spain, Switzerland, and Algeria. As a sprinter he also participated in handicaps and teamed up with other marquee riders for tandem racing.

Banker entered the 1898 world championships in Vienna, the capital of Austria, determined to finally win the professional sprint title. About midway through days of qualifying heats progressing to the finals, the city's calm was shattered by the assassination of Empress Elizabeth by a knife-wielding Italian anarchist. Her murder on a quiet afternoon, on a street in the center of Geneva, Switzerland, aroused outrage across Europe. In Vienna masses of men and women ran weeping into streets. Flags across the city hung at half-mast.

The city plunged into mourning. The worlds program was in jeopardy. A special train brought the Empress's body back to Vienna. After a delay of several days, the worlds program resumed. Banker defeated Franz Verheyen of Germany and France's national champion, Edmond Jacquelin, for the world pro sprint title. Banker couldn't get a train out of Vienna for a week.

He remained on the Continent for the 1899 season and won several grand prix events, including the Grand Prix de Bayonne in southwest France. He was presented with a bronze objet d'art called "The Peace." Late that year, Banker sailed back to America. He returned to Pittsburgh as a conquering world champion. He subsequently married a New Haven socialite.

Banker was credited with winning more than eighty grand prix events. He invested his prize money with brother Arthur to open one of Pittsburgh's early auto dealerships—the Banker Brothers Company. The brothers also founded the Banker Wind Shield Company, producing heavy plate-glass windshields in the era before tops were added. Their windshields were factory installed in luxury autos including Pierce-Arrow.

• • •

While Banker and Zimmerman were dazzling crowds in 1894 in Paris, fifteen-year-old Major Taylor in Indianapolis warmed up on the Capitol City Velodrome to challenge the mile record set by Walter Sanger. Any black rider going faster than white wheelmen risked severe backlash. Bylaws of the LAW prohibited blacks from joining in every state chapter but Massachusetts.

Taylor followed the track's rules under the guidance of his mentor, Louis Munger. A former world record holder, from twenty-five miles to twenty-four hours in the high-wheel era, Munger had retired to manufacture high-quality bicycles in Indianapolis. He arranged for the requisite three timekeepers and secured permission from track officials for his protégé's one-mile time trial—a muscle-burning, lung-bursting solo effort against the clock. Taylor was a scrawny five feet seven, and about 125 pounds. An arm-wrestling contest between him and the brawny Sanger would prove no contest whatsoever. Yet the bicycle was an equalizer: a shorter, lighter rider could pedal a smaller gear more rapidly and go faster.

When Taylor rocketed around the track, the timers at the finish line held stopwatches. As soon as his front wheel hit the line, timers clicked their watches off together. All three agreed: Taylor beat Sanger's time by an impressive seven seconds.

Instead of earning praise for his feat, Taylor was jeered by a big group of white riders, angry that a black cyclist usurped the record from a white man. Taylor was barred from competing on any track in Indianapolis.

Zimmerman was swaying in the belly of trains on his way to San Francisco in August 1894 to ship out to Australia with a contract for a season of racing Down Under. He stopped to visit Munger in Indianapolis.

Taylor, one of eight children of a coachman and a maid in service for a wealthy family, was employed as a valet by Munger, thirty-one and single. Before telephones were common, Taylor served as a company messenger. They rode together when schedules allowed, and Munger suggested basic training and racing tips. Taylor impressed Munger as having the right talent and attitude. Munger advised his protégé that if he trained rigorously and applied himself he could become the fastest bicycle rider in the world. This encouragement and guidance turned into Munger's legacy, outlasting all of the steel machines he produced.

Reports in newspapers of Zimmerman's visit to Indianapolis brought a throng of admirers to the train platform. A brass band played to welcome the international star. Munger dispatched Taylor to meet him. It is easy to imagine the rush of excitement Taylor must have felt. At the train station, everybody hoped to catch a glimpse of Zimmerman. Taylor stepped through the crowd and passed the band performing on the platform to hand Zimmerman a note of introduction. They climbed into a horse-drawn coach that took them to Munger's house.

• • •

Taylor was lured into racing by a publicity stunt. There were no secondary schools for African Americans in racially segregated Indianapolis and around age ten Taylor worked for the bicycle shop of Hay & Willits. His duties involved sweeping, dusting, and taking care of minor tasks from 9 a.m. until 4 p.m. Sometimes he donned a military-style uniform with brass buttons and stepped outside with a bicycle to perform exhibitions in front of the store. His fancy mounts, stunts, and dismounts—like kids on BMX bikes today—caught the attention of passersby, encouraging them to enter the store. His uniform and the precise way he executed lively drills earned him the nickname Major, which he used from then on in place of his given name, Marshall.

For several years, Hay & Willits hosted a ten-mile handicap race on Memorial Day. It was a festive affair and attracted more than a hundred regional riders. A band played energetic music near the starting line. Red, white, and blue bunting decorated homes and storefronts, and thousands of folks lined the dirt road to cheer. In 1892, thirteen-year-old Taylor went to watch. His employer, Tom Hay, told him he was entered with a fifteen-minute lead on the scratch riders, who had no handicaps and started last. Hay put the surprised youth on his bicycle and pushed him to the start line before Taylor could protest.

He could see that he was being made the butt of a joke. He was expected to line up with experienced riders, fall behind, and struggle in their dust for the amusement of onlookers. Frightened, he began to cry. But when Hay whispered in his ear that he could quit after he had gone down the road because nobody expected him to finish, Taylor choked back tears. No matter what it took, he made up his mind to go the distance to spite Hay.

What Taylor's skinny legs lacked in stamina he made up for in fierce determination. He bolted from the starter's gun. With his handicap lead, he gritted his teeth and endured the pain when his leg muscles burned. At the five-mile point, Hay approached on a bicycle toward him and dangled the gold medal that would be awarded to the winner. Hay shouted the medal was his if he kept his lead. Taylor knew he was being chased by white riders. He dug deep until at last he crossed the finish line in first place. As soon as he dismounted, he passed out and fell, a jumble of arms and legs on the dirt road. He woke to find the gold medal pinned on his shirtfront.

Taylor joined the city's black cycling club, See-Saw Circle, and started to distinguish himself. Meeting Zimmerman and listening to the way Zimmerman and Munger talked, their guest casually referring to his friend as "Birdie," after Munger's beaky nose; Taylor appreciated their deep yet casual friendship. They discussed faraway cities they knew from racing. Cycling champions had unusual travel opportunities. No doubt that fueled Taylor's ambitions. He remarked later in his autobiography, *The Fastest Bicycle Rider in the World*, that he was impressed with the way the two distinguished white men treated him as an equal. He made up his mind to become a champion himself.

After Zimmerman departed for Australia, Munger's mentoring of Taylor became a source of contention within management of his company. Munger moved in early 1895 to Worcester, Massachusetts, and took Taylor with him. Taylor joined the Albion Cycle Club, for African Americans. Northeastern riders were more liberal about blacks in competition.

Taylor developed as Munger predicted, and soon he was winning regional races. He had even features, a square jaw, and intelligent eyes. On his bicycle, he looked shorter than he actually was, because his legs were long, his torso short. He took advantage of his strong upper body and his access to Munger's machine tools to design a metal extension that fitted into the head of the steel diamond frame and put the handlebars several inches over the front wheel. This extension, standard today, let him ride with his back lower, more aerodynamic, than contemporaries.

As Taylor's muscles filled out, he rose up the amateur ranks and set his sights on turning pro. By 1896, pro racing in the United States entered its third season. The LAW reluctantly tolerated promoters offering money, in response to a new upstart, the National Cycling Association, dedicated to pro racing and Sunday programs.

While Taylor ascended, Zimmerman declined. He'd followed his Australian campaign by returning to Europe, although he no longer could live up to his reputation. Breyer speculated that Zimmerman no longer even tried. In his ninth season, he may have suffered burnout.

After Zimmerman's mediocre 1896 season in Europe, the French press compared the sharpness of his sprint in his prime years to the spring of a kangaroo, but he lost that asset. Yet his name still had cachet. Paris promoters invited *le grand Zim* back several more years to ride exhibitions.

By 1905, however, he felt it was time to watch races rather than suit up and participate. He returned to New Jersey with his wife and daughter. They settled in Point Pleasant, near Asbury Park. He invested his savings in a hotel and turned his attention to the hospitality business.

• • •

Taylor turned pro at eighteen to ride in the December 1896 six-day race, one of the last one-man grinds, in New York's Madison Square Garden, the famous Palace of Play. This grueling competition began precisely at one minute past midnight on Monday morning—in respect for the Sabbath—and went around-the-clock through to 10 p.m Saturday. It was an excruciating test of stamina, made worthwhile by a purse of $10,000 in gold double-eagle coins weighing sixteen pounds. Taylor joined twenty-seven accomplished riders from the United States, Canada, Denmark, Germany, Scotland, Wales, Ireland, and England.

The New York Six, raced around the banked board track, ten laps to the mile, went for 142 hours of nonstop competition. Each rider had a support crew to look after him, repair punctured tires and take care of other equipment, cook food, provide beverages, and keep his mind alert so he could keep circling the track. Entrants otherwise decided when to eat, sleep, and take care of personal business. Whoever pedaled the greatest number of laps would win.

Taylor, now eighteen and the youngest entrant, was better suited for short events. His impressive performance tells as much about his athletic ability as his character. He learned quickly and gained press attention. "The wonder of the race is 'Major' Taylor, the little colored boy who serves as a professional mascot for the South Brooklyn Wheelmen," the *New York Times* said.

Fighting monotony and debilitating fatigue, Taylor churned out 1,732 miles, the distance from New York to Houston, for eighth place among fifteen finishers. He won $125, plus $200 for capturing the half-mile sprint event that preceded the main event (his $325 prize money today would be worth about $10,000). The winner was Teddy Hale, promoted as an Irishman although he came from London. He won so much gold he had to put it in his hat and carry it away with both hands.

The Six proved to be a strenuous rite of passage into the pro ranks for Taylor. Experts warned the prolonged effort would dull his sprint. But when the 1897 season began in March, he showed he was as sharp as ever. His stamina had improved so he could hold up better against the other pros on the Grand Circuit.

• • •

Professional cycling appealed to entrepreneurs. At the vanguard of these promoters stood a fast-talking, creative impresario: William A. Brady. He grew up over a Bowery saloon with sawdust on the floor and became one of Broadway's most prosperous theatrical producers. In his youth he had acted on stages. Short in stature, he knew how to jut his chin out, jam his thumbs in his vest, and command attention. He developed an eye for spotting talent. For several years he had a winner in world heavyweight boxing champion James "Gentleman Jim" Corbett, until March 1897 when Bob Fitzsimmons pummeled Corbett with his fists for the title and knocked Brady out of a job.

Brady found a new prospect—not in the square boxing ring, but around cycling ovals in the person of Major Taylor. Brady became Taylor's manager. Brady also constructed a one-third-mile concrete oval in Brooklyn, the Manhattan Beach track. His events drew more than twenty thousand spectators. Brady offered audiences top names and all-out racing: the purses were as much as 50 percent of the gate. He also took over the December Sixes in Madison Square Garden—an imposing, lavish Moorish castle made of yellow brick and white Pompeian terra-cotta with a grand entrance off Madison Avenue.

Taylor's gunpowder sprint made him an attraction in meets at Manhattan Beach and around the Northeast. Like Zimmerman, he preferred to wind up his sprint from the back of the pack. When rivals boxed him in against the inside rail, he dropped back, went wide around everyone, then charged away—a difficult move to execute but he had the capacity to pull it off. The Fourth Estate coined nicknames for him: the Black Whirlwind, the Ebony Streak, the Flying Negro, and the Worcester Whirlwind; the name he said he liked best was the Black Zimmerman.

Taylor was earning as much as $850 a day, more than double what his coachman father, Gilbert, earned in a year. Brady also negotiated $1,000 bonuses for records that Taylor set. Brady, a gambler at heart and a battler by instinct, took advantage of racial prejudice and Taylor's prowess. Brady made $1,000 side bets, which paid off handsomely for him and Taylor.

When the outcome of a race, and its payoff, is determined by a margin sometimes as narrow as the thickness of a tire, tempers flare and fists fly. As the rare African American competing against whites, Taylor suffered abuse. One rider he defeated jumped off his bike, clamped his hands around Taylor's neck, and choked him until police broke up the attack. Officials ruled that both men should re-ride the race, but

Taylor was unable to do as a result of his injuries. The incident drew protests from many newspapers.

Some riders, like Eddie Bald, "drew the color line," as the expression went, and refused to ride against him. Judges at times gave Taylor second place—and less prize money, or none in a winner-take-all match—when he won by a wheel length. Worse, promoters in the South rejected his entries in the 1897 national circuit.

The following season got off to a tumultuous start when riders revolted over the issue of Sunday racing. Commercial interests in favor of Sunday sports—including baseball games—were gaining over traditionalists adamant about preserving Sunday as the Lord's Day. LAW officials opposed Sunday racing, only to find large numbers of riders and race promoters abandoning LAW for the fledgling National Cycling Association.

The issue hit Taylor personally. A devout Baptist, he carried a copy of the Bible in his traveling bag and read passages of scripture in his training quarters before a race. His religious beliefs were instilled by his mother, Sophronia. She strongly opposed her son riding a bicycle on Sunday. From the beginning of his career, she repeatedly asked him not to race on Sunday. He promised he would never race on Sunday—a vow that was to cause him difficulties when the NCA eclipsed the LAW.

Despite obstacles, Taylor kept improving. He was a big attraction on tracks from Manhattan Beach to Green Bay, from Boston to Peoria, from Asbury Park to Ottumwa, Iowa. Some folks attended to see him get beaten by white riders; others went to see how good he was. Newshounds described his style as smooth, with a compact body held in place by strong arms; his acceleration down the final stretch was so explosive that he transformed races in the final yards.

Race programs typically involved men's amateur and professional events, with distances often from the quarter mile to twenty-five miles. Promoters like Brady organized the next race soon after the last one ended to keep the action lively and spectators entertained. Bands on the infield, featuring as many as fifty musicians, performed jaunty tunes.

Taylor specialized in the match sprints, the purest form of competition, representing a confluence of speed and cunning, where two men competed against each other for a mile. Spectators like match racing for the early-race drama as riders poise on their bicycles, waiting to see who makes the first move. On banked board tracks, riders play cat-and-mouse up and down the shallow slope of the straights and steeper turns. The tactics, the maneuvers, the feints, serve as just the preliminaries for the final 200 yards. Racers shoot off the final turn and sprint over the final straight where the entire race comes down to who can accelerate most sharply, hit the fastest speed. Match sprints have long been the high point of the program. Taylor was winning his share of best-of-three match races, paying $500—worth nearly $20,000 today.

It wasn't long before he saved enough money to buy a seven-bedroom Victorian home in the fashionable Columbus Park section of Worcester. Despite a heavy race schedule, Taylor was an avid letter writer and kept in touch with his family in Indianapolis. When his sister, Gertrude, fell ill with tuberculosis, he moved her to Worcester and had her taken care of in his home.

Taylor must have felt confident he was ready to fulfill Munger's prediction that he would become the fastest bicycle racer in the world, a lionhearted prophecy. Blacks in American society were, as author Ralph Ellison later noted, invisible. When a black West Indian heavyweight boxer named Peter Jackson won Australia's championship and came to America as an obvious contender for the world heavyweight championship in the late 1880s, reigning champion John L. Sullivan refused to meet Jackson because he was black.

• • •

In 1899 Taylor seized a chance to go where no black athlete had yet gone. The world track cycling championships, after a round of European cities, went to Montreal. The Montreal worlds were held August 7–12 at the Queen's Park velodrome in the borough of Verdun. More than eighteen thousand fans filled the grandstand and bleachers; thousands more were turned away. Big white tents were pitched around the park for riders from Canada, the United States, Australia, Belgium, England, France, and Italy. Vibrant-colored silk streamers on the grandstand spires danced in the wind. Vendors hawked food and beverages. Bands blared merrily.

On opening day, twenty-year-old Taylor decisively won two heats in the half-mile race and advanced to the final. There he lined up against five others including Nat Butler of Cambridge, Massachusetts, and Charles McCarthy of St. Louis. From the crack of the starter's pistol the cyclists flew away, bunched together around the one-third-mile board track. Off the final turn, they fanned out shoulder-to-shoulder, heads down, legs churning.

The spectators jumped to their feet and yelled. All six finalists crossed the finish line so close the judges had to huddle for several minutes before reaching their decision: McCarthy first, followed by Taylor, then Butler. The press and spectators saw it differently—some claimed Butler had won, others insisted on Taylor. A riot broke out in the stands.

Differences of opinion, however, failed to influence the judges.

The next day saw the premier event, the mile. Taylor had to sharpen his wits. Twenty-one riders competed in five heats; only winners qualified for the final. Taylor clinched his quarterfinal and semifinal heats to vie for the title race against Canadian champion Angus McLeod, French champion Gaston Courbe d'Outrelon, who wrapped the French flag around his torso, and Nat Butler and his brother Tom, the reigning U.S. champion. With both Butlers in the final, the other three men worried the brothers would conspire against them.

For the first two laps, everyone rode aggressively, then eased at the beginning of the bell lap for a tactical race. Along the backstretch, McLeod attacked and opened a sizeable gap. The others chased like hounds after the hare.

"It was a beautiful sprint," said the *Montreal Star*. "McLeod was caught at the turn, and Tom Butler drove down for the finish at a great rate. Taylor caught him ten feet from the line, and just managed to hold out, while d'Outrelon made a close third."

Before the announcer picked up the megaphone, which was so long he gripped it in both hands, to deliver the judges' verdict, the *Star*, carried away with colors, noted, "The crowd, fearing that their dark-skinned, white-haired boy was going to get the worst of it, began to be a little demonstrative. The hold which Taylor has taken upon the sympathies of the people in the grandstand is something wonderful."

The announcer declared that Taylor won. The standing-room-only audience responded with boisterous approval.

"I never felt so proud to be an American before," Taylor wrote in his autobiography of the lap of honor he rode while the national anthem played.

He also captured the two-mile championship. He had risen to the top of cycling as Munger had forecast. He beat the best. He had conquered racial prejudice, though he had not set out to become a pioneer. Soon lucrative invitations came in telegrams inviting him to compete in Europe.

His manager, Brady, was also overseeing the new heavyweight boxing champion James J. "the Boilermaker" Jeffries, who had defeated Fitzsimmons in June to claim the title. Brady was inducted into the International Boxing Hall of Fame as the rare boxing manager of two world heavyweight champions; even more remarkable (and considerably less known) is that he also managed the world professional cycling champion.

Tradition held that the new pro and amateur champions would face one another for a match race. Taylor refused. He protested that amateurs were beneath the standard of pros.

• • •

As the twentieth century dawned, cycling as a sport and industry underwent profound changes. Sufficient numbers of LAW members opposed Sunday racing and voted that LAW withdraw from sanctioning competitions and concentrate instead on advocating for recreation activities. LAW officials signed papers that relinquished the sanctioning of races to the National Cycling Association.

LAW's membership plummeted, parallel to bicycle sales dropping as cycling's popularity fizzled in the manner of fads fading. Once-avid cyclists swapped two-wheelers for golf clubs, shifted to photography, or hit the roads driving new motorcars or motorcycles. Velodromes in Indianapolis and dozens of other cities closed. But the sport continued robustly in the Northeast, on the Eastern Seaboard, and in Chicago, St. Louis, Salt Lake City, and San Jose.

In early 1900 Taylor had his pick of offers as he continued to watch over his ill sister Gertrude. One particularly enticing invitation, from a consortium in Paris, guaranteed him a $10,000 contract to race in

France. As much as he wanted to follow in Zimmerman's wheel marks there, Taylor declined because the offer included Sunday races. He didn't ride on Sundays and refused to permit his mechanic to do any bike repairs on that day.

Iver Johnson's Arms & Cycle Works of Fitchburg, Massachusetts, signed Taylor up with a $1,000 annual contract to ride their bikes for the next two seasons. The company featured his photograph in advertisements. Taylor also rode in vaudeville home-trainer races on stationary treadmills against "Mile-a-Minute" Murphy before sold-out theaters.

Taylor's 1900 season got off to a slow start when his sister died in April. Around Memorial Day he resumed racing on tracks from Waltham, Massachusetts, to Washington DC, to Pittsburgh. His steady string of triumphs and good manners earned him respect. To the *New York Times* and other newspapers, he was no longer "the little colored boy," but "the colored champion."

His victories earned him a commanding lead in the season-long contest for the NCA national professional sprint championship. Taylor's greatest rival turned out to be nineteen-year-old Frank Kramer.

• • •

Kramer's introduction to cycling, like Taylor's, came by happenstance. When Kramer was in his early teens growing up in Evansville, Indiana, his parents worried that he might contract tuberculosis. They bought him a bicycle for exercise to improve his breathing. They reasoned that the air near the seacoast was more beneficial for his health than in southern Indiana and sent him east to New Jersey. He lived in the home of family friends in East Orange, near Newark.

In his first race, at age sixteen, he showed no sign of promise—he finished dead last. Yet he enjoyed cycling. He rode longer distances and tried to go faster. From a frail youth he grew to five feet eleven. He had a barrel chest and held himself as straight as a sword, which made him appear taller. He inherited the family's protruding chin, the source of his nickname, Chisel Chin. In 1898, at seventeen, he won the LAW national amateur title, and the NCA amateur title the next year.

Kramer shared the secret of his success to a reporter writing it down with a stubby pencil on his notebook: "I have worked, and worked hard. I did nothing else but try and try again. Each defeat that I got made me more determined to conquer until finally my determination became a part of me."

After a race program in Philadelphia, Kramer and Taylor met in the aisle of a swaying train car bound for Newark. Kramer proudly showed Taylor the trophy he'd won. Taylor grinned, reached into his suit trousers, and pulled out a fat roll of cash amounting to several hundred dollars. Dollar bills were longer and wider than today (the U.S. Treasury downsized the bills in 1929). Kramer later recalled that Taylor displayed a handful of dollar bills so large they could trip an elephant.

Taylor told him that he had what it took to ride pro.

In early 1900 Kramer took out a pro license.

In some respects, Kramer was single-minded to the point of eccentricity. He rarely fraternized with fellow riders and had few close friends. Marriage was not a consideration until after he retired at age forty-two. Nothing interfered with his regular habits, particularly sleep. Kramer was so punctual about going to bed every night at precisely 9 p.m. that the cop on the beat said he could set his watch when the light went out in his bedroom. His regular habits paid off, for he always had the vitality to win.

Kramer established himself as a contender early in his first pro season when he nipped defending national NCA champion Tom Cooper. The Pierce Cycle Company in Buffalo advertised their bikes with their trademark of a flinthead arrow going through the name Pierce, and the company signed Kramer to ride their machines at a salary of $40 a week (worth about $1,000 today).

On September 3, 1900, Kramer and Taylor faced one another in Newark for the NCA quarter-mile championship, capping the season-long series that counted toward determining who would score the most points to become national champion. Most fans put their money on Kramer, the White Hope.

Before a crowd of ten thousand spectators, the season's highest attendance, filling the Newark grandstand, cramming the surrounding bleachers, and standing on the infield, the two Hoosier hotshots faced one another for the best of three matches on the banked wooden velodrome, a lap and a half dash around the oval.

Taylor and Kramer stayed so close that there was no daylight between them. When they swooped down the banking of the last turn, spectators stood as one and shouted. Kramer led down the final straight. In the final yards, Taylor whipped off his rear wheel and zipped ahead for victory, a blistering thirty-three seconds flat.

The second match went the same way—Kramer leading down the final straight only to see Taylor pop around to beat him. "Taylor had hardly dismounted when the crowd swarmed over the track and onto the arena to pay homage to the wonderful colored cyclist," wrote Kramer's biographer Harry Mendel in *Motorcycle Illustrated.*

Taylor captured the NCA quarter-mile race, which clinched his national championship title based on a season-long series of sprints awarding points in the quarter-mile, one-third-mile, half-mile, and the one-mile races. He received another $500 roll of cash. Kramer went home empty-handed. "The final of this quarter-mile race was one of the most popular victories I ever won," Taylor wrote in his autobiography.

Reports of Taylor's national championship were transmitted across the Atlantic. Paris promoters cabled him again. This time, their offer for him to come and race for the 1901 season agreed to his stipulation: no Sunday races. That amounted to an enormous concession, for Sunday was prime time in Paris and cities around Europe. As an African American, Taylor was a novelty. As an athlete, he was a proven winner.

Paris journalist Breyer negotiated a $5,000 contract (worth $150,000 today) for Taylor, plus all expenses, and he could keep his winnings. That enticed him overseas to start the 1901 season. It turned into a profitable spring of racing in sixteen cities in Belgium, Denmark, France, Germany, Italy, and Switzerland. He won forty-two races over various distances against dozens of stars, including national champions Thorvald Ellegaard of Denmark, Willy Arend of Germany, Louis Grognia of Belgium, Tom Gascoyne of Britain, and Palmo Momo of Italy.

The tour culminated in Paris at the Parc des Princes velodrome in southwest Paris. Taylor was matched against the reigning world champion, Edmund Jacquelin, a swarthy Frenchman famous for lightning acceleration. Some thirty thousand people paid to see the two sprinters compete for the grand prize of $7,500, a huge amount and worth $220,000 today.

Taylor had studied Jacquelin's style on the Parc des Princes—named for generations of Bourbon princes who had hunted in the area when it was a forest. The track—constructed for tandem-paced racing, measured 666.66 meters, about 700 yards, one of the largest in Europe—would be used as the finish of the Tour de France from 1903. It featured a pink concrete surface in tribute to the stylish red high heels introduced by King Louis XIV. Taylor observed that Jacquelin launched his sprint off the final turn and upped his speed on the long finishing stretch to the line.

In their first match in the best-of-three series, Taylor timed his sprint off the final turn at the same time as Jacquelin. They both tore down the long straight in a drag race. The crowd went into a frenzy. Taylor won by four lengths.

The second match started twenty minutes later. "I worked in a bit of psychology after both of us had mounted and were strapped in," Taylor wrote. "I reached over and extended my hand to Jacquelin and he took it with a great show of surprise. Under the circumstances, he could not have refused to shake hands with me." Taylor wanted to show "Jacquelin that I was so positive that I could defeat him again that this was going to be the last heat."

So it was! After crossing the finish line, Taylor pulled a small silk American flag from his waistband and waved it as the two racers took advantage of their momentum to circle the track to boisterous adulation.

• • •

To American blacks, Taylor became a national figure. After he returned to Worcester in 1901, he courted a black socialite, Daisy Victoria Morris. The couple had met in October 1900 at a church social. Their courtship was noted with interest in the Negro press.

To Europeans, Taylor was an awe-inspiring athlete. Paris promoters Breyer and Robert Coquelle offered him another appearance fee of $5,000, again agreeing to no Sunday racing. Taylor and his fiancée married in March 1902. The newlyweds recognized that professional bicycle racing was a business, and four days after their marriage Taylor left his bride with relatives. He embarked alone on a second European racing excursion. He scored another forty victories against the best riders in Belgium, Denmark, France, and the Netherlands before sailing home in June.

Taylor became one of America's best-paid athletes, but he was just another Negro in a segregated society. Youthful resilience helped him endure harassment and humiliation. Nevertheless, the divide between blacks and whites left him often unable to check in to hotels near tracks where he was to compete. The same problem persisted in getting service in restaurants. As a result, he had to commute across town to the African American neighborhood and either stay in a hotel that catered to blacks or with a black family.

Taylor's most outspoken nemesis was Floyd MacFarland of San Jose, California. MacFarland, a year older, stood an imposing six foot four. He had dark hair, expressive deep-set eyes, and such long arms and legs that he sat on a bicycle like a gargoyle perched on a roofline. He drew international acclaim for winning the 1900 Madison Square Garden six-day in the modern two-rider team format created by William Brady; each team alternated with one partner pedaling around the track while the other ate, rested, or took care of personal business. The rule was that neither partner competed more than twelve hours a day. Mac and his partner covered 2,628 miles—the distance from Boise, Idaho, to New York City.

MacFarland, customarily convivial and charming, was a natural leader. Many men took their cues from him. Fans flocked to the track to see him in action, especially in handicap races. He started on scratch—behind everybody set ahead at intervals—and could almost always catch all of them and still win.

But MacFarland, as prejudiced as many other whites against blacks, harassed Taylor in the changing room. Taylor defended himself by pulling a Bible from his traveling bag to wave as he quoted scripture at him.

MacFarland's sprint lacked Taylor's punch, but he knew other tactics. MacFarland persuaded others to ride in concert to stymie Taylor's moves. The tall man knew how to taunt Taylor until the black champion's usually restrained behavior suddenly erupted in anger.

When the 1902 season wound down after Labor Day, Taylor turned twenty-four and contemplated retirement. His diary showed he had won $35,000 that season (worth more than $1 million today), making him the best-paid athlete in the nation. He'd set seven world records on top of his national and world championships. His idol, Zimmerman, had counseled retirement while "still at the top of the heap," if he could afford it, which Taylor could.

Sales of bikes, meanwhile, collapsed. A. G. Spalding and other retailers exited cycling. Taylor's mentor, Louis Munger, changed careers for the automobile business. (Munger made a fortune from inventing a removable car-wheel rim.) William Brady soon left sports altogether, after James J. Jeffries retired from boxing in 1905, and produced Broadway plays.

While Taylor contemplated retirement, he received a cable inviting him to compete for the winter in Australia for a $5,000 contract, full expenses for him and his wife, no Sunday racing, and lucrative prizes. Australia appealed to Taylor because Zimmerman had raced there. Taylor felt that his own career would not be complete without also racing Down Under.

4

John M. Chapman, Czar of Cycling

'Tis on Market Street away from all the cornfields
Mistress Mihlon draws the amber clear and cool,
Oftentimes I think I'd like to have a schooner,
And receive my lessons there in Nature's school.
There is not one thing that's missing in the picture,
Her smiling face makes everything complete,
And makes me long to see her in the doorway,
Or standing by the bar, her boys to greet.

—ANONYMOUS

When Brigham Young led his small band of Mormon pioneers into a flat river valley near Utah's Great Salt Lake in July 1847, he knew he had found what he was looking for. To the east were the peaks of the Wasatch Range, reaching 8,000 feet toward the sky. To the west, more mountains—the Oquirrh, topping out at almost 11,000 feet. On the northwest side of the valley stretched the Great Salt Lake. "This," Young said to his people, "is the place."

The Mormons laid out a town there in the valley, built a fort and houses, explored the valley and the mountains, irrigated the land, and planted crops. More Mormons moved into the area, and in three years there were five thousand of them. By 1868 the town was Salt Lake City, and the city became a mining center. As more settlers and more businesses came into the valley, so did railroads (the golden spike joining lines from the east and west was driven not far away at Promontory Point in 1869) and railroad builders. Young's brother-in-law, architect

Truman O. Angell, decided that the wonders of Utah needed a showcase. The one he built in downtown Salt Lake City became the fabulous resort known as the Salt Palace, which opened in 1899.

It was indeed a palace—a glistening pleasure dome composed of rock salt from the lakeshore. Slabs and blocks of salt provided the building materials for the structure. Salt-encrusted wood was used for exterior wall panels and molding. Salt was mixed with plaster for the wainscoting. The exterior lights were set in sparkling crystal-covered bells covering the palace towers. An electric star topped the dome. At night, the Salt Palace twinkled in the dark like an enormous jewel.

The interior of the dome was not salted, yet it was as spectacular as the rest of the Palace. Each of its sixteen panels was painted in iridescent colors to display the name of a western state. One was Utah, which had been a state for only three years when the Salt Palace opened.

Besides exhibits of Utah's copper, gold, zinc, and other mineral resources and displays of agricultural industry, the Salt Palace offered on the grounds an outdoor wooden velodrome one-sixth of a mile around, where races were held twice a week. Sellout crowds of five thousand were common; the ninety thousand people of Salt Lake City included a high proportion of fans.

Fifty years after Young and his followers arrived in the valley, Salt Lake City had become one of the stops on the bicycle racing circuit. For the riders, the city meant speed: its thin air at almost 4,400 feet let them ride faster. For the fans, speed records became expected. For the sport in general, Salt Lake City meant something more. For if it was *the* place for Young and his Mormon followers to found a city, it also turned out to be the place for one itinerant racer to learn the promoting business, which launched the sport into its golden era.

That racer was John M. Chapman, who became what the *New York Times* described as the "undisputed czar" of the sport. "More than any other man," the *Times* said, "he was responsible for the growth of the sport as a popular attraction in this country."

Today, among all the figures in American sports, Chapman is one of the most overlooked. In many ways, he was the quintessential Horatio Alger character—from a humble background he earned great fortune.

He was even born in a log cabin with a dirt floor, in College Park, just south of Atlanta. His father was celebrated throughout Georgia for the excellent brandy he distilled from peaches grown on his farm. In 1894, at the age of sixteen, young John bought a bicycle, which began his involvement in the sport that would be his life.

Two years later, he started racing in Atlanta. He showed promise in his first year, and the next year found him also competing on the Southern Circuit in Atlanta, Nashville, Memphis, and Chattanooga. By the end of the season, he was a regional star, with an income of $800—impressive at the time.

Chapman was good, but not in the same class as another Georgian—Bobby Walthour. They were the same age and competed against each other often. Walthour, a few inches taller than Chapman, was five feet eleven, and won so many races that newspaper accounts indicate he was as well known in Georgia as legendary Confederate general Robert E. Lee.

Walthour and Chapman competed on the track, and, as it turned out, in romance. Chapman fell in love with a petite redhead named Blanche Bailey. She accompanied him to races and cheered. Somewhere along the way she and Walthour met. In 1898 Walthour's competition with Chapman gained another dimension. On a soft summer night when the moon was full Bobby and Blanche eloped on a tandem bicycle.

The next day an Atlanta newspaper carried a picture of the couple riding their tandem, Cupid perched on the handlebars. Accompanying the artwork was a verse that went:

> He was a champion scorcher
> She was a lady true;
> They sped away at the close of the day
> On a bicycle built for two.

Walthour's descendants, and a number of contemporary newspaper accounts, say that the elopement inspired the popular song "Daisy, Daisy," sometimes known as "Bicycle Built for Two." It's a pleasant romantic notion, but records at the Library of Congress show the song was copyrighted in 1892, when Bobby was thirteen and Blanche ten.

The elopement caused a rift between Walthour and Chapman. Chapman left the South to compete on tracks from New York to Michigan to British Columbia, then to San Francisco. Finally, in 1899, he arrived in Salt Lake City, where he lived for most of the next eight years.

At the Salt Palace velodrome, Chapman had his best racing years. The local press dubbed him the Georgia Cyclone. Thistle Bicycles hired him to ride their brand with Thistle emblazoned across his jersey front. He befriended a Swedish immigrant named Iver Lawson, a tad under six feet—taller and twenty pounds heftier than Chapman. The Swede had a contract to ride Cleveland Bicycles. He was struggling to speak better English, and Chapman offered pointers. They traveled together to Australia to take advantage of races in the Southern Hemisphere's summer. In 1901 in Salt Lake City they teamed up and set the world tandem five-mile record of 9 minutes, 44 seconds, topping 30 mph; it stood for more than fifty years. The year-round schedule, however, overwhelmed Chapman. Midway through the 1902 season he retired.

Chapman accepted the job as manager of the Salt Palace velodrome. He knew how to set up race programs involving amateurs and pros, arrange merchandise for amateurs and purses to entice pros, and publicize events for spectators to buy tickets and watch. He became so confident that at the end of the 1903 season he left the Salt Palace and invested savings in another track in the Salt Air Amusement Park on the shore of the Great Salt Lake. The enterprise flopped in 1904, and Chapman went broke. Out of money and a job, he headed to Goldfield, Nevada, to look for gold. There he met another prospector, a former cowpuncher and marshal from the Lone Star State named George Lewis "Tex" Rickard.

Rickard—whose sharply defined nose and chin gave him the visage of a banker or Shakespearean actor—had already struck it rich in the Klondike gold rush in northwest Canada's Yukon Territory. With that money, he had set up a saloon and gambling hall that made him even richer, only to lose everything on a bad bet. He swung an axe as a lumberjack long enough to earn the funds he needed to open another saloon in Alaska, even more profitable than the first—until he lost that as well in worthless gold claims. Rickard had won and lost enough money to make Chapman's losses seem like small change.

The two became friends. Eventually they agreed the gold rush had ended. Rickard invested what cash he had left in another gambling house, the Northern Bar saloon and casino, in Goldfield; Chapman returned to Salt Lake City where he landed employment as manager of Hogel's Saloon. Another twelve years were to pass before the two prospectors met again at the other end of the country, to strike it rich at the top of American sports.

• • •

While Chapman was changing careers, his former rival Walthour was charging to the top of cycling. In 1899 when Chapman had arrived in Salt Lake City, Walthour and wife, Blanche, settled in Newark, a thriving metropolis. Walthour competed in many races that William Brady put on at Manhattan Beach. In December Brady helped promote the six-day in Madison Square Garden. The Northeast press embraced Georgia's Walthour as a darling and called him the Dixie Flyer. The *New York Times* later said, "Bobby Walthour was to bike racing what Babe Ruth was to baseball."

The Garden sixes had been held yearly since 1891. The Garden itself grew synonymous with sports and entertainment in New York City—from Annie Oakley shooting glass balls out of the air in Buffalo Bill's Wild West Show to circuses to beauty contests; and six-day bike races were among the attractions.

Critics complained that the sixes punished the body. In 1898 the New York State legislature passed a law forbidding any competitor to ride more than twelve hours a day. Fans feared the law would kill the event, but with a showman like Brady involved, opportunity beckoned. He introduced two-man teams, with each rider competing only twelve hours a day; like tag-team wrestlers, the teams could use their discretion on when each partner would race. This made sixes more exciting than ever and drew even bigger crowds. Two-rider team races have been known worldwide ever since as Madisons—and Madisons have become a medal event in the world championships and the Olympics.

In the 1901 New York Six, Walthour teamed with Archie McEachern of Toronto against fifteen other teams. After 142 hours of nonstop racing, Walthour and McEachern were tied with four other teams for the lead. They had covered 2,555 miles—the distance from Atlanta to

San Francisco. When the bell rang for the final lap, a tenth of a mile, Walthour surged ahead so sharply that only one other racer could stay with him. They shot into the final turn before Walthour blasted ahead to win and clinch the race for himself and McEachern, earning $4,000 in prize money, worth $125,000 today, plus product endorsements.

Reporters covering races consistently singled Walthour out in their dispatches. When he raced, everyone was assured of action. After the turn of the century motorcycles were introduced, and cyclists pedaled behind them for motor-pace racing, Walthour became the top motor-pace racer. In 1902 he won nearly every competitive motor-pace event, including the national championship, which he captured again the next year.

He found that by reversing the frame's front fork and using a smaller diameter front wheel he could lower his center of gravity to gain a better wind shield, pedaling 50 mph and faster, at a time when cities had speed limits of 10 mph on the streets. In a motor-pace event on the one-third-mile Charles River board oval in Cambridge, Massachusetts (on the grounds of what is now the MIT campus), Walthour set twenty-six world records in a thirty-mile race.

Motor-pace racing was glamorous but dangerous. Falls were common—bicycle tires tended to burst at speed, chains snapped, and engines suddenly conked out. Cyclists wore neither helmets nor gloves. They depended on fast reflexes, the rude health of youth, and luck. Despite having all three in his favor, Walthour collected an impressive (or dismaying) inventory of injuries over his career: twenty-eight fractures of the right collarbone, eighteen of the left, thirty-two broken ribs, and sixty stitches to his face and head. Once, according to family history, he was given up for dead in Paris and taken to a morgue, where he regained consciousness on the cold-steel slab.

Injuries are only one measure of how much Walthour put into his vocation. Victories are another. In December 1903 he teamed with Bennie Munroe of Memphis to win the New York Six. By then Paris race promoters Victor Breyer and Robert Coquelle wooed the Dixie Flyer with lucrative contracts. In the spring of 1904, Walthour shipped to Paris. He won sixteen out of seventeen motor-pace events—such an impressive record that the international star was put under another contract through the end of the season.

That led to his entering the 1904 worlds, now under the auspices of the Paris-based Union Cycliste Internationale. The championships took place late in the summer on the grounds of London's Crystal Palace, a Victorian architectural marvel made of glass and steel. Before an audience of fifteen thousand Walthour competed against a field of riders from nine countries in the 100-kilometer (62.5-mile) motor-pace championship. French national champion César Simar commanded the lead. Walthour caught him at forty miles, one hour later. They then dueled for a half-hour until the last miles when Walthour pulled ahead to win.

• • •

Other Americans at the 1904 worlds kept the Stars and Stripes flying. Iver Lawson, now a naturalized U.S. citizen, streaked through qualifier heats to face three-time defending world pro sprint champion Thorvald Ellegaard of Denmark and burly German champion Henri Mayer in the final. Ellegaard and Mayer were expecting cat-and-mouse tactics of balancing-act track stands and surging feints to force someone to lead. But when the start gun fired, Lawson took off like a thief fleeing the police around the quarter-mile track. He built a big lead before his opponents gave chase and crossed the finish line fifteen yards up on Ellegaard, with Mayer in third.

Marcus Hurley, a striking six feet tall crowned with a forest of red hair parted neatly down the middle, captured press attention in the amateur sprint championship. English journalists remarked he was a vegetarian, as though indicating an eating disorder. A New Yorker from New Rochelle and enrolled at Columbia University, he'd shipped to England after capturing his fourth straight U.S. amateur sprint title along with four gold medals and a bronze at the 1904 St. Louis Olympics. Although his Olympic successes are unrecognized by the International Olympic Committee for lack of foreign competition, his performance at the London worlds remains undisputed.

Twenty-year-old Hurley reached the final against Englishman Arthur Reed, the defending champion, and his countryman Jimmy Benyon.

Hurley, who wore a black jersey bearing the white Mercury logo of the New York Athletic Club across his chest and back, sprang off the start line. Reed caught and passed him, provoking applause from the home audience. At 300 yards to go, Hurley bounded ahead. Reed countered again to lead around the final turn. Up the straight, Hurley went wide and pulled alongside in the last five yards.

"The final effort landed the American an inch or two ahead on the winning line," wrote *American Bicyclist*. "Hurley was loudly cheered as he made a tour of the track, the band playing 'Yankee Doodle.'"

• • •

What is remarkable about Lawson's victory is that he had nearly lost the chance to qualify. In February he had been matched against Major Taylor in a two-mile race in Melbourne, Australia. Twenty thousand spectators watched Taylor fall heavily at a brisk clip on the back straight of the concrete track. He suffered multiple cuts and abrasions that put him in the hospital for two weeks. Lawson was charged with deliberately hooking Taylor's handlebars and knocking him down. A board of the League of Victorian Wheelmen found Lawson guilty of unfair riding and imposed a twelve-month, worldwide suspension.

Lawson immediately appealed to the Union Cycliste Internationale. He pleaded in his thick Swedish accent that the suspension would deprive him of his livelihood and jeopardize his contract with Cleveland Bicycles. He was desperate to attend the worlds. He'd grown frustrated after finishing second for three years to Frank Kramer in national championships and thought he could win the world title.

After another inquiry involving twenty witnesses, the Victorian Wheelmen board told Lawson they considered him guilty of careless riding, but reduced his punishment to three months, making him eligible for the London worlds seven months later.

• • •

Taylor had mixed feelings about his 1904 Australian tour. His wife, Daisy, gave birth to their only child in Sydney, a harbor city the couple loved so much they named their daughter Sydney. His Australian tour the previous year had been a great success—his diary showed he won more than $23,000 in four months (worth $700,000 today). But his 1904 Australia tour was spoiled by hectoring and interference from his nemesis, MacFarland. Taylor felt—with justification—that Mac enlisted others to team up together and ride against him.

The stress of prolonged international travel and intense competition ground away at Taylor's mind and body. Before leaving Australia in June 1904, he accepted another contract to compete in Europe, where he was planning to race in the London worlds. But he was increasingly distraught. His return to America was marred soon after disembarking the ship in San Francisco when he and his family were refused service in a restaurant. The contrast between his celebrity treatment abroad compared with being snubbed in his homeland left him upset.

Taylor returned to his house in Worcester, intending to take a brief vacation. Instead of resting, he suffered a nervous breakdown, forcing him to cancel his fourth annual European tour. French promoters Breyer and Coquelle, disappointed over missing out on their expected box-office bonanza, sued him for $10,000 for breach of contract. The National Cycling Association agreed with the French promoters and suspended Taylor for not fulfilling his contract.

When the track racing season culminated at the London worlds, Taylor called it quits. He was more interested in raising a baby kangaroo, a joey, which he had brought back from Australia as a pet for his daughter, Sydney.

• • •

Chapman seized another chance at race promotions in 1907 at the Salt Palace velodrome after management went through lean times and asked him back. His first act was to import talent. From his racing Down Under, he knew Jackie Clark, the Australian champion famous for his exceptional sprint. Chapman sent him an invitation plus expenses for first-class ship's passage across the Pacific, a three-week voyage, and train fare from the West Coast to Salt Lake City.

Clark lived in Shepparton North, Victoria, where nobody attracted notice for carrying a rifle as they strolled along the dirt streets. He was twenty-one, handsome, and dressed like a fashion plate. In Salt Lake City, he found the thin air to his liking and set a succession of premium world records—the quarter mile, half mile, and two-thirds of a mile. Clark loved women, and his carousing the nightclubs made good newspaper copy. He attracted the kind of attention that Chapman needed to fill the velodrome seats again.

Today we get a feeling for the atmosphere at the Salt Lake Palace races from John Held Jr., destined to become one of the best-known magazine illustrators of the 1920s. His stylish drawings graced the covers of F. Scott Fitzgerald's books in defining Jazz Age flappers in dresses and sheiks in tuxedos dancing the Charleston. Held grew up in Salt Lake City where races were a summertime fixture on Tuesday and Friday evenings. As the bandleader's son he lugged the large portmanteau holding concert sheets for the fifty-piece orchestra.

"The parts for a full band for an evening's concert in most cases weighed more than I did at the time, but my custodianship of the sheet music always admitted me to the races," Held wrote in his memoir, *The Most of John Held Jr.* "The 'Echo Quartet' was a feature of these concerts. Dad was also very fond of a composition called 'My Creole Sue,' and he would beat the living bejesus out of it on his cornet."

Clark, ballyhooed as the big draw, had gutsy competition from dozens of other pros. Former world champion Iver Lawson set world records on the Salt Palace track. A San Jose native named Hardy Downing, a veteran of tracks around the United States and Australia, won his share of races. A bearded Russian, Teddy Denesovitch, consistently placed well. News dispatches about the dramatic level of competition on the Salt Palace velodrome encouraged pros from the East and West Coasts to board trains for Salt Lake City.

After a year, Clark grew restless to see more of America. He wanted to take on Frank Kramer, who was burning up the competition in the Northeast.

Word of Kramer's top-end speed reached Europe. In 1905 Paris promoters Breyer and Coquelle, irritated with Taylor, enticed Kramer with a $10,000 appearance contract for a series of well-paid races. Kramer's French tour peaked at the Grand Prix de Paris, an event that rivaled the prestige of the worlds. First prize was $1,500—worth $45,000 today. Kramer faced two of France's most flamboyant sprinters: Gabriel Poulain, who would win the worlds later that summer in Antwerp, Belgium, and national champion Émile Friol.

Their contest was tactical all the way around the 666-meter Parc des Princes velodrome. They flew around the final turn in a tight formation—Kramer tucked behind Poulain as Friol sped furiously to burn Kramer's legs into submission. Up the finishing straight, Kramer swung wide as Poulain and Friol surged ahead shoulder to shoulder. Kramer on the outside drew even and pulled ahead to nip them by a half-wheel.

The crowd shouted boisterous approval.

Promoters Breyer and Coquelle invited Kramer back the next year, and he won another Grand Prix de Paris. Both European trips were great successes. His first trip abroad had resulted in a notable fourteen wins in twenty-three starts; his second trip concluded with seventeen wins in twenty races. He proved a great athlete, but never availed himself of the City of Light's famous nightclubs. The French public found him a bland Puritan.

Kramer was content to return home to New Jersey. After he had lost the national championship to Taylor in 1900, he claimed it in 1901 and defended the title each year after, as though he had a lock on the title. It was open to foreign challenges. That appealed to Jackie Clark.

• • •

In August 1908 Chapman left Salt Lake City with Clark for the Northeast. Clark promised to be the biggest threat in years to break Kramer's hold on the national championship. Clark and Kramer matches filled the grandstands and bleachers on tracks in Newark, New York, and Boston leading to the national championship on September 12 in the revered center of entertainment, Madison Square Garden. Chapman arranged a lively program of amateur and professional races, culminating in the professional national sprint championship—two matches, a half mile and the mile, between Kramer and Clark.

In the opening half-mile match, Clark jumped away early and gained a half-lap in the four-lap contest. The Aussie appeared to have stolen the race, which meant that a foreigner could tie Old Glory around his waistband for a year. But the race was still in progress. Kramer put his head down and chased. He and Clark circled the board saucer in a pursuit contest for a couple of laps. Then Kramer reeled in Clark with a lap remaining. Off the final turn, Kramer flew around his adversary's rear wheel and won by a bike length. In the mile contest, Kramer trailed until the last lap when, again, he swept outside and defeated Clark.

New York's fifteen daily newspapers informed readers how Kramer had fought off a foreign contender to claim his eighth straight national title.

Chapman visited Newark to check out its outdoor board track in the Vailsburg neighborhood, a regular stop on the Grand Circuit since 1895. The Newark Velodrome was only a few miles by trolley from the downtown hubbub. One afternoon on Market Street, near Broad, in central Newark, Chapman ambled into the Long Bar Saloon for a tall schooner of beer and a thick beef sandwich. They cost only a nickel.

The tavern boasted an elongated bar with a brass foot rail and a selection of brews on tap. Chapman rested an elbow on the polished hardwood slab. He could look around at electric lights hanging from the bare high ceiling. The entire wall facing the bar was festooned with ten-point buck antlers, moose heads, and other game harking back to Newark's rustic past now greeting patrons entering from Market Street. Here was an ideal man-cave, sawdust on the floor. Behind the bar stood Frank J. Mihlon, a crisp white apron tied high around his waist.

It was inevitable that Chapman and Mihlon struck up a conversation. Mihlon had grown up in the saloon business. He worked there with his widowed mother, the venerated Mistress Mihlon. He would have spotted Chapman as a stranger—someone to get to know. Over the years, Mihlon culled through the sluice of coins he handled in transactions and accrued a complete collection of Indian head pennies issued every year going back to 1859, Liberty Head Double Eagle twenty-dollar gold coins from the 1849 Gold Rush days, and a treasury of all coin denominations in between. He may not have attended events on the Newark Velodrome—he preferred shooting handguns in target practice.

Chapman respected Mihlon as an established businessman. A second velodrome had been built near the first one in Vailsburg. Chapman pitched a proposition. He suggested the network of railroads linking Northeast cities offered a franchise based in Newark and radiating like spokes in a wheel to tracks in New York, New Haven, Providence, Boston, Worcester, Springfield, and Philadelphia. Pros would have daily competition, and amateurs would compete in the preliminaries. Ticket sales would net Mihlon a percentage of each box office. After careful calculations, Mihlon agreed to put up the capital for a joint venture.

As manager of the Newark Velodrome and director of the 1909 franchise circuit, Chapman earned a salary of $50 a week—a comfortable wage. His races paid $50 to the winner, down to $5 for fifth place, and each meet served up two to four races for pros, plus merchandise purchased at discount from local businesses for amateurs. Pros earned a decent living when men's haircuts and movie admissions cost twenty-five cents and you could purchase a three-bedroom house for $2,000.

Among professional athletes, cyclists earned top dollar. Major League Baseball players were routinely underpaid by stingy team owners, setting the conditions for the notorious Chicago Black Sox scandal after Chicago White Sox players threw the 1919 World Series to the Cincinnati Reds for easy money. Professional football struggled as a raffish, underworld sport; basketball remained decades away from cash ranks; hockey still existed as a Canadian phenomenon; and boxing had the louche reputation of a red-light district.

Chapman explored other opportunities. He wintered in Europe and frequented indoor six-day races where he acquired contacts with foreign promoters and riders, many looking to come to America to join his circuit. They included a future world champion from Germany, Walter Rutt, and legendary Dane Thorvald Ellegaard, on his way to racking up six world titles.

Yet there were snags. Chapman had an austere manner and kept his distance from riders—they complained he tried to make them feel subservient. Photos show a stern-looking Chapman in a starched white shirt and collar, necktie fixed in place, button shoes, and rimless eyeglasses, peering imperiously at the camera lens. He was notoriously tightfisted with money and, except for rare instances, such as with Kramer and Clark, refused to pay appearance fees.

What kept riders loyal to him was his reputation for honesty. When each race ended, Chapman punctually handed over the envelopes containing all prize money as promised. His circuit increased in importance as fast-talking characters now and then appeared with happy talk about big money for their races only to vanish soon after the events began, the box office cleaned out to the last penny.

There is no denying that Chapman spotted talent. As he had done for Clark, Chapman paid expenses for Alf Goullet, an up-and-coming Aussie. Goullet was nineteen when he came to the United States in 1910. He went on to win more than four hundred pro races on three continents and set dozens of world records, from short bursts to grueling six-day races.

Chapman persuaded Mihlon to fund the construction of a third velodrome in Newark's Vailsburg district. This board track of six laps to the mile, like its predecessors, offered a larger, deeper grandstand and more bench seats to accommodate an audience of 12,500 instead of the previous 10,000 capacity. Its groundbreaking in early 1911 marked Newark's becoming known worldwide as the home of cycling.

• • •

Major Taylor in 1910 was winding down his career in Salt Lake City when fire destroyed the great Salt Palace on August 29—eleven years to the day after it had opened.

He'd settled out of court three years earlier with the Paris promoters after they agreed to drop the lawsuit in exchange for his return to Europe, including the stipulation that he participate in Sunday events. Taylor protested, but the balance of power had shifted. Robert Coquelle had traveled to Worcester from Paris to get Taylor to sign a new contract, and Coquelle held the upper hand. Taylor wanted to get back to competition to support his wife and daughter. The personal price he had to pay was racing on Sundays.

Taylor had gained forty pounds, and the extra weight showed. He trained diligently, trimmed down. And once he got his racing legs and lungs back, he beat all the crack sprinters of Europe, except for France's world champion Edmond Jacquelin, who beat him early in the summer. Jacquelin then sacrificed fitness in wine-flowing cabarets with admiring women. His speed on the bicycle declined. He was getting trounced by lesser talents. When offered a revenge match against Jacquelin, Taylor declined out of respect.

At the close of his 1907 European tour, Taylor had announced his retirement. It could be that he fully intended to hang up his wheels. He'd always wanted to go out as a champion the way Zimmerman had advised. Two main factors, however, influenced the proud Taylor to change his mind and accept the many offers coming his way. One was his growing resentment at the widely held perception of black inferiority, a view that he did everything he could to dispel. The other was the responsibility he felt toward his wife and daughter. Offers from Breyer and Coquelle kept him returning to race in Europe. But his last trip, in 1909, was so disappointing to the thirty-year-old Taylor, consistently beaten by inferior men, that he regretted ever going.

He might have retired then, too, except that in America's highly charged racial climate he didn't want to appear to back down. Black boxer Jack Johnson defeated Canadian Tommy Burns in 1908 for the world heavyweight championship, which prompted the white public nationwide uproar for a "great white hope" to regain the title.

Tex Rickard, choosing another way to prospect for gold, promoted a fight between Johnson and James J. Jeffries. Jeffries, overweight and out of shape, came out of retirement as the highly touted Great White Hope. Rickard built a special arena in Reno and refereed the fight on July 4, 1910. Johnson won with a knockout. The outcome bitterly disappointed whites around the country while African Americans were euphoric. Large-scale race riots broke out in Los Angeles, Kansas City, Washington DC, Norfolk, and Jacksonville.

When Taylor returned from Europe for the final time, he decided to race one last season in America "with those dirty sandbaggers," as he wrote in a letter to his wife, describing those who let his nemesis Floyd MacFarland influence them at his expense. In August 1910 Taylor competed at the Salt Palace velodrome against Iver Lawson, Hardy Downing, Jackie Clark (back in Salt Lake City with a new fiancée), and MacFarland.

For Taylor, it was the beginning of the end. His first appearance was on August 5, a quarter-mile exhibition behind a motorcycle. According to the *Salt Lake Tribune*, "The Negro rider was not the hero of any wonderful performance, but he gave a good exhibition behind the motor."

Two weeks later, a match between Taylor and Lawson, two former world sprint champions, packed the stands outside the fabulous resort with five thousand people. The two men competed in Taylor's specialty—the best of three one-mile matches for an $800 purse: $500 to the winner and $300 to the loser. Taylor, a master bike-handler, maneuvered behind Lawson at the start of the first match. Lawson countered by taking Taylor up and down the steep banking to tire Taylor's legs and possibly get around behind him, to take advantage of drafting and to monitor his every move. Taylor followed Lawson closely as they snaked up and down the banking for six and a half laps.

They were high up the banking when Taylor abruptly cut down the inside of the track and burst for the finish. He opened a lead of several bike lengths and built speed before Lawson could react. Such a move between two riders of nearly the same ability normally would have been decisive. But Lawson shot down the banking, quickly caught Taylor, then hastened ahead to win.

The second race was a similar, and humiliating, defeat for Taylor. He was shut out of his specialty by a man two years older. Three days later in a match race against Clark he was again crushed.

On August 28, he joined others in a benefit program to start a fund for riders injured on the Salt Palace track. The races drew another full house. Four world records were set in the course of the evening program. One rider, S. H. Wilcox, clipped a second from Taylor's world quarter-mile motor-pace record while Taylor watched from the sidelines. Taylor managed a second-place in a half-mile race against three others. Later, against two others, he finished last.

At three o'clock the next morning, a fire broke out in a concession stand of the Salt Palace. A heavy wind fanned the flames to overwhelm the entire Palace and spread the short distance to the velodrome. Remarkably, as soon as the track fire was doused, the manager dispatched a gang of carpenters to repair the damage; racing resumed three days later under the Utah sky.

On Labor Day, the concluding race of the season, Taylor won his heat in the quarter-mile race. In the final, he had a bad start and quit. Next came the mile handicap for pros. Taylor started but pulled out rather than lose badly.

He went home to Worcester and retired from racing.

His distinguished sixteen-year pro career ended profitably. He owned his home and his records show savings of $75,000—worth $1.9 million today. What next interested him the most was learning a mechanical trade. Taylor applied for admission to Worcester Technical School, but he was turned down because he lacked a high school diploma. He turned his attention to automobiles and became fascinated with developing shock absorbers for trucks. He used his capital to found the Taylor Manufacturing Company to manufacture shock absorbers.

He had every right to expect success. America in 1910 had almost three hundred motorcar companies in twenty-four states. A majority of the car companies, like Pierce, were former bicycle manufacturers, opening the way for the Auto Age.

• • •

Chapman's franchise out of Newark was a big commercial success for him and Frank Mihlon, except for the New Haven track, which closed after the 1911 season. Australians were willing to travel twenty-two days by ship and six days by train to race in Newark. Europeans traveled a week across the Atlantic to dock in New York and then take a short train ride to Newark. The city was settled by immigrants from Germany, Russia, Italy, Poland, and Ireland, all eager to watch racers from their homeland.

When the 1911 season wrapped after Labor Day, Chapman faced an unexpected crisis. Floyd MacFarland breezed into Newark intending to cash in on his experiences and reinvent himself as a promoter. Big Mac had distinguished himself against top international competition in cities around the United States, in Sydney and Melbourne in Australia, and across the Atlantic in London, Berlin, Paris, Brussels, and Vienna. He was especially esteemed by New Yorkers for his hard-fought victories at the sixes in Madison Square Garden in 1900 and 1908.

Most pros admired MacFarland. He was gregarious and, when the opportunity arose, he drank and told colorful stories late into the night. He was considered well educated for the period, a high school grad, and he had the knack of talking to anybody about anything. Yet he had a violent temper. At a champagne reception in Camperdown, Victoria, in Australia, Mac was reputed to have deliberately insulted Bull Williams, a professional boxer. The two men squared off and MacFarland knocked his opponent flat.

In early 1912, before the racing season began, thirty-six-year-old Mac launched his promoting career by following Chapman's example. Mac went west and took over the management of the Salt Palace velodrome. Attendance there had fallen off after the fire two years before.

Mac had a vision to expand franchises in the West and in southern Canada, modeled after what Chapman did out of Newark. First, he prevailed on old friendships. In the spirit of camaraderie, Mac easily persuaded many of Chapman's best pros to leave Newark for Salt Lake City. Mac recruited about twenty pros, a good number for the Salt Palace venue.

Chapman, meanwhile, created a plan from behind his roll-top desk in his office upstairs from Mihlon's Long Bar Saloon. He wrote letters and sent transatlantic cables to contacts cultivated on trips to Paris, home to the Union Cycliste Internationale. The UCI awarded the 1912 worlds to him in Newark. That gave him enormous clout in signing contracts with international greats.

From France came two-time world champion Émile Friol and French champion André Perchicot. Also arriving were Australian champion Ernie Pye, Alfred Grenda of Tasmania, Fred "Jumbo" Wells of New Zealand. Chapman secured a top lineup for his circuit and a season culminating in the UCI worlds.

• • •

In Salt Lake City, MacFarland enjoyed a successful launch. A local newspaper account proclaimed the 1912 season "the best season of racing which Salt Lake City has ever seen." Alf Goullet led with the first of a dozen new world records. On his first day he won $150 in silver coins. (He told me he was never paid with paper money in Salt Lake City.)

Reports of the stream of national and world records set on the Salt

Palace velodrome ran over newspaper wire services nationwide and across the Atlantic. According to Goullet, during a series of interviews I had with him in his apartment in Red Bank, New Jersey, between 1985 and his one-hundredth birthday in 1991, MacFarland was the best promoter he knew. "If a race began at 3 p.m. on a Saturday, then the stands were packed at 2 p.m."

The main distinction Goullet drew between MacFarland and Chapman was personality. Mac's friendliness came across to the riders and the audience, while Chapman remained aloof. Mac had a better idea of the capabilities of individual riders so their races were close. Then, as now, spectators lose interest in a race when the outcome is obvious. Mac was in his element when devising a racing schedule for the audience and cyclists alike.

Word of his popularity and revenue from ticket sales reached Newark, where riders were chafing under Chapman's authoritarian rule. So many riders expressed their dissatisfaction that they sent Mac a cable, which a Newark newspaper published: "Great majority of riders favor your immediate presence here. We are prepared to race at motordrome across the street under your management. Motordrome people will reconstruct track and also install lights upon advice from you. Proposition looks good. Chapman must be canned."

The motordrome, a quarter-mile board oval, had opened on July 4, 1912. Motorcycles were the new rage. Motordromes hosting motorcycle races were proliferating in cities around America and drawing big audiences. The owner of Newark's Vailsburg Motordrome was Inglis Moore Uppercu, an automobile distributor.

MacFarland, however, declined to discuss details until the season closed.

• • •

Compared with today's world cycling championships, the 1912 worlds, held over six days late in the summer, were simple. There were no road races, nor competitions for women; the Nineteenth Amendment granting women the right to vote was still eight years away. Radio was in its infancy and television coverage was still decades away; media was restricted to newspapers and magazines. Chapman offered only three championship events on the Newark Velodrome for the right to claim the title of world's fastest cyclist: a 100-kilometer (62.5-mile) motor-paced race for pros, the amateur 1-mile sprint championship, and the professional 1-mile sprint championship.

Kramer had ruled the national pro sprint title since 1901 and became America's highest-paid athlete. In 1911, Ty Cobb of the Detroit Tigers held out all winter on signing a new contract to boost his salary from $4,500 to $10,000. Kramer was already making more than $20,000 in prize money in addition to his $2,080 annual stipend from the Pierce Cycle Company. He personified the motto on Pierce bicycle head badges: "Tried & True."

He acknowledged the pressure he faced to win the worlds. Among friends, the man they called Big Steve, after a popular newspaper cartoon, confessed concern about getting too nervous and failing to race up to his ability.

From August 30 through September 4, twenty thousand people daily passed through the turnstiles to watch the worlds at the Newark Velodrome, exceeding its official seating capacity. Chapman allowed overflow spectators to stand in the infield, along with the orchestra, trainers, newshounds, and illustrators.

There were dozens of races to watch. The amateur and pro sprinters from ten nations went through a gauntlet of elimination heats, with winners advancing to three semifinals, then the three-man final.

On the opening day, Kramer's chances literally crumbled beneath him. Émile Friol talked him into partnering with him in tandem races, an exhibition to warm up the audience. Wiry and jovial, Friol had won four French national titles, the Grand Prix de Paris three times, and a brace of world titles. Kramer protested that he had never planned to ride a tandem in the worlds, and if he were to do so, he would choose an American compatriot.

Friol, easily spotted off the bike by wearing a broad-brimmed hat, reminiscent of d'Artagnan leading the three Musketeers, charmed the stolid Kramer by explaining they were forming a Franco-American all-star team. In their tandem race, the Franco-American All Stars appeared to clinch the event as the bell rang to mark the final lap.

They were winding up their sprint on the back straight into the far turn, where the banking veered from twenty-five degrees to fifty-two degrees on the top of the turn. All of a sudden, their rear wheel collapsed. They slammed onto the boards, slid down the banking, and careened into spectators standing on the infield. Friol was knocked out cold. His face was scraped, his right eye swollen nearly shut. Kramer's right arm and elbow suffered abrasions.

The next day, Friol lined up for his first elimination heat against Australian champion Ernie Pye and two others. Friol's face remained swollen, his right eye almost closed. Yet he gamely won his quarterfinal heat, advancing to the semifinals three days later. He was matched against compatriot André Perchicot for a French runoff—Perchicot of Paris versus Friol, a former car mechanic from Lyon. Perchicot nipped Friol to advance to the final.

The men's amateur sprint championship and the professional motor-paced contest lacked the foreign delegation that characterized the pro sprints and served as preliminary events. Donald McDougall, son of a *Newark Evening News* photographer, was noted for his cat-like acceleration. McDougall won the amateur sprint title. The motor-pace championship went to George Wiley of Buffalo.

Kramer's first elimination heat pitted him against Fred Wells of New Zealand and two Americans. Kramer won decisively. In the semifinal he defeated Walter DeMara of Portland, Oregon, who had finished second in the tandem race. Kramer lined up in the final against André Perchicot and Alfred Grenda of Tasmania, a broad-shouldered six foot one.

On the last day, it was Kramer, Perchicot, and Grenda set to battle it out in the main event for the world pro sprint championship. The winner would claim the title plus a check for $1,000—today worth more than $26,000.

The velodrome grandstand, bleacher seats embracing the oval, and the infield were a crammed mass of humanity. Twenty thousand people focused on the home straight in front of the grandstand where trainers held the three finalists on their bikes to push them away for the start of the six-lap contest.

At the boom of the starter's revolver, Kramer set a brisk clip for three laps before Grenda surged ahead. Perchicot tried to catch Grenda's slipstream, but Kramer reacted quicker and displaced the Frenchman. For the next two laps, Grenda kept his head down, arms locked in a streamlined position, and strategically quickened the tempo and towed Kramer and Perchicot.

As they filed in front of the grandstand, the bell clanged to declare the last lap. The audience was screaming in fear that Kramer would let them down. The *Newark Evening News* reported:

> "Make your jump now, Frank!" and "Go on, Kramer!" were shouts that were heard from all quarters as the men swung to the first turn on the last lap, and everybody who hadn't already stood up jumped to their feet. Everybody knew that within a few more seconds a world's championship would be won and lost, and pretty near every mother's son and daughter of them wanted Kramer to win it. They thought he could win it, too, but the tardiness made them fearful. Should he falter after the twelve years of campaigning when the crown was in sight should be disheartening.

Midway through the first turn, Kramer surged up to Grenda's shoulders. Grenda pedaled faster to force him wide while Perchicot drafted. They were barreling at more than 35 mph and accelerating on the back straight when Kramer pulled even, wheel-to-wheel with Grenda. The man from Tasmania upped the tempo to hold off Kramer in their poker game on wheels. Leaning into the fifty-two-degree banking high off the final turn, Grenda kept Kramer on the outside and gained a length when they flew down the final straight. It was do or die when Kramer unloaded his sprint approaching 40 mph.

The *Evening News* continued: "First, his advance was slow, and then he came faster, but come he surely did, and as each yard passed under him he was nearer Grenda's front wheel and after the halfway mark in the stretch was reached it was seen that he could win. There were already exultant shouts from the spectators, and, as Kramer came on, they increased, so that when he finished a yard from the tape they broke into bedlam. The race was over. It was a great race and fairly won and fairly lost."

Grenda trailed by inches. Perchicot, in the outside lane, was only a wheel behind.

The *New York Times* proclaimed: "The contest furnished all that cycle fans could wish for of spectacular riding."

In the worlds tradition for the professional and amateur champions to race an exhibition, McDougall was expected to challenge Kramer. But Kramer trounced him.

The next year McDougall set a national amateur record for the quarter-mile, 28.2 seconds, on the Newark Velodrome. He retired at the end of the season for a job in the Newark Police Department repairing motor vehicles.

• • •

Chapman's worlds reaped a handsome profit for him and Mihlon. Yet as they tallied their receipts, there was no time to sit back and relax.

On the next Sunday afternoon at the motordrome, two drivers flying around the saucer lost control of their Indian Motocycles and smashed at 90 mph into the audience. Both drivers were killed along with six spectators. Thirteen others were injured. The crowd stampeded out of the grandstands.

Days later, fire destroyed the motordrome.

In the public turmoil over the motordrome tragedy, owner Inglis Uppercu announced that he was prepared to build a velodrome for bicycle racing and ready to hire the riders necessary to challenge the Newark Velodrome. A battle was shaping up between Uppercu and Mihlon to determine whose track would survive the next season.

• • •

At the conclusion of his prosperous Salt Lake City season, Mac took his crew, including Goullet, off to Europe for a 1912–13 winter tour. Mac arranged indoor programs in Berlin, Prague, Brussels, Copenhagen, and Paris.

Within two weeks of arriving in Paris, Mac organized a six-day in the famed Vélodrome d'Hiver, in the shadow of the Eiffel Tower, from January 13 to 19. Mac had no trouble signing up sixteen two-rider teams boasting international headliners. They included Tour de France winners Octave Lapize and Lucien Petit-Breton of France, along with such outstanding racers as Frenchman Maurice Brocco, Belgian César Debaets, and American Bobby Walthour.

Goullet teamed with Joe Fogler of Brooklyn to win. They pedaled 2,751 miles—a world record, and the distance from San Francisco to New York.

For a race program in Berlin, Mac wanted to sign up his friend and former German national champion Walter Rutt. Rutt had won two sixes in Madison Square Garden. But twenty-nine-year-old Rutt had dodged the draft for Germany's compulsory military training; he could not return to his homeland without risking arrest at the border and imprisonment.

Mac called on his friendship with the German emperor, Kaiser Wilhelm II, a cycling fan. He'd given Mac and his partner Jimmy Moran, from the Boston suburb of Chelsea, each a pair of gold cuff links for winning the 1909 Berlin Six. Mac and the Emperor Kaiser quickly solved the problem in a telephone conversation. Rutt could return to his native country under Mac's management.

In April 1913, Mac returned with his entourage to Newark. He visited friends and quickly learned about the friction between Mihlon and Uppercu.

Mihlon had risen socially, eased through money flowing from cycling connections. The velodrome circuit out-earned the Long Bar Saloon. He upgraded his pub with polished brass fixtures everywhere. The latest electric lights hung from the ceiling of pressed tin and cast a warm glow. Animal trophy heads on the wall near the Market Street entrance were replaced by framed velodrome photos. The sawdust had been swept from the floor, replaced by polished hardwood. A room for family dining had been added while the long bar still served the faithful.

Mihlon abandoned his barman's apron for custom suits. Clean-shaven, a silk tie anchoring a fresh collar, he strode around Newark's business community as one of the moderns, breaking from bushy-bearded patriarchs. He was thirty-five, a bachelor courting the lovely

Minnie Yetter, a model for Gibson Girl drawings, the era's ideal of feminine beauty and poise and independence. Yetter acted in silent movies filmed at Fox Studio in Fort Lee, New Jersey. When the studio planned to move west to Hollywood, Mihlon proposed and they married. They were seen as the smart couple, sitting on the velodrome's front row over the start/finish line.

His cycling ties extended to the Madison Square Garden sixes. He received a percentage of its profitable extravaganzas. Mihlon understood what he risked by going against Uppercu, whose Cadillac Motor Company dealership earned him a cut of all Cadillacs sold from New York to Washington DC. Uppercu also had a hefty share in a growing aircraft company. When Mac suggested a plan to avoid a confrontation, Mihlon wanted to hear more.

Mac brought Mihlon and Uppercu together. He recommended that Mihlon let Uppercu buy a half-interest in the Newark Velodrome in exchange for Uppercu not building his own facility. Mihlon preferred to have Uppercu on his side and graciously agreed to Mac's recommendation.

Mac's strategy was self-serving. Now that he had prevented a commercial war, the new co-owners hired him to take over the Newark Velodrome.

Chapman was discarded from the franchise he'd created and developed. There was nothing he could do but return with his wife, Martha, to the family farm, with 350 head of cattle, in Georgia.

5

A Bizarre Twist

There is always another story, there is
more than meets the eye.

—W. H. AUDEN, "Twelve Songs," 8

Floyd MacFarland became America's undisputed cycling promoter. He paid out more appearance money than ever. In 1914 Alf Goullet received $3,000 in appearance fees, won another $5,000 in cash prizes during the summer, and earned $3,500 more in the Madison Square Garden six-day that November for a total year's income of $11,500 (worth $300,000 today). That amounted to a comfortable income when Henry Ford's workers took home the unprecedented figure of $5 for an eight-hour workday (worth $125 today).

In 1985, Goullet was ninety-four, a widower living in Red Bank, New Jersey. He had a clear, resonant voice, a remarkably unlined visage, trimmed birch-white hair, and blue eyes so sharp that he did not need glasses for driving. (He quit driving when he turned one hundred and his insurance premium spiked more than he thought was necessary.) He speed walked three or four miles in the morning. On some evenings he had a beer and a bump with friends, although he adamantly denied doing so to his grown daughter, Suzanne Goullet Klein. Once, when dining out in a restaurant with me, he was asked by a young waitress if the food was to his liking. He sat back in his chair and startled his server when he proclaimed, "Best meal I've eaten in a hundred years!"

Born in 1891, Goullet grew up on a farm in Emu, 150 miles north of Melbourne, Australia. He described watching Floyd MacFarland in a race in Melbourne, which he said inspired him to make his own dirt cycling track. Goullet hitched a horse to a heavy log, dragging it to clear away grass on sloping ground for natural banking. In 1908 he competed in his first race, a quarter-miler, which he entered as a professional. It was a near disaster. The trainer holding him up on his bicycle became so nervous that the firing of the starter's gun scared him and he pushed Goullet to the ground. He scrambled back on his bike, finished third in the heat, and went on to win the final. More triumphs that followed earned him an invitation to go to Newark in 1910.

"If you were a bicycle racer, you went to Newark to prove yourself against the best," he told me. "Chapman sent me the money for travel. I came."

The transition from Australian racing to competing in America was enormous. Goullet had to ride faster and smarter.

• • •

At the 1914 six-day in Madison Square Garden, he teamed with Alfred Grenda, a Tasmanian, a head taller than Goullet. Grenda stood out among slender cyclists with his beefed-up shoulders and biceps from off-seasons spent in northern Australia, earning money chopping down trees ten hours a day for furnaces generating steam power to operate train cars carrying coal out of mines. In late 1911 Goullet had returned to Australia to win the Melbourne and Sydney sixes. Chapman cabled him to sign up two riders. "I signed up Grenda, figuring that was all that was needed."

The Aussie and the Tasmanian had dispositions that made them natural foils: Goullet was high-strung and inclined to fret; Grenda didn't worry as long as he ate six or seven meals a day and could take an occasional nap.

The Garden's six-day was the major event of the year for racers, a box office bonanza for the Palace of Pleasure, and a big social opportunity for the city. At any time of the day or night there was at least one band playing lively music on the infield. Crowds attended around the clock to watch the riders. Every day New York's fifteen daily newspapers compared the present teams' mileages to those of past racers. The crowds drew "song pluggers," who hired pianists and sang through a megaphone on the bandstand in the track infield; sometimes they had accompaniment from cabarets. When the Harlem cabarets closed for the night, the jazz bands and combos headed for the action at the Garden and played till dawn. While the racers were pedaling, the song pluggers were peddling songs like "For Me and My Gal," "Peg O' My Heart," and "Road to Mandalay" when the ink of the sheet music was still fresh to promote the songs.

The nightclub atmosphere, combined with the cyclists' fierce competition—which invariably opened with riders covering fifty or so miles in the first two hours—generated so much excitement that riders rarely slept in the first twenty-four hours. On the second day, they became saddle sore while wrists, arms, legs, and necks began to ache. Discomforts usually continued to the final day. Then the racers approached the finish in a rush of adrenaline. The last hours turned into one hard chase after another. Audiences relished these "jams."

At the 1914 six-day, from November 16 to 21, MacFarland was the general manager. Wearing a dark three-piece suit and bowler hat, he seemed to be everywhere—up in the stands and down at trackside—always monitoring the race. He kept the pace pumped with a purse of more than $2,000 (worth $51,000 today), which he doled out for designated sprints; for teams that "lapped the field" (that is, flew away from the front and went all the way around to catch the others from behind, thus "stealing" a lap); and for teams leading in distance.

Mac also introduced a new ending. Instead of the traditional last-mile sprint, he increased it to racing over the final hour. Teams a lap or more behind the leaders would be withdrawn to leave the leaders to sprint every fifteen laps (1.5 miles) for points: six to the winner, five to second, down to one for sixth.

Most of Mac's sprint premiums were ten dollars cash, although some from audience members, eager to spur action, jumped as high as $250. The premiums—called by their French name "primes" (pronounced "preems")—kept the riders sprinting.

Soon after the 1914 New York Six began, the leaders were on pace to surpass the world record that Goullet and Joe Fogler of Brooklyn had set the previous year at the Paris Six. By the fourth day, the assertive pace took a toll on the original eighteen two-rider teams. Crashes forced several cyclists to quit. Those whose partners dropped out formed new teams after losing a penalty lap. On the fifth day, many surviving riders banded together and threatened to withdraw if Mac did not stop offering primes. They complained they could not get any sleep because of all the primes, that the competition was becoming distorted. Lagging teams could hit up a terrific pace during the sprints to win money and then rest by dropping back a few laps, while teams in the lead had to fight to keep up the brutal pace or get dropped and lose laps.

Mac reminded them that they had known about sprints for the primes when they entered the race—it was too late to change. He also warned that, if they quit, they would be ruled off all tracks for violating their contracts. Dissatisfied riders grumbled, but all continued.

"That was the hardest race I ever rode," Goullet recalled. "Usually in the early-morning hours, after midnight and before six o'clock, we had an unofficial truce and riders on the track pedaled easy. But Mac offered bonuses to the teams that had lost laps. They tried to gain back their laps. That kept the pressure up."

Between accidents and the relentless pace, a majority of the riders incurred injuries. They rode with white bandages and gauze on skinned arms, legs, and their heads like war casualties in triage. Through it all, the team of Goullet-Grenda stayed in control of the race. By 5 p.m. Saturday, with the finish still five hours away, the Garden's stands and infield were filled to standing room only. The *New York Times* commented: "The arena was one vast mass of humanity, packed in as close as sardines, as every available seat was taken, and the crowd was literally hanging on the rafters. Early in the evening the place was kept in an uproar by the desperate efforts of Clark and his partner, Root, to make up the lap which they lost Friday night, and which divided them from the six leading teams."

Nobody in the top six teams wanted to contend in the final hour with Jackie Clark, nicknamed the Australian Rocket for his sprint, who had ridden on the winning team in Garden sixes in 1909 and 1911, or Eddie Root, a six-foot Swede, lean yet muscular, and lady-killer handsome. Root had won four Garden sixes, between 1904 and 1910, with different partners and other sixes in Atlanta and Toronto, and he won a six in Brussels. At this six, each time Root or Clark launched off the front to break away and try to make up their team's lost lap, the pack sped up to pounce on them like cats after mice. Root, thirty-four, had a taste for the ironic and for years insisted on wearing superstition-busting number thirteen on his back.

Attacks and counterattacks in the 1914 six continued hour after hour. The hot pace and taut drama kept spectators yelling and on their feet. Riders with rested legs circled on the upper rim of the Garden's oval track and swooped down to take over from their tired partners, creating an atmosphere resembling a frenetic beehive. Not even Root and Clark could make up their lost lap; they had to pull out and let the top six teams fight it out in the final hour to determine who would win the $1,600 for placing first, $1,000 for second, down to $350 for sixth.

In that final hour, the audience was electric with excitement. Grenda was struck with an attack of appendicitis, forcing Goullet to carry their team. He won eight of the sprints to lead his team to victory with 2,759 miles and one lap—the distance from San Francisco to Buffalo. They set the world record for sixes, which stood for the rest of the twentieth century.

• • •

MacFarland's success in the Northeast affected Salt Lake City. Area pros either went east or quit. The Salt Palace velodrome closed. Hardy Downing, a native of San Jose and age thirty-six in 1914, retired and opened a boxing gym in Salt Lake City, holding amateur and professional cards on Monday nights. In 1915, a reedy-voiced Mormon youth calling himself Kid Blackie asked Downing for the chance to break into professional boxing. A few years earlier, Kid Blackie had polished shoes for Downing and Goullet. Kid Blackie won his first bouts in Downing's gym, changed his name to Jack Dempsey, and soon was slugging his way into sports history.

Mac had several plans in store for the 1915 season. The Union Cycliste Internationale had suspended its worlds programs indefinitely with the outbreak of war in Europe in the summer of 1914. Mac devised his own ambitious world championship series in Newark, Philadelphia, and Boston in 1915—until whenever the war ended and the UCI sanctioned races again. He also established a track in Chicago, with a homegrown promoter named Paddy Harmon, to open with the 1915 season. Another track was planned for Toronto.

Big Mac gained weight like a bourgeois. He sported a bowler hat and suit with a gold watch chain. He enlisted Chapman to manage the Toronto franchise with a racing circuit modeled after what he had done in Newark.

In April Chapman climbed down from a train pulling into the Newark station. He came to discuss details with Mac and Mihlon. Nobody could have anticipated that Chapman, exiled from the sport for two years, would take it over.

• • •

On Saturday, April 17, 1915, the weather was chilly. Newspapers that day reported Ty Cobb was on his way to a ninth straight American League batting title, and a field of seventy-five runners had signed up for the nineteenth annual Boston Marathon to be held in two days' time. In Newark, about 150 men and boys bundled up to watch cyclists in wool clothes practice on the velodrome that afternoon for the next day's season-opening races.

Those at the track saw Mac get into a heated argument with David Lantenberg of Brooklyn, proprietor of a concession selling refreshments at the track. Lantenberg, a twenty-seven-year-old with dark hair, had been mounting posters on a velodrome wall when the advertising manager, Wally Howes, told him the signs were not allowed; the screws that Lantenberg used to mount the posters could loosen, fall to the track, and cause tires to puncture. Lantenberg protested that he was authorized to post the signs to promote his business. The two argued until Howes left to take the matter up with Mac, who angrily rushed over to Lantenberg.

Lantenberg stood only to MacFarland's chest and weighed 120 pounds. He shouted that he was going to put up his signs, turned away, and used the screwdriver he was holding to drive a screw into the wall. Mac grabbed his arm. Both men lost their tempers. Witnesses told police that Lantenberg lashed out with the screwdriver and Mac quickly ducked his head but could not avoid the blow. The point of the screwdriver struck the back of Mac's head behind his left ear, pierced his skull, and penetrated his brain. He dropped to the ground.

Alfred Grenda rushed to the quarrel in time to pick up Mac, with Lantenberg's help. They carried him to Lantenberg's car, parked nearby, and rushed him to Newark City Hospital.

The screwdriver had penetrated five inches into the back of MacFarland's skull. He never regained consciousness. At his bedside were his wife, Frank Mihlon, Frank Kramer, and Alf Goullet.

MacFarland died at 9 p.m. He was thirty-nine.

"I felt empty," Goullet said. "It was a real loss."

Lantenberg was arrested at the hospital and taken to the Seventh Precinct police station. He was initially charged with assault, then with homicide, and finally with manslaughter; on June 23 he was acquitted.

News of MacFarland's death was published the next day on page 1 in newspapers from Newark to New York City. A crowd of fifteen hundred attended the funeral at the home of Frank Kramer, who escorted Mac's widow during the service. A thousand gathered at the cemetery where the casket was kept temporarily until it was sent for burial in Buffalo, his wife's hometown. Eighty-five floral offerings were received, requiring three horse-drawn wagons to carry them to the cemetery. European and Australian cyclists sent horseshoe-shaped floral arrangements bearing the colors of the countries they represented.

A week after Mac died, the *New York Times* ran a feature on his career, complete with a portrait two columns wide, a practice reserved for important figures. The *Times* acknowledged that he was a master at arranging a race program and could suggest more new turns to a race than anyone else connected with the sport.

The start of the racing season at the velodrome was suspended. Co-owners Mihlon and Uppercu discussed the situation with Chapman, who had signed a contract to manage the Toronto velodrome. On April 22 Mihlon and Uppercu announced that Chapman would succeed Mac as manager of the Newark Velodrome, and a resident manager would be appointed in Toronto under Chapman's supervision.

The *Newark Evening News* printed the announcement as the day's lead sports story. It acknowledged the "dissension in the ranks of the cyclists" in 1912, when a majority of the riders wanted Chapman canned, but the newspaper endorsed Chapman: "With a vast amount of money and great fortune at stake, it is no time to experiment with an inexperienced man." Comparing the two promoters, the *Evening News* observed, "Chapman lacks the magnetism of MacFarland. He is more of the cool, calculating business man."

The newspaper said others had been briefly considered for the post but praised Chapman as "the best man for the position," adding, "Chapman knows the game thoroughly. The present success of cycling in America is largely due to his ideas, and it was the foundation laid by him in 1911 and the two years following that put the sport on a firm basis here in Newark."

Through a bizarre twist and by being in the right place at the right time, Chapman was back in charge.

He reclaimed his former office over Mihlon's saloon on Market Street and resumed overseeing the franchise. The managers of the other velodromes tended to be retired pros, like Walter Bardgett, operating the Providence track, and Nat Butler, managing the Revere Beach track near Boston. Bardgett and Butler had competed all over America and in cities across Europe, against Bobby Walthour, Major Taylor, MacFarland, and other greats.

• • •

Over the next few years, Chapman supervised race programs and strengthened his grip on the sport. He found an enterprising confederate in Chicago: Patrick "Paddy" T. Harmon. Harmon grew up as one of ten children on the West Side and quit school at nine to work snuffing out nine hundred neighborhood gaslights before bounding away to hawk newspapers on street corners. He recognized that people always looked for entertainment. "It's not hard to please the public," he said. "All you have to do is to remember that we were all born children, that we all die as children, and that in between we are children."

Harmon hustled to provide what people wanted. He rented a dance hall, hired a band, and the place filled with music and dancers happy to pay admission. He opened roller skating rinks. He managed prizefighters. Bicycle races were another entertainment. In 1915 he promoted spring and winter sixes in a capacious building downtown with riders supplied by Chapman.

An engineer friend of Chapman named Pat Mulvey had construction of indoor tracks for the sixes down to a science. Mulvey's velodromes measured six laps to the mile. His tracks called for sixty thousand feet of pine or spruce, cut one-and-a-quarter inches thick and two inches wide, planed on all four sides. An army of a hundred carpenters erected the support structure for the towering turns banked forty-five degrees—rising to fifty-two degrees at the summit—and straights of twenty-seven degrees, then laid the boards on edge, smooth as a bowling alley. Carpenters hammered two thousand pounds of eight-penny nails into the boards from underneath so nothing poked through.

Construction typically started promptly after a Saturday night hockey game or a boxing card. When the track was completed by Saturday evening, amateur cyclists rolled over boards in preliminary events. They preceded the six-day for pros, launched at the stroke of midnight Monday morning.

• • •

Chapman's crony Tex Rickard blew into New York City after a detour down to Paraguay where he raised cattle for six years. Rickard now managed Jack Dempsey and was turning into boxing's biggest promoter. He and Chapman cruised saloons together once again. Rickard gave Chapman a small trophy of a boxer as a paperweight for his rolltop desk. Chapman introduced him to bicycle races. Rickard became a fan, especially of the sixes in Madison Square Garden.

Bobby Walthour was still racing in Europe. The Continent had been consumed by war since August 1914, chiefly in northern France and across Belgium and the Netherlands while the United States officially stayed neutral. Yet Walthour remained in demand in Paris, Leipzig, Berlin, and Milan, where audiences sought relief from wartime horrors.

For a decade Walthour had won every European motor-pace classic. After winning the 1904 motor-pace worlds in London, he defended his title the next year in Antwerp, Belgium; he placed third in the

1910 motor-pace championship in Brussels. By 1917 he'd also won fourteen sixes on both sides of the Atlantic, the most of any cyclist in the world.

Late in the summer of 1917, in a motor-pace event in Paris on the pink concrete of the Parc des Princes, he suffered his worst crash. His front tire blew out, throwing him to the track where other riders and heavy motorcycles ran into his prostrate body. By the time rescuers ran to him, his head was split open, his left shoulder was broken, and both arms and legs were severely lacerated.

French physicians gave up hope. They didn't reply to his anxious wife's cables from Newark asking about his condition. The U.S. Embassy in Paris had been instructed to take care of his remains if he died and to see to ordering the flowers.

Three weeks passed before Walthour opened his eyes. Another four weeks went by before he climbed off his hospital bed and boarded a ship for home.

Aside from Kramer, Walthour was the last American professional to have won a world championship and still be competing. Iver Lawson, thirty-eight, was employed as Chapman's personal assistant. Lawson hung up his wheels the year before after a bad crash in the Kansas City Six almost cost him an eye. He had earned a fortune, but what he didn't spend on good times he lost in a disastrous marriage in Salt Lake City and a failed tobacco shop there. He had a drinking problem. His alcohol abuse was attributed to grief over the death of his younger brother, Gus, in a motor-pace accident in Cologne, Germany, and the previous demise, from meningitis, of his older brother, John, nicknamed "the Terrible Swede."

Newspaper columnists scolded Iver Lawson in print for falling down stairs in his house and waking up in the hospital. Chapman doted after him like an older brother, care that puzzled those who knew Chapman.

Sad news came from Pittsburgh. George Banker, after his brilliant cycling career, marriage to a socialite, and business success selling automobiles, had suffered the death of his wife and was languishing in a hospital bed with terminal throat and tongue cancer that would take his life on September 7, at age forty-four.

Arthur Zimmerman still managed his hotel in Point Pleasant, New

Jersey. Goullet told me that he occasionally went there with friends to drink a pint.

Major Taylor lived in Worcester, and word in the cycling community circulated that he was going broke. Apartments he rented weren't panning out because tenants refused to pay rent. And the Taylor Manufacturing Company and a home-heating company he owned were draining his savings.

In the spring of 1917 President Woodrow Wilson declared war on Germany in response to German submarines sinking U.S. ships in the Atlantic and killing hundreds of U.S. passengers. America, allied with France and England, sent a million U.S. troops to France "to save democracy."

That summer the inevitable happened—Kramer finally lost the national sprint championship, breaking his skein of sixteen consecutive years. He was dethroned by twenty-year-old Arthur Spencer of Toronto.

Kramer's defeat, news of Taylor's reversal of fortune, Banker's demise, Walthour's brush with death, and grim war reports from France, published in the *New York Times* and the *Newark Evening News*, that French sprinter Émile Friol, a wartime motorcycle messenger, was killed in action in November 1916 during the Battle of the Somme, may have moved the usually stoical Chapman. Or perhaps he saw a commercial opportunity. For whatever reason, he organized an old-timers' race at the Newark Velodrome for Sunday, September 16.

Goullet said it was the only old-timers' race he ever heard of in Newark. "There should have been more races like that to help generate public interest in the sport."

Chapman invited Taylor. Sports writers questioned whether Taylor would accept because he'd opposed Sunday racing and tightfisted Chapman refused to pay travel expenses. But Taylor cabled back that he had returned from a hunting trip and would be in Newark for the race "with both feet."

Zimmerman, forty-eight, declined to attend, citing rheumatism. Mile-a-Minute Murphy, forty-six, had pulverized a kneecap on duty as a New York City motorcycle policeman when he drove into a concrete bridge abutment. He gamely used crutches to board a train to Newark and served as official starter.

Taylor's mentor Louis Munger arrived from Middletown, Connecticut. On the way, Munger was in in a car wreck, borrowed another auto, and drove through the night and next day—typical drive time for the period's road conditions—to arrive in time to hold Taylor up on the start line.

Taylor appeared older than thirty-eight years. In street clothes he looked ordinary, but once he pulled on wool racing shorts and a tight jersey the extra weight showed. Goullet loaned him a Redbird bicycle made by the Columbia Bicycle Company. All the components came from Europe—indicating how the American bicycle industry had withdrawn. Goullet, five feet seven, recalled that his bike fit Taylor without adjusting the seat height.

The stands were filled with 12,500 spectators on the day of the old-timers' one-mile race, Goullet said. Taylor was relaxed as he rode warm-up laps and waved to the audience, cheering for him and the others.

Eleven old pros entered. The *Newark Evening News* in a preview story unmercifully labeled their event as the "Rheumatic Stakes Feature." Chapman entered along with Taylor's rival from the 1899 worlds, Nat Butler.

The *Newark Evening News* declared, "Major Taylor is the best of ancient pedal-pushers," and added, "The dusky demon won and won as he pleased with yards to spare, making a show of his Caucasian brethren."

During the program, Goullet won the half-mile and five-mile handicaps for pros. Kramer lightheartedly lined up for the start of the old-timers' race until photos were taken. He won a one-mile match race against two opponents.

• • •

By December Walthour recovered enough from injuries to sign a contract for the Garden six. Even when he was getting back to fitness he was a better rider than most others on their best days, and he had crowd appeal. Not long after the New York Six got underway, however, his partner took ill and both men withdrew. A week later, Walthour slipped on ice while walking near his home. His left leg broke in two places, between the knee and ankle.

The Garden's six had a bigger following than ever. The fulsome audience attracted Tin Pan Alley song pluggers. They introduced patriotic tunes like "Over There" and "It's a Long Way to Berlin, But We'll Get There!"

• • •

In 1917, Chapman lengthened the Garden sixes from 142 hours to 144 so they concluded at midnight Saturday. He also introduced the Berlin points system to heighten the action. A series of ten two-mile sprints were introduced for the matinee, evening, and late-night shows. For these sprints, six points were awarded for a win, four for second place, two for third, and one for fourth. From 11 p.m. to midnight, the stakes went up—a sprint every mile, awarding seventy-two points to the winner, then decreasing to five points for second, down to one for fourth. In the last hour, the six's outcome could change drastically.

That year, boxing lost at political roulette when New York State declared boxing was illegal. Tex Rickard was shaping the career of the sweet science's latest sensation, Jack Dempsey, legendary for punching power. Born in Manassa, Colorado, he could knock an opponent out with either fist, inspiring his nickname, the Manassa Mauler. Rickard took him to Toledo, Ohio, and set up a world heavyweight championship bout for July 4, 1919. Dempsey, six feet one and a taut-muscled 193 pounds, challenged world heavyweight champion Jess Willard, six feet six and 260 pounds. Willard, from Pottawatomie County, Kansas, and billed as the Pottawatomie Giant, gained fame in 1915 for knocking out Jack Johnson to claim the heavyweight title.

The Ohio Ministerial Association denounced Rickard's fight. The Ohio legislature passed a resolution demanding that the governor ban the bout. Instead of closing down the match, all the clamorous opposition promoted Rickard's event and boosted ticket sales. Dempsey won in a third-round knockout. He seized the world heavyweight championship.

In 1920 New York State senator James J. Walker, who would be the mayor of New York City a few years later, helped arrange passage of what was known as the Walker Law, which accepted boxing as legal again. Rickard moved fast. Before the governor signed the law, Rickard leased Madison Square Garden from the New York Life Insurance Company for ten years at $200,000 a year and took over as manager. With Dempsey the reigning heavyweight boxing champion, and his old prospector friend Chapman in charge of bicycle racing, Rickard was ready to usher the Roaring Twenties into Madison Square Garden.

Rickard said his slogan was, "Give the public what they want, the way they want it, and not the way you think." It served him well. He watched the sixes in his hallowed temple of sport and felt the audience's phenomenal passion. After witnessing Goullet win the December 1919 New York Six with New Jersey teammate Eddie Madden, Rickard tallied the box office receipts and ordered Chapman to hold a springtime six, beginning in March 1920, to augment the winter six.

The team of Goullet and New Yorker Jake Magin won the March event. For Magin, it was his third New York Six triumph and second with Goullet.

Of the twenty-nine sixes Goullet entered on three continents, he said the Garden was his favorite venue. "New Yorkers really knew what they were looking at," he told me. "They applauded and cheered style and class. They didn't hesitate to boo and heckle when they saw someone slacking. There was no fooling New Yorkers."

In the six's round-the-clock hoopla, he thrived on two-hour naps in the small cabin on the inside perimeter of the track, waking up feeling refreshed. "Every time the bell rang to announce a sprint, I responded like a firehouse Dalmatian." The effort left him exhausted. "Every six-day I was in was my last," he admitted. "They were always so hard. Then after a rest of two or three days, I was all set for the next one. Forgetting the physical discomfort was a blessing."

On August 1, 1920, Rickard signed a five-year contract with Chapman to jointly hold two sixes a year in the Garden, each with purses of $50,000—an eye-popping sum worth more than $600,000 today. Rickard announced plans to import more foreign talent than had ever been seen in sports. Cycling's golden days were rolling in high gear.

6

Wonderful Nonsense in the Jazz Age

Men and women enthusiasts, thrilled by the spectacle of the cyclists tearing around the pine saucer at breakneck speed, yelled themselves hoarse in a din which transformed [Madison Square] Garden into bedlam.

—*New York Times*, March 3, 1921

It was estimated that close to 150,000 persons passed through the turnstiles, leaving their dollars and sense behind.

—*New York Times*, December 11, 1927

In 1920, eleven football teams that would eventually form the National Football League went on sale for $100 each. All the NFL teams could have been purchased by one person for $1,100.

The better bicycle racers made almost that much—$700 to $1,000—in a good week. Chapman's programs improved to pay $200 to the winner of the open race, $100 for second, down to $10 for sixth, and $100 to the winner of the handicap race, tapering to $10 for sixth. Stars like Goullet and Kramer made up to $350 more for winning match races. Chapman upped prize money in 1919 after raising general admission price to fifty cents, the cost of a movie ticket.

Fortune favored Chapman. He bought a hilltop mansion in Summit, New Jersey, just outside Newark, and improved his family's College Park farm in Georgia where he and his wife spent winters. The log cabin with a dirt floor he was born in was torn down and replaced by a modern house. He apparently had second thoughts and built another log cabin on the property to show how far he had come.

Construction started in 1920 on the New York Velodrome, which opened in May 1921. Located at 225th and Broadway, the wooden track sat at the end of a rail line, which cost five cents to ride. People who drove cars to the velodrome parked for free. Chapman managed the velodrome for co-owners Uppercu and circus entrepreneur John Ringling.

The circuit Chapman managed featured eight outdoor programs a week for the seven warm months each year. Racing began Sunday afternoon on the Newark Velodrome, then moved Sunday night to the New York Velodrome. On Monday night events were held in Providence, Rhode Island, or the Revere Beach Velodrome in Boston, followed by Tuesday again in New York, Wednesday in Newark, Thursday in Philadelphia, Friday night in New York, and Saturday night in Newark. Cycling was so popular that Massachusetts also had tracks in Worcester and New Bedford outside Chapman's franchise.

With cash on the line, races were aggressive. In open events, fields of fifty to sixty went hard and fast around the velodromes, twenty-two feet wide. Racers zipped around these tracks at speeds approaching 40 mph, when legal city speed limits for cars were under 20 mph. There was a lot of bumping of knees, shoulders, and elbows through the turns. Bike races on the boards resembled hockey on wheels. Riders slammed each other into the boards of the outside railing or crunched together in mass pileups, which twisted wooden wheel rims like pretzels and wrecked steel frames. Falls could be serious. Dan Pischione, formerly a pig farmer from Providence, Rhode Island, was killed by a splinter that drove into his abdomen when he fell.

The action, and the attendance, appealed to Tex Rickard. Wearing his trademark broad-brimmed Stetson and sauntering with his cane, he was seen often at the races. Leading sports and entertainment celebrities were traditionally official starters for the Garden sixes. For the March 1921 event, Rickard took the liberty of firing the starting pistol. The following March, boxing heavyweight Jack Dempsey had the honor. Others included Oklahoma humorist Will Rogers, toting his own six-gun to start a six; Al Jolson, whose movie *The Jazz Singer* introduced sound to film; entertainers Eddie Cantor and Jimmy Durante; and striptease artist Gypsy Rose Lee.

Chapman's outdoor velodromes measured six laps to the mile. The New York Velodrome boasted the largest seating—twenty thousand folks filled the stands three times a week. Publicity generated by the outdoor circuit helped bolster enthusiasm for the winter and spring indoor sixes.

By the late teens, Chapman created an international circuit of sixes—in cities such as Buffalo, Philadelphia, Pittsburgh, Cleveland, Toronto, Montreal, Detroit, Indianapolis, St. Louis, Kansas City, and Chicago. Riders rested two or three days before climbing aboard a train to the next event. Promoters in western cities also held sixes sanctioned by Chapman through the National Cycling Association, which he ran out of his office over the Long Bar Saloon. North America offered as many sixes as Europe.

All this gave Chapman international clout. His races were among the best paying in the world, and the circuit he controlled offered the best opportunities anywhere. The $50,000 purse for each of the two annual Garden sixes afforded him the pick of the best racers from three continents.

Chapman took a tip from Rickard, far more generous about putting up money. Beginning in 1920, Chapman paid Alf Goullet $1,000 a day as appearance money to ride in sixes in New York and Chicago. Goullet was so fast that the Fourth Estate christened him the Australian Bullet. His personality appealed to Chapman; he was flamboyant on the track, which attracted crowds and the press, and off the bike he was modest, convivial, and a natural raconteur. Goullet set five world records, all unpaced, from two-thirds of a mile to fifty miles.

"That dark and sinister villain, Alfred Goullet, again held the center of the stage last night in the six-day cycling drama at Madison Square Garden," reported the *New York Times* on March 13, 1920, telling how he helped his American partner Jake Magin win. "While the fans booed and groaned with their usual gusto, he circled the track in front four out of six sprints, and maintained the team lead despite repeated onslaughts by the other ten combinations."

Fans spotted Goullet in his trademark scarlet silk jersey, black trim on the sleeves. When he sprinted, his back low, he stayed on the saddle while the middle of his back arched up like an attacking cat.

The 1920s were wonderful nonsense, and the Garden's sixes were part of good times. Actress Peggy Joyce—whose wealth and bravura prompted songwriter Cole Porter to pen, "My string of Rolls-Royces is longer than Peggy Joyce's"—served up $200 primes several times a night, presumably to stir up the action but more to gin up publicity for herself. Once, while the band played "Pretty Peggy with Eyes of Blue," she had a grand time watching the riders tear around the track for her $1,000 prime. According to Goullet, the actress didn't put up the money: "One of her boyfriend chumps was happy to have that honor."

Reporter and columnist Damon Runyon of the *New York American* wrote about another wealthy spectator, Mike Delores, whom he called the Mad Hatter from Danbury. Arriving in the Garden at the end of one evening sprint session, Delores was allowed to extend the sprints as long as he posted two and three C-notes at a time until he turned his pockets inside out. He then came back for the morning session with an even bigger money roll. The Mad Hatter from Danbury put up a fat roll for a two-mile sprint prime. It came to $2,400—worth $60,000 today.

The Garden sixes grew so popular, so rollicking, that it was not unusual for two bands to perform along the backstretch and another two on the homestretch, each band playing a different tune as the riders charged round and round on what sportswriters called the human squirrel cage. Crowds streamed through the Garden's doors until the fire marshal ordered them closed.

Star entertainers who regularly attended were Enrico Caruso, Mary Pickford, Douglas Fairbanks, John Barrymore, Bob Hope, and Jimmy Durante. Theatrical impresario Florenz Ziegfeld Jr. rented a box by the week and filled it with beautiful showgirls. Crooner Bing Crosby went often and was known to pick up hospital costs of injured riders. Others who stopped by to watch—and not necessarily cover the event—were celebrated newspaper writers James M. Cain, Walter Lippmann, and Damon Runyon. Before Cain became famous for his hardboiled novels and successful movie adaptations—*The Postman Always Rings*

Twice, *Mildred Pierce*, and *Double Indemnity*—he wrote editorials on sixes for the *New York World*, the city's largest-circulation newspaper.

After Goullet's dramatic victory in the Garden's December 1921 six, Runyon, remembered for his colorful stories of Broadway characters, devoted an editorial in the *New York American* to the bicyclist, pronouncing him "king of the six-day racers" and proclaiming, "Long live the king!"

• • •

Into this flamboyant, endless whirl popped young Bobby Walthour Jr. In 1921 he won the national amateur track championship at age nineteen. Soon afterward he turned professional to follow in his father's tire marks.

"He was really proud of his dad," Bobby Walthour III told me. "My dad used to brag about him. My dad took a big chance trying to fill his dad's shoes, but he gave it a good try."

The son had his father's easygoing disposition and straw-blond hair. He grew up around velodromes on both sides of the Atlantic and lived in Germany long enough to speak fluent German. The Walthour family originally came from Austria. The first Walthours settled in Georgia, and a Walthour built the first railroad line connecting Atlanta to Savannah. The family became wealthy landowners fifty miles from Savannah, where they founded the town of Walthourville in the late eighteenth century.

After Walthour Sr. had recovered from his broken leg, he received a commission in 1918 to head the YMCA Division formed for service with the French Army in France during the Great War. He returned to Newark after more than a year of duty abroad to find his wife involved with another man.

Too many long absences from the hearth ended the marriage of the couple who had pedaled to a parson on a bicycle built for two. Just after Valentine's Day in 1920, Walthour traveled to Atlanta and filed for divorce in Fulton County Superior Court. He charged that his wife had become infatuated with another man and alleged that she tried to kill him with a butcher knife.

Walthour Sr.'s career was for the most part over, although he still received contracts for exhibition rides in Germany, where he went to live.

When Bobby Walthour Jr. won the national amateur track championship at the end of the summer of 1921, he posed for photos on the Newark Velodrome, clutching a bouquet of flowers, the American flag wrapped around his shoulders. Next to him also wrapped in the flag and holding flowers was the professional champion, Frank Kramer.

• • •

Kramer was still on top at the age of forty-one. His defeat for the national title in 1917 interrupted his reign but didn't end it. When he'd lost the championship, thirty-seven-year-old Kramer realized his legs had slowed slightly so he converted to a bigger gear, from one that propelled him as though he were riding a high wheeler ninety-one inches in diameter to a gear equivalent to a wheel that was 104 inches in diameter. The bigger gear took getting used to, like a baseball player swinging a heavier bat, but after he mastered it, Kramer found the bigger gear packed more wallop. He came back to win the title in 1918 and again in 1921.

In 1922, when Walthour Jr. was moving up the pro ranks, Kramer still ruled as monarch of bikes. He advertised Cadillacs in newspapers and national magazines: "Frank Kramer, Cycle King, Drives a Cadillac—Why Don't You?"

Kramer was on course to capture yet another national title. In performance and longevity he was in the same class as Major League Baseball's Christy Mathewson, Cy Young, and Ty Cobb. But that summer he began having difficulty falling asleep. His physician told him insomnia was mental, but he felt it came from all the years of training and racing.

In the third week of July, Kramer performed well in the preliminary heats of a championship race that earned points counting toward the national title, but he faltered in the semifinals and was eliminated. He thought sleepless nights were affecting his performances. It didn't help that some spectators razzed the champion, called him an old man, told him he'd lost it. In his dressing room—its door bearing the words "Number One" for twenty-one years—he was unable to hold back tears. He protested to close friends that he didn't deserve harassment.

Kramer emerged from his dressing room to announce one last ride, appropriately, against the clock. He was going to shoot for a world record on which to end his career. He chose to go after the world record of one-sixth of a mile—one lap of the Newark Velodrome, his home track.

His retirement, at age forty-two, was treated as a national event. The *New York Times* ran stories for three days leading up to his last ride as cycling's sultan of speed, on July 26. The *Newark Evening News* assigned four reporters, two photographers, and a cartoonist.

Jack Brennan of Irvington, New Jersey, recalled Kramer's final ride with gusto. Brennan's father, John "Pop" Brennan, was a master bicycle mechanic and virtually an institution on the infield of sixes around the country. He took his sons Jack and Bill to witness Kramer's last ride on the Newark Velodrome.

"I was just a kid," Jack Brennan told me. "But I remember the excitement at the track. It was like the second coming of Jesus Christ."

When the grandstand, bleachers, and infield were crammed, Kramer was feted with one photo after another and one more award after another. Goullet had taken donations from the pros. "We collected about two hundred dollars," he said. "Kramer liked to smoke occasionally in the off-season. We knew a jeweler in town who could give us a good deal, so we bought Kramer a gold cigarette case. When I presented Kramer with the case, I teased him, 'Don't smoke too much.'"

Even Kramer's former trainer, Jack Neville, who hadn't spoken to him for years, came. After winning the 1912 world championship Kramer had returned to race in Europe in 1913 and 1914. On the last trip he thought his carefree, party-going trainer needed discipline and relegated him to steerage class while he himself traveled first class. They parted ways. They finally shook hands at Kramer's final ride; the band at the center of the velodrome struck up a rousing rendition of "Hail, Hail, the Gang's All Here."

At last Kramer swung a leg over his nickel-plated bicycle and warmed up for several laps around the velodrome. In the days before chrome was available, he preferred nickel-plated frames to enameled frames. He rode with Alfred Grenda, who paced him for a flying start. When the champion was ready, Grenda led him to within a few feet of the start line and then peeled away. Kramer flew at the crack of the starter's pistol.

Attired in his usual white silk jersey over black wool shorts, Kramer hurtled through the first turn. His legs rolled sharply as they had through so many title victories and so many races. He was considered the oldest professional athlete in the country, the highest paid, with an income topping $20,000 a year for twenty-two years. He was credited with winning 550 pro races on both sides of the Atlantic.

As he streaked down the back straight, the crowd boisterously cheered. He was trying to break the world record of 15.4 seconds set in 1911 by former rival Albert "Musty" Crebs in the thin air of Salt Lake City. As Kramer barreled through the final turn, the twenty-thousand throng jumped to its collective feet, yelling. They were witnessing Kramer sprinting for the last time in his career down the final straight.

When he flashed across the line, an official fired another shot in the air and all went silent. Everyone in the grandstand and bleachers and infield held their breath until announcer Willie Sullivan picked up the megaphone in both hands and bellowed that Kramer had equaled the world record. A brief silence followed. Then pandemonium.

It was an emotional moment that brought tears to many eyes. The band played "Auld Lang Syne," then "The Star-Spangled Banner." Kramer wrapped Old Glory over his shoulders and clutched it tight to his chest with one hand for his last lap of honor in front of a tumultuous crowd.

It was a high note on which to end his long competitive career. He was retiring as the incumbent national champion and ended by tying a world record while lowering his own personal mark for the distance by two-fifths of a second.

When Kramer finished cooling down he alighted from his bike in front of the grandstand. Well-wishers engulfed him. Kramer's remarks were characteristically brief. Ever methodical and uncomfortable speaking before the public, he stood next to Frank Mihlon and read from a prepared statement.

"I want to thank you for your interest shown in me and your appreciation of my efforts in the last twenty-seven years," he said. "I'm only sorry that I am not fifteen years younger, so that I might continue to entertain you. However, I have no alternative, and must bow to Father Time."

Another thunderous ovation followed. Hats and programs were tossed in the air. The band once again struck up the national anthem. It was a fitting tribute to a champion athlete who embodied the American ideals of integrity, perseverance, and courage. The following day reporter George Bancroft Duren published this poem in the *Newark Evening News*:

> When dusk creeps in and silence treads the bowl
> And shadows crouch in every vacant seat,
> He will come back in fantasy to ride
> Each winning and defeat.
> His last race run, the crown upon his head,
> And yet I know, though others look in vain,
> A silent form bent low across the bars
> Shall ride that track again.
> He will still come, a watcher in the crowd.
> And yet in mind, in heart, in soul, I know
> He will be there beside the panting men
> Who ride in the bowl below.

• • •

Tex Rickard borrowed a strategy from Chapman and reached across the Atlantic to France to sign up the dashing European heavyweight boxing champion Georges Carpentier. On July 2, 1921, in Jersey City, Rickard put his world heavyweight champion Dempsey against Carpentier. Rickard unabashedly billed the bout as "the Fight of the Century."

He nearly quadrupled the previous gate record, to $1.8 million (worth $25 million today). Not only was this the first million-dollar gate, when revenue came from tickets sold to the ninety thousand spectators passing through the turnstiles, it also was the first commentary broadcast over the radio.

Dempsey knocked Carpentier out in four rounds to keep his title. Rickard recognized a golden opportunity in whatever unexpected shape it might appear. He exploited the power of stars to sell tickets. He arranged another bout for Dempsey—against Luis Firpo of Argentina, who was called the Wild Bull of the Pampas. On September 14, 1923, in front of eighty thousand spectators at the Polo Grounds in New York City Firpo gave Dempsey a wild fight, twice knocking down the champion before Dempsey knocked Firpo flat for the ninth and final time in two rounds. That bout produced Rickard's second million-dollar gate.

After the battle, Goullet had lunch with Dempsey to talk about old times when Goullet had raced in Salt Lake City and young Dempsey polished his shoes in a barbershop. "As a youngster, Jack Dempsey wanted to race bikes more than anything," Goullet said. "On Decoration Day [Memorial Day], he was about fifteen or sixteen and he wanted to ride a race. He told the barber that he wouldn't be at work the next day. Then the barber said, 'No, you can't because tomorrow I will start you off with your own chair.' He wouldn't give Dempsey the day off. So Dempsey had to quit his job to race. It was twenty-five miles each way, out and back. Dempsey got to the turnaround when his chain broke and he had to walk all the way back. After that, he got involved in boxing."

• • •

Track races were simply another form of entertainment—a show for customers to watch riders on two-wheeled rockets dashing around banked tracks. To keep going fast, riders routinely took drugs. Nobody thought about drug testing any more than quizzing actors about spelling the words in their scripts.

Drugs have a shady tradition in cycling, back to the 1890s when riders began pedaling for cash. During the 1903 Madison Square Garden six the *New York World* published a cartoon of the Grim Reaper in hooded robe and carrying a scythe pedaling on a track ahead of riders who had died from ingesting strychnine. Taking a little strychnine in a strong-tasting drink to mask its bitter flavor improved muscle tone and stimulated cyclists to keep going. Prolonged use turned the drug lethal—the murderous potion propelling Agatha Christie mysteries.

Bobby Walthour III grew up in the 1920s and '30s as a child playing around tracks where his father was racing. He recalled in the 1980s how the smells of ether-doused sugar cubes, cognac (poured into milk), brandy, and absinthe—all favored by Europeans for dulling muscle soreness—hung in the air.

For decades cocaine, originally hailed as a cure for morphine addiction, was sold by prescription from drug stores, typically located on street corners. Cocaine powder inhaled or poured into drinks delivered a quick boost of energy and a sense of exhilaration. Cyclists called it eagle soup.

Cocaine produced unintended consequences for Eddy Root. In the summer of 1915, before a race on the Newark Velodrome, he was pumped up on cocaine before rain cancelled the program. He was long remembered by Newark residents as a madman with number thirteen on the back of his jersey, sprinting on his bike for hours along city streets in a downpour. News hawks didn't write he was a cheater on dope—he was only burning off eagle soup.

• • •

Bicycle racing led as one of America's best-paying sports for those at the top of a steep pyramid. Sam Gastman of Irvington, near Newark, was paid $150 a day, plus winnings, for the twenty-two sixes he rode for Chapman in the 1920s. Gastman, in his mideighties in 1985, walked with spring in his step and, still lean, looked race-ready. He said the money was very good but always hard earned.

Once, to help promote the November 1923 six-day in the Chicago Stadium, Chapman ordered Gastman and nine others to pedal their track bikes—which lack brakes and have a fixed gear that doesn't permit coasting—from Newark to Chicago, about 850 miles. Chapman intended their ride would attract the attention of newspaper reporters looking for a novelty story.

"The roads were horrible," Gastman recollected. "There were a lot of cobble roads. Most of the roads that were paved had broken pavement. Sometimes we rode through backyards because the roads were so bad. After we got to Chicago we rested three days. Then we had to race the six-day. There was a lot of competition to get into Chapman's races. There was a limit to the number of teams in the six-days, with fifteen to eighteen teams [two riders each], and half the riders came from this country, the other half from Europe and Australia. When you rode for a living, you had to do what Chapman said."

In 1925 the New York Giants football team was sold for $500. The February 13 *New York Times* trumpeted that Chapman signed burly Dutch sprinter Piet Moeskops to race in the spring Garden six for twenty times that amount. Chapman brought the four-time world sprint champion to America.

About the time Moeskops arrived, New York Life Insurance Company officials told Rickard they planned to demolish Madison Square Garden and replace it with a forty-story building that would become the company's main office. Never one to shut off a money machine, Rickard came up with nearly $6 million (worth $83 million today) from Wall Street backers to construct a new entertainment mecca twenty-five blocks uptown. It would accommodate his passion for boxing, as well as other indoor sports, like hockey, which he recently discovered and promoted. (He named the New York Rangers hockey team after the Texas Rangers. For a while they were known as Tex's Rangers.) To keep tradition, he called the new building Madison Square Garden.

The old Garden closed its doors forever on May 5, 1925. Its successor opened in November with a six-day that set a new attendance record: 15,475 men and women attended the final night's action to watch Belgians Gérard Debaets and Alfons Goosens take the win.

It was Goullet's farewell. Now thirty-four, he hung up his wheels. He'd won four hundred races on three continents. He and his bride, Jane, the daughter of a Newark council member, sailed to Paris for their honeymoon.

When I interviewed him in his apartment sixty years later, he told me with pride that he had won ten sixes—eight in Madison Square Garden, including the December 1922 edition partnered with Italy's great road racer, the frizzy-haired Gaetano Belloni, winner of the 1920 Tour of Italy. The other two sixes Goullet claimed were in Paris and Sydney. When I returned a couple weeks later, I said that the record books indicated he had won fifteen sixes. He shrugged and frowned. He didn't give a whoop about victories in Melbourne, Boston, Newark, or Chicago.

• • •

First Kramer, then Goullet. Chapman's stalwarts were retiring. He depended on foreign talent. America was headlong into its love affair with automobiles. Two hundred auto companies like Pierce-Arrow, Marmon, Duesenberg, Oakland, Flint, Star, Hupmobile, REO, Maxwell, Nash, and Moon were producing more cars every year. The U.S. Census of 1900 had put the number of motorcars in the country at 8,000; an Automotive Industries census in 1928 put the number of cars in the U.S. at 17.7 million.

Fewer adults pedaled bicycles. Fords or Chevrolets cost around $600, compared with $100 for a racing bike. Consumers sought luxury, not fitness. Chapman saw no need to build a farm system, like those run by baseball teams to cultivate young talent. He imported proven talent, a propensity that contributed to American cycling's downfall.

Goullet liked accompanying Tex Rickard to watch the New York Giants football team play and considered buying the franchise after he retired from cycling. "I talked to John Chapman and asked him to rent me the Newark Velodrome after the season closed following Labor Day. He became very suspicious and asked what I had in mind. I told him how I enjoyed watching the New York Giants play, and I wanted to purchase the franchise. The velodrome's grandstand and bleachers made for good sight lines. I would put up goalposts on either end of the center field and lay down the gridiron. But John Chapman wouldn't hear of it," Goullet said. "He turned me down. Said football was for high school kids and college boys. Chapman said nobody would ever pay to watch professional football."

• • •

It was widely acknowledged that Chapman was grooming Bobby Walthour Jr. to succeed Kramer as the next big name in the sport. Walthour's parents separated and he still lived at home with his mother, although under reduced circumstances. Chapman quietly provided groceries for the family and paid utility bills. Race results indicated that the youth lacked his father's top-end speed, but his quick recovery made him an intrepid six-day racer.

When eighteen-year-old Freddy Spencer of Plainfield won twenty-eight consecutive two-mile races as an amateur on the Newark Velodrome in the 1923 season, Chapman paid attention. Only a close second-place finish broke Spencer's streak. But the robust, raven-haired Spencer rallied and won the next fourteen two-milers.

Around this time Spencer had a brush with greatness. On a training ride he overtook an old gent pedaling an outmoded cycle. "All of a sudden this guy I had passed pulled up next to me and said I was riding real good. Before I could say anything, he introduced himself as Arthur Zimmerman! We stopped and shook hands. He said I could be a national champion."

Spencer didn't win an amateur title. "In 1924 Chapman turned me professional," Spencer told me. "Didn't even ask me about it. I was nineteen going on twenty. I had to lie about my age to ride in my first six-day because you had to be twenty-one to ride in them."

He jumped straight to the top—just what Chapman needed, although at the expense of depriving Spencer of trying out for that year's Olympics. Newshounds welcomed him with the nickname "the New Jersey Jammer." He had a round face with jug ears, and friends teased him for looking like a potato head. Spencer admired Kramer and emulated the master by riding shiny, nickel-plated frames. When chrome became available after the mid-1920s, Spencer had some of the country's first chrome-plated frames.

"I don't know why Kramer preferred the nickel-plated frames," Spencer said. "But I rode them because he looked so good on them, and I found I could look at the down tube of the frame and see the reflections of the riders behind me, like looking in a [rearview] mirror. That helped me keep track of what was going on behind me."

At the March 1925 Garden six, Dutchman Piet Moeskops was paid a $10,000 appearance fee, which newspaper writers declared made him the Garden's top moneymaker. The Dutchman was formidable. Not only was he six feet three and 230 pounds, he also reigned as the world pro sprint champion for four consecutive years. A former wrestler, he liked to playfully lean against rivals to push them around, like naughty children. That didn't work for Alfred Grenda, physically developed enough to hold his own.

Spencer, paired with Bobby Walthour Jr. as "the Little Old New Jersey Team," beat a sterling international field to win—the second six-day victory for the team of Spencer-Walthour.

Moeskops didn't figure in the grind. He took advantage of his visit to New York. Instead of returning to the Continent, he stayed with the intention of adding the U.S. professional sprint title to his accomplishments. The Dutchman was in for a surprise when he met Spencer for a one-mile match race in April. Spencer's preferred style was to take the lead, which suited the Dutchman. Spencer kept Moeskops even with his hip as they covered the inconsequential early portion of their first heat, and when the world champion made his move to surge ahead, the American matched pedal strokes down the banking and all the way to the line. Spencer repeated in similar style to win the match.

The first off his bike to congratulate him was Moeskops.

Chapman initially signed Spencer up for forty match races at $200 each (worth $3,000 today). He went undefeated, taking the U.S. title along the way. Chapman upped Spencer's appearance fee to $350 (worth $5,000 today) a match for the next six years, with a guarantee of at least thirty matches a season.

Moeskops returned to the Netherlands at the end of the season without the American national championship. Yet he won a fifth worlds in 1926 in Milan.

• • •

In October 1925 Spencer teamed up again with Walthour and captured the Chicago Six. A total of more than one hundred thousand fans watched them ride to victory in the March six-day in New York. Nearly as many people saw them win seven months later in Chicago. Walthour became celebrated in Chicago for scoring five consecutive six-day victories. Spencer got a lot of attention when he became the first racer to win a six-day and the national championship in the same year.

Spencer and Walthour Jr. were such big celebrities they were invited to the White House to meet President Calvin Coolidge. In 1986, at his house in Rahway, New Jersey, Spencer told me about the meeting. His hair mostly white, he walked with ease at age eighty-one.

"The way President Coolidge shook my hand, I thought he had a broken finger because he had a funny grip. President Coolidge was not a cycling fan. But being that Walthour and I were so popular, the president wanted to meet us." (Spencer explained the president shook his hand by curling his second finger toward the palm of his hand, a technique for reducing pressure in a hard squeeze.)

After meeting Coolidge, Walthour and his fiancée, Margaret Murray, hailed a cab, eloped to Alexandria, Virginia, and got married in Alexandria City Hall—to keep up the family tradition.

Spencer and the newlyweds traveled by car to Atlanta and Chapman's velodrome farm in College Park for a rest.

• • •

A crack showed up in the sport's structure when velodromes in Worcester and New Bedford went out of business in 1926. The tracks were not part of Chapman's circuit. Observers said they failed because his circuit had the best competition and Bay Staters stopped attending when they saw inferior riders, or races that were fixed.

At the top of the sport, six-day purses at Rickard's "Castle of Competition" jumped 50 percent to $75,000 (worth $1 million today), and attendance records were climbing. Rickard exploited star power with Hollywood celebrities. The March 11 *New York Times* chronicled that, after midnight, Hollywood sweethearts Douglas Fairbanks and Mary Pickford went to the Garden, followed by Theodore Roosevelt Jr. Fairbanks donated $200 primes for two one-mile sprints. Pickford posed for a photo with Fred Spencer.

On July 12, 1926, fire swept the grandstand and a section of the track at the Newark Velodrome. Firefighters responded quickly. They worked under constant danger that electric trolley wires would drop on them. Tongues of flames lit up the skyline. The heat was so intense that steel bicycle frames in a shed buckled and bent. Damage to the track was estimated at $25,000; insurance was limited to $10,000.

Inglis Uppercu paid for the repairs. Since becoming involved in the sport, he had made more than a million dollars from the Newark and New York velodromes. Five months older and slightly shorter than Chapman, Uppercu had fine facial features and blond hair, combed straight back. He was born in Evanston, Illinois, the son of a lawyer.

After graduating from the Brooklyn Polytechnic Institute he attended Columbia University Law School. Fascinated with cars and combustion engines, he gave up law to become an auto mechanic. He also owned gold, silver, and manganese mining interests in Mexico, Montana, and North Dakota.

During World War I, he was president of a company manufacturing seaplanes for the federal government. The government paid him a salary of a dollar a year and issued him a paper barring his arrest or delay under any circumstances. From 1914 to 1917 he operated a passenger airline connecting Miami, Nassau, Cuba, and Key West. A yachting enthusiast, he reconditioned a full-rigged clipper ship, the *Seven Seas*, and sailed it.

He influenced John Ringling to invest in the New York Velodrome in 1920. Ringling was renowned for common sense. He trusted Uppercu's judgment and spent $50,000 to buy into the venture, an investment that paid each man back more than tenfold.

In 1925, Uppercu became president of the National Cycling Association. Promoting sports was a relatively new enterprise. Yet as Rickard had demonstrated in boxing and Chapman in cycling, the attendance and money were there for the taking.

Once the Newark Velodrome was repaired and back in operation Chapman resumed bringing world-class riders to Newark. Today it is hard to reconcile the city's renown as the Home of Cycling. Yet for the first three decades of the twentieth century, Newark hosted every world professional champion and most national pro and amateur champions from Europe and Australia.

The Garden's sixes had an even more passionate following. *New York Times* sportswriter John Kieran examined the phenomenon in his March 10, 1927, Sports of the Times column:

> There are several problems that still baffle the scientists, and one of them is the dreadful six-day bike bacillus which twice a year ravages the peaceful population of this more or less fair city. Once bitten by the "bike bug," the victim bids his family farewell, takes up a leaning position on a rail at Madison Square Garden and for an entire week alternates between periods of coma and hysteria.

> At times the patient gives no sign of life at all. That is during those hours when the weary pedal-pushers circle the track at a funeral pace. But as the riders come to life the patient goes into fits of delirium. While a "jam" is on he shouts, weeps, gnashes his teeth, stamps on his coat, tosses his hat in the air and subsides exhausted only when the clanging of the bell tells him that some luckless rider has crashed to the track and the pace is slowed down to pick up the wreckage.
>
> If the spill occurs at the end of the track the patient is in his glory. He will buttonhole everybody coming into the Garden and tell about it, with gestures.
>
> "Mac tried to cut inside—clipped Dinale's hind wheel—down they went—Goosens rode into the pile—turned a somersault—landed on his nose—murder! Sure, I was standing right there—MacNamara had Dinale's front wheel around his neck when they picked up—here's a couple of spokes for souvenirs."
>
> And thus the dread disease runs its course.

What kept the riders in the race? Kieran suggested there was no logical answer but added there was at least a plausible explanation:

> Money makes the wheels go round. Except for a trifling matter of breakage in bones, bike riding is a profitable profession.
>
> "We must have bloody noses and cracked crowns," said Harry Hotspur in *King Henry the Fourth*, and bike riders turn these necessities into profit. An ordinary six-day pedal-pusher might average $5,000 or better during any given year. Reggie MacNamara sometimes makes as much as $25,000 or $30,000 a year, but Mac plays more circuits than most riders. And he's the flower of the six-day flock.
>
> New York is not the only city which suffers from the six-day fever. It's an international disease. There are six-day grinds in Chicago, Berlin, Antwerp, Brussels, Paris, and Milan. This clearly indicates that no nation has a monopoly on insanity.

Spencer corroborated Kieran's explanation: "What kept me going so well was the money that I earned. It was very exciting. I liked the fans. They treated me real nice."

In December 1927 Spencer was teamed with New Yorker Charley Winter and was hard at it in the Garden's forty-third international six. Winter had taken up cycling on a dare. His brother-in-law told him it was a rich man's sport and training took all day, every day. Winter acquired a racing bike, won two national amateur championships, and set a national record for one-third of a mile. He was a rookie pro teamed with Spencer in the Garden six.

They were five laps down on the leaders, a team from France, when Spencer was awakened from a nap as Winter raced around the track. Spencer woke up surprised to discover his guest was Major Taylor.

"He said I was aces," Spencer said.

Taylor was apparently enjoying himself that day, although he was having a tough time personally. With his fortune dwindling, he and his wife sold off most of her jewelry by 1925 and disposed of their seven-bedroom house for a smaller residence in Worcester. These changes created marital friction. Their daughter, Sydney, had graduated from the Sargent School of Physical Education in Cambridge (now the College of Health & Rehabilitation Sciences at Boston University) and left home for a teaching career. Taylor attempted to recapture his achievements by composing his autobiography, dictated to a student from the local business school. His wife moved out to live with friends in New York City.

Alone and broke, but with his spirit intact, Taylor completed his manuscript by the time he met Spencer. Taylor was unable to interest a publisher, so he published the book in 1928 at his own expense through the Commonwealth Press of Worcester, and listed the publisher as the Wormley Publishing Company: *The Fastest Bicycle Rider in the World: The Story of a Colored Boy's Indomitable Courage and Success Against Great Odds*, in 430 pages, with photos. He dedicated it: "To my true friend and advisor, Louis 'Birdie' Munger."

Taylor's faith in Spencer was justified. The Spencer-Winter team rallied to overcome their deficit of laps on the leaders and turned the race in their favor. Spencer won the final sprint by six lengths to capture another Garden six-day. Twenty-one thousand fans, a new record attendance, went wild in appreciation to show that they, too, thought he was "aces."

• • •

A short time later, Rickard invited fifty millionaires to a banquet he organized to celebrate what he called the "Kings of Sport." His banquet, at the Waldorf-Astoria Hotel, Manhattan's premier luxury hotel, remains memorable for hosting the greatest single gathering of America's top athletes of the 1920s.

Babe Ruth, who in 1927 had belted sixty home runs for the Yankees, was there. So was Gene Tunney, the new world boxing heavyweight champion after defeating Dempsey in two bouts that produced more than $3 million for Rickard. Also in attendance were Bill Tilden, the first American to win Wimbledon, who had already notched up six U.S. singles tennis championships; Atlanta golfer Bobby Jones, who was well on his way to winning thirteen U.S. and British championships and achieving golf's grand slam—winning four major tournaments in one year; Bill Cook, a hockey star on the New York Rangers, who scored the team's first goal in Madison Square Garden history; and Johnny Weissmuller, the Olympic swimming champion, who was soon to become best known for his Tarzan movie roles.

Joining these Kings of Sport were Spencer and Winter. When the eight monarchs of sport assembled for the photographer, Spencer sat next to Jones, a golfing buddy. Jones gave him a pair of steel clubs, which Spencer had bike mechanic John "Pop" Brennan use as seat stays for a bike frame Brennan made for him.

• • •

The year 1928 began like a highly spirited six-day jam. In January Rickard announced to the Fourth Estate that Chapman was appointed vice president and assistant general manager of the Madison Square Garden Corporation. On February 5 Rickard proclaimed that Chapman was representing him on a trip to London to "look over the situation" for a title bout in White City Stadium, famed for holding most of the 1908 London Olympics events. Then Rickard left for a vacation in Miami where he owned property and spent winters.

Around that time Kramer stepped off the gangway of a ship in New York harbor and told reporters that the Union Cycliste Internationale in

Paris had awarded the 1929 worlds to the United States. Kramer, chairman of the board of the National Cycling Association, said officials at UCI member countries assured him they would send their outstanding talents to the worlds, set for August 1929. Newark would host the professional and amateur track sprint championships, and New York would hold motor-pace events.

The news was warmly received in Newark. Howard Freeman, a cartoonist for the *Evening News*, wrote, "The two-wheeled racket does not need any stimulation, for it runs along on an even keel from season to season, paying great dividends to the moguls. But Chapman believes in serving the customers with a delectable dessert once every decade just to break the monotony of a menu that's pretty much the same year in and year out."

Freeman predicted additional stands would be erected to accommodate a bigger audience than 1912. He published a cartoon of Chapman, in spats, greeting Kramer, gripping a bundle labeled "World's Bicycling Championships."

But the biggest fumble in American cycling was about to happen.

7

Sputtering to an End

From surfeit to loss is a short line.

—CAROL SHIELDS, *The Stone Diaries*

American popular culture underwent changes. Millions of listeners could hear in the comfort of their homes radio broadcasts of six-day races from Madison Square Garden's station, WMSG. In 1928, radio had become such an accepted way of life that E. M. Statler invested a million dollars to equip 7,700 rooms in his six Statler Hotels with loudspeakers and headsets so that guests could "feel at home." Some visionaries were predicting that sports fans would watch sixes without leaving home, thanks to a new device called television. Prototype television used a screen four inches high and eight inches wide to receive a picture that made a squealing sound when transmitted.

At the same time, the relationship between Rickard and Chapman was cooling. Rickard, seven years older than Chapman, was renowned for the thousands in cash he carried in the pockets of his custom-tailored suits. He never hesitated to give money to an athlete in need, or to lay a wager. In a relaxed moment with Fred Spencer, Rickard pulled the engraved metal handle out of his cane to reveal the grip of a pistol; he carried the cane as much for style as for protection.

Chapman never carried a cane, or much cash. He paid a few select riders well and let everybody else fend for themselves. Even though attendance swelled at the new Garden's sixes, Chapman paid his star Spencer only up to $800 a day—less than the $1,000 he paid Goullet. Most riders were grateful just to compete in his races. Chapman took advantage of them. They ruefully nicknamed him Stingy Johnny.

He was notorious for appropriating national team sweaters that riders from France, Italy, Belgium, and other countries brought with them to ward off the chill of drafty, cavernous arenas where the sixes were held. Stingy Johnny snitched sweaters without asking, like a tithe, and collected them by the trunk-load. Each winter he took them to his Georgia farm to give to farmhands.

Chapman's publicist, former *Newark Morning Star* reporter Harry Mendel, published a story in the *Newark Evening News* about the first night he spent at Chapman's Georgia farm. Mendel looked out a window the next morning and saw so many workers scurrying around doing chores in foreign team sweaters that he thought a bike race was about to start.

Spencer and Goullet said Chapman, to his credit, always paid promptly, no questions asked. According to Spencer, Chapman required that money for the primes, which riders valued so highly, had to be paid up front before any announcement was made. "Mr. Chapman never accepted an IOU," Spencer said. "When you won a prime, you got an envelope with the money right away."

Chapman's tenure under Rickard led to clashes. The biggest involved how to promote sixes. Rickard insisted on handing choice tickets to his legion of friends. Chapman protested that sixes were doing fine without giving away free tickets. Following the December 1928 six-day, he resigned after nearly a year as vice president and assistant general manager of the Garden's corporation.

Ostensibly, he quit over his sense that customers would be deprived of their chance to purchase choice seats to sixes if tickets were given to cronies. Within the corporation, Chapman never blended. He was regarded as one whose position was patronage for the high profits of the Garden's bicycle races. They proved a reliable revenue source, but not enough over the whole year compared with national and state political conventions, bathing-beauty contests, new-car shows, boy-scout jamborees, dog shows, and other high-profile affairs.

Chapman had the personality of a vaudevillian straight man. He lacked social polish. Small talk was not in his repertoire. His growing up in a log cabin with a dirt floor and an education from a rural one-room primary school left him like rainwater to the refined oil of clubby, urbane Ivy League corporate trustees. They praised him in public as he left to devote more time to cycling interests.

On New Year's Day 1929, Rickard was operated on in Miami Beach for acute appendicitis. His appendix had been aggravating him for seven years, but he dreaded surgery so much that he ignored all suggestions—and constant pain—to go under the scalpel. Following the operation, infection from his gangrenous appendix spread through his abdomen. He died on January 6, age fifty-nine.

He lived and died with superlatives. His body returned to New York aboard the Havana Special train, in a bronze casket that weighed 2,200 pounds. Eighteen policemen and firefighters were required to carry it. His body lay in state in his beloved Garden's arena in keeping with the character of the myriad events he staged there. Jack Dempsey covered the arena with a blanket of orchids six feet deep and the message "My pal."

Rickard had elevated boxing from a fugitive sport to one where thousands from the Social Register filled the audience alongside common folk. Five of his prizefights generated million-dollar gates, sums unmatched for nearly half a century, until the advent of closed-circuit TV. Rickard died leaving an estate valued at $2.5 million (worth $40 million today), including $1 million in cash.

Among his pallbearers were Dempsey, John Ringling, and John M. Chapman. Although it was widely speculated that Chapman would succeed him as president of Madison Square Garden, he never had a chance. That post went to John Reed Kilpatrick, a former All-American end on the Yale football team, a decorated army officer, and a member of the Garden's board of directors.

• • •

For the rest of the country, 1929 opened auspiciously. The stock market's first day of the year started with a new record of 5,413,610 shares sold. The rush of orders established big gains. General Electric was the best seller, up twenty-three points. In Detroit, the Ford Motor Company plant in early January hired 600 out of an army of 25,000 jobless applicants shivering outside the gate. The company publicized that it planned to add 30,000 more to the payroll when the factory went to a six-day workweek to increase production by 20 percent.

Paddy Harmon in Chicago envisioned his greatest promotion as a sports palace: the Chicago Stadium. He'd turned himself into one of the Windy City's most colorful personalities. Everywhere he went he was recognized for his gray fedora, an aw-shucks grin, sometimes motoring behind the wheel of his beloved Packard, a pricey luxury car he favored over Cadillacs.

He invested $2.5 million of his own money in the stadium's $7 million budget. He wanted to build the Chicago Stadium as the biggest entertainment center in America, with seats for 20,000—surpassing Madison Square Garden by 5,000. His stadium boasted an unobstructed view from every seat, with clear sightlines for hourly paid laborers in the cheap seats and executives filling the best seats in the house. The architectural plan was so large it violated Chicago's building code—until the city council amended the code to permit construction.

The stadium went up as a state-of-the-art steel-and-concrete structure erected in 1928 in the West End, close to the downtown Loop. The stadium's symmetrical, rectangular lines filled a city block and featured classic Greek architectural design. Eighty-nine feet above the ground were panels of sculptured naked athletes—carved in a style of ancient Greeks—including a track cyclist. Inside, a hundred feet above the floor, a mighty pipe organ nestled in the steel trusses to provide what Harmon deemed as "psychological accompaniment." Organ music filled the stadium as though God were performing from the ceiling.

The 1929 cycling season opened unevenly. Attendance at the New York Velodrome remained robust, unlike the Newark Velodrome where box office revenues declined so much that Chapman abandoned Saturday events and cut the velodrome program to two days of racing a week. Worse, steady rainstorms forced cancellation of many programs on his Northeast circuit.

Chapman expected the 1929 worlds to set new ticket sales records, but the program was in jeopardy. The Union Cycliste Internationale had added separate road races for amateurs and pros to the worlds program. Road racing failed to interest Chapman. Getting permission from city, county, and state governments to allow cyclists to compete on their roads seemed like too much bureaucracy. He was content to rely on velodrome programs.

Amateur racing had fallen into neglect following the demise of the League of American Wheelmen in 1900. The LAW transferred its membership in the international governing body to the NCA. For the 1920 Olympics in Antwerp, Belgium, Chapman and NCA officers held the authority, granted from the NCA's UCI membership and the International Olympic Committee, to select the eleven road and track cyclists to represent the United States, but riders and their clubs had to pay all travel expenses. Olympians and their clubs expressed outrage.

After the Antwerp Olympics more than two dozen grassroots cycling clubs, from New York to San Jose, revolted. The clubs banded together to create a new organization in 1920 committed to amateur racing: the Amateur Bicycle League of America, incorporated in 1921 in New York. Years of bitter jurisdictional bickering followed before NCA officials begrudgingly tolerated the ABLA as long as it stayed off velodromes and never held pro events.

Chapman and NCA officials insisted on organizing the 1929 worlds like it was 1912. The UCI required host countries to organize a full program of track and road races. Without holding road races, the only compromise would be for Chapman to put on velodrome events and make a substantial cash contribution to the UCI, something not in Chapman's parsimonious nature.

The *New York Times* and *Newark Evening News*, which had trumpeted the news of the 1929 worlds awarded to the United States, kept mute on what followed. But retired pro rider Walter Bardgett, associate editor of *American Bicyclist and Motorcyclist*, suggested, "The running of the road championship was probably the straw that busted the camel's suspenders."

The UCI awarded its 1929 worlds to Zürich, Switzerland. The venue change represented a pivotal moment for American bicycle racing, like a plot point in a novel, a movie, an opera. The National Cycling

Association remained fixed on track racing, unlike the organization's counterparts in Europe—which had been sanctioning annual one-day classics and multiday stage races for decades.

Thus began American cycling's decline and fall.

• • •

With attendance dwindling at the Newark Velodrome, Chapman, now fifty, skimped on maintenance. A standard temporary repair was to cover a bad spot on the board track with a car license plate. Nineteen-year-old Sergio Matteini of New York's Greenwich Village, who won both the NCA and ABL championships in 1929, told me that the Newark Velodrome had several such patches where the pine surface was worn. Matteini and Spencer recalled that the practice with license plates was common at that time.

"The splinters were terrible at the Newark Velodrome," Matteini said. "After crashes there, I was always pulling out splinters. It was an old track and needed a lot of repair. But they used to get some good crowds watching."

About the time the worlds program would have been held in Newark, the city commission discussed the advisability of removing the velodrome to build new streets to relieve motor traffic congestion in the neighborhood. The issue was raised because the lease that Frank Mihlon and Inglis Uppercu had to the land the track was on was set to expire on January 1, 1931.

Then came Black Tuesday. On October 29, 1929, Wall Street was swamped with 12,894,650 shares of stock up for sale; the ticker lagged for hours. Within two days, $15 billion in stock market "value" had vanished.

Wall Street's debacle rattled the country. Paddy Harmon's dream for Chicago Stadium turned into a nightmare. His Chicago Six, usually so robust its box office practically printed money, couldn't sell tickets. One company had pre-ordered 5,400 tickets, but then laid off all the employees for whom the tickets were ordered. Despite a classy international field of six-day racers and the mighty organ shaking the rafters with rousing music, the music fell down on battalions of empty seats. Stadium trustees were irate over the financial failure and held Harmon, president and general manager, responsible. He was sacked.

Attendance at the Newark Velodrome declined through 1930. Chapman cut the prize money to seventy-five dollars for first place, and upped the general admission fee to a dollar. Sports promotion, which took a blow when Tex Rickard died, took another hit that July when Paddy Harmon was killed in a car accident. Then, on a sweltering August night as the whole Northeast was suffering one of the worst heat waves on record, the New York Velodrome went up in flames.

The three-alarm blaze was reported at 3:30 a.m. on August 4. It lit up the sky for miles and woke up residents in the vicinity. The fire spread fast. Firefighters abandoned efforts to save the velodrome and fought to keep the blaze from spreading. Showers of sparks rained on hundreds of residences and businesses. Hundreds of homes lost electricity as fire destroyed electric lines.

The cause of the fire was reportedly a lighted cigarette left over from the race the night before. Goullet shook his head when discussing the blaze. "It was a deliberate fire," he said. "There was no question about that."

The fire followed the opening two weeks earlier of the Coney Island Velodrome. On July 19 the new velodrome—with seats for ten thousand—began operation with a full card of twenty-three events. Like the Newark and New York velodromes, it was six laps to the mile. Chapman granted NCA sanction to Coney Island's velodrome management, but he neglected to authorize top riders to compete there. The fire eliminated the new track's main competitor.

The owners of the New York Velodrome declined to rebuild. In 1928, Inglis Uppercu invested in the Uppercu Cadillac Building in Manhattan, a twelve-story structure to store the Cadillac and LaSalle cars his company, the Uppercu Cadillac Corporation, sold and serviced. The new building took a considerable financial commitment, which put him in a bind when the Depression began and car sales nose-dived. According to the *New York Times*, velodrome co-owner John Ringling, age sixty-four, was then mainly interested in acquiring "the biggest and best art collection."

The Newark Velodrome, its property lease set to expire at the end of the year, appeared destined for oblivion. It was generally expected that Frank Mihlon would build a new velodrome on the six-acre plot he owned directly behind its present location because he had netted a fortune. When Prohibition took effect in 1920 and the sale of alcoholic beverages became illegal, Mihlon sold the Long Bar Saloon. He bought land around Newark to provide for family members.

On December 4, 1930, the Newark Velodrome, on which so many stirring battles had been fought and world records set, was torn down so the site could be returned to its owners in the same condition as when leased. The location that had been so vital in cycling circles for thirty-five years was knocked to pieces by the wrecker's ball.

All winter, rumors circulated about the fate of cycling in Newark. On February 13, 1931, *Evening News* columnist Willie Ratner wrote that there was a move underway to fund a new velodrome in the aptly named Dreamland Park section of Newark, with Alf Goullet as manager. Riders themselves raised $38,000 to fund the venture. But the sum fell short. Chapman was not willing to invest. Uppercu could not. Ringling wasn't interested. Mihlon was equivocal.

The source of Mihlon's indecision that winter may have been across the Atlantic, in Berlin. Frank Mihlon Jr. recalled that his father had lost a considerable sum in Berlin where a velodrome he had invested in burned down in 1930 not long after it opened. It was the Rutt Arena, named after Walter Rutt, the German champion who won the 1913 world professional sprint championship. Mihlon and Rutt knew each other well over the years because the German raced in Newark and New York before and after World War I. When Rutt retired in the 1920s, he prevailed upon Mihlon for capital.

"I recall that Mother and Dad got into an argument over the amount of money that Dad took in a suitcase over to Berlin to finance construction of the track," Frank Mihlon Jr. told me. Hyperinflation exceeding 200 percent a week hobbled Germany; construction costs would have been exorbitant. "Dad dropped a lot of money there, a suitcase full of cash, and he didn't get any of it back."

Not until early March 1931 did Mihlon make up his mind. Bill Wathey, sports columnist for the *Newark Star-Eagle*, wrote on March

9 that Chapman told him that Uppercu and Mihlon could not afford to rebuild a track in Newark.

Soon after, Chapman and his wife, Martha, boarded a train to travel around the South. He was in New Orleans when he suffered a mild coronary. The couple returned to Newark where he recovered.

• • •

The 1920s roared, but the 1930s whimpered. American cycling tumbled into a downward spiral. The Depression stifled the economy: one-third of the American workforce could not find jobs; business failure rates tripled from 48 per 10,000 listed enterprises in 1920 to 154 in 1932; suicides hit a rate of 15.6 per 10,000 population in 1930, the highest in American history for eighty years.

The Revere Beach track in Boston closed in 1931, its boards sold for firewood. The same fate happened in Providence and Philadelphia. Only the Coney Island Velodrome remained, its attendance modest. All Chapman had left were sixes in New York and other cities.

Sergio Matteini got an invitation from Georges Kaiser in Paris to race for him in 1931. Kaiser, billing himself as "Agent of the Stars," maintained a stable of outstanding sprinters. They included English champion Syd Cozens, French champions Lucien Faucheux and Louis Gérardin, Italian champion Mario Bergamini, and Belgian icon Jef Scherens.

Matteini's pedaling style was smooth, his torso steady as a statue—he rode like he was floating. He was short and small-boned. With movie-idol features, he became known on both sides of the Atlantic as Adonis of Bikedom. He settled outside Paris for most of the next four years.

His 1931 season was remarkable for winning a three-man match race on the Vélodrome Buffalo in Paris, like Major Taylor, Arthur Zimmerman, George Banker, and Frank Kramer had earlier. Matteini beat Belgian champion Scherens and former world amateur champion Willy Falck Hansen of Denmark to raise expectations for another American medal at the worlds. Two weeks before the worlds, however, Matteini wound up in a Paris hospital with typhoid fever. Falck Hansen won the 1931 worlds, with Scherens third.

Matteini became good friends with Scherens, winner of the world pro sprint title in 1932, and again in 1933. Matteini accompanied him in 1933 for the celebration Scherens received in Brussels, with horse-drawn carriages and a ticker-tape parade. Scherens dominated sprinting each year until the outbreak of World War II.

Like Scherens, Matteini was a pure sprinter and specialized in match races. Agent Georges Kaiser secured his racers with matches paying them $200 to $350 a race, even during the depths of the Depression, and they raced often.

Matteini competed all over France, Italy, and Denmark, and he crossed the Mediterranean to race in Casablanca, Morocco. He became an honorary citizen of the French city of Niort, near Bordeaux, where he won the Grand Prix de Niort.

• • •

Major Taylor was reduced to selling copies of his autobiography door to door. Those close to him in his glory days couldn't offer him aid. Louis Munger had died suddenly at age sixty-six of a heart attack in 1929 in New York City. Taylor's former agent, William A. Brady, lost everything in the stock market collapse. Brady, sixty-five, was putting on plays to get enough money to retire.

Word of Taylor's predicament reached a former competitor, James B. Bowler. Bowler got in touch with Taylor in 1930. An alderman for Chicago's twenty-fifth ward, Bowler told Taylor he would get him a job if the old champion would come. Taylor sold what possessions he had, including his house and collection of American and French bicycles. His daughter, Sydney Taylor Brown, told me he piled a cart high with copies of his autobiography and left Worcester.

Chicago held promise for Taylor. He had a brother living there, and he was remembered from his racing days. Taylor took up residence in a YMCA and took a job. Photos taken in Chicago show him dapperly dressed in a suit and tie, but with sad eyes, often downcast.

By age fifty he suffered health problems. In the spring of 1932 he was admitted to Provident Hospital. He remained a patient there for a month and then was moved to a charity ward in Cook County Hospital. On June 21, 1932, Taylor died of an apparent heart attack, age fifty-three.

His death went largely unnoticed, except for the *Chicago Defender*, a weekly newspaper for African Americans. It ran a story on July 2 titled:

“Major Taylor Dies Here in Charity Ward.” According to an article by Robert Lucas in the May 1948 *Negro Digest*, “barely enough mourners to fill a single automobile” accompanied his body to Mount Glenwood Cemetery—a sad end to the young man who won two world championships so well attended that thousands were turned away at the gate. The athlete who drew as many as thirty thousand paying fans to a meet was buried in an unmarked grave.

After the mid-1940s, the Bicycle Racing Stars of the Nineteenth Century Association, in Chicago, joined distinguished black athletes to give Taylor a better resting place. On May 23, 1948, a memorial service was held in the Mount Glenwood Cemetery. It was attended by members of the association, black athletes, and members of the Olde Tymers Athletic Club of the Wabash Avenue YMCA. They had Taylor’s body moved to the cemetery’s Memorial Garden of the Good Shepherd.

Delivering the main address at the memorial service was Ralph Metcalfe, the black track-and-field star sprinter who won four medals at the 1932 Los Angeles Olympics and the 1936 Berlin Olympics and would become a congressman. Other black athletes were National Football Hall of Fame players Claude “Buddy” Young and Frederick “Duke” Slater, and 1936 track-and-field Olympian John Brooks. Walter Bardgett, a former rival, covered the memorial service for *American Bicyclist and Motorcyclist*.

Frank Schwinn, president of the Schwinn Bicycle Manufacturing Company, provided a tombstone for Taylor. The cycling association donated a bronze tablet with Taylor’s sculpted image. It was placed on his grave with the inscription: “World’s champion bicycle racer—who came up the hard way—without hatred in his heart—an honest, courageous and God-fearing, clean living gentlemanly athlete, a credit to his race who always gave out his best—gone but not forgotten.”

• • •

American cycling appeared to revive in Nutley, a residential community northeast of Newark. On June 4, 1933, the Nutley Velodrome opened. Twelve thousand fans packed the grandstand and bleachers.

Frank Kramer had recommended that it be seven laps to the mile so the turns would be sharper and tighter to provide more speed and excitement for spectators. For a while a track cycling renaissance seemed possible.

Even though admission was only forty cents, official programs going for ten cents, attendance was so high the track paid for itself by the second season, rather than in five as planned. Velodrome owner Joe Miele, a local businessman, said he wanted to give bike fans a break and promote the sport. Managing the velodrome was Harry Mendel, a gregarious former *Newark Evening News* scribe turned entrepreneur—he also managed a car-racing track, promoted prizefights, and helped Chapman promote sixes.

A new generation of pros was dazzling audiences. William "Torchy" Peden of Canada, Cecil Yates of Texas, Norman Hill of California, local rider Tino Reboli, and the versatile Belgian national road racing champion Gérard Debaets became stars in Nutley.

The first two auspicious seasons were only an Indian summer before the cold winds of January 1935. Mendel had a falling out with Miele and left to manage the Coney Island Velodrome, a split that harmed both venues. Mendel and Miele discouraged pros from signing contracts with their rival, a departure from the past circuits. The Nutley and Coney Island velodromes scraped along fitfully for a few years, more by memories of cycling's heyday than by receipts.

• • •

At the end of the 1934 season, Sergio Matteini returned to the United States. "Something was in the wind," he told me. "Crowds at the races were falling off. People were preoccupied—they had no money and they were tightening their belts. You could see the war was coming."

• • •

The last American sprinter in Europe was Bill Honeman, NCA pro champ from 1934 to 1936. He grew up on a chicken farm outside Newark and went into the city with his parents to watch races at the Newark Velodrome. Inspired by watching Frank Kramer win match sprints, he entered races in his early teens. After Kramer retired he took Honeman on as a protégé.

"Kramer suggested sprinting in the saddle," Honeman told me. "Getting out of the saddle to stand on the pedals was something the six-day riders did. But the pure sprinters, like Kramer, stayed in the saddle. He also emphasized quality training at peak speed over the last eighth mile [220 yards]."

In 1924 Honeman won the Amateur Bicycle League of America national junior championship at Humboldt Park in Buffalo. He turned pro at nineteen, in the spring of 1928, and specialized in match sprints in Newark and New York. He refined his skills against visiting pros from Europe and Australia. He looked up to Australian Bob Spears, the 1920 world pro sprint champion. A six-feet-five tower of a man, Spears stretched over his bike frame—both hands gripped the handlebar drops ahead of his front wheel hub. Walter Bardgett nicknamed him the Drake.

Honeman told me he felt devastated when he learned that fire destroyed the New York Velodrome. "All my ambition and enthusiasm for the sport just went down the drain when that track burned to the ground. And the Newark Velodrome was soon to go, too."

As the wrecking ball smashed Newark's track, Spears and his wife, a Newark native, sold their house. Spears invited Honeman to ship out with them to Paris. "Spears knew a lot of people in Europe, where he raced in the early 1920s. He acted as my manager and secured some contracts for me around Europe."

They traveled on trains to cities on the track circuit across France, Belgium, and Denmark. Spears was in demand for having won several grand prix events and silver medals at two worlds. "Match races were sure money," Honeman said. "We were paid a hundred dollars to win, seventy-five if we lost."

Honeman rated Paris as his favorite city for racing indoors, in the spacious Vélodrome d'Hiver (the Winter Track), often shortened to Vel d'Hiv (pronounced "vel d'eve"), with its skylight, and outdoors on the Parc des Princes. His scrapbooks show that he was a headliner.

In 1934 Honeman returned to northern New Jersey. He received star treatment on the Nutley Velodrome and won the NCA national pro sprint title. That autumn he boarded a ship one last time to Paris for the winter indoor season of 1934–35, which proved momentous for American cycling.

The Vel d'Hiv promoter informed Honeman that instead of the plain white jersey he wore in homage to Frank Kramer, still remembered there by the public, Honeman needed a proper national champion's jersey. "The United States did not have one at the time," he said. "But all the European national champions had their championship jerseys, made of silk and using the colors of their national flags. A Paris sports shop called Unis designed a jersey that featured a blue field with white stars on the upper part and vertical red-and-white stripes below. I wore it for the first time in races on the Vel d'Hiv."

He wore that jersey on the Nutley Velodrome. The design soon was adopted as the jersey of U.S. national champions.

• • •

In 1936, the United States was gasping from the chokehold the Depression had on the economy. Even baseball, the nation's pastime, strained to survive. Major League Baseball's payroll had been scaled back 25 percent in five years, from $4 million in 1931 to $3 million in 1936, according to a spokesperson for the National Baseball Hall of Fame and Museum in Cooperstown, New York. The average annual salary for players dropped from $9,800 to $7,500.

Cycling's leaders were passing away. August Zimmerman died in Atlanta on October 20 at sixty-seven of a massive heart attack while walking along a sidewalk with his grown daughter. Shortly after Christmas, Frank Mihlon succumbed at fifty-nine to a heart attack in his home in Belmar, New Jersey.

Chapman kept busy promoting winter sixes. With the economy staggering, the two annual New York Sixes brought a welcome cash flow to Madison Square Garden shareholders. Twice a year the galleries packed with multitudes coming to watch dazzling performances of the best Australian, European, and U.S. riders.

Chapman signed up foreign luminaries like Alfredo Binda, Italy's legendary three-time world pro road champion and five-time Tour of Italy winner. The German duo of Heinz Vopel and Gustav Kilian, a legendary team, won sixes in Madison Square Garden, Pittsburgh, Chicago, Cleveland, and a half dozen other cities around North America.

Parisian Alfred Letourneur (known as Le Diable Rouge, or "the Red Devil") thrilled audiences. On the morning of May 17, 1941, he streaked into the history books when he broke Mile-a-Minute Murphy's legendary speed record. Letourneur pedaled his Schwinn behind a racecar as motorists were driving to work on a highway near Bakersfield, California, for a new speed record of 108.92 mph.

In December 1936, yet another Walthour burst into the Garden's winning circle. Jimmy Walthour Jr., the son of Bobby Walthour Sr.'s twin brother, Jim. The three Walthours garnered seven national titles, and each won a Garden six.

Chapman promoted sixes in places like the Butler Field House at Butler College in Indianapolis, municipal auditoriums in St. Louis and Kansas City, and the Washington DC Armory. On December 7, 1937, he announced in Madison Square Garden that he was finally retiring. Garden president John Reed Kilpatrick tried to persuade him to remain, but Chapman was adamant. Harry Mendel succeeded him as promoter of the Garden sixes.

Chapman's departure also hastened that of Frank Kramer, chief referee at indoor and outdoor races. Kramer announced he wanted to leave the sport with Chapman. Their departure signaled the end of an era.

The next year, Mendel held only one six in the Garden—the first time in nineteen years. In December 1939, the Garden's sixty-sixth and final international six took place. And because of previous Garden bookings, the race was shortened to five days.

Consistent with the parade of celebrities firing the starting gun, New York Yankees star Joe DiMaggio did the honors. Only half the seats were sold. Since Great Britain and France had declared war on Germany that year, foreign talent was cut off, which effectively dealt a coup de grâce to the sport already waning.

• • •

A boisterous era in sports sputtered to an end. Kramer and Chapman had enough money to live comfortably the rest of their lives. In 1924, Kramer, forty-four, had married Helen Hay of East Orange. He was a natty dresser and smoked cigarettes in a gold holder. Kramer became police commissioner for East Orange and afterward managed a nonprofit ambulance service in Orange. He was active in the Boy Scouts movement and became a member of its National Court of Honor. Kramer had a fondness for cars, partial to Cadillacs, and worked as a special inspector in the New Jersey Department of Motor Vehicles.

Neither the Kramers nor the Chapmans had children. Chapman and wife, Martha, moved to the West Coast in 1940 and bought a house in Santa Monica. It was said that Chapman preferred the sea view; it is more likely that he wanted to be near Bobby Walthour Jr., then living in Santa Monica with his wife and children.

Walthour Jr. worked in the MGM studios film library in Culver City. He landed the job through Dore Schary, once a rival of young Bobby in Newark before Schary moved to Hollywood. Schary won an Academy Award for Best Writing as co-writer of the *Boys Town* screenplay. He headed MGM production.

Chapman's voice became grave from smoking. He joined the Santa Monica Pinochle Club and started playing at 9 a.m. Acquaintances called him Colonel, homage to his Georgian roots. He traded old bike stories with racers who migrated to the Golden State, but he never attended any sporting events. When summer came he and his wife traveled east to visit friends and relatives.

His great niece, Charlotte Winsness, in 1993 recalled him fondly for handing out five-dollar bills like they were candy to nieces and nephews. He grew too weak to travel, so frail that he could hardly raise his hands to play pinochle. On March 20, 1947, Chapman, sixty-nine, died in Santa Monica.

• • •

By 1947 cycling's focus had shifted to Europe. Road races were drawing audiences and press attention at the expense of velodromes. The National Cycling Association's metal filing cabinets gathered dust in a Newark warehouse.

When Bobby Walthour III came of age, all the wooden velodromes in the United States had disappeared. The competitions held by the Amateur Bicycle League of America on roads in parks and remote locations on early weekend mornings to avoid car traffic continued as all that remained of competitive cycling.

About the time Walthour III was setting swim records for Santa Monica High School and St. Mary's College of California, a *Newark Evening News* reporter interviewed Kramer. The old champion's head of hair had turned totally white. When asked what he thought it would take to revive bicycle racing as a spectator sport in this country, Kramer replied, "Only one good American rider."

The story of U.S. cycling turned into individuals working against overwhelming odds to become that rider.

TWO

"Spit and Scotch Tape"

8

L'Américain

L'étape Vichy-Saint-Étienne est gagné par Magnani
(The stage from Vichy to Saint-Étienne is won by Magnani).
—*L'Auto*, June 17, 1938

During Europe's golden age of road racing when riders carried a spare tire wrapped in a figure eight over their shoulders and back, a lone American competed against the sport's giants: Joseph Magnani. He rode from 1935 to 1948 on French and Italian pro teams and earned standing as one of his generation's best. French journalists called him L'Américain.

In the 1947 world pro road race championship in Reims, northeast of Paris and famed for its Champagne vineyards, Magnani, at age thirty-six, placed seventh, the final finisher. He pedaled 170 miles through torrid heat that forced most of the starters, including legendary Fausto Coppi, to abandon. When the news reached the United States, where his performance should have been celebrated, Magnani's name caused bewilderment.

"If anyone knows who he is or where he came from to represent America, we would like to hear about it," wrote Otto Eisele, secretary of the Amateur Bicycle League of America, in the trade publication, *American Bicyclist*. To Eisele, a savvy cycling official, the notion of a U.S. road racer competing at the worlds stretched credibility.

In 1948, Magnani returned to America. He brought his French wife, Mimi, and their son, Rudy, to visit relatives in Chicago. The Schwinn

Bicycle Company recruited him to ride the indoor winter six-day circuit. In his first six, in Buffalo, he fell and sustained injuries that forced his retirement from racing. He went to work right away for Schwinn and settled in the Windy City with his family.

Eisele's question about who Magnani was went unanswered. How could an American earning his livelihood as a pro racer in Europe become overlooked?

"My father lost a whole box containing newspaper and magazine clippings, team jerseys, racer-leader jerseys, and photos," explained his son Rudy, a Chicago resident born in France. "Everything my parents and my father's sister had saved from his years of riding was in a box that got lost on its way from Nice, France, to Chicago. That box just disappeared. And my father had a quiet, self-effacing personality. He didn't draw a lot of attention to himself."

For more than a decade, I had been teased by brief articles published in the 1930s and '40s in *American Bicyclist*, which I read in the Library of Congress in Washington DC. Rudy Magnani said his father had died in 1975, age sixty-four, taking his remarkable experiences with him to the grave—or so I thought.

One day in 1994 in Washington DC, I visited Coppi's Vigorelli, an Italian restaurant on Connecticut Avenue, slotted among chic boutiques, world-class hotels, sedate apartments, glass-and-steel office buildings, sports bars galore, and statues as magnificent as those on the Avenue des Champs-Élysées in Paris. Connecticut Avenue runs into Lafayette Park, across the street from the White House. One of my first lessons in the nation's capital is that it keeps no secrets—there are only head starts. Seated in a comfortable booth, I discovered I had at last caught up to Joseph Magnani, thanks to a restaurant proprietor intent on bringing the glory of his Italian idol, Fausto Coppi, to the banks of the Potomac.

• • •

The co-owner of Coppi's Vigorelli was Pierre Mattia, an Italian native, trim in his forties with a salt-and-pepper mustache, gold-rimmed eyeglasses, and the bemused expression of a professor. Mattia grew up revering Coppi, known as Il Campionissimo (the Champion of

Champions), like Americans idolizing Babe Ruth, Joe DiMaggio, or Ted Williams.

Coppi had a narrow face and delicate, almost birdlike bones, thigh muscles bulging like wine casks, and raven-black hair blowing back as he rode. He won the Tour de France twice, dominated the Italian grand tour, the Giro d'Italia, with five victories, and captured world titles in the road race and track pursuit (in which two riders start on opposite sides of the velodrome and chase one another for five kilometers for the fastest time). Coppi also set the world hour record, considered the most prestigious of all cycling marks, by pedaling 45.871 kilometers (28.5 miles) in sixty minutes at Milan's Vigorelli velodrome, as hallowed in cycling as Yankee Stadium, Fenway Park, and Wrigley Field are to baseball diamonds. He ranks among cycling's all-time greats. In post–World War II Italy he transcended sports as a national hero. His visage was the model for the cyclist in the 2003 French-Canadian animated comedy, *Les Triplettes de Belleville.*

"Had it not been for World War II, which forced him to take five years off, he may have been the rider with the greatest accomplishments," said Mattia.

When Mattia and his business partner, Elizabeth Bright, decided in the early 1990s to open a new restaurant, specializing in pizzas and calzones baked the old-school way in a brick oven, in the District of Columbia, they chose a distinctive European motif. Mattia went back to his birthplace of San Remo, a tourist destination on the Mediterranean coast, in search of photos of Coppi and his rivals. He met a photographer whose family had operated a studio for four generations. Mattia acquired a collection—some originals, some copies—of cyclists in sharp black-and-white images. He traveled to Bordighera, on the Italian Riviera bordering France, to visit Jean Veneziano, a contemporary of Coppi. Veneziano donated a trove.

"He gave me the photos because he loves the sport. This is a way to contribute to cycling being better known in the United States."

Trendy Washington brasseries usually display framed and signed photos of presidents, senators, and members of Congress, augmented by Hollywood celebs and rock stars. The best and the brightest from both sides of the political aisle ply their talents as politicos, trade-industry lobbyists, media mavens, policy wonks, Pentagon brass and staff, and other livelihoods. They unwind after laboring long hours in offices by going out to eat and drink in social get-togethers.

The Coppi's Vigorelli restaurant presented cycling greats. Fausto Coppi and squads of legends were captured pedaling on dirt roads soaring into clouds in the Alps and Pyrenees. In some images, cyclists are stalked by snub-nosed cars and motorcycles carrying photographers and journalists motoring past crowds of applauding spectators. Many photos capture exuberant victors charging over the finish line, faces jubilant, to the chagrin of foes wilting behind over their bikes.

Mattia's father, Tommaso, operated a restaurant, La Botte (the Barrel), in San Remo, near the finish of Italy's annual classic road race, from Milan to San Remo. Held annually since 1907, the 181-mile event is the longest one-day race on the pro calendar. Mattia grew up inculcated with cycling lore and the restaurant business.

His photo collection was professionally framed, each rider eternally in his prime. Soon after Coppi's Vigorelli restaurant opened, a dignified woman entered, intrigued by the name. Upon seeing an image of Coppi in his wool jersey, the name Bianchi for the bicycle team he rode for stitched across his chest, she became overwhelmed with a flood of emotion.

"She recalled when she was young and a fan of Fausto Coppi and burst into tears," recounted Mattia. "Most of my customers are not cyclists. But customers who never saw a bicycle race in their life look at the photos and become mesmerized."

I plumped down after the lunch throng had cleared out and mentioned that Magnani might be among the images. Mattia nodded. He picked up a phone and tapped numbers to call Jean Veneziano, living in Monaco, six time zones away. To our surprise, Veneziano answered. Mattia chatted softly in Italian into the phone briefly and listened for long minutes, punctuated by an occasional grunt of surprise. I sipped a cappuccino. At last he paused to say that Veneziano and Magnani were close friends.

They were teammates in Nice, on the French Riviera. Veneziano had saved everything from his racing career, which included material about Magnani. When Magnani had married his fiancée in 1941, in Nice, Veneziano attended as best man. On the phone with Mattia, Veneziano said there were a dozen photos of Magnani—he was staring down upon us.

Soon I was able to answer Otto Eisele's question about who was Joseph Magnani and how he came to represent the United States at the 1947 worlds.

• • •

Magnani (pronounced Mahn-yan-ee) was born in 1912 to an Italian-immigrant family in LaSalle, Illinois, a coal-mining town in the middle of the Prairie State. He grew up in the village of Mount Clare, between the state capital in Springfield and St. Louis, according to his youngest brother, Father Rudolph Magnani, a Catholic priest in Bethesda, Maryland.

In 1928, sixteen-year-old Joseph Magnani, the second child in a family of eight, and his elder sister, Angelina, were sent to live with relatives in France. "His father had fallen on hard times in the mines," said Joseph's widow, Mimi, in Chicago. "Joe and his sister were sent to France to make the family smaller."

They lived on a farm in Cap d'Ail (the Cape of Garlic), a small town near Nice, within sight of the purple-colored Maritime Alps bordering Italy. "Joe and his sister lived across the street from my family," said Mimi. "He delivered coal and wood to residents in the area."

Magnani joined the amateur Club Cyclo-touristes, sponsored by Urago Cycles, a family-owned bicycle company in Nice. François Urago gave the company publicity when he won the 1930 national motor-pace championship in Paris, pedaling 50 mph in the slipstream of a motorcycle. In 1934 Magnani, twenty-two, won the Grand Prix Urago against a field of eighty-five. In fifteenth place was his Italian friend Fermo Camellini, who was destined to win Tour de France stages.

Magnani stood an inch under six feet with sturdy shoulders. The French press described him as thin and strong. He had a wide forehead, a small chin, and a thick mat of dark hair parted in the center and combed back.

Two dozen other French bicycle companies—among them Peugeot, Terrot, and Automoto—supported trade teams. Thousands of hopefuls vied for only a small number of berths. "Getting a contract to race for one of the pro teams was tough," said Mimi.

In winter months, Magnani chopped firewood and shoveled coal for hours before hauling loads around on deliveries, which strengthened his upper body while earning money. He told an interviewer that he prepared for the next racing season early by training for four thousand kilometers (about 2,500 miles).

In 1935 Urago Cycles offered him a coveted pro contract. Entry-level pros like Magnani received bare basics: a bicycle, a set of wrenches, an allowance of tires, a couple jerseys and shorts inscribed with the sponsor's name. Neo-pros lived on prize money. Sometimes the sponsor paid a small bonus for victories—if press coverage mentioned the brand, or if the rider's photo in his team jersey appeared in the newspaper. Pros with victories could negotiate appearance fees, which promoters doled out to drum up publicity.

Magnani needed a racing license from the American governing body, the National Cycling Association, in Newark. He wrote to the NCA and received his license, issued by Frank Kramer.

• • •

One of the first 1935 regional spring classics along the French Riviera was the 125-miler from Marseille to Nice. Dating back to 1897, Marseille–Nice winners included Frenchman Gustave Ganay, mentioned in Ernest Hemingway's memoir, *A Moveable Feast*, and 1920s Italian superstar Alfredo Binda, three-time world road champion. The hundred entrants in the 1935 edition rode bicycles equipped with new five-speed derailleurs. Derailleurs offered unprecedented choices of gears to pedal up and down hills; by reaching a hand to flick a lever on the frame, riders shifted the chain from one to another of rear-wheel sprockets—a major upgrade over one-speed bikes pedaled by Ganay and Binda.

Frenchman Lucien Juy had invented a double-pivot derailleur. His game-changer invention featured two spring-loaded pivots, which kept the chain taut underneath the rear hub where the chain could be shifted up and down as many as five sprockets. Lucien Juy invented the Simplex derailleur, which became a household name in French cycling. Riders pedaled faster than ever, and competitions became increasingly more tactical.

Derailleurs transformed road racing and ushered in road cycling's golden age. Cyclists could choose an easier gear for pedaling up hills; on descents or aided by tailwinds, they had access to bigger gears to go faster. Instead of contestants on one-speed bicycles straggling like a ragged line of refugees trailing the front-runners through the hills, more stayed together in packs, which created the *peloton*, French for "pack." Derailleurs remodeled road racing as radically as the advent of sound changed movies.

Competitors in the peloton, like birds swarming in flight, create a cocoon of reduced wind resistance, which allows nearly everyone behind those at the head of the pack to pedal a little easier. To bystanders watching the peloton roll by, it can appear permanently in place, even though individuals constantly shift positions to shield themselves from undulating and curving roads and the ever-changing wind direction. Ambitious competitors surge off the front to break away in a bid to win. Without slipstream protection, most breakaways fizzle.

In the final kilometers of the 1935 Marseille–Nice, five hours after departing from Marseille, Magnani slid back through the peloton and dropped off the rear unobserved before he jinked, squirrel-like, and rushed up on the outside, faster than the peloton. He escaped and bowled up the road as though he could see the finish line. Alone, he gambled. If the peloton caught him, his legs would have little left for the dash to the finish line in the harbor in Nice. All he needed was to stay away for about ten minutes. He sliced the tangents of turns faster than the peloton could manage. Spectators lined the road and yelled encouragement. Every quick turn of the pedals took him closer to the finish until at last he flew across the line in a solo triumph.

He had become the first American to win a professional road race on the Continent. Marseille–Nice was last run in 1959, yet it is still listed in *VeloPlus*, the Belgian cycling record book, citing the 1935 winner: Joseph Magnani (USA).

That season Magnani also won the Grand Prix Waldorf in Nice. In 1936 he joined Urago teammates in the seven-day Tour of Switzerland, up and down the Swiss Alps on a 1,070-mile course. Its topographical profile resembled a row of shark teeth. On the fifth stage, he scored third place. He finished the Tour of Switzerland eighteenth in general classification, based on total elapsed time.

Magnani impressed French journalists. *L'Auto* published a feature about him by José Meiffret, himself illustrious for setting motor-pace records into his late forties as the fastest cyclist in the world. Meiffret exclaimed to readers: "Attention! Follow this man! Urago has on its hands a rider of great quality."

• • •

"There wasn't much money in the 1930s," said Mimi. "The Great Depression was on. What kept him racing was that he was making a pretty good living."

Earning a good living meant persevering despite horrendous weather, such as his 1938 victory in the 149-mile Marseille–Toulon–Marseille Riviera classic during a torrential rainstorm. All but four of eighty entrants quit. That same year Magnani drew considerable press attention in the 940-mile Tour de l'Est Central, sponsored by Dubonnet wine. It boasted a hefty prize list of 90,000 francs. On stage 5, from Vichy to Saint-Étienne, Magnani shot off the front of the peloton up the last hill after 110 miles and time trialed the remaining few miles to the finish on the Vélodrome de l'Etivallière. He won by a minute. That boosted him to second overall, which he kept when the race concluded three days later.

One enduring result came in the early-season Paris–Nice, still a major event. Since it starts in chronically overcast Paris and heads south for eight days to the sun-splashed Riviera, it is called the Race to the Sun. On the last stage, Magnani attacked up a hill and into a headwind with five others to forge a successful breakaway. The time he and cohorts gained on the peloton that stage lifted him to finish ninth overall.

He also competed in the Italian classic, Milan–San Remo, for the second time in 1938 and, after his twenty-second place the previous year, he finished a respectable twenty-ninth. That summer Magnani won the two-day Circuit of Lourdes, featuring steep climbs up the highest peaks of the Pyrenees bordering Spain, and menacing descents at breakneck speeds down narrow, snaking dirt roads hugging cliff edges. He set a new hour record for the Nice velodrome, pedaling forty-two kilometers (26.25 miles). The monarch of the Nice velodrome was L'Américain.

At the top of bicycle racing then, as now, loomed the Tour de France. A stage winner gains lasting social status, like the basketball player who sinks that championship-clinching shot just before the buzzer sounds. Unlike today's trade teams, Le Tour in Magnani's day involved national teams. It was an era of heightened patriotism across the Continent in what Europeans call the period between two world wars. National teams excluded the lone American. Yet he earned consideration to join an international composite squad. Its members had to pay for meals and lodging, recalled former racer Al Stiller of Boulder, Colorado, a work colleague of Magnani in the 1950s at Schwinn, who told me: "A Canadian who came up with more money bumped him off the team."

In 1939 Magnani joined the Terrot-Hutchinson team, headquartered in Dijon, famous for mustard. He won the first leg of the eleven-stage Tour of Southeast France, which covered 1,250 miles. He wore the leader's blue jersey, the color of the sponsoring newspaper's pages. He also snatched third place in stage 3. After the first week, he lost the lead and finished seventh in general classification, based on total elapsed time. He also won the Lyon–Saint-Étienne one-day race for Terrot.

Magnani, twenty-seven, was riding at the top of his game when German soldiers and tanks invaded Poland. Hundreds of thousands of civilians fled with belongings they packed on a moment's notice. Great Britain declared war on Germany, mobilized its military, and drafted tens of thousands of young men into service to fight across the English Channel.

In the spring of 1940 German tanks blitzed across northern France and overwhelmed the French army. Nazi troops commandeered thousands of French farmsteads for their barracks. German troops marched into Paris and seized government buildings. The Union Cycliste Internationale headquarters was relocated to Berlin. The crisis canceled the UCI worlds set for Italy, wiped out the Olympics scheduled in Japan, and scrapped Le Tour de France.

Northern France under occupation of German troops functioned differently from southern France, which remained free and bicycle racing continued. The German occupiers in the north encouraged sports to offer a semblance of life as usual. Magnani moved to an Italian team, Martini, sponsored by the wine company, and joined his friend Fermo Camellini. Magnani won the opening stage of the 1940 Grand Prix de la Côte d'Azur. He and Camellini posed with Magnani's fiancée, Mimi, for a celebratory photo.

In 1941, Magnani was hired by the France-Sport team, offering greater resources than he ever had. Magnani won a stage of the Circuit du Mont Ventoux. The course scaled the Ventoux, the region's highest mountain, at 6,263 feet elevation, and called the Beast of Provence or the Bald Mountain for its summit of bare limestone. He finished fourth overall. He also achieved a respectable tenth place in the Grand Prix des Nations, an individual time trial 140 kilometers (87.5 miles) long in suburban Paris, the de facto world time trial championship.

Magnani's career was thriving against a backdrop of worsening war. Nobody knew how long the fighting would continue. It was a time to seize life and make every day count. In October 1941 he and his fiancée, Mimi, a petite dark-haired ingénue, married.

• • •

On December 7, 1941, Japan launched a surprise bombing attack on the U.S. naval base in Pearl Harbor, Hawaii. President Franklin D. Roosevelt declared war on Japan. Then Germany and Italy declared war on America. The U.S. armed forces rapidly ballooned to more than 12 million men and women serving in uniform, with millions of them deployed to Europe, North Africa, and the Pacific.

War ruptured France's economy. Food and fuel were in short supply and had to be rationed. Yet Magnani and teammates maintained a full racing schedule over the 1942 season in southern France. He scored ten top-ten finishes.

Then thousands of German troops stormed southern France. Their occupation turned severe. Magnani became marked. To outward appearances, he appeared inconspicuous, spoke French like a native. But he carried a U.S. passport. To armed German occupiers he might as well have been wearing a bull's-eye on his chest and back. He began the 1943 season auspiciously, signaled by third place in the Grand Prix de Bergerac. His freedom, however, timed out. "The Germans arrested Joe because he was an American," Mimi said. "They put him in a concentration camp in the north of France."

"Joe was practically starved in the concentration camp," said Father Rudolph Magnani, Joseph's younger brother. "Our family sent him care packages with food, but we had no way of knowing how much got through to him. His weight dropped from 170 pounds to 98 pounds."

On June 6, 1944, the biggest armada invasion in world history launched with 160,000 U.S. and British troops assaulting a fifty-mile stretch of the heavily fortified Normandy coastline in northwest France. On August 24, Allied Forces rolled into Paris, liberating the City of Light.

A short while later, Magnani was rescued. Finally, after eighteen months of incarceration as a prisoner of war, he joined his wife in Nice. Their son was born in July 1945, named after Joseph's brother, Rudolph.

• • •

Cycling events, like much of everything else suspended by the war, finally resumed. The Union Cycliste Internationale headquarters relocated to Geneva, Switzerland, a haven for centuries from wars in Europe. Magnani joined others getting back in shape to pick up their careers.

He was nourished back to health by his wife's cooking. "Mama Magnani cooked wonderfully rich French food in the Provençal style," testified Richard Schwinn, a fourth-generation bicycle maker. "I dined often at maison Magnani. That woman didn't know the word hungry. Nobody went hungry around her table."

Joseph Magnani on the France-Sport team participated in a full 1945 racing schedule along the Riviera and around Paris. He scored thirteen top-fifteen finishes, including the regional classics Paris–Reims, Paris–Limoges, and Dijon–Lyon.

His comeback was noted by a former adversary, Giuseppe Olmo. A gold medalist on the Italian cycling team in the 1932 LA Olympics,

Olmo turned pro to ride for Bianchi. He set the world hour record on the Vigorelli velodrome (which Coppi would break a decade later by about 700 yards), twice won the Milan–San Remo spring classic, and racked up a robust twenty stage victories in the Giro d'Italia. He'd retired to found a company to manufacture bicycles. In 1946 he hired Magnani to ride in the pink-and-white colors of his Olmo squad.

Magnani delivered on Olmo's faith with three victories, two seconds, and five other top-ten finishes. Italy's three-week grand tour, the 2,250-mile Giro d'Italia, had been suspended for five years, making the 1946 Giro a passionate theater for all Italian teams. Olmo picked Magnani to ride the Giro, thus adding that grand tour to his lengthy list of firsts for U.S. racers on the Continent.

Italy was passionately divided in support between Fausto Coppi, back from his time as a prisoner of war captured by British troops in North Africa, and Gino Bartali, a devout Catholic nicknamed "the Pious," who risked his life in the war working for a secret network to protect Jews and other endangered people from the Nazis. Other pros, such as Fermo Camellini, a short man and formidable climber in the mountains, and Fiorenzo Magni, the shockingly bald three-time Giro winner and model advertising Nivea skin-care products, also fought for attention.

According to Jean Veneziano, Magnani rode support for Camellini, whose swiftness in the mountains and the punch he had for sprinting made him the team captain and a Giro contender. During the second week, Camellini wore the race leader's pink jersey for three stages. Then Magnani fell heavily in a pileup.

"He banged up his knee and couldn't race because of infection, so he came back home to recover," said his wife. Camellini lost the leader's jersey while Coppi and Bartali dueled, with Bartali victorious.

Over the 1947 season, Magnani scored ten top-ten results, including a second in the final stage of the Tour of Normandy. At the Tour of Switzerland, he scored ninth in the time trial stage, won by Coppi; Magnani ended in seventeenth overall in the event won by Gino Bartali.

Magnani entered the world road race championship in August in Reims over thirty-five laps of a twisting 7.8-kilometer (4.9-mile) course designed for grand prix car racing. Among the field of thirty-one pros were Coppi, Magni, Albert Sercu of Belgium (father of 1964 Olympic gold medalist sprinter and six-day racing legend Patrick Sercu), and Dutch star Theo Middelkamp.

"The amateur race was held in the morning when the weather wasn't bad, but by the time the pros started after noon, it was really hot," recalled Al Stiller, who paid his expenses to Paris to represent the United States in the amateur track worlds at the Parc des Princes. "The temperature hit 100 degrees Fahrenheit, with humidity to match. The heat knocked Coppi out."

After racing seven and a half hours under the relentless burning sun, Middelkamp won, with Sercu in second and Magni fourth. Ten minutes back, Magnani was the last man to finish, hanging on for seventh place—the best U.S. performance for the next twenty-nine years.

• • •

For the 1948 season, Magnani rode for the AS Monaco team, sponsored by the posh Mediterranean principality. Now thirty-six, he talked about retiring. "In July 1948, we came to the United States on a vacation trip," said Mimi. "Joe hadn't been back to visit his family since he had left so many years before."

"When he came back," said Father Rudolph Magnani, "I was an adult, eighteen, seeing him for the first time. I was really thrilled. I wore my best shirt."

Following the family reunion, Magnani presented a letter of recommendation from Urago Cycles to the Schwinn Bicycle Company, Mimi said. Of the half-dozen bicycle brands in the United States, Schwinn alone supported racing. Pros were limited to winter indoor six-days. Schwinn hired Magnani to ride in its red-and-white colors.

The 1948 circuit opened with the Twelfth International Buffalo Six, October 5 to 11, downtown in Memorial Auditorium. Fifteen two-rider teams signed up for the whirl around a portable Masonite hardboard track, a precariously steep bowl, eleven laps to the mile (160 yards around). Entrants included Hugo Koblet, the blond Swiss with a silky-smooth pedaling style who would triumph magnificently in the 1951 Tour de France. Koblet was paired with compatriot Walter

Diggelman, a future Tour de France stage winner. Magnani teamed with Bill Johan, Chicago's hot young talent, both riding their first six.

"Joe was really out of his element," said Bill Jacoby of Chicago, paired with Alf Letourneur, the iconoclastic Parisian calling himself the Red Devil and easily spotted wearing number thirteen on the back of his red silk jersey. "That track was a far cry from the roads of Europe, which Joe rode so well."

Crashes day and night on tight turns pulverized the field to just six teams. Among the casualties were Magnani, his partner Johan, and Swiss ace Koblet. Jacoby and his partner Letourneur finished fifth.

Magnani's Chicago vacation turned permanent when Schwinn offered him a full-time job. The handful of American bicycle companies concentrated on the juvenile market, growing from the baby boom. Schwinn catered to juveniles, yet the family-owned business allocated a portion of profits to promote racing. Schwinn was America's only company producing handmade racing frames, branded Paramount. They carried a lifetime guarantee and were cherished.

"Joe worked for me in the Paramount room, a large warehouse space with a high ceiling off the assembly line," said Al Stiller, the amateur racer who was an engineer with a college degree. "Joe and two or three other guys assembled Paramount track bikes and tandems. In the early 1950s we started building Paramount road bikes. Joe assembled all of them for years. When he put a Paramount together, it was ready to race in America or anywhere in Europe."

Magnani devoted himself to his family and job. Al Stiller, Bill Johan, and Bill Jacoby—all Chicago born and bred—talked about him among friends. Gradually his accomplishments seeped through the Midwest cycling community, about a homegrown cyclist who had competed in the Golden Age of road racing against Fausto Coppi, Gino Bartali, and the third great man of Italian cycling, Fiorenzo Magni. Hearsay swirled around the mystique of a Schwinn employee as the first U.S. rider in the Tour de France—the equivalent to Elvis sightings.

9

Jack Heid, America's Premier Cyclist

Hot and overcast. I take my gear out of the car and put my bike together. Tourists and locals are watching from side cafés. Non-racers. The emptiness of their lives shocks me.

—TIM KRABBÉ, *The Rider*

On a summer night in 1948 five-year-old Jack Simes III sat at a desk in the living room of the family's vacation cottage in Beaver Lake, New Jersey, tuning a shortwave radio for the BBC broadcast of the Summer Olympics from London. He heard a news report about a rider his father coached, Jack Heid, in a qualifying heat of the 1,000-meter match sprint. The winner would move up to the quarterfinal in his quest for an Olympic medal.

Simes listened attentively as the BBC announcer told how Heid had won his earlier qualifying match by twenty yards. Now Heid faced Clodomiro Cortoni of Argentina—South America's fastest cyclist. On the Herne Hill Velodrome, an outdoor concrete oval in a tree-shaded residential borough of Victorian homes in south London, Cortoni led with 400 yards remaining and set a brisk tempo. Heid drafted behind Cortoni's rear wheel and in the final 200 yards surged to pass. The Argentine accelerated to keep his rival at bay. But Heid pulled alongside. Both sprinters were so close, elbow to elbow, heads down, backs arched like fighting cats when their front wheels flew over the black finish line, judges had to consult a photo before they ruled for Heid.

That same summer, sixteen-year-old Art Longsjo in Fitchburg, Massachusetts, was planning to quit high school and train full time to make the Olympic speed skating team. Fifteen-year-old Nancy Neiman in Detroit was taking courses in shorthand and typing to prepare for a secretarial career. Herbie Francis, eight years old, was getting ready to move north from Miami with his parents to New York City. Perry Metzler, seven years old, was living in Yazoo City, Mississippi. In Los Angeles another seven-year-old, Mike Hiltner, was learning to play the flute. Five-year-old Audrey Phleger was turning cartwheels in La Jolla, California.

They would all follow Heid in stoking U.S. cycling through its leanest years.

• • •

Amateur cycling had languished in the shadow of pro racing for decades. Since the League of American Wheelmen quit sanctioning competitions in 1900, the authority over races in the United States belonged to the National Cycling Association, dedicated to pros. The collapse of outdoor velodromes after 1930 dealt a blow to the commercially driven NCA.

The ABLA, fostered by dedicated volunteers, counted fifty-two clubs in thirty-five states with about 1,500 men and women members. ABLA races were free to anyone willing to line up for weekend start times at dawn, usually on the outskirts of town to avoid car traffic. Sometimes while events were underway police shooed organizers away for waking up neighbors; as a result, finish lines had to be moved farther out of town while races were in progress.

Clubs established year-round weekend rides, highlighting autumnal one-hundred-mile "century" jaunts, and developed spring and summer handicap races of twenty-five to fifty miles. Competitors took off in groups of similar abilities—novices were given a head start of up to twenty minutes, intermediates followed about ten minutes later, and the elite last on scratch. The groups charged down a public road for half the distance, turned around a designated official standing in the middle of the road, and doubled back. Wannabes fought for places while those on scratch battled for the quickest times. Prizes were bragging rights.

ABLA state chapters held championships of four events, called an omnium, over an early-summer weekend. Omniums ranged from one mile to twenty-five miles; points awarded to the top five finishers counted toward determining the gold, silver, and bronze medalists. Each state's three medalists qualified for the national omnium championship in August.

The inaugural 1921 nationals in Washington DC were held on a polo field for men seventeen and older. The next year, on the streets of Atlantic City, the junior boys category was added for sixteen and younger, competing in a one-miler on Saturday and a five-miler on Sunday. National champions took home a gold medal with a diamond chip glinting from the center, plus a new stars-and-stripes jersey to wear in races.

The 1930s Great Depression squeezed the ABLA. In 1931 the ABLA had less than a paltry $1,500 for its budget, which meant cancelling its national championships. They were lost again in 1932, an Olympic year. The U.S. Olympic Committee and the Cycle Trades of America, an industry trade group, rescued the ABLA with donations to hold selection trials for the cycling team that would compete in the Los Angeles Games. Thus, the ABLA held four sets of track sprints, and 100-kilometer individual time trials for the road race, beginning with state qualifiers, followed by regionals and the national qualifier.

Aspiring Olympians paid their own expenses. Twenty-year-old Victor Fraysse of New York City had placed high in the East Coast qualifiers, but traveling to the final near San Francisco put him in a dilemma. "My father had a job on Wall Street with Hornblower & Weeks, making nine dollars a week," recalled his son, Mike Fraysse. "My grandfather told him that he was crazy to take time off his job and risk the opportunity to work his way up Wall Street just to go to California for the Olympic trials. My grandfather assured my father that there would be plenty more Olympics."

Victor Fraysse, like uncounted others trying to keep their jobs, missed his chance. Four years later, a bad spill kept him from entering the 1936 Olympic trials. The 1940 and 1944 Olympic Games were casualties of World War II.

• • •

Looking to spread the ABLA's grassroots base, officials introduced the girls category for all ages of women at the 1937 nationals in Buffalo's Humboldt Park. It was a first-ever sanctioned cycling nationals for women, more than half a century after the inaugural men's championship in Newport, Rhode Island.

Fifteen-year-old Doris Kopsky, daughter of Joe Kopsky, a bronze medalist in the team road race at the 1912 Stockholm Olympics, went to Buffalo. For her thirteenth birthday, her father had built her a track bicycle in his bike shop in Belleville, New Jersey. He painted a big *D* for Doris on the crown and coached her.

"I did my sprint training on a flat half-mile stretch of road between Nutley and Belleville," she told me. "My father used to tell some of the old bike riders who came into his shop to race me. He told them, 'She will beat you.' I did, too."

How did her mother, Genette, react to her daughter, an only child, racing bikes? "My mother was mad at my father for getting me into cycling. She didn't consider cycling ladylike. But it was only natural that my father would get me into the sport. I was the son my father never had."

Doris raced for a couple years in events in the Northeast and Middle Atlantic. She won the 1935 ten-mile National Capital Sweepstakes around the one-kilometer Ellipse behind the White House in Washington and received a china tea service. "My mother was pleased with the prize," she said.

The 1937 nationals offered three races for women: a half-mile and five-mile on Saturday, and twenty-five miles on Sunday, with points to the top five in each race. "There were about a dozen of us, including a few girls from Canada," she said. "My sprint training on that half-mile stretch paid off. I won the national championship."

Triumphing in the men's open was Charley Bergna of Paterson, New Jersey. The junior boys' winner was Furman Kugler, a neighbor from Somerville and occasional training partner.

"After winning the national championships, Furman and I really celebrated," Doris Kopsky said with a laugh. "We broke training and went out to eat a banana split and a strawberry soda."

National championships were suspended during World War II. For the war effort, the Schwinn Bicycle Company converted machinery that had made steel bicycle frames and components to turn out bullet shells, munitions, and devices for shipboard electronic communications.

Frank W. Schwinn, a second-generation bicycle manufacturer, looked to the future. In 1944 he negotiated with ABLA president Otto Eisele, a recreation cyclist and an executive with the New York Rail Road, to provide $5,000 a year for five years—a substantial amount of money then (worth more than $70,000 today)—to underwrite nationals when the war ended.

Hostilities ceased in Europe when Germany surrendered in May 1945; on August 14, the Japanese Empire capitulated, and the war finally ended. Over the previous fourteen years, the ABLA had held nationals only six times, once under the auspices of the Amateur Athletic Association governing track and field. The Schwinn family came to cycling's rescue. The ABLA held its national program on the weekend of August 18–19 in Chicago's Humboldt Park.

With the ABLA's prospects looking up, its nemesis, the National Cycling Association, was disappearing. The NCA still retained membership in the Union Cycliste Internationale for sanctioning Olympians and riders going to the UCI worlds. ABLA president Eisele capitalized on social connections in the U.S. Olympic Committee, then headquartered in New York City, to grant the ABLA official recognition. Before 1945 concluded, the ABLA was admitted to represent amateurs and have equal voting power with the NCA.

Yet the amateur organization was no Cinderella. It depended on volunteers, one-dollar annual license fees, and donations. American cycling was held together, in the words of one ABLA official, "with spit and Scotch Tape."

• • •

Postwar racing had no frills. Local ABLA clubs and volunteers held events. Every summer ABLA clubs put on state championships for men, sixteen-and-under boys, and women. Medalists qualified for the nationals, which rotated to different cities.

Every four years came the Olympics, for male cyclists only. To earn a berth on the team, and the chance to compete against the best amateurs in the world, represented American cycling's peak—unlike Europeans with professional teams and three-week grand tours in France, Italy, and Spain. Getting on the Olympic team earned you an official U.S. Olympic Committee navy blazer. It was adorned with the red-white-and-blue USA stars-and-stripes embroidered shield and the five Olympic rings on the breast pocket to wear in the opening and closing ceremonies where all national teams marched in the Olympic stadium behind their country's flag. Some men requested they be buried in their Olympic blazer.

The 1948 Olympic cycling trials were held in July in Milwaukee to select the men to represent the United States at the London Games. These trials, like the Olympics, were the first in twelve years. More competitors than usual were determined to make the team.

For Victor Fraysse, the Milwaukee trials were his last chance. Now thirty-six, he was more concerned about providing for his wife and family. He realized his Olympics dream was over. "My father opened a bike shop in Ridgefield Park, New Jersey," his son, Mike Fraysse, said. "Guys would come into the shop and moan that they couldn't take the time from this or that to travel to a race. My father would tell his nine-dollar-a-week story and end by saying if they didn't go, they might not get another chance."

Jack Heid, a navy veteran, was twenty-four and seized his chance. He had sharpened his sprinting talent under the tutelage of Jackie Simes II, the 1936 national ABLA champion; Simes had turned pro later that year to race in the San Francisco six-day, but suffered a career-ending crash. Heid, handsome with dark curly hair and a broad smile in the way of the actor and dancer Gene Kelly, had a sturdy neck like a boxer and sloping shoulders with muscles that danced under his shirt. Before his death at age sixty-two in 1987, in a house fire, he could still do twenty-five chin-ups with form that would cause any football coach to crack a grin. On the Brown Deer Park track Olympic trials in Milwaukee, Heid overpowered the other competitors to earn his place on the cycling track team in both the match sprints and the 1,000-meter time trial.

Nineteen-year-old Ted Smith of Buffalo, wearing his stars-and-stripes jersey as the ABLA national champion, won the 138-mile road race in a solo break, pedaling a one-speed bike with a fixed gear (no coasting). Derailleur gears were still not allowed in American road racing.

Heid and Smith led the ABLA's U.S. Olympic team of five track and five road racers. ABLA president Frank Small, a veteran of the 1920 Antwerp Olympics, served as team manager. The coach was Chester Nelson Sr. of St. Louis, a veteran of the 1928 Amsterdam Olympics. On the road team was Nelson's son, Chester Jr.

Amateur rules governing cycling were so strict that if Heid had worked in a bike shop he would be disqualified as a professional for participating in the Olympic trials. In London, after he defeated Argentinian Clodomiro Cortoni, Heid advanced to the quarterfinal. He wanted to be the first U.S. cyclist to win an Olympic medal since the 1912 Games in Stockholm, Sweden, when cyclists won two bronzes.

Heid next drew a match against Axel Schandorff, Denmark's national champion. Schandorff towered over Heid by six inches and had finished second in the 1946 worlds. The Dane was the first world-class competitor Heid had encountered. Schandorff eliminated him in their match and went on to win the bronze medal. "Losing to Schandorff really inspired me to do whatever I had to do to improve so I could later turn the tables on him," Heid said.

Next Heid tightened his leather toe straps for the kilometer time trial, an assault against the clock—fractions of a second counted. He was muscling his bicycle from a standing start to full speed when a tire, inflated to 110 pounds of pressure, burst as loud as a pistol shot. Judges allowed him another turn.

"I had to wait hours for a second ride, at dusk in a drizzle," he said, noting that water on the track created drag on tires. His time of 1 minute 16.2 seconds put him in seventh of twenty-one competitors. The time was a fraction of a second slower than he'd ridden in the trials, when he set a new national record.

Heid, impressed by Schandorff and other Europeans, considered the London Olympics as his stepping-stone to Europe. He refused to go home after the Games closed on August 14. He approached the team manager, Frank Small, to request reimbursement for his round-trip ship fare.

"At first, Frank Small refused to listen," Heid said, his voice thick with emotion. "I used to say that I would eat shit if it would make me ride faster."

Small, a 1924 Olympian dedicated to the ABLA raising its racing standards, tried to persuade Heid to return with the other Olympians. Small, a theatrical manager, had had experience with temperamental performers. He pleaded for his star sprinter to compete in the nationals in Kenosha, Wisconsin.

Heid had heard Victor Fraysse tell his nine-dollar-a-week story and remained adamant. "Frank Small told me I owed it to the cycling community to go back to the States and race in the nationals. I asked him who would pay for my way back here. We argued back and forth until I told him I was prepared to give up my U.S. citizenship to stay. He saw I was determined and finally saw it my way. I got $210 return fare for the USS *America*, the ship we went over on, and with the $600 I had saved, I went out to conquer Europe."

• • •

Born to a hardscrabble family on Manhattan's crowded, boisterous Lower East Side in 1924, John Sebastian Heid used to watch six-day racers as they cruised the roads around Central Park in New York a few days before the next Madison Square Garden six. He became fascinated by the way men in brightly colored jerseys pedaled their bikes with a honeyed fluid motion while maneuvering casually around traffic, spinning up hills and zipping down them as though the bicycle was as much a part of their body as arms and legs.

When his family moved to northern New Jersey he bought a track bike so he could emulate six-day riders. In 1941 he won his first race, a half-mile handicap on the Coney Island Velodrome, the last East Coast track still standing before it was dismantled for scrap during the war. He grew to five feet eight. His leg muscles gained mass and definition as his career began to take shape in 1942, his first year of open competition at age eighteen.

His early mentor was Jackie Simes II, a second-generation pro before he retired to open a bicycle shop in Westwood, the northern New Jersey town where Heid grew up. Simes went to watch all the local races. His wavy red hair became a familiar sight in the crowd. He loved stories about racers, their personalities, and tactics. Heid liked hanging out in Simes's Westwood shop to ask questions and soak up the atmosphere.

In 1942 Heid beat Furman Kugler of Somerville, New Jersey, the 1940 national ABLA champion and three-time state champion, for the state title. Soon afterward, with the country at war, Heid and Kugler enlisted in the U.S. Navy.

"Most guys in the service dreamed of their girlfriends back home, but I dreamed of my bicycle and what I would do when I resumed my racing career," Heid said.

He was stationed as an aviation mechanic at the navy base on Treasure Island, near San Francisco, when a fellow New Jersey rider, Ray Blum of Nutley, also in the navy, received orders for the base. Blum, dark-complexioned and a few inches taller than Heid, had begun racing on the Nutley Velodrome. Blum added to his repertoire wintertime speed skating, which uses similar leg muscles and drafting tactics. Blum established a national reputation in both sports. He and Heid shared the sole rental bike at a local cycling shop for several months until Blum was transferred to the Great Lakes Naval Station in northern Illinois.

When the war finally ended in 1945, Heid and Blum were released from the navy and resumed their friendly rivalry. American riders still used one-speed track bikes with a fixed gear on the roads, even though the stiff frames of track bikes are jarring to ride on anything other than a smooth surface. Europeans had switched decades earlier to road bikes featuring longer wheelbases, more comfortable than track bikes on roads.

American racers pedaled rear wheels equipped with a different sprocket on each side of the hub. One sprocket had the standard fixed gear; the other sprocket allowed the rider to coast, called freewheeling. Standard practice in hilly road races was for everyone to pull over on an arduous climb, stop, dismount, remove the rear wheel from the frame—either by snatching a wrench from a hip pocket to unscrew the nuts holding the rear wheel to the frame or unfastening wing nuts—pull the wheel out, turn it around, and reinsert the freewheel side with a smaller gear for pedaling more easily uphill, then coast down the descent. Later, riders stopped and reverted to their fixed gear.

Derailleurs were difficult to come by in America. Prevailing wisdom dictated that fixed gears made riders better pedalers. But fixed-gear pedaling could be hazardous. Some veteran fixed-gear riders were spotted by their missing a joint or two from the index finger of the right hand from getting the finger caught between the chain and front sprocket while tightening a toe strap.

One of the earliest proponents of derailleurs in this country was James Armando in 1929 during a sixty-two-mile race in New York. Jackie Simes II was among the spectators lining the road when they discovered that Armando had broken into the lead alone, riding a bicycle with three speeds. Simes recalled the moment with enthusiasm: "Armando rode a Cyclo derailleur, made in England. It was a crude contraption that literally had a complete figure eight in the back to keep the chain tension, and it sounded like a coffee grinder. But the crowd just loved it! They kept yelling at him, 'Throw it in high gear! Let's see what you've got! Throw it in high!'"

The United States led the world in industrial advancements like Thomas Edison's incandescent electric light bulb and Henry Ford's moving assembly line, but lagged behind Europe in cycling. The first significant changes in America's bicycle racing in the 1940s were shiny aluminum rims replacing dull yellow wooden rims, and the 1946 ABLA helmet law requiring amateurs to strap on leather helmets resembling hairnets and filled with sponge. Armando may have been an early supporter of derailleurs, but he complained out loud that helmets made cycling look dangerous and would discourage newcomers.

The chief influence on cycling—and all amateur sports in America—after the war was Avery Brundage of Chicago, known disparagingly as the "Mother Superior" of amateur athletics. The *New York Times* described Brundage as "the most powerful figure in the history of international sports." He was influential in the International Olympic Committee—as vice president from 1945 to 1952 before moving up to IOC president through the 1972 Munich Olympics.

Brundage had been a track star at the University of Illinois, studying civil engineering, and competed in the 1912 Stockholm Olympics in the pentathlon and decathlon. He finished out of the medals yet remained with the Olympic movement for the rest of his life. After college he founded a construction company in Chicago and earned a fortune, which funded his wide-ranging travels, first for the U.S. Olympic Committee then the International Olympic Committee.

Reporters called the zealous defender of amateurism names like "Slavery Brundage," "the nation's No. 1 common scold," and "a male Carry Nation, hacking away with a hatchet of righteousness at those who are trying to undermine the amateur idea." He was notorious for being brusque, prompting one critic to describe him as resembling Oliver Cromwell's idea of God—righteous and inflexible. Yet he was privately respected for backroom deals that kept the Olympic Games going through fierce political rifts and angry racial divisions.

American cyclists often packed four into a car to drive ten hours one way to compete in races. Often the prize might be a bicycle that was completely dismantled: the winner was awarded the frame, second place received the rear wheel, third took the front wheel, on down to the steel toe clips and leather toe straps. Afterward, still sweaty and dirty from their exertion, everybody squeezed back into the car, drove back home, and got up early to be at their job as usual on Monday morning.

"We all went because we loved the sport and money never entered our minds as it just wasn't there," Heid said. He got around the lack of a shower by packing a hand towel to wash his face and hands before the drive home.

When Heid accepted invitations in 1947 and 1948 to compete in the Caribbean Olympics in British Guiana (now Guyana), the British Guiana Amateur Cycle and Athletic Association covered all expenses—flight, accommodations, meals—with no expectation that the ABLA would return the favor. (The Olympic-style Pan American Games for countries in North and South America were introduced in 1951 in Buenos Aires, Argentina.)

Heid and Blum trained and raced to get ready for the Olympic trials. On early Sunday mornings without any weekend race they joined a group of Olympic hopefuls' rides of fifty to a hundred miles on hilly roads around northern New Jersey and southern New York. Most in the group, including Don Sheldon and Don McDermott, trained diligently. When a member of the group missed the Sunday morning ride—usually sleeping in after a Saturday night date—somebody would joke that the absent rider was "out painting a barn."

Blum was the first to make the Olympic team, in 1948, as a speed skater bound for the Winter Olympics in St. Moritz, Switzerland. In the 1946 ABLA nationals in Columbus, Ohio, where Heid had finished second, Blum had scored third place behind Heid and Ted Smith in the twenty-five miler. Blum's skating and cycling versatility attracted nationally syndicated cartoonist LeRoy Robert Ripley. The result was a *Believe It or Not!* cartoon in which Ripley pronounced Blum "the World's Most Decorated Athlete," a sketch showing him smiling in skating tights with medals pinned head to foot.

Setting the New Jersey Sunday morning pace and regaling everyone with stories and advice was Gérard Debaets, the admired Belgian who had won the December 1925 New York Six in Tex Rickard's new Madison Square Garden. Debaets, a John Chapman import, appreciated America so much he became a U.S. citizen. Debaets had thick dark hair combed straight back, a prominent nose, and he exuded charisma. He endured severe economic hardship from German occupation during World War I. He worked as a laborer until he earned more money from racing bicycles and achieved stardom on both sides of the Atlantic.

Debaets endeared himself to audiences at track races with stunts like flying along one of the straights, pulling his feet from toe clips, lying flat on his stomach on the saddle, with legs and arms out straight like he was flying. The *Newark Evening News* called him "cycling's jester." When spectators offered up cash primes, Debaets beat the competition and added to his prize money—carefully edging opponents to heighten the drama.

In 1930 Debaets fell ill after winning the Chicago Six. Hospital tests revealed a congenitally bad heart—his aorta valve leaked with each beat. That meant his heart wasn't supplying his body normal amounts of oxygen and nutrients. Despite the physical shortcoming, he was a prolific winner. He still rates among Belgium's greats for twice winning the Tour of Flanders, his country's springtime one-day classic notorious for fiendishly steep hills, one after another for hours, sections of bone-jarring cobblestones, narrow roads, and harsh weather. He won Belgium's national road race title and seventeen sixes.

Heart surgery to correct his leaky heart was still decades away. At the time of his diagnosis, Debaets was thirty-one and had no career alternative but to keep up a full racing schedule until pro cycling waned in his adoptive country. When the Nutley Velodrome closed in the mid-1930s, he retired from racing and opened a bike shop in Paterson, in north-central New Jersey.

"I went to Debaets for help because I wanted to stay in Europe to race after the Olympics," Heid said.

Debaets gladly helped. He mentored Heid on strategies and introduced him to massages to speed the recovery of tired muscles. A bike rider's legs are the pistons of his engine; they have to be treated carefully. Cyclists shave their legs to help keep them clean and aid massages. Debaets's counsel took some getting used to. In the 1940s no American man would shave his legs, let alone have them rubbed by another man in a massage. The Belgian told Heid that if he wanted to get to the top in cycling he had to think differently.

Debaets offered something more—contacts with promoters he knew in Europe, and a sister in Antwerp who would give Heid a place to live while he made his start on the Continent.

Any doubts Heid had about going to Europe to compete he dismissed during the 1948 Olympics. Teammate Ted Smith was the best prospect for a medal in the road race until he incurred the wrath of ABLA officials. Smith had won two national championships, once narrowly beating Heid in second place, and decisively captured the 138-mile Olympic trials road race in Milwaukee to claim first spot on the road team. When athletes arrived in London, Smith entered several races, which also drew other foreign Olympic cyclists. The ABLA Olympic coach ordered his riders not to race because an injury from a bad fall could knock them out of the Olympics.

Smith performed well in local races. He entered them to test himself against the competition he would face in the Olympic races for medals as well as to adjust to using his first derailleur. To punish him, the ABLA officials gave Smith's berth in the road race to another teammate.

"I trained eight years to make the Olympic team," Smith told me in 1985. "The Olympics were my dream. I won the Olympic trials qualifying race by a minute and got replaced in the Olympic Games by some ham-and-egger."

None of the four U.S. riders in the 121-mile road race finished. Smith was put on the four-man, 4,000-meter (2.5-mile) team pursuit; it was doomed when one rider broke a wrist in a fall and pulled out.

Another of Heid's Olympic teammates liked the idea of staying in Europe. Al Stiller of Chicago had ridden in the tandem event but was eliminated early. Stiller agreed to join Heid. A graduate of the University of Utah and a skier, Stiller was powerfully built but nowhere as aggressive as Heid.

"I used to say that Al was too nice a guy to be a bicycle racer," Heid said. "I was an animal."

Olympic cycling team manager Frank Small granted Stiller permission to remain behind with Heid.

• • •

Following the Olympic Games, Heid and Stiller made their way to Antwerp and met Debaets's sister, Ernestine, who helped them set up a base residence. The Yanks signed up for a team race on the Antwerp Velodrome. They wore Olympic jerseys and won their first foray.

The next stop was Amsterdam for the 1948 world cycling championships. Heid got the full effect of what he was up against. He discovered that cycling at the top level was unforgiving. Europeans were hardened from years of wartime food and fuel shortages. Heid rode against men who knew what the value of a single potato or a trivial centime coin meant to a family. Their only way to improve their lot in life was by riding their bike faster than anybody else. They played for keeps. National teams went to the worlds with full-time coaches and trainers, masseurs, and mechanics. He and Stiller only had each other.

Heid realized that he had to reassess basics. He was eliminated early in the match-race heats and was left, with Stiller, in a ten-kilometer (6.2-mile) consolation race under the track lights after midnight. Sixty riders made an aggressive pack tearing around the concrete oval. In the final two laps, the pace was sizzling, tires hissing over the track like serpents. Heid positioned himself behind the rear wheel of Australian Sid Patterson, who had finished a fraction of a second ahead of him in the 1,000-meter Olympic time trial and was trying to win so he could stay on the Continent.

When the pack surged around the final turn, Patterson jumped to the front, Heid in tow. The Aussie put his head down and went all out. Patterson held off a challenge by another rider to win, with Heid a close third. That result got Heid an invitation, expenses paid, to race in Copenhagen on the Ordrup Velodrome, an outdoor concrete track. Stiller accompanied him.

In Copenhagen, Heid won a race, which generated more invitations. After a couple of weeks, he and Stiller returned to Antwerp to break into the Belgian circuit. They won some team omniums—four events—but found the going faster than they had ever experienced. On occasion, Heid could hardly walk after a race.

The transition from racing in the United States to competing in Belgium was abrupt as a result of America's decline of the professional class in the 1930s and the complete loss of domestic pro racing during the war. The continuity of high-performance standards that developed in the United States from the 1880s into the 1930s had vanished. Regaining that level would take the next three decades.

European amateurs were paid modest allowances. Everyone had more use for money than shiny trophies. Track racers signed contracts for every race. A standard contract at the Antwerp and Ghent velodromes was about thirty dollars a program for four events, and the prize money was theirs to keep.

Heid and Stiller found that Belgians fondly remembered Debaets. "All I had to do was mention his name and doors opened," Heid recalled. Belgium's world sprint champion Jef Scherens—Sergio Matteini's friend—and national hero and world road racing champion Stan Ockers sought the Americans out for friendly training rides. Thanks to Heid's association with Debaets, he and Stiller were welcomed into the club.

Shortly before Christmas, Heid won a miss-and-out (the last rider at the end of each lap drops out until only one is left) on the Antwerp track. He won twenty-five dollars and a bouquet of flowers. Stiller, in tenth, wasn't as determined to make it in Europe and left to return to Chicago. Heid remained the lone American to prepare for a full next season in Europe.

• • •

Arthur Matthew Longsjo Jr. in Fitchburg, Massachusetts, burned with the same competitive hunger as Heid. As an eleventh-grader in 1948 at Fitchburg High, he was impatient to quit classes and train full-time to shoot for a berth on the next Olympic speed skating team. He had been inspired in the early 1940s when Carmelita Landry of Fitchburg won the women's national championship. She was so popular that local kids bought speed skates with the long blades, instead of hockey or figure skates.

Longsjo grew by sixteen to a wiry six feet one, deep chested. His parents stood only to his shoulders; thereafter the family dubbed Arthur Senior as Shrimp. Junior had a light olive complexion and chestnut hair, defined but not delicate facial features, a chiseled nose and cheeks. His mother, Ann, taught him to speak Finnish. She said that if one word characterized him it was *sisu*—for guts and a stoical determination to persevere through adversity and failures to accomplish a goal. Fitchburg itself was named after John Fitch, a colonial-era explorer synonymous with heroism. In Fitchburg, fifty miles northwest of Boston, refrigerator magnets and car-bumper stickers today tout *sisu*.

A quiet, high-spirited youngster, Longsjo was a protective older brother to his sister, Penny, and brother, Tom. At eleven Arthur Junior joined the Mirror Lake Skating Club, his entry into competitions on frozen lakes, ponds, and indoor rinks around New England. He raced age-group events from 220 to 880 yards.

Dick Ring remembers accompanying Longsjo to the Boston Silver Skates Derby in Boston Garden, the speed-skating equivalent of boxing's Golden Gloves tournaments. "We clipped out an entry from the *Boston Record-American* and sent in twenty-five cents. We got back a postcard and a number. We were just in awe at the Garden. There were fifteen-thousand-plus people packed into the stands. As youngsters we got buried by the veteran salts. But we came back the next year and did better. Eventually we became some of the heavy hitters, too."

By 1947 Longsjo was under the tutelage of Alex Goguen, winner of several national five-mile championships since the 1930s. Goguen, twelve years older, was regarded as a fox when it came to racing tactics. He lived near Longsjo and gave the youngster rides in his car to races to have company and help Longsjo work on his form.

"He could hardly stand on his skates as a youngster," Goguen said. "But he was happy going to meets. He had a ball. He always thought he would do well because he was a Finn."

Finland has turned out a high proportion of world-class athletes for such a small country. That sports streak was continued by a colony of Finns settled in Fitchburg, which has long supported a Finnish-American newspaper, *Raivaaja* (the Pioneer). In 1925 when Finland's great Olympics gold-medalist runner Paavo "the Flying Finn" Nurmi toured the United States, he stopped in Fitchburg to compete in a track meet. The elder Longsjo was twenty and won a sprint event. Nurmi captured the handicapped mile—he ran a mile and a half against competitors who specialized in the mile.

Longsjo Senior competed for the Reipas Athletic Club, a Finnish association. Members discussed stories of track and field, skating, and skiing the way baseball and football stories are bandied about in American Legion halls.

Goguen coached Longsjo to skate more smoothly. "I saw the kid was slowing down on the turns because he was digging the front of his skate blade into the ice on each stroke as though he were running," Goguen said. He advised the youngster to lift the blade front up first as he pushed the skate blade level on a stroke at right angles from the body. Speed skates are set lower to the ice and harder to balance on than hockey or figure skates.

"Sometimes I couldn't tell if he was listening to me," Goguen said. "He had his own ideas about things. But then I would watch him and I could see he was trying it."

Goguen also broadened his protégé's competitive radius to major events around New England and upstate New York. They often won races in their divisions. Longsjo felt that he had what it took to make the Olympic team. He complained that attending school interfered with his training.

His parents were anxious that he talked about dropping out of school at sixteen, contrary to the prevailing emphasis on getting more education to improve job prospects and economic mobility. The region was home to many abandoned textile mills. Windows that had let in natural light when the mills employed hundreds decades earlier stood derelict with broken panes—haunting reminders of businesses that moved away as workers were replaced by mechanized looms.

Longsjo's mother understood his dilemma. She was born Anna Elizabeth Lapisto in Michigan's Upper Peninsula. One of seven children of Finnish heritage, she grew up speaking Finnish at home. She lost a young brother in a house fire, and her mother died in the 1918 influenza epidemic. Her father moved the family to Bellefonte, Pennsylvania, and changed their name to Hill from Lapisto (which translates as "hill"). Anna loved music and dancing. She left home at sixteen in 1926 for the glamour and bright lights of New York City to try her luck as a dancer. She went by Ann Hill, waited tables, and did domestic work for fashionable families to earn money for dance lessons.

A dancing classmate was chain-smoking Bette Davis, the future actress. Ann regarded her as stuck up, hopelessly clumsy: "Bette Davis was the worst dancer in our class," she said. "No talent whatsoever. But she never let that bother her one bit."

In New York City Ann met her future husband, Arthur Longsjo, also drawn to the glamour of the Big Apple. He was five years older and handsome in his hotel bellhop uniform. He was a first-generation Swede (Longsjo means "long lake" in Swedish). They fell in love and kicked up their heels dancing the Charleston, the fox-trot, and the Lindy in hip nightspots like the Cotton Club. Ann and Arthur married in Brooklyn, his uncle performing the ceremony. After Arthur Junior was born in October 1931, they moved to her husband's hometown, Fitchburg. He found a job operating a lathe at Simonds Saw & Steel Company.

"I went to his school and talked with the principal," Ann Longsjo told me. "He said that I could make him go to school, but I couldn't make Art study. He used to get up at three o'clock in the morning to go practice skating. And he couldn't understand why other kids his age smoked cigarettes in the locker room."

Ann couldn't miss following the ascent of Bette Davis, pushing her way to become one of Hollywood's greats. Ann understood his skating passion. "I thought my son showed a similar drive as hers. He could go from skating to something greater."

She and her husband reluctantly acquiesced to their son's dropping out of Fitchburg High in his Olympics quest. This big change in Longsjo's life coincided with Goguen moving to Pittsfield, snuggled in the Berkshires a hundred miles west. Goguen, twenty-eight, was hired by the parks department in a job that included coaching a speed skating team. After a talk with Goguen, Longsjo's parents let him go. Longsjo could get coaching, and Goguen could get him a seasonal job with the parks department. Later, Longsjo told reporters he thought that was "heaven on ice."

• • •

Heid adapted to austere postwar Europe and learned to speak French and Flemish. He lived in the home of Ernestine Debaets, on a street near a dock where heavy loads were hauled by horses as they had been for centuries. The house lacked a flush toilet. The cuisine took some getting used to, particularly large amounts of fried food and horsemeat. "A specialty of the house was cow udders dipped in grease," Heid said. "I got so I liked sandwiches made with cow udders."

He evaded Belgium's cold, rainy winter by training and racing indoors on velodromes. On occasion he entered road races up to sixty-five miles in Belgium and the Netherlands to build stamina. Newspapers called him the Antwerp Yank. Some training rides turned into shopping trips; he cycled across the border to the nearest Dutch town, twenty-five miles away, to purchase cold cuts, cheese, and smoked fish, all cheaper than in Antwerp. With the purchases in his knapsack, he pedaled home.

Back in America, the cycling community circulated news of Heid's progress. Don Sheldon of Nutley, New Jersey, liked what he heard. Sheldon had set national records at seventeen in 1947, won the ABLA national men's open championship the same year and twice won the Tour of Somerville, a fifty-mile criterium in north-central New Jersey offering a treasure trove of merchandise prizes that attracted the top riders from around the United States and Canada.

Millions of Americans learned about Sheldon one Sunday morning from Ripley's syndicated "Believe It or Not!" cartoons, showing Sheldon in the national champion's stars-and-stripes jersey. He was cited for winning his second Tour of Somerville "from 134 crack riders, including Ted Smith, the national champ!" Sheldon followed Heid to Antwerp.

Early in the 1949 season, Heid and Sheldon traveled to England, where they raced on the Herne Hill track in southeast London, the Fallowfield track in Manchester, and Butts Stadium in Coventry. They lived on what they earned from races. When their prize was a merchandise certificate, they sold it at discount for cash. Heid supplemented his income as an underground entrepreneur—he smuggled watches. He would purchase a wristwatch for five dollars in the Jewish quarter of Antwerp or Ghent and sell that watch in England for five times as much.

"England had a 100 percent luxury tax," Heid said. "So this actually saved the English who bought from me for twenty-five dollars. When I went from Belgium to England, I would take ten to fifteen watches with me. They would be good watches, shockproof, but not too expensive because nobody would buy an expensive watch."

He wrapped his contraband in paper and put them in a dirty old tool pouch, which he placed on top of the contents of his knapsack. Customs officials pushed the tool pouch aside for their inspection. "I was willing to risk a fine or jailing, or whatever it was they would have done if they had caught me, just to stay in Europe to race."

Heid also took derailleurs and cycling jerseys and shorts, all in short supply in England. "It was quite an adventure. I wasn't greedy. It was surviving." Souvenir programs at velodromes where he and Sheldon competed featured their photos on the cover. In England during the outdoor track season, he beat so many national champions that the local press dubbed him the Yankee Clipper. One of Heid's best wins came in July at the Manchester Wheelers Meet, an international competition.

Sheldon gamely struggled to adapt to the faster pace. He accompanied Heid to Denmark for the circuit on outdoor concrete tracks.

"The Danes were very enthusiastic," Heid said. "We rode an international sprint, a handicap, a miss-and-out, and a Madison [two-rider teams]. There was also tandem racing and motor-pace. Pros and amateurs raced separate events." Danes had pari-mutuel betting on cyclists, like at horse tracks. "If the people made money betting on you, they would take you out to eat."

When he and Sheldon went to the worlds in Copenhagen in August 1949, Heid's performances proved a highlight of his career as well as a high spot in post–World War II U.S. cycling. Sheldon was eliminated early in the heats, but Heid got his momentum going by dispensing with two opponents to advance to the eighth-finals. There he came up against Britain's national amateur sprint champion and a silver medalist in the 1948 Olympics track tandem race, Alan Bannister.

On the bell lap, the Englishman led Heid up the forty-eight-degree banking of the 370-meter (400-yard) concrete track. Heid climbed higher, between Bannister and the outside fence, before suddenly dropping down as Bannister continued up. Heid gained six bicycle lengths before Bannister could react. The Englishman chased until he saw it was hopeless and lifted his hands from the handlebars, a surrender.

The quarterfinals pitted Heid against his nemesis, Axel Schandorff, the Dane who had eliminated him from the Olympics sprint. Schandorff had the advantage of racing before a home audience. The preliminaries over, qualifiers competed in the best of three matches. A sharper Heid faced the Danish champion. In their first match, he pipped Schandorff by three inches. Their second match was much better—Heid won by a length and a half. He had come a long way.

Yet he still had lessons to learn. The following day in the semifinal, Jacques Bellenger of France beat him in two straight matches to put Heid in the runoff for the bronze medal, against another Frenchman, Émile Lognay, winner that season of the Grand Prix de Paris. This was high-stakes racing. Heid was so fired up from his loss to Bellenger that he entered the best-of-three match races already a winner in his mind. The first he won decisively. The second turned into another photo finish, which judges ruled he won by the width of a tire.

So, Heid, America's premier sprinter, won the first world championship medal for the United States in thirty-seven years, and he became the first American since Bobby Walthour, Iver Lawson, and Marcus Hurley in 1904 to win a world championship medal abroad.

Sid Patterson of Australia defeated Bellenger to win the world amateur crown. With Englishman Reg Harris dethroning Dutchman Arie van Vliet for the pro sprint championship, 1949 turned into the year of the English-speaking invasion in Continental cycling.

Life as a top amateur in Europe had many advantages that would have been unavailable to Heid if he had returned to America after the Olympics. He earned a modest living. Frequently he negotiated such perquisites as transportation expenses, an appearance fee, and carte blanche to sign for meals in restaurants. In Copenhagen, the Ordrup Velodrome promoter let Heid's fiancée, Julia De Witte of Antwerp, watch him race from a private box in the grandstand.

After the worlds Sheldon followed cycling's migratory route to warmer weather in Morocco, then a French colony, where Italian, French, and Belgian cyclists spent the winter racing. Heid accepted an invitation to compete in Paris where he won enough to afford to marry his fiancée. But before the wedding came a three-month racing trip to South Africa.

10

The Allure and Agony of European Road Racing

Ever tried. Ever failed. No matter.
Try again. Fail again. Fail better.
—SAMUEL BECKETT

A group of New Yorkers, directed by the spherical James Proscia, renowned as Jimmy the Whale, rented the 168th Street Armory to put on six-day races. Proscia also held sixes in Buffalo, Cleveland, and Chicago. He and his partners envisioned that sixes would one day return to Madison Square Garden.

Ted Smith recalled that after he had won his third ABLA national title in 1948 he was paid $25,000—worth more than $260,000 today—to turn pro and ride sixes. "My first six-day was in Memorial Auditorium in Buffalo. I took one look at the velodrome and thought it was so small that for a moment I wondered if I was going to run around it or ride. It was a lot different racing than I thought it would be. Going around and around like that affected my stomach and I couldn't eat."

Smith was partnered with Jules Audy from Montreal, nicknamed the Blond Flash for his haystack-yellow hair and aggressive attacks off the front of the pack. "Jules had ridden in a hundred sixes, won fourteen," Smith said. "He knew his way around the track. Women loved Jules. He always had a pair of nice leather gloves to give them."

Buffalo began Smith's pro career, and Buffalo proved to be the last stop for Joseph Magnani. Smith's compact body and sharp acceleration out of the turns suited him on short tracks. In Jimmy the Whale's March

1949 New York Six in the 168th Street Armory, Smith was impressed with Swiss star Hugo Koblet.

After the winter sixes, Smith migrated to eastern Canada where Albert Schelstraete, a Belgian immigrant, held professional races in the Ontario towns of Delhi, Simcoe, and Shawinigan Falls. Schelstraete built a portable velodrome, twelve laps to the mile, which he transported on trains and installed on hockey rinks. He knew how to attract audiences, especially Belgian expats working on tobacco farms.

"Schelstraete one time called me up and asked, 'Do you want to race a horse for two hundred fifty dollars?'" Smith said. "So I went up there to Delhi for the race on a horse track against a sulky. The people there are Belgians and they bet on anything. They will bet on where a fly will land. Well, the race was the best two-out-of-three matches, a mile each race. I rode behind the sulky. I had to be careful because the horse was kicking up a lot of dirt in my face. But I came around and beat the horse in two straight. The driver wanted me to ride in front of the horse. But I didn't want any of that. The horse would bite off my ear."

Another who competed in Schelstraete's races was Jimmy Lauf, a dark-haired Maryland farm boy. To enliven a race program, Schelstraete persuaded Smith to lie down on the track and let Lauf jump over him on a bicycle. "I lay down on my face on the straightaway," Smith related. "Jimmy got speed up and jumped his bike over me. He touched me just a little."

Lauf succeeded Smith as national amateur champion. Like Smith, Lauf chafed against ABLA rules. "When I won the nationals in San Diego in 1949, a Schwinn company vice president offered me two Schwinn bicycles if I would come to Chicago," Lauf said. "I went out at my expense to the corporate headquarters, but the deal fell through because the ABLA officials said they would turn me professional by taking the two bikes that were offered. That is how crazy things were in those days. If you took a bicycle, they turned you pro."

Schelstraete had a laissez-faire approach to prizes—cash to all, pro and amateur alike. Lauf, twenty-two, saved his prize money in a Canadian bank, a compromise ABLA officials made after they threatened to declare him professional if he spent his winnings in the United States. At the end of the 1949 season, Lauf withdrew his savings and bought a ticket on the RMS *Queen Elizabeth* ocean liner to cross the Atlantic. He made his way to Antwerp and moved into the house where Heid and Sheldon had lived.

Smith in the spring of 1950 also shipped out to Belgium. He lived in Deinze, near Ghent, as a guest of a Belgian coach, Jules Verschelden, a friend of Albert Schelstraete. Smith discovered that local newspapers had published his photo in a story announcing his arrival.

"People came up to me and said my name like they knew me all my life," Smith said. "Then they would talk to me in Flemish, which I don't understand at all. I would shake their hand if they were a man, or kiss them on the cheek if they were a woman. It was a lot different than I thought it would be. In my day, our riders were scared to go to Europe because those European riders were so superior. When I got to Belgium, I was treated nicely. The Belgian people were still grateful because the American soldiers had pushed the Germans out during the war."

Smith found that while the United States offered races on weekends in the summer, every day in Belgium he had an abundance of pro races to choose from. He could usually pedal to the events, compete, then cycle home.

In Antwerp, Lauf had his choice of ten to fifteen races every day within a thirty-mile radius. Like his American cohorts, he was well received. He had contract offers to ride track events as the incumbent U.S. national champion. Track events paid as much as thirty dollars a meet—as good as top professionals, enough to live on for a week or two. He supplemented his income with road races.

The Americans expressed shock at the racing and living conditions. Smith said the roads were terrible. "I never saw roads like them in my life. They were all cobblestones and bricks. When you race seven hours at a time on them, that is tough. I'm not talking about just riding on those cobbles for seven hours. I'm talking about racing on them. Going hard. Your wrists, your back, your whole body takes a pounding."

Amateur races in America usually had pelotons of fifty to a hundred riders, but in Belgium there were up to two hundred. "The packs strung out for a kilometer on the sides of the cobblestones," Lauf recalled. Every rider constantly had to fight for his position on narrow cinder paths that bordered cobblestone roads. Beyond the cinder paths were ditches with sewage flowing. "I'll never forget the first time I rode an open race. I tried to pass somebody on the cycle path and fell. I got dumped into the sewage beside the road."

After the first week, Smith felt like going back home. But he had paid his own way to Belgium. He also realized that staying and racing against other pros was part of paying his dues to follow his dream and join the big show.

The amenity he and Lauf missed most was taking a shower. After a race, the manager of a local café would fill a tub with cold water in the back courtyard. Riders then stripped down and sponged off the sweat and grit.

"If you finished the race first, you got clean water," Smith said. "But it was strictly first come, first served. If you got there last, all you got was dirty water."

He realized the Superman reputation of the European cyclists was overstated, yet had some foundation. Belgian races were far longer, much faster, and more competitive than anything he knew. Popular American road-race fare featured fifty-milers around a downtown circuit or city park—mostly a cruise until the final miles when the pack jostled to wind up for the finishing sprint in the era of stick-and-kick. In Belgium he was racing sixty to a hundred miles every day, until he got so tired that he grasped he was overdoing it and cut back. American races usually had ten or so contenders, but Smith felt like all of the Belgians were so strong and fast that everyone seemed capable of winning.

In the town of Waarschoot, outside Ghent in East Flanders, he won a 140-mile pro race. That was in June. Victory generated contracts to compete on the velodromes, which made for smoother riding, much to his pleasant surprise.

• • •

In 1950, when Smith and Lauf were breaking into European racing in Belgium, Jack Heid married. He and his bride, Julia, moved from Belgium to England when the weather warmed and the English outdoor track season opened. Heid earned a more comfortable living. He was taking home about fifteen pounds a week, double what the average English worker received. He had help with equipment from Claud Butler, a bicycle manufacturer near London. The company even produced a frame named after him, the Jack Heid Special. (The best that Frank Kramer, riding for Pierce Arrow Cycles, had was a frame bearing his initials, FKS, for Frank Kramer Special.)

Two factors helped endear Heid to the public in postwar England: his keen competitive nature, and he was an American. He also fit in with the best riders; his regular training partners were world champions—Englishman Reg Harris and Aussie Sid Patterson. Harris's classroom education had ended after grammar school, when he went to work polishing cars. His athletic career was thus his fortune, and he selected training partners judiciously to reduce his risk of crashing. Harris's choice of Heid as a training partner indicated that he trusted the latter's bike-handling skills and increased stature in cycling.

Harris, Patterson, and Heid developed a regimen. They warmed up on a half-hour ride in the afternoon, the pace getting progressively faster, followed by a light ride for a half-hour. Then they raced four sprints on the Fallowfield track in Manchester, each man taking a turn leading out the others.

• • •

Back in the United States, the dwindling survivors of American cycling's glorious 1890s had formed the Bicycle Racing Stars of the Nineteenth Century Association, based in Chicago, and counted on Heid to win the world amateur championship. The elders wanted him to show once again that their country was a force in international bicycle racing.

The old corps was dying off. The original world champions, August Zimmerman, George Banker, and Major Taylor, were gone. Early national champion and founder of Indian Motocycles George M. Hendee died in 1943. Eddie Bald, the first national pro title holder, passed away in 1946, a few months before Ohio-state-cycling-champion-turned-pioneer-racecar-driver Barney Oldfield, the first to pilot a car a mile under a minute. In February 1950 Charles "Mile-a-Minute" Murphy died.

The association sent Heid $200 (worth $2,700 today) for expenses. It looked like Heid was going to fulfill their hopes as well as Frank Kramer's prescription for "one good American rider" to boost the sport in America. But Heid's idyllic life was upset in mid-May when he lost his balance living on the fine line between amateur and professional. British cycling officials hit him with a six-week suspension for an infraction involving expense money from a race promoter. His chance to win the world amateur title was in jeopardy.

A representative of the Claud Butler company offered him a covert stipend to help him through the suspension as he kept training. His wife, Julia, heightened the dilemma when she announced she was pregnant. Reg Harris told him that if he turned pro he would guarantee Heid fifty pounds, almost $170, from race promoters every time he raced. Heid considered this possibility, knowing he had good mentors. He held Gérard Debaets in high esteem as a great racer and devoted father bringing up two sons when his wife fell ill with tuberculosis and had to be hospitalized. Debaets had raced pro, like Harris. So had Jackie Simes II.

Heid's hesitation about turning pro was that there wasn't much money in sports. He knew that a world champion fared well. Harris had his Raleigh sponsorship, which paid him a base salary, plus bonuses for records he set; he also negotiated appearance fees, and he kept the prize money he won. Harris reigned at the summit of a steep pyramid. Many pros on the Continent earned less than Heid.

Riding professionally would liberate him to negotiate his own deals. He felt responsible for the hopes of the Bicycle Racing Stars of the Nineteenth Century Association, yet he had family responsibilities. He made the leap to go pro.

• • •

When the worlds came up in late August 1950 in Moorslede, Belgium, someone asked Ted Smith if he was there to ride the amateur road race. "I replied, 'Not me. I'm riding with the big boys.'"

Smith became the next U.S. rider after Joseph Magnani to compete in the world pro road race, 178 miles on roads featured annually in the Tour of Flanders classic. Among the forty starters were such legends as Stan Ockers of Belgium, Louison Bobet of France, Gino Bartali of Italy, and Hugo Koblet and Ferdi Kübler of Switzerland.

The pace was hot from the start. After four hours of racing, a tire on Smith's bike blew. He wore a spare tire in a figure eight across his back and dismounted to change tires, only to find he neglected to attach his frame pump. "I was glad to get that flat," he admitted. He hitched a ride in the "broom wagon," a truck that followed far behind the peloton, after the phalanx of team-support vehicles. The broom wagon stopped to "sweep" riders and their bikes from the road when they dropped out and needed a lift to the finish.

Inside the broom wagon, Smith sat next to Swiss ace Koblet. Smith asked why he was there. Koblet replied he "got tired." The man, who would win five stages of the 1951 Tour de France and the entire Tour by a historic twenty-two-minute margin, said he was tired. "No excuses," Smith said.

At the sprint matches on the Rocourt velodrome in Liège, promoters were hoping for a sentimental match, preferably in the final, between the aging Belgian Jef Scherens, in his swansong worlds, and French ace Louis Gérardin, not only France's nine-time national champion, but also the lover of France's singing star Edith Piaf. Scherens and Gérardin had finished one-two at the world pro sprint championships in Paris in 1947. They were still drawing crowds.

Heid in his first qualifier match drew Scherens. "I had great respect for Scherens," Heid said. "He was fifteen times Belgian national sprint champion. Seven times world champion. He used to do a sprint with me when we trained on the same velodrome—a friendly sprint, the experienced pro helping to bring up a younger rider, because I was a friend of Debaets. But I could see that I was matched as a lightweight at the worlds against Scherens."

When Heid warmed up he found the banking so steep he had to file his right pedal to keep the bottom from scraping the concrete surface. Part of his warm-up consisted of imposing his opponent's strategy on the banked turns and the straights to figure out his own tactics. Scherens had such sharp spring in his acceleration he was called the Cat. Audiences were thrilled at how smartly he dashed from behind an opponent's rear wheel to take the lead. Heid calculated where Scherens would make his move in their match race.

In the qualifier match, Heid led and turned his head around to look behind and eye Scherens. Around the final turn, Heid jumped a split-second ahead of Scherens. They blasted for the line, one sprinter beginning his pro career, the other ending a long and distinguished one. The fans packing the stadium jumped in unison to their feet. Scherens moved up to Heid's elbow down the final straight. But Heid was prepared. He had another jump and beat Scherens by a wheel. Belgium's favorite sprinter was eliminated by one from the New World.

In the next round, Heid eliminated Jacques Bellenger, who had leveraged his silver medal from the previous amateur worlds to go pro.

Next, the Antwerp Yank drew Arie van Vliet, the Flying Dutchman—who had won the gold medal at the 1936 Berlin Olympics kilometer time trial, then added the world amateur sprint title. He also won the world pro title in 1938, again in 1948. And in 1950 he was still a serious contender.

Heid didn't know Van Vliet and wasn't sure how to beat him. Belgian coach Aloïs De Graeve had studied Van Vliet and told Heid to lead the Dutchman up and down the velodrome banking to tire his legs. Unfortunately, De Graeve knew Van Vliet better than he knew Heid.

"I had never ridden like that," Heid recalled. "I was a pure sprinter. I depended on my jump. I would get in front and stall a long sprinter. But I tried running Van Vliet up and down the track. It really messed me up. I was too tired to sprint."

Heid wound up eighth in the worlds. Van Vliet lost the final to Harris. The Englishman kept his promise to Heid and made sure promoters paid him fifty pounds a race in England. When the summer ended, Heid and his wife, Julia, moved to Antwerp for the birth of their first child.

• • •

Sheldon traveled widely to races around Europe. About the time Heid turned pro, Sheldon moved to Paris. He used connections he had made in Morocco to negotiate a slot in the Vélo Club de Levallois, supported by Peugeot Cycles. It was a big break, because VCL riders received food and lodging, road and track equipment, shoes, and plenty of Peugeot apparel. Sheldon posed for a studio portrait in his VCL jersey with

Peugeot across his chest; the photographer touched up his image to smooth over rough acne scars.

The summer of 1950, however, saw the compulsory military draft reinstated when the United States went to war with North Korea. In October, Ted Smith was drafted into the U.S. Army Air Corps. He returned to Buffalo and served a year of duty in South Korea.

Jim Lauf went to Mexico for the Tour of Mexico, a fourteen-day race of 1,200 miles. It drew teams from Europe and South America. On the ninth stage, to Guadalajara, Lauf sprinted out of a small breakaway to cross the line first.

He was thrilled with the race—an estimated 1.5 million spectators lined the streets in Mexico City. The contingent of U.S. riders Lauf rode with found the race more than they could handle. His teammates abandoned early, leaving him alone. Following his win in the ninth stage, Lauf was misinformed about the next day's starting time and missed the start.

Lauf went back to his home on a farm in rural Hydes, Maryland. He enlisted in the U.S. Coast Guard and was stationed at a New Jersey supply depot. The base commander was unusually supportive and allowed him to train during duty hours after Lauf assured him that he would make the Olympic cycling team.

Sheldon, twenty-one, went to Paris from the Centennial Games in Christchurch, New Zealand, where he had gone for refuge from Europe's winter. In May 1951 he enlisted at the U.S. Embassy in London for four years in the U.S. Air Force. He was stationed in England and assigned to a Special Services athletics division to prepare for the 1952 Olympics in Helsinki.

• • •

Heid hustled to make a living in Antwerp. He competed in road races, entirely different from the racing he had been in for more than a year. Pro races paid down to thirty places.

In early September he pedaled twenty-two miles to a ninety-mile race in which he finished seventh and received seventeen dollars—enough to support his family for a week. His wife had borne a son, John. Fatherhood heightened his need to earn more money. The onset of winter meant hitting the indoor track circuit in Belgium, France, Germany, the Netherlands, and Switzerland. He found that the smaller velodromes favored his sprinting ability as the riders laid over on the steep turns and accelerated on the short straights.

In late February he was racing on the roads, frequently in the rough winds and cold, numbing rain. Twelve months earlier the sun had been shining on his career. But 1951 turned grim. For the first time, Heid felt discouraged.

"Van Vliet saw me riding and said, 'You've been racing on the roads. Your pedal action shows it.' He was right. I wasn't pedaling with the round smoothness of a track rider, more of a road rider pedaling squares."

Heid performed as well as anybody else in the long races—at least until about halfway through when he noticed a major transformation unfold in the peloton. "Some riders began drinking out of a different bottle they carried," he said. "Then they got revved up, which made the races harder. I'm sure that some guys were taking steroids or amphetamines, but I didn't want to go that route."

Late in a seventy-five-mile race in March, Heid surged with another rider and broke away. The two men worked together—each taking a turn leading the other for some 250 yards before swinging out to let his partner come through and catch the slipstream to recover. If they could keep their lead, Heid and his breakaway partner were guaranteed decent prize money. As a sprinter, Heid could play to his strength and win; the peloton would battle for third place.

One moment Heid was bumping over the cobbled road and peering ahead to gauge where he would end his turn pulling so he could swing out to recover behind his partner. A moment later, he heard the sharp sound of steel snapping apart. Heid fell and slid on his side along stones, bruising his hip and scraping skin from arms and legs.

His bicycle frame, weakened by the constant pounding on coarse pavement, cracked and broke. He barely had time to drag himself to the side of the road to avoid being run over by the peloton whooshing past, followed by a caravan of team-support vehicles and journalists.

In the blink of an eye, he went from leading the race to lying on the ground—filthy, arms and legs scraped and bleeding. "I realized I had to move my family back to America and get a job to support my family," Heid said.

• • •

Heid, twenty-six, settled his family in the northern New Jersey town of Rockaway. He found a full-time maintenance job with a Swiss pharmaceutical company. Instead of training rides or traveling, he wore a uniform, fixed broken windows, climbed a ladder to replace burned-out lights, and took care of the building. He and Julia bought a house. Another son was born in 1953 and given the popular Belgian name of Rik. Heid added a part-time job. He didn't join his former riding buddies anymore. They referred to him as "painting a barn."

He had a strenuous cycling apprenticeship in Europe, but in America that game had gone bust. The sixes that Ted Smith broke into as a pro before he shipped out for Belgium had fizzled. Jimmy the Whale Proscia gave away the velodrome in the 168th Street Armory, plus a pair of big power saws, to two teenagers and ordered them to cut it up and toss the pieces into the East River.

Under ABLA rules, Heid had to wait five years to apply for amateur reinstatement. "Jack Heid was a great bike rider," observed Jackie Simes II. "But he was born thirty-five years too late."

11

Outside Normal Limits

If you aren't in over your head, how do
you ever know how tall you are?

—T. S. ELIOT

Art Longsjo pulled off his shirt in October 1950 and stood barechested for the physician in the Selective Service System office in downtown Fitchburg, a rite of passage under law requiring men to register with the draft board when they turned eighteen. He had wire-hanger shoulders and skin stretched tight over muscle and bone. Alex Goguen had trained him in a series of strenuous speed-skating sprints from 220 yards to two miles, repeated over and over again on alternate days, a common regimen today but rare in the 1940s. Years of these drills sharpened speed and increased stamina. Longsjo had been sweeping his age-group division in major meets, setting state records, and he won a national championship.

The physician pressed a cold stethoscope against Longsjo's warm chest and heard an unusually slow heartbeat. The doctor announced he detected a heart murmur. Longsjo was classified 4-F, unfit for duty.

Goguen saw him differently: "He could stay with you and stay with you, and then take off so fast that you would wonder what was wrong with you."

That is what he'd done in the national two-mile championship in late 1949 in St. Paul. Two days of events drew four thousand faithful spectators, bundled up like grain silos to withstand the severe wind chills of a Minnesota winter in order to watch the best skaters in the country. Jack Heid's former training partner, Ray Blum, won the men's open national championship. In the juniors' two-mile race, for sixteen-to-seventeen-year-olds, Longsjo broke away at the mile. He won by a big margin and chopped nine seconds from the state record.

After flunking his draft physical, Longsjo returned to Pittsfield to skate another season with Goguen and work for the parks department. Turning eighteen promoted him into the men's open division. He was good, but just another one of the bunch. Wanderlust had a tighter grip. At the end of February 1950 Longsjo and another skater picked up their final paycheck and hitchhiked south to Florida.

His buddy left the Sunshine State to go home. Longsjo hitchhiked west alone. He spent a week in Texas picking cotton in a field under a burning sun. He wrote notes with a fountain pen to family and friends on the back of picture postcards. He signed them in a neat, loopy script, Artie.

Eventually he reached San Francisco. He waited on tables and worked odd jobs. Spotting Bay Area cyclists on racing bicycles with dropped handlebars influenced him to take up cycling, a sport popular among speed skaters in warm weather. Racing bicycles meant track bikes, which sold for a hundred dollars, more than he could afford. He called home for the money, more than his parents, supporting his younger brother, Tommy, and sister, Penny, had on hand. But they had confidence in his athletic abilities and took out a bank loan.

Longsjo returned to Fitchburg with his bike and stories about travels and life in Florida, Texas, and San Francisco. He stayed in Fitchburg rather than return to Pittsfield. For fitness he rode twenty-five to forty miles a day when he wasn't working at the United Farmers' Cooperative hauling grain bags. When the weather turned cold and a pond near his home froze, he tied on skates.

Longsjo traveled to the Olympic skating trials in January 1951 in St. Paul. Officials picked him as alternate for the Olympic team—an honorary choice, but he missed the traveling team. He was advised to stay available to fill in case someone was injured. Skaters were selected a year early to give them time to adjust to the European-style skating in the Olympics.

American skaters grew up on a diet of massed-start races, pushing and shoving off the line at the crack of the start pistol, and the first over the finish line wins. Europeans had a format in which two skaters at a time competed individually on opposite sides of two concentric tracks. At the end of each 400-meter (437-yard) lap, skaters switched tracks through an open lane on the home straight. They skated for the fastest time. The format was totally new to Longsjo.

He was recognized wherever he went to meets, often with Goguen. Longsjo was winning big Silver Skates competitions from Boston to Chicago to Lake Placid in upstate New York. But he didn't want to repeat as an alternate. He returned in late 1951 to train under Goguen and work for the Pittsfield Parks Department.

• • •

Longsjo and Goguen planned a four-year program to prepare him for the next Olympic trials. In January 1952 they started with the national championships in St. Paul. To be on the safe side, Goguen took Longsjo for a physical. The doctor checked his heartbeat, pronounced it too slow, and prescribed that Longsjo go home and rest. The diagnosis appealed to Longsjo's taste for irony. The next week at the nationals in St. Paul, he won three races.

But not without prodding. The first day he stayed in the pack. Goguen, frustrated, demanded to know why they had driven all the way and spent hard-earned money to get to St. Paul only for him to slack off. The next day, Longsjo won the one-mile, two-mile, and five-mile races. That got him runner-up in the nationals, which drew 15,500 spectators. Goguen placed sixth.

In February they drove to the North American outdoor championships for two days of racing in Alpena, Michigan, in the northeastern corner of the state, on Thunder Bay. On the first day, after skating in races from 440 yards to two miles, Longsjo tied in points with Ray Blum. The next day, both skaters watched each other closely as a severe snowstorm blew in from Lake Huron. Blum and other skaters folded newspaper pages and stuffed them under sweaters against their chests to cut down on the wind chill as they skated. Terry Browne, a Detroit firefighter, sprinted off the front of the three-mile race with a group of Detroit skaters to nearly lap the field and win the race. The points Browne collected put him in a three-way tie for first. Afterward, everyone flocked into a heated building for awards and photos. They heard a radio broadcast that Don McDermott of the U.S. Olympic speed skating team won a silver medal in 500 meters at the Winter Games in Oslo, Norway. McDermott, originally a cyclist, had participated as a regular in the Sunday morning training rides with New Jersey cycling and skating buddies—including Blum, Jack Heid, Don Sheldon, and Gérard Debaets. McDermott continued to ride but focused on speed skating as his primary sport.

"I accidentally sprayed a shower of confetti in the air when we heard the news about McDermott's silver medal," Blum said. "I took off my sweater by crossing my arms over my chest and pulled the bottom of the sweater up. The newspaper under my sweater had become soaked with sweat, then dried, and became brittle in the frigid air. The shower of confetti in the air was like a celebration of McDermott's Olympic medal."

• • •

On a blind date in 1952, Longsjo met Terry L'Ecuyer, a tall, willowy brunette from Fitchburg. She was attending Becker Junior College in Worcester, studying to be a medical secretary. It was the beginning of a five-year courtship, which spanned three continents.

"He was my first love," she explained. "I went with him sometimes to watch his morning workouts. I helped him shovel snow off the ice. He was dedicated to sports, sometimes too dedicated. But he didn't sit around and talk about doing something he wasn't going to do. I knew he wasn't going to change, and I was willing to help him excel."

Their romance kept Longsjo close to Fitchburg. He landed a job as file clerk at the Fitchburg General Electric plant and joined the Leominster Center skating club near Fitchburg. In the next skating season, Longsjo emerged as a dominant skater in the Northeast and a contender for the next Winter Olympics skating team.

As part of his training regimen he ramped up cycling. Both sports use similar leg muscles—particularly quadriceps—in the same motion. And both cycling and American-style speed skating use related tactics:

competitors are jostled in packs around turns and along straights. In both sports, drafting behind competitors, keeping presence of mind in a speeding pack, and timing a sprint under pressure require concentration and skill.

Longsjo's debut as a bicycle racer at the 1953 Massachusetts ABLA state championship was talked about for years in the Bay State. When twenty-one-year-old Longsjo showed up at the Westboro Speedway, a steeply banked concrete track made for midget-car racing, he looked out of his league, a rube. He wore cutoff wool skating tights, a loose-fitting, white cotton T-shirt, and brown penny loafers—his standard cycling gear. People looked at him and rolled their eyes. All the other racers wore close-fitting, bright-colored silk or wool jerseys imported from Europe, black wool shorts, and imported bike shoes with a metal cleat on the sole to fasten over the pedal for better drive.

He caught the looks and played along. He didn't have a car, so he rode his bike to the race, pedaling an hour and a half to get there, longer than usual because he had to make frequent stops to pump up his front tire, which had a leaky valve. Everybody else arrived by car to keep their legs fresh. What chance did he have against the better-rested riders? His bike wasn't shiny and new like the others, so he referred to it as "my truck." He came without a helmet, the leather hairnet apparatus required under the ABLA rules, so he had to borrow one. He could get through the mile and three-mile races in the championship with the leaky valve in his front tire, but he would be at a disadvantage in the last race, the twenty-five-miler. How could he compete against better-equipped riders?

It's a wonder that nobody picked up on the slight hustle in Longsjo's deadpan modesty. If they had, they might have realized that his legs were muscular and strong and perfect for cycling. They might have noticed, too, that his "truck" was really a Schwinn Paramount, put together by the hands of Joseph Magnani. Longsjo's dirty bike needed cleaning, it needed oiling, it needed new tires, some of the paint had been nicked by stones, but it was one of the best.

Longsjo also was good. In his first event, a qualifying heat for the mile, he won impressively. Somebody loaned him a tire to replace the one with the leaky valve. He then went on to win all three races.

Success didn't end there. Longsjo's state championship victory qualified him for the ABLA national championship in St. Louis—and he qualified for some expense money as well. The ABLA granted Longsjo sixty dollars, which wouldn't begin to cover round-trip gas for a car, food, and staying three nights in a motel. Moreover, for a national championship, Longsjo needed proper cycling clothing and, some fans and friends believed, a better bicycle.

The *Fitchburg Sentinel* ran an article about his state championship victory and the financial predicament he faced for traveling to the nationals. The *Sentinel* announced a fund drive. Mayor Peter J. Levanti opened the campaign with a five-dollar donation, and Police Chief Carlisle F. Taylor served as fund treasurer.

A total of ninety-seven dollars was collected. All but five dollars was spent to buy him a racing uniform. A veteran racer performed much-needed maintenance on Longsjo's "truck," for a nominal fee. A second fund drive raised a hundred dollars expense money to supplement the ABLA allowance to St. Louis.

At the nationals in a city park—an omnium of one-, three-, five-, and twenty-five-mile races—Longsjo the novice bike racer spilled twice. He suffered gouges and scrapes to his arms and legs. Yet he won points for third place in the three-mile and wound up in a four-way tie for ninth. In the one-mile run-off, the other three rivals cruised in anticipation of sprinting over the final 200 yards, but Longsjo exploded away at 350 yards to clinch ninth in his first nationals.

Three weeks later, Longsjo rode in his third bike race—the New England track championships in Lonsdale, Rhode Island. He won all four events, from one to twenty-five miles. It was a short but brilliant cycling season. Nobody gave much thought to the possibility that he could make two Olympic teams in one year, but the potential existed.

• • •

In January 1954, Longsjo packed his skates, not his bicycle, and went to West Allis, Wisconsin, to compete in the Great Lakes Open. He was so popular that skating officials proposed he race instead at the Midwest Championship, in Detroit's Belle Isle Park and sponsored by the *Detroit Times*. Officials agreed to cover his expenses to the national championship coming up in St. Paul.

The switch had another payoff. In Detroit, Longsjo won four of the meet's seven races and earned the "Skater of the Day" award. The *Detroit Times* acclaimed him as one of the greatest skaters ever to race in the championship, which had attracted top U.S. and Canadian skaters for thirty-two years.

At the nationals in St. Paul, Longsjo set a new U.S. record in the two-mile. He also won the five-mile, sprinting out of the lead pack after the final turn. However, falls in the 220-yard event and the mile cost him potential points. He finished the national championship in second place.

Next came the North American outdoor championship in February in Pittsfield, the highpoint of the city's annual Winter Carnival. The city common was flooded to create an ice rink with a track measuring six laps to the mile. There were eighty races for men and women in assorted age groups.

The most thrilling event was the men's open two-mile, in which Goguen led until two laps before the finish. Then Longsjo flashed past his mentor, followed closely by Olympic silver medalist McDermott. Goguen chased. The pack strung out behind him like a game of crack the whip. McDermott and Longsjo, the same size, skated stroke for stroke around the final turn. In the final straight, Longsjo opened up two strides on McDermott to win. Then Longsjo captured the 880-yard event to own the North American outdoor title.

Longsjo duplicated Carmelita Landry's 1941 victory—fitting, because her victory inspired him to become a speed skater. Yet he felt he hadn't reached his potential. He set his sights on the North American indoor championship in four weeks in Lake Placid. No male skater had ever won both indoor and outdoor championships in the same season. He decided to try for the double.

More than three hundred skaters from the United States and Canada, ranging from seven to fifty-six years old, entered the two-day North American indoor championship in Lake Placid. Longsjo skated to first in four races from the half-mile to five miles. He also scored second in two others. He totaled an overwhelming number of points to win—and clinch both North American titles.

Longsjo's versatility in two sports attracted press attention to the bike races he entered in 1954. Newspapers mentioned that he was two-time winner of the North American speed skating championships. Sports pages proclaimed "Skater Cycles to Victory" and "Champ Skater Shows Heels to Cyclists." The publicity directed new attention to the usually overlooked sport. He appeared to be that "one good American rider" Frank Kramer had prescribed.

Press coverage no doubt enhanced his personal satisfaction, but it gave him little material value. Sometimes he won wristwatches, cycling equipment, an occasional piece of luggage. International Olympic Committee President Avery Brundage liked to say that amateur sports would remain unchanged. Cyclists, skaters, and athletes in other Olympic sports grumbled as Brundage ignored their pleas to permit better prizes and more travel expenses so they could devote more time to training.

Longsjo, the son of an hourly paid factory worker and a homemaker, was determined to compete and to be the best. His pursuit of excellence in two sports, both minor compared with ball sports or track and field, bound him to a year-round regimen. Folks in Fitchburg, a working-class town, worked regular jobs, married, raised families, and drove cars. People used to call Longsjo an outsider. He shaved his legs. He trained every day before adult exercise was accepted. Some motorists drove past when he was cycling and chucked soft-drink bottles out the window at him. Any day job he had was secondary to making the Olympic team. He had no hesitation about taking time from work without pay to drive someone else's car to a race that took him out of town for days.

A frequent summertime Sunday ride he devised when he didn't have a race took him 180 miles. At dawn he pedaled west across Massachusetts into New York along the Mohawk Valley, then north and east over mountains in southeastern Vermont to Keene, New Hampshire, before curving south into Massachusetts and back to Fitchburg, reached sometimes after dark. He concluded his four-state jaunt with a climb up Wachusett Mountain, a ski resort near Fitchburg topping

2,000 feet, the highest point east of the Connecticut River in Massachusetts, on flat landscape. His one-speed bike had a fixed gear so he never coasted. "Art treated that long ride like it was his sundae," his friend Dick Ring said. "The finale climbing up Mount Wachusett was his big cherry on top."

In the summer of 1954, to peak for the Olympic skating trials, Longsjo raced in all the major cycling events he could reach. The fifty-mile Kugler-Anderson Memorial Tour of Somerville in New Jersey, founded on Memorial Day 1940, had become an American cycling classic. It was touted with some justification as the Kentucky Derby of American bicycle racing.

The event attracted a who's who of riders from across the United States and Canada. They came for a chance to take home the choicest prizes—dozens of bicycles, merchandise including household furniture, washers, dryers, and, the year before, a gleaming new Chevrolet. Merchants of the borough of Somerville, population twelve thousand, donated the goods out of civic pride to make their town a destination. Crowds lined Main Street six deep to cheer.

Longsjo finished fourth—a remarkable debut.

He soon after won his second Massachusetts state championship by sweeping all four events from the half-mile to ten miles.

As state champion, he went again to the ABLA nationals, in Minneapolis. He finished third in the twelve-miler and second in the ten-miler. During the one-mile, he rounded the final turn in a good position in the pack when his bike went out from under him. He fell and slid on the asphalt. When he scrambled back to his feet, both elbows and one knee bloodied, he discovered the worst damage—both tires were ripped from the rims. He grabbed his bike and ran, *click-clicking* in bike shoes with a steel cleat on the sole, 150 yards to the finish, and still came in fifth. That gave him enough points for fourth overall.

• • •

His fearless performance in Minneapolis generated buzz in cycling's subculture. He then began building a legend in September in eastern

Canada, in the 170-mile road race from Québec City to Montreal. Sponsored by Montreal's *La Presse*, the newspaper touted it as the longest one-day event for amateurs in the world. Québec-to-Montreal, introduced in 1931, was ebulliently compared to the Stanley Cup in hockey. Only two U.S. riders had won it.

Ninety cyclists lined up for the 6:30 a.m. Sunday start in front of the Hotel Frontenac in Québec City. The pace was lively. After only a few miles a group of eight broke away.

"I drove my Plymouth in a caravan of vehicles that followed the riders," Goguen remembered. "We passed a Catholic church on the way and I stopped in to attend mass. When I got back out and caught the caravan, I decided to go on past the pack where Art was and check on the breakaway. I kept driving and driving. I was surprised to see the breakaway had a lead of two miles, so I pulled over to the side of the road and waited for the pack to pass. When I spotted Art, I shouted, 'Hey! You better get somebody to work with you to catch the breakaway. Otherwise, you're racing for ninth place!'"

Only Pat Murphy, a Canadian national champion from Delhi, Ontario, was interested in pursuing with Longsjo. They worked in a relay, taking turns drafting behind each other for twenty miles, until Murphy's rear tire went flat.

Goguen drove up in his car and saw the two stopped to change the tire. Goguen pulled his bike from his car trunk and gave it to Murphy. It was a little small, but the two riders resumed their chase. They caught the breakaway over the next twenty miles while Murphy's support crew made a wheel change and got him back on his own bike again, fifty miles from Montreal.

Several in the breakaway were fatigued. They had been out in front for 120 miles, more than five hours. The pack revved up its chase. Longsjo took long pulls at the front of the breakaway to maintain the record tempo.

When Goguen spotted Gothic church spires piercing the Montreal skyline, he became concerned that spectators lining the course blocked the landmarks he and Longsjo had identified earlier. Goguen was concerned that Longsjo didn't know exactly where the finish was in Montreal—in front of city hall. He turned around and drove back to the breakaway. He signaled Longsjo that he would stand on the side of the road 300 yards from the finish line.

The outcome after 170 miles came down to a ten-man sprint. From the outskirts of Montreal to city hall, people stood ten deep on each side of the road. In the last mile, one rider after another charged away, attempting to capitalize on the other riders' fatigue after seven hours and twenty-two minutes of racing. One by one, Longsjo caught them, drafted, and waited as the breakaway came back together. Meanwhile, the pace quickened, crowds grew louder.

At last Longsjo spotted Goguen on the side of the road, waving both arms like he was doing jumping jacks. Longsjo rose from the saddle and sprinted with all he had left. He won by five lengths over Murphy and cut the course record by seven minutes. Nearly four minutes behind came the pack, reduced to thirty-one.

Longsjo's cheerful manner as he signed autographs and answered reporters' questions helped make him a new star. The Association Cycliste Canadienne named him Canadian cyclist of 1954.

Québec-to-Montreal paid cash prizes, something that ABLA officials publicly disparaged. The U.S. and Canadian governing bodies agreed not to tell each other how to conduct their own affairs. Longsjo was discretely handed an envelope stuffed with $300 in cash, worth more than $3,000 today. The prize he accepted before a scrum of newspaper photographers was a tall shiny brass trophy topped with a brass cyclist. He also was awarded a new Italian road-racing bicycle, with the latest derailleur offering eight speeds.

• • •

When the Olympic skating trials were scheduled for February 1955 on Lake Como in St. Paul, Longsjo, twenty-three, was a contender. Hedly Bray, the new mayor of Fitchburg, helped raise $300 so Longsjo could go a few weeks early and train where he would skate in the Olympic trials. Two other skaters accompanied Longsjo—Dick Ring, who financed his trip by spending money he had saved to buy furniture for his upcoming marriage, and Arnold Uhrlass of Yonkers, New York, a rival. After the three arrived in St. Paul, Longsjo's hopes were nearly dashed during a rigorous workout on Lake Como. His right skate blade caught a crack in the ice, causing him to fall. His knee was wrenched.

Longsjo was prescribed to rest and take daily whirlpools at the University of Minnesota's physical education facility. The treatment kept him out of the Eastern States qualifier in mid-January. He applied for a waiver and submitted a medical report to the U.S. Olympic Committee. The USOC granted him an automatic qualifier for winning nine of eleven national-level meets in 1954.

He'd spent a week in whirlpool treatments when a professor who had been watching him approached and asked him to follow. As Ring told the story, Longsjo figured that as a guest using the facilities he should follow: "He had only a towel wrapped around his waist, and the professor led him down some hallways. Pretty soon the professor stops and opens a door. Suddenly, Art is staring at a whole classroom of students. He's embarrassed. He's standing there in front of them with only a towel around his waist and everybody's staring at his legs. They were art students and they couldn't believe the definition in his legs. They had never seen an athlete's legs like Art's before."

Longsjo was still pampering his swollen knee when it came time to skate in the 5,000-meter (3.1-mile) time trial, the event he wanted to win.

Ring recalled the momentous occasion in vivid detail: "Art began slow. He had a talent for winding up easy. He got very low on the ice and built his speed up. He was like a symphony in motion, moving low and fast. Faster and faster. And then he exploded all the way to the finish line. He just croaked everybody. He won the 5,000 meters. That put him on the team."

Records show he skated the distance in 8 minutes, 56.4 seconds to beat twenty-five other finalists. Uhrlass was second, six seconds behind; Ring was fifteenth.

Under an idiosyncratic rule of the U.S. Olympic Committee, Olympic skaters were kept out of skating competitions for the rest of the season to prepare, on their own, for the European-style format in the Olympics. (A rule since abandoned.) He let his swollen knee recover and prepared for an ambitious cycling season.

Not until May was his knee completely healed, just in time for the Tour of Somerville on Memorial Day. The official starter was Olympic-gold-medalist-swimmer-turned-actor Buster Crabbe, wearing the gaudy outfit from his blockbuster Flash Gordon movies. Longsjo finished a close second to Canadian Pat Murphy.

Longsjo won or placed well up in whatever bike races he entered. He captured his third consecutive Massachusetts state championship. That qualified him for the ABLA nationals in Flushing Meadows, in the New York borough of Queens, on what is today a parking lot for Citi Field, home to the New York Mets. On a half-mile concrete track, Longsjo won the ten-mile, came in second in the five-mile, but failed to place in the mile and half-mile races, which favored sprinters. His tally at the 1955 ABLA nationals put him second overall.

At this point, Longsjo had already secured a spot on the Olympic speed skating team and appeared likely to make the Olympic cycling team. He became a cult-leading actor in both sports. Yet he barely scraped by financially. The *Fitchburg Sentinel* published a letter on the op-ed page, written by someone identified only as a local businessman, which defined Longsjo's predicament: "It is indeed unfortunate that Art's greatness is achieved in a sport as little supported as speed skating or bicycle racing, for the result is complete lack of support and interest in his achievement. Were he a track and field man, a football, baseball, or basketball player, his name would be heard the world over and the city of Fitchburg would proudly claim him as one of her own."

The letter writer noted that Longsjo was overlooked in his hometown, "a city which he, alone, today is putting on the map," and added, "I remember the celebration in honor of Miss Carmelita Landry when she won the North American outdoor speed skating championship, a feat well deserving of the tribute bestowed. Yet my memory fails to recall any similar celebration in honor of the man who brought that same crown in the men's division, plus the indoor championship, to Fitchburg, and then to really top it off with a berth on the Olympic speed skating team."

From time to time Longsjo told friends he felt he should give up amateur sports and work for a professional ice show "to earn a little money for a change." Other times he said wistfully he would like to go to France and ride on a professional cycling team "for the experience," Goguen recalled.

He never complained about lacking money. He said the traveling he did and friends he made compensated for economic difficulties. Occasionally, Longsjo received unexpected support. In early January 1956 he walked into a Fitchburg department store when the owner—Lester Kimball—asked him why he wasn't in Norway with Olympic skating team members who went there early to train. Longsjo said he couldn't afford to go until the U.S. Olympic Committee gave him plane fare. Kimball promptly wrote Longsjo a personal check; it enabled him to fly there ten days earlier than the USOC would have sent him.

Skating in Norway presented a new world for Longsjo. Skaters were popular, well known. People in the stands pulled out stopwatches to clock skaters, and they appreciated subtleties in skating styles.

Longsjo studied the way skating meets were conducted, as well as the European form of skating, which stresses technique. From Norway the U.S. Olympic skating team flew to Davos, Switzerland, for pre-Olympic competition.

He was enjoying himself. At times he could be stubborn. He and coach Del Lamb, a veteran of the 1948 Olympic skating team, argued about training methods. Lamb wanted him to skate all-out every day, but Longsjo disagreed because he said he needed some recovery time. After Lamb reprimanded Longsjo at the end of one session, Longsjo told teammates that if Lamb thought he skated slowly that day, the next day in a 500-meter race, which was not his event, he would skate even slower. Longsjo finished seventy-fourth out of seventy-five. He said with straight-faced irony to friends the competition was so hard he could only manage seventy-fourth place.

The Cold War between the East and West was fought on ice rinks, running tracks, and boxing rings. In 1951 the Soviet Union applied to the International Olympic Committee to participate in the Olympics. The application came too late for the Winter Olympics, but the USSR sent athletes to the 1952 Summer Games.

The 1956 Winter Olympics in Cortina d'Ampezzo, a ski resort high up in the Italian Dolomites in northeastern Italy, were the first Winter Olympic Games for the Soviets. Their skaters came prepared. Russian coaches were the only ones taking motion pictures of their skaters, wearing bright buttons on the hips, knees, ankles, and arms of their uniforms so that techniques could be analyzed and improved. This practice intimidated many athletes, including Longsjo, aware his team lacked anything close to that level of support.

A few days before Longsjo was to compete in the Olympics, he was stricken with the flu and lost 7 pounds from his usual weight of 160. He finished fortieth in the 5,000-meter (3.1-mile) race, won by Boris Shilkov of the Soviet Union. If he had been healthy, Longsjo said he still would have done no better than twenty-fifth place. The Russians were very good. Longsjo noted in an interview that three U.S. skaters set new national records in four events, but still the team went home empty-handed.

Russian athletes held a dark fascination for the American public. When Longsjo returned home, a *Fitchburg Sentinel* reporter immediately asked him what the Russians were like. The story ran over the Associated Press wire. "The Russians are terrific, both from a personal and a competitive standpoint," said Longsjo. He said the Russian skaters were like anybody else and won by training hard. Russian athletes were the least argumentative, the most subdued athletes, he continued, unlike athletes from other Iron Curtain countries like Poland and Czechoslovakia who "scrapped constantly."

The interview gave him a forum to speak out on two issues that put him years ahead of his time. "I think we will eventually have to resort to government sponsorship of our teams," he said. "Especially in a sport like speed skating, where there is such a demand on training to produce stamina and endurance. I feel that the amateur must be given a break. He must be given the time and opportunity to get himself in as good shape as his fellow contestants. Almost every European country does it. Why can't we?"

He also attributed the poor showing of U.S. speed skaters in the Olympics primarily to the different style of competition. He called for adopting the European format in the Olympics. More than twenty years would pass before that happened.

In the meantime, Longsjo began training for the Olympic cycling trials. They were to be held in mid-September near San Francisco to determine who would make the team flying to the Summer Olympics in Melbourne, Australia.

No one had ever competed in two separate U.S. Olympic teams in the same year.

12

America's First Woman National Champion

> When I won the national girls' championship for the second time in 1954, I told the ABL officials that I was twenty-one and was no longer a girl. I said I wanted the name of the division switched to women's, and it was.
>
> —NANCY NEIMAN BARANET

Up until the 1950s bicycle racing had been predominantly a men's club—even though women had been riding bikes almost since they were invented. Before the turn of the nineteenth century when cycling was a nationwide craze, adventurous women had taken to cycling for recreation spins and some racing in sufficient enough numbers to influence fashions, such as divided skirts, or short capes that were removed from the shoulders after a ride and fastened around the waist to cover the divided skirts. Around 1850 Amelia Bloomer of New York advocated and adopted a form of athletic apparel with a short skirt extending to the knees, below which were loose trousers fastened about the ankles—which became known as bloomers after she publicized them in the women's newspaper she edited. They became popular with women cyclists, who, however, were subject to sharp criticism, even ridicule, in newspaper editorials and from the pulpit.

A century later, the 1950s turned into a landmark decade for an American woman to compete in a European stage race: Nancy Neiman Baranet of Detroit. She first made her mark by getting ABLA officials to recognize her as the national women's champion, rather than girls' champion.

Neiman Baranet, a slender, five-feet-two brunette, was one of about 250 American women racing cyclists, compared with some 1,250 men. Her mother didn't think racing was ladylike. "Her main objection was not the consequences of a spill," Neiman Baranet said. "But what the neighbors would think."

Recognition has come slowly for women athletes, including bicycle racers. Women usually entered competitive cycling either through their families, like Doris Kopsky, the 1937 national girls' champion, or, like Neiman Baranet, by joining a local club. She began cycling as a tourist in 1951 on an American Youth Hostel trip in Massachusetts that toured Cape Cod and Martha's Vineyard.

Afterward, she joined a Detroit club. It offered coaching from an Italian named Gene Portuesi. His discipline corresponded with the name, the Spartan Cycling Club. The next season's training began as soon as the mercury rose above five degrees Fahrenheit. Members rode in small groups, and Neiman Baranet worked out with the men. By April they were riding about three hundred miles a week. The Spartans pedaled two thousand miles in May, when they added sprint exercises.

"The level of women's racing in this country in the 1950s was as good as we could get," Neiman Baranet pointed out. "The drive was there, but we had no facilities to take advantage of like there are today. We worked regular jobs from nine to five, and trained after work. I was a secretary. We lived for the sport, but we had to put food on the table. Nobody took care of that for us."

Neiman Baranet followed Jack Heid's example and looked to Europe. In 1955 she flew across the Atlantic to race for the summer because she felt that was "the thing to do." She wrote to Eileen Gray of the Women's Cycle Racing Association, who set up a racing itinerary in England and France for the American.

Neiman Baranet paid her way from savings without any expectation for reimbursement. "Absolutely nobody even *breathed* the word money in those days," she said. "You didn't want to lose your amateur status."

She discovered just how sensitive amateur status was when her plane first landed in London. The flight's passengers remained seated as she was called to the front cabin to meet Eileen Gray, who boarded with special permission. She told Neiman Baranet that a Claud Butler Cycles representative was waiting in the airport to give her a new frame, which she could accept as long as she quickly covered up the name and never mentioned anything about it. After Gray briefed Neiman Baranet, they and the rest of the passengers were free to leave their seats.

The highlight of her three months of competing in Europe came in August when she tied the world record for 200 meters at the Paddington track in London. Neiman Baranet went 14.4 seconds to equal the mark set by Daisy Franks of England. The American also visited Paris and raced on the Parc des Princes velodrome—following in the wheel marks of Walthour, Taylor, and Heid.

In 1956 Neiman Baranet returned to France to compete in the Critérium Cycliste Féminin Lyonnaise-Auvergne, billed as the women's Tour de France, an eight-day stage race in late July on narrow secondary roads in central France.

"I had some amusing problems with the French language," she recalled with a laugh. "I was trying to introduce myself as America's woman champion, but I said the French word *champignon*, which means mushroom, so it came out that I was introducing myself as a mushroom. My French got along very well with kids five and under."

Neiman Baranet was the sole U.S. entrant in a field of eighty-seven starters from Great Britain, France, Belgium, Switzerland, and Luxembourg. Her previous racing had been limited to weekend events up to ten miles, but in France she had eight straight days of competing up to fifty miles a day.

"Did I ever suffer!" she said, recalling her experience. "I was a trackie. I had absolutely no experience in road racing and mountain climbing. At the base of the climbs, I started at the front of the pack and then lost places as we went. The longer the hill, the more I lost on the leaders. But once I got to the end of the stage, my track experience helped me sprint for a good place."

For the twenty-mile time trial stage, officials refused to let Neiman Baranet wear her silk stars-and-stripes jersey. Officials said silk's reduced wind resistance gave her an unfair advantage over others wearing wool. (What would they have thought about today's teardrop helmets and skintight Lycra body suits?) She borrowed a wool jersey.

At the end of some stages her legs felt rubbery. Her hands were so tired from gripping the handlebars that she was unable to close them for hours. Yet as the race went on, she grew stronger. In the seventh stage she finished second, losing the sprint in the final fifteen yards.

America's first woman stage racer in Europe ended up fourteenth out of forty finishers, based on total elapsed time. She followed up with more events around France before heading to England for ten days—where her track races were rained out every day. Neiman Baranet went back to the United States in time to win her third national championship, in Orlando, Florida.

• • •

In early 1956 the ABLA reinstated Jack Heid and Ted Smith as amateurs. Heid resumed Sunday morning rides with northern New Jersey friends, who didn't mind that he had been away "painting a barn." Smith, in Buffalo and nervous about new talent coming up, trained for three years to get competitive. The big change in American racing in their absence was that European and Schwinn Paramount road bicycles with derailleurs had taken over from track bikes and fixed gears. Derailleurs had been refined to ten speeds.

While the two former pros returned to the peloton, former expats Jim Lauf and Don Sheldon had left the sport. Both competed in the 1952 Olympics in Helsinki, Finland. Lauf was dismayed when ABLA officials shifted him from the kilometer, the track event he won in the trials, to the 4,000-meter (2.5-mile) team pursuit, which also included Sheldon. They were eliminated in the first round. Sheldon doubled in the 112-mile road race, finishing twenty-second. After the Olympics, both hung up their wheels, as Lauf put it, "to get on with life."

For Heid and Smith, reinstatement allowed them to compete in all amateur events except ABLA nationals. But the de facto national title event was the fifty-mile Tour of Somerville on Memorial Day. The borough's population tripled on race day. Crowds cheered riders charging around downtown streets closed to traffic. Somerville became to bicycle racing what the Boston Marathon was to running.

At the 1956 event 130 riders from around the United States, Canada, Mexico, and Japan lined up. Winners of the previous six editions came, plus six Olympians. They were competing for glory and a prize list starting at $500 in merchandise plus a top-of-the-line racing bicycle valued at $200 for the winner, descending to $100 in merchandise and a trophy to tenth place. To heat up the pace were generous lap primes plus $150 in merchandise for the rider who led the most laps. Frank Kramer, looking like a banker in a suit, would present the prizes.

A shiny new Thunderbird, Ford's stylish two-seat answer to General Motors' Corvette, served as pace car. After the racers blasted away, thirty-two-year-old Heid shot to the front of the pack. He knew from experience that the best way to avoid getting caught in crashes that were inevitable around the 174 right-angled turns was to stay at the head of the pack. He also controlled the race by chasing down breakaway attempts—dashing up to each break with the peloton in tow.

The hard-hitting pace shredded the field down to seventeen with a half-mile remaining around the final turn. They surged onto the last stretch, a long flat straight paved with bricks and asphalt, bordered by spectators. Racers scattered from curb to curb as they sprinted.

Smith recounted drafting behind Heid's rear wheel somewhere in the middle of the peloton with 300 yards left. Heid swiftly led him up the left side of the trolley tracks. Smith was getting knocked on the elbows by rivals challenging him for the "sleigh ride." Smith held his place as they sped past everybody and burst into the lead. Smith tried, unsuccessfully, to move up on Heid.

"When we hit that line," Smith said, "I shouted, 'I got second, buddy! You won. I got second!'"

Three lengths back, Longsjo followed, in third.

After they coasted past the finish of their first race in five years, Heid put his hand on Smith's shoulders, leaned over, and kissed him on the cheek.

Photos show Longsjo sprinting with his elbows bent slightly, hands pulling at the handlebars like he was picking up the engine block from a car. "Longsjo's form was good," Heid said. "He used a more European approach to bicycle racing. He attacked more frequently during the races. In the 1950s, most of the races had bunch finishes, and the sprints at the end were shorter than now. Longsjo was a long sprinter. He improved later on because he rode those long races in Canada."

That season, Longsjo won nearly every race he entered. In a sixty-two-mile race in Valleyfield, Québec, he toppled over on a turn, got up, chased unaided to catch the field, and still won. Afterward, he had to be treated for cuts and bruises to his left leg.

He won another Massachusetts state title, but passed up the ABLA nationals to compete instead in the Canadian national road race championship. It ran 110 miles from Montreal, north over the Laurentian Mountains to Sainte-Agathe-des-Monts and back. The Laurentian Mountains, famous for winter skiing, include a particularly majestic, steep, and long ascent accurately called Mont Sauvage (or the "Wild Mountain").

Guy Morin of Montreal had competed on the Canadian national team in the 1954 British Commonwealth Games in Perth, Australia, and in the 1955 Pan American Games in Vancouver, Canada. The way he told the story, unlike most others in the pack, Longsjo wasn't intimidated by Mont Sauvage.

"Art got out of his saddle and began sprinting as though the finish was only two hundred meters away. We had more than eighty miles left. And he's sprinting madly down the road. I began yelling, 'You crazy American! It's too early!' He didn't listen. All the rest of us decided, What the hell, let him go. He'll run out of steam. His lead got bigger and then we lost sight of him.

"Up at the top of Mont Sauvage was my trainer, Fioro Baggio. He was a retired Italian professional who raced twenty-five six-days. He moved to Montreal and had a bicycle store. Baggio watched Art climb up Mont Sauvage all alone. Then, that crazy American, you know what he does? He takes his feet off his pedals, lets his legs hang, and coasts. Then he gets off his bike, walks over to Baggio. 'Excuse me,' he says to Baggio. Not hurried. Like he's sightseeing. 'I'm looking for the mountain. Can you tell me where it is?' Baggio just looked at him for a moment. Nobody in the race was in sight. Baggio smiled. He said, 'I think you just passed it.'"

Longsjo won the race.

In other races, Morin tried to figure out Longsjo's riding. "I forced him into a long sprint, but that was a mistake. He beat me easily. I stalled him to a short sprint near the finish of a race with thirty others. But he nipped me a few yards from the finish and won. Finally, I thought I had him when we went into the final turn of a race. I'm much shorter than Art. I used my lower center of gravity to take the turn tight and get the inside, open a gap. Ah, I thought, I've got him now. I got twenty lengths on him. Then with fifty meters left, he went by me. I yelled at him, 'You crazy American!'"

Baggio, the Canadian distributor for Torpado Bicycles of Italy, sponsored a team, Baggio-Torpado. Morin couldn't beat Longsjo, so he invited him onto the team. Each member received two road frames and two track frames every year, a big deal in those days.

On Labor Day, Longsjo entered the fifty-mile criterium around Colt Park in Hartford, Connecticut, a major Northeast race. He had racked up a string of fifteen consecutive victories for the season. In the last half-mile, he was in a group of six, which included Smith. As the riders flashed down the descent of a short hill that bottomed to the finish, Smith broke one of his steel toe clips.

"I overreacted and pulled the toe strap so tight it broke, too," Smith recalled. "All I had left was the cleat on the bottom of my shoe. We were flying down that hill, I want you to know. I had to concentrate on riding as smoothly as I could and manage to beat Longsjo. I did. I just beat him out in the sprint. When we coasted past the finish, he congratulated me and said, 'I'd like to see what you could do with both legs.'"

• • •

The U.S. Olympic cycling trials consisted of two road races of 116 miles each on a six-mile course around San Francisco's Lake Merced, three days apart. On the first day, ABLA officials selected the top three finishers for the Olympic road team. Then the top two from the second qualifier. During the intervening days, sprint events were held in San Jose, on a velodrome built in 1950.

Longsjo's bid to make his second Olympic team appeared to end with a loud bang when his rear tire burst a short distance from the start line of the first early-morning race. His rear derailleur was also acting up. He pulled out and returned to the start line in time to go to breakfast with race officials.

For the second road race, Longsjo had new tires and his derailleur was fixed. He and Dick Ring succeeded in joining the breakaway of twenty from the pack of a hundred. At the end of 4 hours, 51 minutes of racing, 10 minutes faster than the previous race, Dave Rhoads of San Jose, a veteran of the 1952 Olympic team and national ABLA champion, streaked to the lead with 220 yards left. Longsjo finished half a bike length down to secure second place and a second Olympic team berth.

ABLA officials, however, assigned him to the 4,000-meter (2.5-mile) team pursuit on the velodrome. Selection of the four-rider pursuit team was up to ABLA officials; they picked two road and two track cyclists on the basis of speed and power. (The practice was soon abandoned when the Olympic trials were expanded to hold designated races to determine the selection of the pursuit team.)

Longsjo was disappointed at the assignment, as the road race was the event for which he had qualified. Nevertheless, after he was told to ride the team pursuit, he commuted to Montreal, where he stayed at the home of his friend Guy Morin and dutifully trained on a new velodrome that had opened there.

The XVI Olympiad was celebrated in Melbourne, Australia, from November 22 to December 8—the first Olympic Games hosted in the Southern Hemisphere. Australians were so enthusiastic that they lined both sides of the road to watch Olympic athletes ride buses five miles from the Olympic Village to the competition sites. Spectators paid an admission fee of twenty-five cents to watch the athletes work out, and they besieged them with autograph requests.

The Melbourne Olympics were noted for their pageantry. They also were the first time the Russian athletes stayed in the Olympic Village, which heightened international excitement. The events were low-key compared with media extravaganzas we know today. Television was just coming into homes, and the three U.S. broadcast networks beamed only a limited number of programs; airtime for the Olympic Games was limited to highlights. Coverage in print and over radio and television was modest. One improvement over the past was that U.S. amateur rules had eased to permit the Schwinn Bicycle Company to supply Paramounts, assembled by Joseph Magnani, to U.S. Olympic cyclists.

In the Olympic cycling team pursuit, riders work a close-order drill that begins with the lead rider pedaling about a hundred meters with the other three tucked behind in a tight file. The leader swings out slightly to let the other three pass through as the former leader catches the end and the new leader pulls another hundred meters. The time of the team's third rider across the finish line is recorded as the team's time. Longsjo rode with Dave Rhoads and sprinters Allen Bell, a powerhouse from Somerville, New Jersey, and Dick Cortright of Buffalo, in his first of three Olympics.

Unlike other squads, Longsjo's pursuit team spent little time together because after the California trials they were on their own until they arrived in Melbourne. Predictably, the U.S. team was eliminated in the preliminary heats.

The year 1956 is remembered for two achievements in sports. Rocky Marciano of Brockton, Massachusetts, became the only world boxing heavyweight champion to retire without losing a professional fight (his 49-0 record remains undisturbed today). And Don Larsen of the New York Yankees pitched the only perfect game—no opposing batter reached base—in a World Series, Game Five against the Brooklyn Dodgers.

Longsjo's feat—competing in two separate Olympics in the same year—went overlooked. He finished out of the medals in both Olympics, as did all of his teammates. But he was remarkable for being among the best in each of two sports that lacked the support they have today.

Twenty-eight years later, many in the media forgot Longsjo's accomplishment when Dave Gilman of the U.S. Army made the 1984 U.S. Olympic team in the winter luge event and the summer kayak event. The media mistakenly credited Gilman as the first U.S. athlete to make the double.

Longsjo's only recognition came from promoters of a new six-day circuit. Shortly after he returned home from Australia, Belgian promoters offered him a contract paying $500 a day for six of their six-days scheduled in America. He readily acknowledged to reporters that he could use the $3,000 (today worth almost $30,000). But he turned down the offer to shoot for the 1960 Olympics. He thought the sixes amounted to a gamble.

Instead, he took a job teaching skating for the Fitchburg Parks Department. Because that employment could be seen as a violation of amateur rules, he worked for free. In a Sunday skating session, he slipped on the ice, slammed full speed into the wooden border of a rink, and broke a leg. He was sidelined for months.

• • •

Jack Heid heard—and heeded—the siren song of the sixes. The youngster who had caught six-day fever in the 1920s was ready in the 1950s. He signed a contract paying a base of $150 a day—enough to buy a new washer one day, a dryer the next, and then new furniture for his home.

In January 1957, the day after President Dwight Eisenhower and Vice President Richard Nixon were sworn into office for a second term in Washington DC, the first new six opened in Cleveland to a crowd of five thousand. Nine nations were represented in twelve teams. They raced a twenty-hour daily format, from 8 a.m. to 4 a.m.

As riders dived down the steep pine-board banking and sped wheel-to-wheel around the short velodrome, several were knocked out from crashes and pileups. "These are supermen to rival the fabulous heroes of any breakfast cereal," Geoffrey Risher wrote in the *Cleveland News*.

The biggest supporter of sixes was the AFL-CIO meat cutters union. In an article in *Butcher Workman*, Ray Dickow pointed out that the cyclists expended as much muscular energy in each race as Jack Dempsey spent in his entire professional boxing career, as much as a Major League pitcher spends in forty games, as much as a basketball player burns up in three-fourths of a season.

That kind of exertion burned up lots of fuel. William "Torchy" Peden of Canada—who had enjoyed an avid following at the Nutley Velodrome in its best years and had won 38 of the 123 sixes he entered—was known to devour four lamb chops, two steaks, and three chickens in two hours on a typical afternoon. Peden also wolfed down a basket of grapes and a dozen oranges a day between meals. The racing commissary following the winter circuit stocked up to 500 chickens, 2,500 lamb and veal chops, 1,000 quarts of milk, and about 1,000 steaks to feed the riders and their support crews.

Attendance in the Cleveland Sports Arena increased night after night. Heid and his partner finished sixth. When he returned to his regular day job, he rested up for the next grind in late February in Louisville.

But the success of the Cleveland Six brought out former officials from the dormant National Cycling Association. They wanted a share of the gate and went to the Louisville Six to collect. Jurisdictional politics between the NCA and the Belgian race promoters flared. Bad publicity resulted in attendance dropping. The Louisville race lost $30,000 (almost $300,000 today).

Next came the Chicago Six. Heid heard the mighty pipe organ from high up in the Chicago Stadium rafters rock the building with invigorating music, like God was performing. When the organist played "Pennies from Heaven," the audience seated in tiers over the track threw pennies. Pennies rained down, pinging and bouncing on the boards. The pennies proved to be all the money Heid saw. The Windy City's six ended without any of the riders getting paid.

Heid completed the Chicago Six in third place (partnered by Italy's Mino De Rossi), with his legs, neck, wrists, and back aching—and all for nothing. The other planned U.S. sixes were scuttled. He walked his bike to where he had parked his car, packed his bike in the trunk, and drove 780 miles back home to New Jersey. He was retiring for good from racing.

• • •

In August 1957, Nancy Neiman Baranet sprinted to her fourth national ABLA title, in Kenosha, Wisconsin. She posed for photos with the men's national champion, Jack Disney of Pasadena, California, also winning a fourth national title. Both were familiar faces in their national championship jerseys. The rider next to them was not only a new face but also the first black rider to win the national amateur championship, and the first black national champion since Major Taylor. He was sixteen-year-old Perry Metzler of Brooklyn.

Perry Metzler and his twin brother, Jerry, took up cycling with several other black youths in 1953 as members of the Crusaders Club of Brooklyn. They couldn't afford fancy equipment; they rode used bikes and did their own repairs. They wore blue-and-white jerseys with a cross on the front.

The Crusaders participated in local races. In May 1954 Jerry was the first of the Crusaders to win a race, capturing the junior division in a twenty-five-mile time trial in Westbury, Long Island; Perry scored second.

The twins took to racing. Amos Ottley, from St. Albans in Queens, another black rider, then in his early thirties, coached them and served as a father figure as the twins' parents had separated after the family moved from Mississippi to Brooklyn.

In mid-1954, the Crusaders' treasurer absconded with the humble treasury and the club disbanded. Many area cycling clubs, including the Century Road Club Association, one of the oldest and biggest in the country, had bylaws that barred blacks. That left the twins and fellow Crusaders few alternatives. Many quit the sport.

The Metzlers kept riding with Amos Ottley. In the 1955 ABLA state championship, Perry finished third. He qualified for the ABLA nationals, held that year on the half-mile oval in Flushing Meadows. The nationals were a matter of local pride because of nostalgia associated with New York and the sport's heyday. ABLA officials brought in retired six-day star Jimmy Walthour Jr. as official starter.

For the nationals, Flushing Meadows took on the atmosphere of the gayest years of six-day history in the Garden. More than two hundred riders from most of the forty-eight states arrived. Each state flew its flag in the area set aside for contestants and equipment. The Department of Parks erected long lines of bleachers, which were filled at the start and finish lines. Attendance over the late-August weekend was estimated at ten thousand daily.

Metzler rode his bike from home in a high-rise public housing project in Bedford-Stuyvesant to Flushing Meadows. He finished out of the points on the first day, but the next day he snatched fifth in the five-miler to earn a point, which placed him ninth overall. At the age of fourteen, he showed promise.

The Metzler twins grew to a well-proportioned five feet nine. Their bodies matured early, with long thin faces and deep chests. The twins raced often and collected a mass of trophies. In 1956 the twins went one-two in the New York State ABLA championship, with Jerry winning. They both qualified for the nationals, in Orlando, Florida. They sought to win a national ABLA medal, but instead came up against a bigger obstacle than the poverty they lived with, and the sport was never again the same for Jerry.

Two years earlier, the Supreme Court had ruled unanimously in *Brown v. Board of Education* of Topeka, Kansas, that racial segregation in the classroom violated the Constitution. The ruling completed the reversal of the 1896 Supreme Court decision, *Plessy v. Ferguson*, which had permitted "separate but equal" public facilities. The Sunshine State remained racially segregated—in schoolrooms, hotels, and restaurants. Throughout the South, newspapers had published separate obituary sections, depending on race. It was not unusual for police in the South to arrest blacks just for being out on the street after sundown.

"I told them not to make the trip down there," Ottley remembered. "I had places in Brooklyn that I couldn't get into. Things were different then."

Segregation was familiar to the Metzler twins. They had lived in Mississippi for nearly ten years before their family moved to New York. They went to Orlando anyway, on a bus. They could not book a room in a hotel or receive service in restaurants near the national championships. They discovered they had to turn right around and go back home. Jerry, always outgoing and quick-tempered, became disgusted and quit racing.

Although Perry Metzler was blocked out of the Orlando nationals, he gave another indication of his talent in 1956 when he won the junior Best All Round trophy, a national season-long contest based on points awarded to top finishers in five designated ten-mile races in Northeast and Middle Atlantic cities.

The black rider Metzler looked up to was Ken Farnum, a sprinter who had immigrated to Manhattan after competing for his native Barbados in the 1952 Helsinki Olympics. Farnum stood a little over six feet and weighed 180 pounds. A smart tactician, in the sport since age ten, Farnum also had power to pedal big gears and wind them up fast. He was a legend in the West Indies for winning their sprint title eight times. In 1955 he had established himself as a force to be reckoned with in New York by winning the state ABLA championship.

Farnum usually trained alone, but sometimes he worked out with Metzler, Ottley, and two black teenage talents—Jeff Wood of St. Albans and Herbie Francis of Harlem. At the 1957 New York ABLA championship, Ottley's friends were the talk of the sprints. Farnum again won the men's open against competition that included Arnold Uhrlass, the champion speed skater.

Wood and Metzler finished one-two in the junior boys' race. Wood, Metzler's age and size, specialized in the speedy yet strategic half-mile. At sixteen, Wood looked like a likely prospect to win the national championship. He was second in the Tour of Somerville juniors' ten-mile race to Metzler's fourth. The two racers often battled for first; all the others were left to fight for third.

The ABLA awarded expenses for the nationals in Kenosha, Wisconsin, only to the state champion, which left Metzler on his own. He had struggled to buy tires; he certainly couldn't afford to travel nearly halfway across the country.

Al Toefield, a New York City police sergeant, had raced on the Nutley and Coney Island velodromes when he was Metzler's age. He served as an ABLA district rep and spotted Metzler in a parking lot a few days before the 1957 nationals. "I asked him why he wasn't in Kenosha," Toefield said. "He said he didn't have any way to get there. So I said he could ride with me in my car."

At the nationals, on the Washington Park Velodrome in Kenosha, on the shore of Lake Michigan, the favorites in the junior boys' race were Wood and Ed Reusing (pronounced REE-sing), the blond Missouri champion. Reusing had won the junior race at Somerville on Memorial Day and was third in the 1956 Orlando national championship. Seven thousand spectators filled the bleachers.

Juniors competed for points awarded to the top five each in the half-mile, one-mile, two-mile, and five-mile races. The first race was Wood's specialty, the half-mile. Fifty of the country's fastest fourteen-to sixteen-year-olds set a brisk tempo around the tight, steeply banked turns and down the straights.

"Metzler was the kind of guy who could rise to any occasion," Toefield contended. "He could find a hole and ride through it. He had no fear."

Metzler rode with his back straight and flat. In a sprint, his chin dropped low over the handlebars, his neck arched, his face turned up like a headlight. He was so admired for an uncanny ability to stay upright when others fell around him that he was called the Magician.

Metzler stole the show with a magnificent ride in the half-mile event, which he won from Larry Hartman of Washington State, with Reusing in third. In the five-mile, Reusing watched the field carefully and won the race from Metzler and Wood, second and third, respectively. This made the standings twelve points for Metzler and ten for Reusing. On Sunday, Reusing refused to ride in the rain, which practically assured Metzler the championship.

Rain forced officials to move races to the street. Metzler was shut out of points in the mile, in which Wood scored second. But Metzler came back in the final event, the two-mile, for fifth place and one more point for a total of thirteen to Reusing's ten. Wood's eight points were good for fourth in the nationals. In the men's open Farnum finished tenth.

Metzler's victory marked the first time that a black rider had won an ABLA national title medal. He was awarded the champion's red-white-and-blue cycling jersey, a hefty trophy to add to his burgeoning collection, and the larger and grander Grenda-Heit Memorial Junior Trophy. "It took up half the back seat on the drive back home," Toefield said. "The memorial trophy was for Perry's high school, Boys' High in Brooklyn, a major force in area sports, to display for a year in the school's showcase."

Patricia Assam, who married Metzler in 1960, said that he wore his silk stars-and-stripes jersey on the streets of Bedford-Stuyvesant for everyone to see. "Perry was so proud of wearing that national champion's jersey," she recalled. "When he got home he wore it to stand around on the corner with. The word went around the neighborhood what Perry did in winning the nationals. I went by and saw him. He was standing there, practically glowing, he was so proud."

• • •

As Metzler's riding career was getting started, Nancy Neiman Baranet decided to retire after her fourth national title. In recognition of her accomplishments, the Detroit City Council passed a testimonial resolution that named her Sports Woman of the Year. She married her weight-training coach. She served as the only woman ABLA officer and as a board member for twenty-seven years, from 1956 to 1983. In that time, American women cyclists were the first to achieve international recognition.

13

Pedali Alpini

Death is no big deal. Living is the Trick.

—RED SMITH

Art Longsjo recovered from his broken leg and embarked on an unwavering victory streak in 1958 in the United States and Canada. "He was really starting to enjoy life," Goguen said. "He was married and things were falling into place. When I was in Fitchburg visiting relatives he would call me up and ask me to come over to fix his wheels. Said they were all banged up. When I went to his home I could see that just some spokes were loose. Two or three. He just wanted to see me. And he would give me a saddle or some other piece of equipment he had won in a race. He would say, 'Here, take this. I've got too many of them.'"

On Memorial Day in Somerville a breakaway of four looked untouchable. "They had about a half-mile on us when Longsjo started to chase," Ted Smith recalled. "I went with him. After we got out alone, he swung out for me to come through so he could draft behind me. But he was much bigger than me and gave me a great windbreak. I didn't want to give that up, so I swung out with him. 'No, thanks,' I told him. 'I don't work on holidays.'"

Longsjo pulled Smith up to the leaders. "Then when we wound up for the sprint, it was his race. Ah, Longsjo was a true champion. I couldn't beat him if I had four legs that day." Smith, tucked behind Longsjo, finished second, again.

As Longsjo won race after race, he tugged at many hearts and imaginations. He attracted droves of spectators to races and inspired much interest for being what sportswriters called "a two-sport Olympian." At twenty-six, he was in his prime.

In July Longsjo won his sixth straight Massachusetts state championship. He skipped the ABLA nationals the next month to take on the biggest challenge of his career—the Tour du St. Laurent stage race, a grueling four-day event in eastern Canada, styled after the Tour de France. Canada's version featured stages of more than a hundred miles in the morning and another twenty-five to forty miles in the evening. The Tour du St. Laurent drew the most ambitious cyclists in North America for the ultimate test of speed and endurance. Those who competed were hardy. One fell off a cliff, climbed back to the road, and still finished.

Longsjo rode on the Baggio-Torpado team, captained by Guy Morin. The defending Tour du St. Laurent winner, René Grossi of Montreal, captained their team of six. Longsjo, Morin, and the rest of the team pitched in to help Grossi to win again: Grossi's teammates would chase breakaway riders and bring the rest of the field up to the break. Baggio-Torpado teammates would ride to protect Grossi from the wind, leaving him fresher for the stage sprint. The group sought to win the team prize, $1,000, a lot of money, to cover their hotel rooms, meals, and gas for the support car in the caravan trailing the peloton.

Morin prided himself on getting Grossi to first place in general classification, based on total elapsed time, by the second day, and the team led the other teams. The next day, Morin and Grossi initiated a breakaway with two others in a 110-mile stage. Fioro Baggio drove up in the team car and informed Morin their lead was seven minutes.

"At first, I thought that was real success," Morin recounted. "Then I realized Art was back in the pack with two other teammates, and that could cost us the team prize because it was three who scored. So I immediately pulled out of the breakaway, turned around, and tore back down the road. I was real mad that Art had allowed himself to fall so far behind. I turned around when the pack came up and I really gave Art a scolding. 'You crazy American,' I told him. 'The race is going on and here you are sleeping in the pack.'"

They dashed away together. A few miles later, Morin felt too tired to work in a relay with Longsjo and just drafted. "I began to regret that I spoke so harshly to him," Morin said. "Then he wouldn't be pedaling so hard. And I didn't dare fall behind after what I said. By the end, we closed to within two minutes of the breakaway. That kept our team in first."

The final stage was a thirty-mile individual time trial, in which riders went off one at a time in a race against the clock; the last rider in general classification departed first and the leader went last. Grossi had a lead of 2 minutes, 24 seconds over Longsjo, in second. Morin urged Grossi, "Go out there and really open up."

Grossi's margin seemed bulletproof. He tried. But his legs were fatigued after more than five hundred miles in four days. He lost 2 minutes, 35 seconds to Longsjo, who won the time trial stage and the whole race by eleven seconds. Longsjo led the team to victory. He became the first U.S. rider to win the Tour du St. Laurent.

• • •

His record time for the Québec-to-Montreal course still stood when Longsjo was invited back for the Canadian classic's twenty-fifth edition on Sunday, September 15.

Ninety miles after leaving Québec, more than halfway to Montreal, the course left the town of Trois-Rivières and yawned in a straight, flat expanse for thirty miles. The wind blew like it owned the country. The sun burned down. Fiery heat shimmered off the road. Longsjo attacked—rising off the saddle to leverage his body weight on the pedals, hands gripping the handlebar drops, he threw the bicycle between his knees to accelerate, tires shushing on the road with each down stroke. Six others joined him. They formed a pace line. Seven can be a magic number in a breakaway: if each rider at the front leads for about twenty seconds while cohorts draft in a file, each has two precious minutes to recover before his next turn at the front.

The last fifty miles wended through villages and curved on scenic country roads. When the breakaway riders saw the Montreal skyline, they had a six-minute lead.

Longsjo spotted Goguen standing near the finish and attacked again. The others were watching him closely and countered. All seven were in a drag race, spread across the road, the crowd yelling. Longsjo's arduous training ride that took him through four states and concluded up Wachusett Mountain gave him an edge over his closest challenger, Roland Williot of Montreal. Longsjo pulled ahead with enough of a margin to sit back in the final yards and cross the line waving a hand to the crowd. He won by three seconds, about ten bicycle lengths.

Only nineteen of the nearly one hundred starters finished. Longsjo garnered headlines. He was invited for a special post-race television interview, so he stayed overnight as a guest at Morin's home. Goguen drove back to Pittsfield.

Longsjo had been driven to the race by a friend, Edward Robinson Jr., a twenty-year-old former Fitchburg High School track and football star. "I didn't notice much about the fellow who drove Art," Morin said. "He was kind of shy around the riders and stayed out of the way. The next morning, we discussed the possibility of Art going to Europe to ride for a professional team. Baggio said he could fix it up and Art said he was interested. Art and I shook hands good-bye about ten o'clock. He got in the car and left. I was the last one to speak with him."

Longsjo fell asleep in the passenger seat, his head resting against the window as they motored south through Vermont. The winding road they took as a shortcut was wet after rain. At about 11:15 a.m., a bee buzzing around inside the car distracted the driver. He removed a hand from the steering wheel to swipe at the bee as the vehicle approached a curve near North Hero, just north of Burlington. The automobile veered into a utility pole and smashed with such force that the pole was embedded in the passenger side.

Rescue workers had to cut Longsjo out of the crunched and twisted metal of the demolished car. He was unconscious and suffered a fractured skull and internal injuries. The driver's back was broken.

That evening Longsjo died.

His death stunned the cycling and skating communities as well as his hometown. More than a thousand people attended his funeral, many comprising a who's who of the two sports in the United States and Canada. Three Olympic speed skaters and three Olympic cyclists served as pallbearers.

In Fitchburg a movement was organized to create a memorial. Suggestions ranged from renaming Mirror Lake to the Arthur Longsjo Mirror Lake, in honor of his start in sports, to naming a city park after him. Morin visited Fitchburg mayor George Bourque to recommend commemorating him with a bicycle race. Morin helped organize the Fitchburg Longsjo Memorial Race. He spread the word to get top riders to come from both countries. Another committee created a marble memorial to honor Longsjo and his accomplishments.

• • •

On Memorial Day 1960, America's best cyclists lined up for the start of the Tour of Somerville. Southern Californian Mike Hiltner ignited the season and ushered in a new era of American cycling when he scorched across the finish line in a new unofficial national fifty-mile record (only records set on tracks are official) in a little over two hours.

Another who influenced American cycling in the next decade had established his bona fides at Somerville the previous year. In the ten-mile junior boys' race, sixteen-year-old Jack Simes III thought his race was blown when a tire burst. He jumped off his bike and looked up to spot a teenager standing on the side of the road with a balloon-tired bicycle. It had a seat jacked up two feet and trendy long-horned handlebars. Simes dropped his prized racing bike to the street, grabbed the other kid's bike, and gave chase, although the metal cleats of his cycling shoes caused his feet to slip off the rubber pedals.

Spectators standing five deep along both sides of the street watched the group of juniors whiz past. Then came Simes, pedaling furiously on a bicycle with handlebars that put his hands up to his chin, like a prairie gopher standing on his haunches. On the next lap, his father stood on the edge of the street with a spare racing bicycle. Simes traded bikes again, time trialed to regain the pack, and won the pack sprint.

• • •

Simes and Hiltner, nearly the same age but vastly different in personality, faced the same difficulties as other aspiring American cyclists.

They each set national records in winning the Tour of Somerville and won national championships in the 1960s—Simes on the track, Hiltner on the road—and made determined efforts competing in Europe.

Jack Simes III was a third-generation racer in northern New Jersey, instilled with a sense of the sport's heritage. He heard stories from his father and grandfather, both former pros, and he learned about recent foreign experiences from Jack Heid. Simes was schooled early by his father in the basics: how to ride and draft, how to time coming off an opponent's rear wheel to dash for the finish. "I grew up thinking that sprinting was the class act of cycling," he said.

His father had introduced him to Frank Kramer in 1958, a few months before Kramer died of a heart ailment that October, aged seventy-eight. "Kramer came to a bike race at Weequahic Park, near Newark," Simes recalled. "He was a white-haired man in a dark suit, very quiet, and standing all alone. My father was the only one who recognized him. Cycling was such an underground sport then. We walked over to him and he said hello. My father told me he was the greatest bike rider of all time. That meant something. It sunk in. I hoped what he had would rub off on me."

Hiltner was a West Coast marvel. When he grew up in suburban Los Angeles, teenagers drank beer, hung around the beach, surfed, or worked on cars for show or drag racing. In the popular American mind—particularly in Southern California—bicycles were for children. Bicycles had balloon tires for a cushy ride, upright handlebars, chrome fenders, and often had a headlight and a horn that worked until the batteries died. Bicycle racing was as European as soccer. A neighbor introduced Hiltner to cycling. He entered his first race, a twenty-miler against eleven others, in Santa Barbara on July 4, 1957. He finished last, but the experience inspired him to take part in every Olympics until he turned forty.

Most of California's racing took place in the northern part of the state. A typical race today with events for various divisions will draw at least four hundred riders. Bill Best of San Francisco, one of the top riders, estimates that in the late 1950s the entire state had only about two hundred racers registered with the ABLA. The organization had sought to increase its presence in the Golden State by holding its nationals in 1941 in Pasadena and in 1949 in San Diego.

"Races were mostly informal affairs on the West Coast then," Best said. "A big event might draw as many as fifty riders. A standard practice was for twenty to thirty riders to get together in a town where we would select a long flat stretch with good pavement and hold five to ten sprints up the street to a finish we agreed on, like the end of a block. We lined up across the road and took off together. We bumped elbows, shoved one another out of the way, and learned how to stay up while we went hell for leather.

"The winner got a pat on the back, or sometimes a trophy. A pair of tires was considered a valuable prize. A race was considered big time if the organizers managed to give the winner a black-and-white television set."

Simes grew up under the tutelage of his father, who stressed pedaling briskly, with round, silky-smooth strokes. Hiltner was self-coached and followed his intuition. He sat low in the saddle and favored big gears, which moved his legs more slowly than Simes pedaled at the same speed.

In 1959 Hiltner won the Tour du St. Laurent at age eighteen. Overnight, everybody was talking about a short, self-effacing Californian in a burr haircut, the youngest to win the most demanding race in North America. If somebody excitedly asked Hiltner what he did to get so good, he was known to blush in modesty and mumble a self-deprecating reply.

The next year he moved to Northern California to train with a group of San Francisco Bay Area riders dedicated to the sport. Several of them had raced in Europe—some while in the army, like Bill Best, stationed in West Germany, or Dave Staub, 1956 national ABLA junior champion. Staub raced for fourteen months with Steve Pfeifer in England, Germany, Belgium, and Italy. Rick Bronson and George Koenig spent enough time in Italy in 1956 to fall under its spell. They returned to San Francisco speaking flowery Italian phrases and whimsically added *i*'s and *o*'s at the ends of English words. They formed a cycling club—Pedali Alpini.

All it took to get along in Pedali Alpini was to race bicycles. Members idolized Italy as their mecca. Their hero was Fausto Coppi, the winner of all the major races in Europe. While Dave Staub and Steve Pfeifer competed in Italy, they shook the hand of Il Campionissimo. He was such an icon to the Pedali Alpini that COPPI was painted in large letters on a boulder near the peak of a long and arduous climb in the Bay Area. When a rider tackled the ascent and felt his muscles burning and his lungs heaving for all he could take, he would look up to read COPPI and renew his efforts to reach the summit.

Hiltner befriended Lars Zebroski, small-framed, his age, a narrow face tapering to a small chin. They rented a little shack on the San Francisco Peninsula, on Tunitas Creek Road, an old secondary road with switchbacks hugging curves of the mountainous coast laden with redwood, pines, and oak trees. In this idyllic setting, they trained with Peter Rich of Berkeley and others. They pedaled hard up hills and, to sharpen speed, every time they spotted a city or town boundary sign, like Half Moon Bay or La Honda, they jumped off the saddle to sprint as though they were going to win a new Cadillac. They wanted races to be a cakewalk by comparison.

Pedali Alpini riders drove sixteen thousand miles in one six-week stretch in 1959 to races—from California to Chicago to eastern Canada. When Memorial Day approached, they drove cross-country, before construction of the national superhighways, to New Jersey. Hiltner won the 1960 Tour of Somerville.

It seemed natural to Pedali Alpini riders that Rome was hosting the 1960 Summer Olympics. At the road racing Olympic trials in July in New York City's Central Park, Hiltner and Zebroski qualified for the team on the first day, with the Pedali Alpini founding member George Koenig clinching a spot the following day. They were not just going to the Olympics in the Eternal City, they were going to the homeland of Fausto Coppi. They saved what money they had earned from jobs they squeezed between training and racing schedules. They planned to stay in Italy after the Olympics and race with the masters.

• • •

Jack Simes III was seventeen when he went to the U.S. Olympic cycling trials in New York. The track events were held on the half-mile oval in Flushing Meadows. There he rode one of the most unusual match-race finals. He progressed through the qualifying heats until at last he rode in the deciding match for a berth on the team against Ed Lynch, of Compton, California, a veteran of the London Olympics with Jack Heid.

Lynch attracted attention with the enormous gear he rode. It was 30 percent bigger than normal, equivalent to riding a high-wheeler more than ten feet tall; his front chainring looked like a third wheel. He also pedaled with crank arms that were half-again longer than usual to give him greater leverage. He was easily spotted at the track because even on hot summer days he wore dark tights to protect his skin, badly burned in a kerosene fire.

The Californian's experimentation didn't end with equipment. Lynch set up a pup tent in the track infield where he kept a tank of oxygen. A lungful of oxygen before each of his match races seemed to give him a temporary physical boost.

When Lynch, the Olympic veteran, and Simes III, the high school student, rode their match, Lynch didn't mind when Simes perched on his rear wheel around the last turn. Simes had developed what he called a snap—the explosion of speed for the finish. In both match races, Simes eclipsed Lynch by inches. Jack Simes III, whose grandfather had taken his father to Newark to watch Frank Kramer's farewell ride in 1922, became the family's first Olympian.

The 1960 Rome Olympics allowed each country to send two match-race sprinters. Simes's colleague was Herbie Francis of Harlem, America's first black Olympic cyclist. Twenty-year-old Francis was big and muscular, like a football lineman, yet on the bicycle he was amazingly quick and catlike. He would rise slightly from his saddle and rely on powerful quads to accelerate sharply. Francis was considered among the fastest one-sprint cyclists.

Perry Metzler had been a likely prospect. After high school, he took a job in New York's garment district and trained after work. His rival Jeff Wood dropped out of the sport. Metzler transitioned to the open division at seventeen. He scored consistently in Northeast and Mid-Atlantic races.

The Century Road Club Association, New York's largest cycling club, sought to recruit Metzler, but somebody pointed out that bylaws specifically prohibited blacks. They got around this rule by having Metzler write on the application form that he was Mexican. From then on, he rode for the CRCA.

Metzler's successful riding was part of the mystique that grew around him. Another part was that he commuted to races in a polished red-and-green Ferrari. The sleek Italian car was at the other end of the spectrum from the boat-like, chrome-laden Fords and Chevrolets that everybody else drove. The Ferrari belonged to Bill Wilson, an older black man with salt-and-pepper hair who smoked a meerschaum pipe and stayed in the background during races. He became a "big brother" to Metzler after the family broke up.

In January 1960 Metzler was drafted into the army. After basic training he was stationed at Fort Jackson, South Carolina. Al Toefield, on the U.S. Olympic Cycling Committee, tried repeatedly to get Metzler assigned to the Army Special Services so he could train for the Olympic trials. Although the armed forces had been integrated in 1952, blacks were not openly received. Toefield later found that a colonel from the South kept blocking Metzler's transfer to Special Services.

• • •

The 1960 Summer Olympics were called the Grand Olympics because of Rome's classical background. They were the Olympics in which Abebe Bikila of Ethiopia, a country formerly occupied by Italy, ran barefoot through the streets to win the marathon, and Cassius Clay—later Muhammad Ali—won the light heavyweight boxing gold medal. Italians won five of the six cycling gold medals.

Hiltner competed in the four-man 100-kilometer team time trial. The Americans finished eleventh of thirty teams—the best U.S. cycling performance of the Games. He also doubled in the 109-mile road race. At eighty-five miles, a Russian and an Italian broke away, causing the peloton to split apart in pursuit. Hiltner, the only American in the lead group of thirty-one chasers, wound up engulfed in a tight bunch sprint. After 4 hours, 20 minutes of racing through a searing Roman heat wave, they fought for the bronze medal. Hiltner crossed the line twenty-third; teammate Zebroski was fifty-third, eight minutes down.

In the velodrome match races, Simes and Francis were eliminated early.

When the Olympics concluded, Pedali Alpini members stayed behind, like Jack Heid and Al Stiller before them. Peter Rich, a cherub-faced rider called Cannonball for the swift way he descended hills, accompanied the club to the Olympics and stayed too.

"Our object was to get to Italy and live in cheap digs, eat as inexpensively as we could, and do what we had to do to get by," Rich told me. The Pedali Alpini crew had a contact in Milan with Cino Cinelli, a former pro on the Bianchi squad in the era of Coppi. Cinelli had a second career making his line of bicycles and parts, all prized for quality, like Apple today. When the 1964 Olympics were held in Tokyo, Japanese cyclists rode Cinelli bikes; their shiny frames were eye-catching pink, dubbed Tokyo Rose for the English-speaking woman who broadcast propaganda in World War II aimed at U.S. Armed Forces.

"Dave Staub and Steve Pfeifer had met the Cino Cinelli family earlier, and they knew we were coming," Rich said. "So the first thing we did was head north to Milan and get outfitted with new Cinelli bicycles. The Cinelli family welcomed us like we were old friends and invited us to dinner. They gave us a feast, with silver on the table and maid service. We hardly knew where our next meal was coming from, or how long we would be able to last overseas. But at last we were in Italy, and we had new Cinellis. That counted for something."

The Pedali Alpini shifted their base to Florence for its big selection of races. Hiltner won a hefty gold medal. He made headlines in the local newspaper as the first non-Italian finisher in an international race of more than a hundred miles. He came in twentieth in a field of some two hundred.

Hiltner and teammates wintered in Florence. The temperatures plunged below what they were accustomed to in California. They bundled up and trained as best they could. Rich left in early 1961 to explore Belgium, the Netherlands, and Denmark for what turned into a fourteen-month sojourn.

Hiltner distinguished himself by winning the first race of the season, a fifty-miler in Florence. He was so excited that he let himself go after twenty-five miles and charged away from the pack of 150. Three others accompanied him on a successful breakaway. When Hiltner saw the finish 275 yards away, he put his head down and went for it. So did his rivals. They spread out across the road and crossed the line close together. The judges deliberated for a half-hour. The decision went to Hiltner.

Hiltner and compatriots found the racing more intense than they had ever experienced. "The Italians were so fast, and there was far more depth in the quality of the fields," Hiltner said. "Those guys were machines."

In April during a 120-mile road race he battled his way into an eight-man break. Near the finish, the others watched one another closely to see who would make the first move. He jumped ahead and won clean.

Success eluded Zebroski. After the umpteenth fall that summer, he flew back home to California.

Hiltner was being written up in local newspapers. He joined a club, Gruppo Sportivo Lastrense-Gizac. It provided a new bicycle, all the tires he needed, and transportation to events. In July and August he won two more races. Victories paid small amounts of prize money. He earned more in other events, paying to fifteenth place, and the club awarded small bonuses when he won or placed well. He was supporting himself.

But Hiltner discovered that reaching the top of the sport was fraught with diversions he never expected. One was performance-enhancing drugs. There was no drug testing back then.

"Mostly we were burning uppers—amphetamines," Hiltner said. "We would get wired for the end of a race. What we called *la bomba*, 'the bomb bottle,' we usually carried in the hip pocket of our shorts. Basically, it was strong coffee, espresso, and guys would doctor it with amphetamines. Guys would start sipping on this after the halfway point in the race. If you were doing well, then you would take a whole bunch of it.

"A couple of times I got injections from my coach before the start of the race. The coach would say, 'This is new stuff from Switzerland,' and give me an injection in the rear. But I grew fearful. Once I made such a fuss that the coach threw away the needle and syringe with stuff in it. There were nights when I had taken large doses before the race and I would stay wired into the night. Once I went around a turn too fast in a race and crashed into a wall. When they carried me away, I was whistling. But sometimes I burned out my energy supply of the drugs before the finish and had a real hard time getting to the finish. Well, it was my first contact with dope and I didn't use it wisely."

By the end of the season, Hiltner's Pedali Alpini teammates had gone home. The following year, he joined another team, Associazione Sportivo Alfa Cure, backed by physicians who prohibited use of stimulants. He managed second places, but no wins. "I think all the dope I took had blown my body," he said. "I just didn't have any poop left."

He caught a flight back to California.

• • •

Amphetamines had been available since the 1930s. On the Continent, they became indispensable for professional road riders to overcome fatigue. English journalist Geoffrey Wheatcroft, in *Le Tour: A History of the Tour de France*, writes that when Italy's idol Fausto Coppi was asked in the 1950s whether riders took *la bomba*, he said: "Yes, and those who say otherwise aren't worth talking to about cycling." Pressed if he took them, he answered: "Yes, whenever it was needed." How often? "Practically all of the time."

The dean of France's cycling journalists, Pierre Chany, covered the Tour de France every year after the end of World War II—a total of forty-nine Tours. He wrote for Paris sports daily *L'Équipe*. His hair white with age, Chany became concerned about the damaging side effects from amphetamines and other stimulants—hypertension, loss of appetite, excessive sweating. He prevailed on compatriot Jacques Anquetil to understand what was going on inside the peloton.

Anquetil, the first ever to win Le Tour five times, between 1957 and 1964, had won hundreds of races. Over his career he appreciated Chany's journalism. Anquetil had high cheekbones and platinum hair barbered precisely like a film star. He rode with a practiced elegance, his poker face concealing the intensity of his effort. Off the bike, he preferred business suits and always appeared as immaculate as President John F. Kennedy.

Chany interviewed him for *L'Équipe* about drugs in the sport. Anquetil said: "You'd have to be an imbecile or a hypocrite to imagine that a professional cyclist who rides 235 days a year can hold himself together without stimulants."

Anquetil followed up with a stint during the 1965 Tour de France writing columns for *France-Dimanche*, an entertainment tabloid for the masses. He said that pros like him took drugs on a regular basis—simply common practice.

Richard Yates in his 2001 biography of Anquetil, *Master Jacques*, said that Anquetil expressed in print what others only murmured in private. Instead of Anquetil being applauded for candor, he was widely denounced. "All in the racing world who had loved and respected him felt betrayed and wanted to hang him," wrote Yates.

Pros were competing to win, or to assist their team leader, to garner publicity that shined on their corporate sponsors. Flattering exposure promoted winners, their teams, and the sport. Fans turned up to support their heroes. The system hummed along on preserving the status quo.

Changing any long-standing customs demanded a radical shake-up.

• • •

Ted Smith turned pro one more time. He couldn't pass up the chance to ride in the first six-day that Madison Square Garden held in twenty-two years. The organizers—led by Jimmy Proscia—lined up a roster of fifteen two-rider teams from all over Europe and South America. U.S. talent was in short supply. Smith, thirty-three, took one last shot at the big time.

Variety, the show business weekly, and New York newspapers ran features and editorials leading up to the September 22, 1961, start. For the Garden's seventy-fifth international six, the slate of contestants was arguably as good as in the sport's best days. Alf Goullet brought authority as chief referee. World champions Oscar Plattner of Switzerland and Rudi Altig of West Germany lined up with Smith for the 9 p.m. Friday start.

Then came a plague of difficulties. The pine velodrome was constructed in sections in the Garden's basement. When workers brought it up for assembly, they discovered the blueprint had been misread. Pieces failed to fit. As a result, the start was delayed for six hours while an army of sixty-two carpenters were paid time and a half to correct the problem.

Ticket refunds and carpentry costs plunged the event $20,000 in the red before the starting pistol finally fired at 3 a.m. The lavish prerace publicity was wasted. As the days passed, the rumble of bicycle tires on the boards was rarely overcome by applause from the spectators. *Variety* had touted the race for "recalling Prohibition's razzle-dazzle." But the song of the wheels failed to entice the new generation.

Red Smith of the *New York Herald-Tribune* attended the six for his nationally syndicated sports column. America's most widely read sportswriter took advantage of a lull to scan the list of competitors and seized upon Ted Smith with an exclamation. Red Smith skipped over famous names in the sport like Wout Wagtmans, Tonino Domenicali, Antonio Barbosa, Bruno Sivilotti, Anselmo Zarlenga, Enzo Sacchi, and Nando Terruzzi. When chance permitted, Smith the columnist interviewed Smith the six-day rider.

The columnist hurried to his office to file his column. It flew over newspaper wire machines, declaring, "Smith Is a Rare Name for Cyclist." Some family members in his native Wisconsin were given to eccentric and stubborn behavior, but none in his branch was a six-day cyclist.

"Under every family tree," the columnist noted, "some shells are found." He told "how a Smith ever got into this dodge," reviewed highlights of the cyclist's career competing on three continents, and told readers that the three-time national champion and Olympian was retiring after the Garden's six-day to embark on a new career in Buffalo as a barber.

• • •

By the time the Garden six concluded, a committee in Fitchburg was planning the third annual Arthur M. Longsjo Jr. Memorial Race, a fifty-mile event around downtown streets. It had turned into a major race in the Northeast.

In the inaugural race on the first Sunday in July 1960, about two hundred riders had converged on Fitchburg in cars with license plates from twenty states and Canadian provinces. Oom-pah bands played with abandon on two ends of the course, navigated thirty-seven times for fifty miles. People went downtown to see what it was and discovered bicycle racing.

Guy Morin was instrumental in setting up the memorial race. He had represented Canada in the 1959 Pan American Games in Chicago. In the first memorial race to his good friend, he had it in his heart to win. He broke away with another of Longsjo's friends, Arnold Uhrlass, and they lapped the field. When it came to the end, Morin flew to the finish and won.

The day of the inaugural race also marked the unveiling of the Longsjo Memorial, a marble slab seven feet tall bearing the name of the athlete and an engraving of the Olympic torch. The slab is flanked on either side by two smaller stones—one depicting a cyclist, the other depicting a speed skater. The stone memorial is one of the few for an athlete in the nation. It is inscribed: "Honored, admired, and respected for his character, ability, and sportsmanship."

The following year, Uhrlass returned to win. Morin had retired from competition to become president of the Québec Cycling Association. He also remembered Longsjo and was back to supervise the race and drive the pace car, something he continued for twenty-five years.

On the first Sunday in July 1962, the third annual Arthur M. Longsjo Jr. Memorial Race was underway. The men's open peloton formed a bright-colored ribbon flashing along Fitchburg's downtown streets when Don McDermott drove into town from his home in Englewood Cliffs, New Jersey. The Olympic skater had finally married, the last to take the vows among the New Jersey group he had trained with on Sunday mornings. He parked his car on a side street, climbed out, and walked around other side streets until he located the robin's egg–blue Ford station wagon he recognized as belonging to Ray Blum, riding in the peloton.

McDermott forced open the wing window of Blum's vehicle, reached in, unlocked the door. He dropped a hefty, crusty paintbrush with stiff, split bristles on the driver's seat. Then he relocked the door, closed it, and without sticking around drove straight back home. It was a whole day's drive back and forth but worth the trouble just to plant the paint-brush on Blum, who had married before him. McDermott was the last of the New Jersey group to give up his bachelorship—after he'd competed in 1960 in his third Olympics. Four from the group had realized their Olympic dream. McDermott surrendered the paintbrush in an ironic, one-off high jinx that would have appealed to Longsjo.

14

The Rainbow at the End of the Crash

The speed of bicycle racing is a blur, but the sound of it is a poetic, seductive thing to Jackie Simes III. Seasoned and scarred at 21, he is going to offer America's first Olympic cycling medal in 64 years.

—BOB OTTUM, *Sports Illustrated*, September 14, 1964

The grandeur and class of athletes in the Rome Olympics had a profound impression on Jack Simes. Two years and many races later, he felt obligated to go back to Europe and find out what made his rivals there so superior. He quizzed Jack Heid about adapting to living across the Atlantic, seeking tips on what he could do to move up in cycling. Heid provided nuanced advice. He wrote Simes a letter of introduction to Jørgen Beyerholm, promoter of the Ordrup Velodrome in Copenhagen, to help him break in on the Continent.

Simes's 1962 overseas sortie showed promise. "I got in on the tail end of the heyday of track racing," he said. He won the Grand Prix Ellegaard, named after Denmark's legendary Thorvald Ellegaard, winner of six world professional sprint championships in the early 1900s and credited with 925 career victories. Simes was awarded a handsome trophy.

Six weeks after arriving, however, Simes's trip ended abruptly and painfully. He suffered a broken nose, a concussion, a broken shoulder, numerous cuts, abrasions, and bruises after a nasty fall in a match race on June 25 against an Italian. His opponent swerved sharply in front of him, a pedal catching Simes's front wheel and tearing out spokes. The wheel collapsed and Simes was thrown face first to the concrete.

He returned to New Jersey to recover. The next year, healthy again and eager, he earned a spot on the cycling team bound for the 1963 Pan American Games in São Paulo, Brazil. Two Northern Californians—Dave Staub, who rode the kilometer on the velodrome, and road racer Mike Hiltner—also made the team. After the Pan-Am Games, the team toured the West Indies.

Hiltner passed up the tour. In the 100-mile road race, he finished eleventh, but he was first in the heart of his new love, Adelina Neide Marchena. He couldn't take his eyes off the beauty and stayed in São Paulo to marry her. Hiltner learned to speak Portuguese, similar to the Italian he knew. When he wasn't courting Adelina, he competed in local races. Six months later, the couple married and moved to Santa Monica, California. He delivered mail for the U.S. Post Office and after work trained to make the next Olympics.

Simes also had set his sights on another Olympic team. He returned to Europe and performed well enough that sportswriters began touting him as a possible medalist in the upcoming Tokyo Olympics. On his second stint in Denmark he finished second in the Danish Grand Prix to Belgian national sprint champion Patrick Sercu—destined to win three world titles and six stages of the Tour de France. Simes beat Danish champion Niels Fredborg in the Dane's hometown of Aarhus. And Simes outclassed France's Pierre Trentin, who twice had finished third in the world amateur championships.

Sports Illustrated, the nation's most widely read sports magazine, featured Simes in a four-page spread—its longest article ever on a cyclist. It played him up as a legacy rider. He was photographed relaxing on the front porch with his father and grandfather. The Olympian was described as "America's foremost hope for a medal," cautioning that the prospect carried "a touch of Walter Mitty in it."

Walter Mitty and his daydreams of being a hero in the James Thurber short story, "The Secret Life of Walter Mitty," was an appropriate, if disparaging, allusion. The only Olympic medal U.S. cyclists had won went back to the 1912 Stockholm Games when the team took home two bronze medals from the torturous 320-kilometer (200-mile) road race around the elongated Lake Malmö. Joe Kopsky of Jersey City, who was twentieth, used to tell friends that he'd finished on splintered wooden rims after dirt roads shredded his tires.

The 1912 Stockholm Olympics road race, an individual time trial, began at 2 a.m. with competitors on one-speed bicycles setting off at two-minute intervals for the next four hours. Carl O. Schutte of Kansas City placed third after toiling for 10 hours, 51 minutes, 38 seconds. Schutte and his teammates Alvin Loftes, Albert Krushel, and Walden Martin scored third in the team competition for the second U.S. bronze medal.

America's best haul was sweeping all the cycling events at the 1904 Olympics in St. Louis, but the International Olympic Committee never recognized the medals won because only Americans competed. (New Yorker Marcus Hurley had scored four golds and a bronze, then shipped out to the worlds in London where he won the amateur sprint championship.) By the 1960s, the U.S. Olympic Committee saw cyclists as "a questionable group."

Although the USOC never directly indicated it would drop cycling from its roster, the threat circulated through innuendo. The USOC oversaw a limited number of sports, usually around twenty-seven, for the combined Winter and Summer Olympics. Sports like downhill skiing, figure skating, equestrian, rowing, swimming, wrestling, and track and field held seniority on the Olympic Committee's list because their athletes consistently won medals and garnered press coverage. Europeans dominated Olympic cycling while Americans didn't score any medals. Cycling lingered about twenty-fifth on the USOC roster. When another sport was served up for consideration, like badminton, archery, or kayaking, ABLA officials had to fight to keep cycling on the roster.

What sustained the ABLA was cycling's distinction as one of only five sports contested in every Summer Olympics since their 1896 revival in Athens, Greece (the other sports are track and field, fencing, gymnastics, and swimming). Also sustaining the ABLA was the Cold War tension between the United States and the Soviet Union. In the 1960s, Communist bloc countries began usurping cycling medals from west Europeans. The USOC saw the political importance to send cyclists in the hope that America's results would improve.

At the 1964 Tokyo Olympics, however, there was no sign of progress. In the 122-mile road race, the best U.S. finisher was John Allis, a Princeton grad with experience racing on his own in France, in seventy-fifth place; Hiltner came in one-hundredth.

Even Simes was eliminated early in the match-race sprints.

• • •

Another Olympian in Tokyo, Oliver "Butch" Martin Jr. of Manhattan, resolved to do whatever it took to get better. He had developed under the tutelage of Perry Metzler and Herbie Francis. Martin was about Metzler's height, but slighter of build, with a slim torso—light yet strong. In 1963 he catapulted onto the national scene at the juniors' ten-mile race in the Tour of Somerville, where he beat a field of ninety. Francis brought sixteen-year-old Martin into the club he rode for, the Unione Sportiva Italiana, one of New York's oldest.

Martin was the son of an Italian mother and an African American father. His parents met when his father fought as a soldier in Italy during World War II. Born in Harlem, young Martin grew up in Manhattan. He lived near the George Washington Bridge, which he rode across to gain access to lightly traveled roads in New Jersey. He also logged thousands of miles in Central Park.

In 1964 he turned seventeen and entered the men's open division. He and Metzler finished near each other in many races. At the Fitchburg-Longsjo Memorial fifty-miler, Metzler placed fifth, one spot ahead of Martin. Then Martin beat Metzler at the fifty-mile Tour of Flemington, in New Jersey. Martin kept progressing and earned a berth on the Olympic cycling team in the 4,000-meter (2.5-mile) four-rider team pursuit.

By American standards, he joined a Dream Team. There was Arnie Uhrlass, the speed skater–cyclist and a double Olympian like

Art Longsjo. Uhrlass rode with the power of a rip tide and was nicknamed the Governor for the way he ruled races. There was Hans Wolf, winner of the latest Tour of Somerville, the first in memory to break two hours for fifty miles. There was Don Nelson of St. Louis, a third-generation Olympian. In the Tokyo Olympics, Martin expected they would beat a team or two around the velodrome. Instead, his Dream Team was only twelfth fastest in the heats and so did not qualify for the quarterfinals.

"After I came back home," Martin said, "I knew that to move up I had to go to Italy." He considered that Italy offered endless opportunities to race, train, and learn the finer aspects of racing. Martin had connections in his mother's hometown in northern Italy. He flew there in January 1965.

• • •

A couple months prior to the Tokyo Olympics, the ABLA at last changed its nationals format and introduced the road race, a 100-kilometer (62.5-mile) event in Encino, California. Road races were standard fare across Europe for generations; the Union Cycliste Internationale had introduced them to its worlds programs in 1921 for amateurs, and 1927 for pros. But the ABLA held off rather than deal with different governmental jurisdictions. The 1964 national road race championship, won by Rob Parsons of Santa Cruz, California, marked the first time in eighty-four years that a U.S. national title race wasn't held on a track.

In 1965 Mike Hiltner won the second annual ABLA national road race championship, a 100-miler in Encino, California. His prize was a plane ticket to the worlds in San Sebastian, Spain. The ticket gave him incentive to race pro in Europe. Hiltner, twenty-four and racing without support, finished out of the medals.

He and his wife, Adelina, purchased a Volkswagen and drove to Ghent, Belgium, for the remainder of the season. He earned money placing in races and received contracts for events in the Ghent velodrome. That led to a contract for a month-long series of velodrome events in Münster, West Germany, in January 1966. In the Münster city championship, he scored third. The Hiltners then motored south to Florence, for the start of the Italian road racing season. By the time they arrived, they had spent the last of their savings.

Hiltner won two races and had another half-dozen second places, but insufficient to attract a pro contract. He occasionally wrote home for assistance. Adelina, meanwhile, grew impatient. They lived in an apartment without any furniture. They slept on the bare floor. They cooked on a hot plate. Hiltner was doing his best, but that didn't compare with top amateurs winning twenty or more races, which drew them pro contracts.

His final big chance came at the worlds in early September at the Nürburgring, in West Germany, over the hilly, twisty circuit designed for grand prix car racing. Disappointingly, he felt burned out and did not finish.

Mr. and Mrs. Hiltner returned to Florence. He completed the season and pondered his next move. The main course of his life was racing. Brazil offered lots of it and seemed alluring as his draft board in California was recruiting men to fight in Vietnam. The couple sold their car and flew to Brazil.

They moved in with Adelina's family in São Paulo. Hiltner rode for a team sponsored by Pirelli, the Italian tire company. But his enthusiasm for competing and traveling waned. During the Tour of São Paulo, he became sick. He pulled out and retired from racing—a decision he later regretted.

• • •

While Hiltner had raced in central Italy, Butch Martin lived in Milan, in the north, and competed as a member of the Società Ciclistica Corsico team. His coach put him on a rigorous, comprehensive approach to training and racing that he would later apply to profound effect on U.S. cycling. He was impressed that high-level racing requires extraordinary concentration—always studying rivals, paying attention to the gears they used, staying alert. "You lose that concentration one moment and the breakaway would be gone up the road," he recalled.

Martin had arrived in Italy accustomed to measuring workouts by miles pedaled—the more the better. Italy's legendary three-time Giro d'Italia winner Fiorenzo Magni counseled him to acknowledge fatigue—not just physically but also mentally. The revered Magni advised him to keep his workouts flexible.

"If I have scheduled a hundred miles and I just don't feel like doing it, I might not even get on the bike that day," he said. "But if I have scheduled 50 miles and it's a beautiful day and I really feel like going hard, I'll go out and do 125 miles." The insight became a tenet of his training and, later, to coaching.

For twenty-three months, Martin raced a mix of road and track events. Over the winter track season of 1965–66, he raced on the Velodromo Vigorelli, including pro-am team races, which sharpened his bike-handling skills and upped his speed. In the 1966 road season, he won five races, and scored eleven runner-up places.

Martin looked to turn pro. "My problem was the Vietnam War," he said. He returned to New York about the time Hiltner settled in São Paulo. Martin was granted a draft deferment when he enrolled in City College of New York. He took light course loads while he kept training. At the 1967 Tour of Somerville, he stoked the pace in a 150-rider pack that sped to a new course record. In the mass sprint for the finish he lost by a half-wheel to Jack Simes.

• • •

Traveling abroad every season for international competition refined Simes's skills and helped him with big domestic races, but his overseas excursions puzzled the FBI. Twenty-four-year-old Simes had no college deferment from the military, although he occasionally took evening classes at a local community college. He was single and lacked a full-time job. To the FBI, he had no apparent means to fund trips to Europe, South America, and Japan.

One day he arrived at his home in Closter, New Jersey, to find an FBI agent in a dark suit and tie waiting to interview him. When he told the G-man he raced bicycles, he was greeted with a frown and asked to explain. Simes was smooth-faced, his curly red hair tamed in a crew cut. He was slight across the chest and shoulders, not tall enough to make a big impression in basketball, but he had the ideal build and quick reflexes to perhaps play Major League Baseball as a shortstop, although he preferred cycling. Simes invited the agent inside to see his bicycle collection. He explained training routines, speed skating in the winter, and by late spring quitting whatever job held to train and race fulltime.

He showed the agent gleaming trophies and silver cups crammed in bookcases in the living room, filling the dining room china cabinet, lining every mantel, stashed in kitchen cupboards. Plaques filled the hallway walls. Medals were stuffed in his bedroom chest of drawers. There were more trophies and cups heaped in boxes in the basement. The agent scribbled notes in a pad.

That autumn Simes received his draft notice. After basic training in Fort Dix, New Jersey, he was held over on the base for two months. Because of the trips he had taken out of the country, he couldn't get a security clearance. Eventually he was assigned as a physical activities specialist and managed a gymnasium at Fort MacArthur, near Los Angeles. He rode for the army cycling team, an early national cycling team.

Butch Martin had lost his college deferment. He was drafted about the same time as Simes and joined him at Fort MacArthur.

Both men made the 1968 U.S. Olympic team, bound for Mexico City. Improvements were apparent in the Olympic cycling team. Members were doing their homework, not just the riders but also management and administration.

Martin competed in the 100-kilometer four-man team time trial on the road. An intestinal ailment sapped his strength; the team finished twentieth.

Simes felt ready to win a medal in the kilometer (five-eighths of a mile) time trial, a lung-bursting individual race against the clock on the velodrome, his specialty. The previous year in the Pan-Am Games kilometer in Winnipeg, Canada, he took home the silver medal in the kilo. But in the Mexico City Olympics he didn't perform at his best. He also was eliminated early in the match-race sprints. He'd always wanted to race pro, like his father and grandfather. But if he couldn't beat the top amateurs, turning pro wasn't an option.

Two weeks later, Simes had another opportunity—at the world track championships in Montevideo, the capital of Uruguay. The 1968 world amateur track championships were held in Montevideo while the road races took place across the Atlantic, in Rome. The Montevideo worlds were his last chance to show he could turn pro.

The trip from Mexico City had been arduous. Yet it was worthwhile for one more kilometer ride in the worlds. In the lottery for the order of the ride, he drew number one, ordinarily a handicap because everyone else has a mark to chase. Simes did not mind. He didn't have the pressure of the Olympics.

As he pedaled warm-up laps around the Montevideo velodrome, officials ordered everyone else to leave the track. Simes realized he had come a long way—geographically and personally. Alone on the track, he got more psyched up thinking of all the trips he had taken around the United States and to cities on four continents, the three Olympic teams he had competed in, the support he had along the way from family and friends. He grew more determined by considering all the American cyclists he knew who would give anything to be where he was.

At the firing of the starter's gun, he gave everything his mind and body had, and more, to pedal the fastest in his life down the straights and around the banked turns until he flashed over the finish line completely spent, gasping. He could barely turn the handlebars on the first couple of turns as he gradually slowed.

Rider after rider chased his time. Janusz Kierzkowski of Poland, Olympic bronze medalist in the kilometer, looked like he would beat Simes's time, but he didn't. As more adversaries failed to better his time, it looked like he would prevail. Finally, Niels Fredborg, the last rider and the Olympic silver medalist in the kilometer, took his turn. At five feet nine and 165 pounds, Fredborg was slightly bigger than Simes and eclipsed his time by three-tenths of a second.

Simes was disappointed with second place. Yet he realized Fredborg's greatness. In third was Gianni Sartori of Italy. Simes had barged into an exclusive club. His silver medal ended America's seventeen-year worlds drought since Jack Heid's bronze. Simes came to Montevideo doubting whether he could turn pro. He was leaving relieved that he could turn pro after his hitch in the army.

• • •

The next year Audrey Phleger, who'd married Scott McElmury, marked a watershed in American cycling at the world amateur road race championships—where women were not included until 1958.

As a teenager, she was an avid surfer in Southern California's upscale La Jolla. With wide-set dark eyes and long, straight hair she looked like the quintessential surfer. She started cycling in the early 1960s to strengthen her leg after healing from an ankle broken while skateboarding. At age twenty in 1963 she and her high school sweetheart, McElmury, went to Europe for the summer on an American Youth Hostel cycling tour, an inexpensive way to explore France, Belgium, and the Netherlands. After the couple returned home, they married. But rather than settle down, they geared up and began racing.

"All the guys were doing it, like my husband, and I got into it too," she said. "I'm crazy like the rest of them. I don't like to sit and watch."

The only competition available to women was track racing at the Encino Velodrome, an outdoor 250-meter concrete track, in the Sepulveda Basin Recreation Area of Los Angeles. The velodrome had opened in 1961, supported by area cycling enthusiasts, friends, importers, and dealers contributing to a not-for-profit organization. Track racing is an ideal way to learn the basics of speed, stamina, tactics, and, especially, the timing of critical moves.

Right away she won races. She was a commando, drawn to the big game of road racing. She joined the guys in group workouts, took her share of pulls at the front while others drafted behind, and gained respect. Occasionally, as the only woman among the men, she was subjected to false hopes, such as being told that a women's six-day circuit was starting in Europe and coming to America. Harassment from men never bothered her.

(Another who believed in integrating the sexes in the sport was Nancy Neiman Baranet. In 1965 she wrote in *American Cycling Newsletter*: "Training with women is a waste of time." She said women cyclists didn't exert themselves as intensely as men. She encouraged the same training program for both genders: "Naturally, the best woman athlete will never be able to defeat the best male athlete, but she can uncompromisingly defeat one-half of the country's senior men's champions." [*American Cycling Newsletter* became *Bicycling* magazine.])

McElmury joined her husband in open competition. Standing five feet eight, she had long legs and rode a frame the same size as many men. "They couldn't push me around much more than the other guys," McElmury told me. "Frankly, I was pretty damned good. I consistently placed in the top ten. We raced a lot of criteriums, fifty miles and under. It wasn't that I was that strong. I could read a race and knew where to go, where to be at different times in the pack. The men got used to me being in the races."

McElmury gained a devoted following among other women riders along with the wives and mothers of guys competing. Whenever she showed up to a race, even in the parking lot as she pulled her bike from the car, women would point her out and exclaim, "She rides with the men!"

Nurturing her talent was Jerry Rimoldi, a grassroots coach. Rimoldi encouraged interval training—short, intense bursts of top-end speed—as well as pedaling behind a motorcycle to get the legs accustomed to going faster than even sprinting, considered avant-garde.

McElmury spoke with confidence and forcefulness, which reflected the way she trained and competed. She worked out in the gym with weights at a time when cyclists preferred to stay outdoors and ride. She weighed 130 pounds and did leg squats, going down deep, supporting the weight bar across her shoulders, and standing straight up with 210 pounds to build explosive strength crucial for climbing hills and sprinting.

During this time, McElmury majored in biology at San Diego State University. She won several state championships and competed in the ABLA nationals, but found road racing more to her taste. In 1965 she graduated from college and went to the worlds in San Sebastian, Spain, with California cyclists Jack Disney and Harry "Skip" Cutting, both national champions and Olympians.

They shared a room without hot water or cooking facilities. McElmury came down with food poisoning and lost fourteen pounds. Hardships never discouraged her. "After the worlds, the airline people sent my bike to Algeria, rather than home with me. I didn't see it for six weeks."

The following year she realized her potential. She won the ABLA national three-kilometer (1.8-mile) track pursuit championship on her way to capturing the omnium track title. She flew to the worlds in Frankfurt, West Germany, for more international experience.

Nationwide, there were only three thousand ABLA members. The organization was still skimping along on an annual budget of about $20,000 and unable to provide full funding for trips abroad. She and all other riders headed to Europe were on their own for support, equipment, and travel.

"I worked a full-time job as a medical lab tech, working in genetics at the University of California at San Diego," she said. "I worked a forty-hour week, with flexible hours that let me train for two hours at lunch. Of course, I trained again after work. My job also let me take leave without pay to go to the worlds."

Only pregnancy, in 1967, kept her from racing, but not from riding. Before giving birth to son Ian in September, she logged four thousand miles. She also continued weight lifting. Two days before giving birth, she squatted with a 135-pound weight bar, less than her preferred 210 pounds. Her obstetrician was aghast.

McElmury resumed racing in 1968 and came back stronger than ever. That year the ABLA nationals were held at the same time as the worlds in Imola, Italy. "I had to fight and fight and fight to get permission from the ABLA to go to the worlds rather than ride in the nationals," McElmury recalled. "The officials weren't going to let me go because they wanted me to ride in the nationals. But they finally decided, at the last moment, to grant me permission."

The decision proved wise. She rode in the women's fifty-five-kilometer (thirty-four-mile) road race. It came down to a bunch sprint—she finished a respectable fifth.

In July 1969 on the Encino Velodrome, McElmury set the women's national hour record—completing 162 laps around the 250-meter concrete oval for 39.872 kilometers (24.8 miles). She rode a standard track bike, the same diamond frame since the turn of the century and before disc wheels and aero frames were invented. On her way, she established new marks every mile from two to fifteen and twenty miles. (Her hour record lasted eighteen years.)

A month later, at the ABLA nationals in Detroit, McElmury captured the women's 3,000-meter national pursuit title and the overall national championship. Right afterward, she went with three other women and eight men directly to Montreal, where they caught a charter flight to Vienna, Austria. There they charted a bus to Brno, Czechoslovakia (since renamed the Czech Republic).

The charter was arranged by Al Toefield, the New York City cop serving on his own time as an ABLA official. Tall and trim in his late forties, he had deep lines in his face and a mat of black hair. His deep voice was freighted with a Queens accent and charged with an undertone of authority. He applied the same NYPD-sergeant-in-the-line-of-duty commitment to ABLA volunteering and managed the team traveling to the worlds.

Brno, a thousand-year-old city, remained a grim testimony to the previous year's Soviet invasion, intended to quell reformist trends, including freedom of speech. "There were tanks going up and down the streets, and military types with machine guns everywhere," McElmury said. "They were expecting trouble."

The American team and support staff were housed in a twenty-story dormitory. They were ordered not to leave it, except for training rides, which they ignored. "One night, Jack Simes dropped a champagne bottle out the fifteenth-floor window onto a tank in the street," she said. "When the bottle smashed, the crew spun the turret every which way, trying to find out where the explosion came from."

McElmury doubled in the women's 3,000-meter track pursuit, followed by the road race. In the pursuit, she finished seventh. Her effort burned off some tension in anticipation of the road race, which she felt was her best chance.

Civilians were unabashedly anti-Communist and pro-American. During races, spectators booed Russians loudly and cheered U.S. riders wildly. When Russians won, the Czechs walked away to shun the medal ceremonies.

At the stroke of midnight on August 21, the one-year anniversary of the Russian invasion, rioting broke out in downtown Brno, population 370,000. A fleet of heavy tanks revved up their diesel engines. "It sounded like a train coming into the room," McElmury said. "We all ran out to the balcony and were confronted by the almost unbelievable sight of tanks rumbling down the street."

The next morning rumors flew that the road races would be cancelled. They were held, but tanks were parked, cannon barrels pointed at the street, among the trees bordering the 8.7-mile hilly circuit. It was devised for grand prix car racing; the middle featured a hill 2.5 miles long.

McElmury lined up for the seventy-kilometer (forty-three-mile) race of five-laps. She and three teammates joined the field of forty-four from sixteen countries, including a strong contingent of Soviets.

"The pavement was somewhat chewed up from the tank treads," she said. "The course was one that suited my riding. I was good in the hills, and I time trialed well."

On the second lap, defending world champion Katie Hage of the Netherlands attacked. An aggressive chase followed, with McElmury in a group of ten that broke away from the peloton. Just as the chasers caught Hage, she punctured.

"On about the third lap, it started pouring buckets," McElmury said. "The breakaway stayed away for another lap, rain pouring. Several riders crashed while descending the hill."

On the fourth lap, she escaped up the hill and gained a lead of about thirty seconds at the top. "But I came from weather-perfect San Diego," McElmury recalled. "I had never raced in the rain. I fell down while putting on the brakes in a corner on the descent. I went down very hard and slid quite a distance."

She jumped to her feet as the field rushed past. She had lost about thirty seconds before she started pedaling and time trialed solo to close the gap.

"The rain was chilly enough that I didn't feel the full effect of my bruised hip, and the rain exaggerated the amount of blood from a cut on my elbows," she said. "I chased the pack with an ambulance following me to see if I was all right."

McElmury bridged to the pack for the last lap and threaded her way through to the front. She attacked at the base of the final hill and broke away, five miles from the finish. "On the descent, I refrained from using my brakes around the turn where I had crashed. On the finishing stretch, I confess I kept looking around, because I couldn't believe I was out in front. I kept thinking the whole time that they would catch me before the line. But when I had the finish line in sight, I knew I had won."

She won clean, seventy seconds ahead of Bernadette Swinnerton of Great Britain and Nina Trofimova of the Soviet Union.

McElmury's victory broke America's fifty-seven-year gap in a worlds' triumph. She became the first U.S. cyclist, man or woman, to win a world road championship. More, she became the first American ever to pull on the winner's rainbow jersey. The last Americans to win world titles—professional sprinter Frank Kramer and amateur sprinter Donald McDougall—did so in 1912, before the introduction of the special jersey in 1921. Wrapping around the chest and back of the white jersey runs a band of bright colors—blue, black, red, yellow, and green—same as the five interlocking Olympic rings; at least one color appears on the national flag of every country worldwide.

McElmury shoved her arms through the sleeves of her rainbow jersey as she stood on the podium and held a bouquet of flowers outside in the pouring rain, next to Swinnerton and Trofimova. They were soaked from more than a half-hour in the rain while officials scurried madly around Brno to find a recording of "The Star-Spangled Banner" for the awards ceremony. So many years had passed since an American had won a world title that officials lacked a vinyl record on hand, and there was no band to strike up the music.

Finally, a record was found and whisked to the ceremony. When the phonograph needle found the appropriate groove, the national anthem blared from gray metal public address speakers, flaring wide like morning glories.

Reaction in America to her victory proved underwhelming. Yet Toefield had contacts in New York. He arranged guest appearances for McElmury on the popular national television game shows, *What's My Line* and *To Tell the Truth*. "Al drove me around and parked his car right in front of the network buildings. He was with the police department, and nobody messed with Al."

Cosmopolitan panelists like Steve Allen and Kitty Carlisle looked at the guest with world-champion legs but couldn't figure her out. Actress? Model?

"They didn't guess me," she said.

When McElmury alighted from the airliner in San Diego, a television news reporter interviewed her about the first anniversary of the Russian invasion.

Her victory reverberated in France. *Miroir du cyclisme* prophetically wrote that American women were the future of American cycling. The magazine published a cartoon depicting a woman cyclist revising popular graffiti on a wall to edit the message from "US Go Home" to "US Go *Femme.*"

• • •

McElmury's gold medal and Simes's silver in two worlds gave something new for Al Toefield, now ABLA president and chairman of the U.S. Olympic Cycling Committee, to leverage with contacts in the Pentagon.

The number of U.S. troops in Vietnam topped five hundred thousand. Every day the war dominated print and TV news. Reports of battles called Con Thien, Hill 881, and Khe Sanh on the other side of the globe were pouring day after day into American living rooms. There were images of troops in outposts made of sandbag bunkers or in jungles with trees stripped bare from napalm. Haggard faces of soldiers and marines with thousand-yard stares and dazed casualties, connected to an IV drip and lying on a stretcher, carried by buddies to a waiting helicopter, were eroding public support for the war. The fighting would kill more than fifty thousand U.S. troops. The Vietnam War polarized America.

Toefield offered the army a public relations opportunity to organize the first fully supported army cycling team and prepare its members to compete in the next Olympics. For many years, the army had created Special Services for athletes. Its advantages were limited to providing time to train, although how much freedom was up to the commanding officer at each base. Olympic hopefuls were isolated on different bases, on their own for transportation to competitions.

Under Toefield's stewardship, the Army Cycling Team was consolidated first at Fort MacArthur in California and then shifted to Fort Wadsworth on Staten Island, New York. There the team had army vehicles at its disposal to drive to better training venues and to races. Toefield encouraged national-class riders to enlist in the army; after basic training, he would get them on the cycling team. His scheme was unprecedented and, considering the pressure to send troops to Vietnam, it seemed risky. But cyclists had been working for years with him, as the manager of ABLA teams going to the worlds and the 1968 Olympics.

"He was concerned about his athletes," Simes said. "You always knew that Toefield was in your corner."

The formation of the army team was not without its problems, as two Olympians from the Mexico City Olympics discovered. Dave Chauner, of suburban Philadelphia, dropped out of Upsala College to get drafted in November 1970. He figured he would complete basic training in early 1971, receive orders for the team, and have plenty of time to prepare for the Pan-Am trials. After basic training, however, he was sent to Fort Polk, in Louisiana, for nine weeks of maneuvers simulating combat in tropical, steamy Vietnam. When Chauner told his company commander that there had been some mistake, he should be on the Army Cycling Team, he was told that he was soon headed for Vietnam.

Chauner had spent the 1969 season racing in the Netherlands, home to Dutch riders who had scored the most medals in the Olympics. Now, in Fort Polk, he was desperate to maintain fitness because he was counting on Toefield to come through with orders for the cycling team. He sent for his Cinelli. He kept it in a storage area at one end of the barracks. When marching in formation and crawling exercises in the sweltering bayou ended for the day, he went riding.

On the other side of Fort Polk, John Howard from Springfield, Missouri, trained all day every day instead of going out on maneuvers. Howard had been a runner on his high school track team when he had seen ABC's *Wide World of Sports* coverage during the Tokyo Olympics of Jack Simes racing on the velodrome. The qualities of cycling, compared with football, basketball, baseball, and track and field offered in school appealed to Howard. Soon after, he purchased a ten-speed Schwinn, rode long distances in the Ozark Mountains, and was coached by a one-armed cyclist in St. Louis named Ray Florman.

At the 1968 Olympic cycling trials—in Encino, California—the road race doubled as the ABLA national road racing championship. Easterners and Californians considered Howard a dark horse. To the cognoscenti, he came from nowhere. Howard had abundant curly blond hair spiking through his leather hairnet helmet. Draping his six foot three body across his bike, he served as a good person to draft behind. The tall stranger upset stalwarts to win the national road racing championship and secure his place on the team going to Mexico City.

When Howard arrived at Fort Polk with his bicycle, the company commander recognized his name. The company commander, a graduate of Indiana University, had competed in the Little 500 bicycle race, styled after the Indy 500. He let Howard ride instead of joining others in the bayou or target practice. Weeks later, however, Howard received orders transferring him to Officer Candidate School in Fort Benning, Georgia. He didn't think it looked like the Army Cycling Team was going to happen.

Chauner entertained the same doubts until he spotted Howard riding in his stars-and-stripes jersey. "I was seated on a bus going out on a bivouac, sitting with my M-14 rifle resting on the floor between my feet, when I looked out the window in time to see Howard ride over the brow of a hill and disappear."

That gave Chauner confidence. He told his company commander that he was going to get orders soon for the Army Cycling Team. Once again he heard a one-word reply: "Vietnam."

Later that day Chauner returned to the barracks and was told to report to the company commander. Chauner saw him seated behind his desk, shaking his head as he stared at papers in his hand. "There was a look of disbelief on his face," Chauner recalled. "He said that my orders had come to report to the Army Cycling Team at Fort Wadsworth on Staten Island."

Chauner and Howard joined Butch Martin and a dozen others at Fort Wadsworth. They had time to train and used army vehicles for going to races. Howard and Chauner were among the Army Cycling Team riders ruling at the selection trials for the team that went to Cali, Colombia, for the 1971 Pan-Am Games.

The Sixth Pan American Games that August were memorable for having a contingent of 138 U.S. officials—more than the number of athletes sent by any other nation. Frank Shorter of Boulder, Colorado, credited with starting the running boom in the United States, won gold medals in the marathon (26.2-miles) and the ten-kilometer (6.2-mile). Chauner, a six-footer, helped power the four-man team in the 4,000-meter (2.5-mile) pursuit to a bronze medal.

The final event of the Games was the 125-mile road race, which stole the show. After the pack of more than a hundred caught a two-rider breakaway at sixty miles, Howard attacked off the nose of the peloton. Brazilian Luiz Carlos Flores charged away with him. They worked a smooth pace line together.

They never gained much of a lead—always less than a minute. More than a million Colombians lined the road four and five deep around the course to applaud and cheer. They kept Howard and Flores motivated. In the last mile, Howard's rear wheel broke a spoke, causing the rim to rub against the brake block every revolution. Flores launched his sprint when he saw the finish a couple hundred yards ahead. Howard drafted till fifty-five yards to go and darted ahead, winning by four lengths.

He scored the United States' 105th gold medal of the weeklong Games. Coming in the final event, Howard's victory drew considerable media. Newspapers across the United States carried wire-service photos of him sitting up on the saddle, raising both arms overhead as he crossed the line. The *New York Times* declared: "U.S. Wins Cycling Breakthrough."

Howard's Pan-Am Games gold following the worlds medals that Simes and McElmury had won gave the U.S. Olympic Committee reason to consider cyclists as a disciplined group.

1. James Armando, far right, and U.S. cycling teammates at the 1924 Paris Olympics. Second from the left is Iggy (Ignatius) Gronkowski, great-grandfather of Rob Gronkowski, three-time Super Bowl Champion on the National Football League's New England Patriots. Courtesy of the Victor Hopkins Collection.

2. George M. Hendee passed up attending Yale to race bicycles and won five straight national championships, 1882 to 1886. In 1905 Hendee founded the Indian Motocycle Company, which rivaled Harley-Davidson. Photograph from the Genealogy Department, Springfield, Massachusetts, Public Library.

3. Arthur Zimmerman appeared on the cover of the New York Athletic Club's magazine in 1892 to celebrate his winning concurrent national championships in America and Britain. Courtesy of the New York Athletic Club.

4. Tom Cooper worked as a registered pharmacist in Detroit until he gave it up to race professionally. After winning the 1899 national championship, he funded Henry Ford to build racecars. Photograph from Janet Brown Drinkwater.

5. Riders set dozens of world records on the Salt Palace Velodrome, in the thin air of Salt Lake City's 4,400-foot elevation, as thousands watched. Courtesy of the Utah Historical Society Library.

6. George Banker in the late 1890s won the Grand Prix de Paris and the world professional sprint title in Vienna, Austria. He invested his prize money to open one of Pittsburgh's first auto dealerships. Courtesy of the U.S. Bicycling Hall of Fame.

7. Major Taylor won the 1899 world professional sprint title in Montreal and captured the 1900 U.S. national championship to lead the way for African American sports heroes. Courtesy of the U.S. Bicycling Hall of Fame.

8. In August 1901 Major Taylor, center, lined up against Iver Lawson, left, and Willie Fenn Sr., in Newark, New Jersey. Courtesy of the U.S. Bicycling Hall of Fame, William Fenn Jr. scrapbook.

9. Marcus Hurley collected four gold medals as a cycling sprinter at the 1904 St. Louis Olympics and soon shipped out to win the world amateur sprint championship in London. At Columbia University he captained basketball teams that won two NCAA championships. Courtesy of the U.S. Bicycling Hall of Fame.

10. Frank Kramer, right, edges French rivals Gabriel Poulain and Émile Friol to clinch the 1906 Grand Prix de Paris. Courtesy of the U.S. Bicycling Hall of Fame.

11. Carl Schutte of Kansas City, Missouri, won the bronze medal at the 1912 Stockholm Olympics road race. He led the U.S. team to another bronze—America's only Olympic cycling medals for seventy-two years. Courtesy of Louis C. Schutte.

12. Floyd MacFarland stands tall as manager of Jackie Clark, dubbed the Australian Rocket for his explosive sprint. Courtesy of the U.S. Bicycling Hall of Fame, Frank Mihlon Jr. Collection.

13. John M. Chapman, left, with Nat Butler—two former racers turned race promoters. Courtesy of the U.S. Bicycling Hall of Fame, Frank Mihlon Jr. Collection.

14. Frank Mihlon Sr. and wife, Minnie, sitting front and center at the Newark Velodrome grandstand. Courtesy of the U.S. Bicycling Hall of Fame, Frank Mihlon Jr. Collection.

TAKEN SEPT 10-1911
EDDIE F. ROOT.
SCRATCH 3RD HEAT ONE MILE HANDICAP RACE (PRO.)

15. Eddie Root immigrated from Sweden to race in America. Courtesy of the U.S. Bicycling Hall of Fame, Frank Mihlon Jr. Collection.

16. Bobby Walthour Sr. enjoyed a huge following in Germany, where he raced on tracks around the country before the outbreak of World War I. Courtesy of Bobby Walthour III.

17. Frank Kramer cracks a hearty grin after winning the 1912 world professional sprint championship in Newark. Courtesy of the U.S. Bicycling Hall of Fame, Jack and Bill Brennan Collection.

18. Inglis Moore Uppercu helped pilot American cycling by putting up the capital to build tracks. Here he prepares to take Jackie Clark up in his seaplane. Courtesy of the U.S. Bicycling Hall of Fame, Frank Mihlon Jr. Collection.

19. Thousands of fans turned out to watch Alf Goullet, left, sprinting against local star Eddie Madden, middle, and Swiss idol Oscar Egg, whose career included three world hour records and stages of the Tour de France and Giro d'Italia. Courtesy of the U.S. Bicycling Hall of Fame, Jack and Bill Brennan Collection.

20. Jack Dempsey, left, used to polish Frank Kramer's shoes at the Salt Palace Velodrome. Courtesy of the U.S. Bicycling Hall of Fame, Jack and Bill Brennan Collection.

21. Jack Dempsey starts a six-day race in Madison Square Garden. Alf Goullet was on the start line, on the right. Courtesy of the U.S. Bicycling Hall of Fame, Jack and Bill Brennan Collection.

KINGS OF SPORT doff trunks and knickers and don "soup and fish" for history's greatest gathering of champions at a dinner in New York. In the front row are Bill Tilden, lawn tennis; Bobby Jones, golf; Fred Spencer and Charley Winters, bicycle racing. Back row: Babe Ruth, home run king of baseball; Gene Tunney, fight champ; Johnny Weismuller of Chicago, who taught the fish how to swim, and Bill Cook, Hockey. 1927.
Alex Hatos, our cycling photographer and historian, came across this old newspaper photo of the famous "KINGS OF SPORT" gathering sponsored by Tex Rickard way back in the 1920's. Tex invited 50 millionaires to a banquet, together with the top-liners in sport. . . . . with this unique result. The gratifying thing about it all, was the fact that not one, but TWO, cyclists were there. And both of them Century men, at that! Charles Winter is on the extreme right front row; Fred Spencer next to him.

22. Only a brilliant promoter like Tex Rickard could gather the nation's most popular sports heroes of the mid-1920s and persuade them to give up their regular uniforms for tuxedos. Standing from the left, are Babe Ruth, Gene Tunney, Johnny Weissmuller, and Bill Cook; seated are Bill Tilden, Bobby Jones, Fred Spencer, and Charley Winter. Courtesy of the U.S. Bicycling Hall of Fame, Helen Winter.

23. Freddy Spencer, left, teamed with Italian great and Olympic gold medalist Franco Giorgetti for victory in Madison Square Garden's December 1928 six-day. Courtesy of the U.S. Bicycling Hall of Fame.

24. Bobby Walthour Jr. followed his illustrious father's wheel marks as a six-day racer. Photograph by Tovio Katilla, courtesy of the U.S. Bicycling Hall of Fame.

25. Jimmy Walthour Jr., first cousin of Bobby Walthour Jr., drew crowds wherever he competed. Courtesy of the U.S. Bicycling Hall of Fame, Jack and Bill Brennan.

26. Frank Kramer persuaded the Union Cycliste Internationale board in Paris to award the 1929 worlds to Newark. Illustration from the *Newark Evening News*, February 16, 1928. The illustrator, Howard Freeman of Portland, Oregon, raced against Kramer in their youth. Money Freeman won enabled him to fulfill his dream of studying in art school in New York City. He joined the Newark newspaper, and his illustrations were syndicated in more than three hundred newspapers.

Taken at the Vel d'hiv. 1934
With Best Wishes to
Pete Nye. Oct. 1985

27. In 1934 a Paris promoter designed the stars-and-stripes jersey for American national champion Bill Honeman to wear in the Vélodrome d'Hiver so audiences could spot him in the pack. The design was adopted to designate American national champions. Courtesy of the U.S. Bicycling Hall of Fame, Bill Honeman.

28. When Jackie Simes II won the 1936 Amateur Bicycle League of America national championship, he moved up to turn pro. Courtesy of the Jeff Groman Collection.

29. Doris Kopsky learned to race from her father, Joseph Kopsky, a bronze medalist from the 1912 Olympics. He holds her as America's first girls' champion, in 1937. Courtesy of the Jeff Groman Collection.

30. Reggie MacNamara at the 1932 Chicago Six, where he was so popular that a fan named a baby daughter after him. Photograph by Tovio Katilla, courtesy of the U.S. Bicycling Hall of Fame.

31. Alf Letourneur, left, of Paris takes over from his partner, Belgian national road champion Gérard Debaets, giving Letourneur a hand-sling push. Courtesy of the Jeff Groman Collection.

32. Joseph Magnani of LaSalle, Illinois, captured the 1934 Grand Prix Urago in Nice, France, to launch his professional career on French and Italian teams. Courtesy of the U.S. Bicycling Hall of Fame, Jean Veneziano Collection.

PARIS-NICE 1938. SPAPERI THIETARD JAMINET MAGNANI
dans la moyenne corniche.

33. Joseph Magnani, on the right, takes his turn pulling the breakaway during the 1938 Paris–Nice. Courtesy of the U.S. Bicycling Hall of Fame, Jean Veneziano Collection.

34. After the 1946 nationals in Columbus, Ohio, Jack Heid poses with Ray Blum holding him. Photograph by Henry Kloss, courtesy of the U.S. Bicycling Hall of Fame, Louise Blum Collection.

35. Jackie Simes II coached Olympians Jack Heid, left, and Don Sheldon, right. Courtesy of the U.S. Bicycling Hall of Fame.

36. Ted Smith in his national champion's jersey in 1945, the first nationals after their suspension during World War II. Photograph by Tatro, courtesy of the U.S. Bicycling Hall of Fame.

37. (*opposite top*) Nancy Neiman Baranet insisted after winning her third national girls' championship to change the title to national women's champion. Courtesy of the U.S. Bicycling Hall of Fame.

38. (*opposite bottom*) In 1957 Perry Metzler, right, became the first African American since Major Taylor to win a national title. Metzler won the junior boys' division in Kenosha, Wisconsin. He joined champions Jack Disney and Nancy Neiman Baranet. Courtesy of the U.S. Bicycling Hall of Fame.

39. (*above*) Road racing on public roads often left cyclists on their own in traffic, such as the Worcester, Massachusetts, fifty-miler in October 1958. Photograph by Gordon W. Lundstrom, courtesy of the U.S. Bicycling Hall of Fame, Louise Blum Collection.

40. The 1956 U.S. Olympic cycling team, from the left: coach George "Bud" Thorpe, Jack Disney, Jim Rossi, Joe Becker, Erhard Neumann, Alan Bell, George Van Meter, Dick Cortright, Art Longsjo, Dave Rhoads, manager Charles Nelson, and Doug Ferguson. Courtesy of the Art Longsjo Foundation.

41. (*opposite top*) Art Longsjo, right, learned drafting as a speed skater and applied the skill to bike racing. Courtesy of the Art Longsjo Foundation.

42. (*opposite bottom*) Art Longsjo won the fifty-mile Tour of Somerville in 1958, the season he won every race he entered. Courtesy of the Art Longsjo Foundation.

43. The Art Longsjo Memorial was unveiled on July 7, 1969, in Fitchburg, Massachusetts. Terry Longsjo presided over the dedication with Jocelyn Lovell, left, a three-time Olympian from Toronto and winner of the 1969 Art Longsjo Memorial Race, and junior boys' winner Harold Gulbransen of Huntington, New York. Courtesy of the Art Longsjo Foundation.

44. Jack Simes III reigned as America's fastest man in the 1960s. Photograph by Al Hatos, courtesy of Jack Simes III.

45. Three generations that influenced twentieth-century sprinters. From left, Gilbert Hatton Jr., Gary Campbell, Jack Disney, and Ray Blum. Photograph by A. C. Brown, courtesy of the U.S. Bicycling Hall of Fame, Louise Blum Collection.

46. Audrey McElmury fell on a rain-slick street in the women's 1969 worlds road race in Brno, Czechoslovakia, but got back up, caught the pack, and won. She became the first U.S. cyclist to wear the rainbow jersey. Courtesy of Sandra Wright Sutherland.

47. John Howard winning the 1971 Pan-Am Games road race in Cali, Colombia. His victory boosted publicity for U.S. cycling. The man in the white short-sleeved shirt and tie celebrating in the street is his father, Harry. Courtesy of John Howard.

48. (*opposite top*) Sheila Young-Ochowicz of Detroit won three world match sprint championships and a gold medal as an Olympic speed skater. Courtesy of Robert F. George.

49. (*opposite bottom*) Sue Reber of Flint, Michigan, won seven worlds medals—two gold, four silver, and one bronze—on the track as well as eight national track and road championships. Courtesy of Robert F. George.

15

50. (*opposite top*) After competing in the 1976 Montreal Olympics road race, George Mount scored a stage victory in France's Circuit de la Sarthe. He helped lead a new generation of American riders in Europe. Photograph from *Vélo*.

51. (*opposite bottom*) Greg LeMond, left, was recruited to turn pro in 1981 by Tour de France champion Bernard Hinault under team manager Cyrille Guimard, while translator Mel Pinto of Arlington, Virginia, helped translate at a press conference in New York City. Courtesy of Mel Pinto.

52. (*above*) Connie Carpenter Phinney, left, and Rebecca Twigg radiate the thrill of scoring gold and silver medals respectively at the inaugural women's road race in the 1984 Los Angeles Olympics. Courtesy of Michael Furman.

USA

RALEIGH
RALEIGH

53. (*opposite top*) Alexi Grewal beams with the gold medal around his neck after capturing the LA Olympics road race. © Beth Schneider.

54. (*opposite bottom*) In the LA Olympics track races, Mark Gorski powered to win the match sprints. ProServ®

55. (*above*) Nelson "the Cheetah" Vails, a former New York City bicycle messenger, won gold in the 1983 Pan-Am Games match sprint in Caracas, Venezuela, and silver in the LA Olympics. © Beth Schneider.

56. Under Eddie Borysewicz, wearing sunglasses, American cyclists won nine medals at the LA Olympics. He held Leonard Harvey Nitz, who took home silver and bronze medals from Olympic track races. Courtesy of Michael Furman.

57. Marianne Martin entered the 1984 Tour de France Féminin as a dark horse, but found her form to win the three-week event. She stood on the podium in Paris with the men's winner, Laurent Fignon. Reproduced by permission from Marianne Martin, Graham Watson Publishing.

58. Eric Heiden, famous for winning five Olympic gold medals as a speed skater at the 1980 Lake Placid Winter Olympics in upstate New York, delighted the crowd when he won the 1985 USPRO Championship in Philadelphia. Courtesy of Michael Furman.

59. Connie Paraskevin captured four world match sprint gold medals, a bronze medal in the 1988 Olympics, and ten national sprint titles. © Beth Schneider.

60. Chris Carmichael, left, listened to advice from Jim Ochowicz during the Coors International Bicycle Classic. © Beth Schneider.

61. The Tour de France and Giro d'Italia always barred women from working on teams until the 7-Eleven squad arrived with masseuse Shelley Verses. She led the way for women masseuses in Europe. Here she massages Estonian-Norwegian cyclist Jaanus Kuum. Reproduced by permission from Graham Watson Publishing.

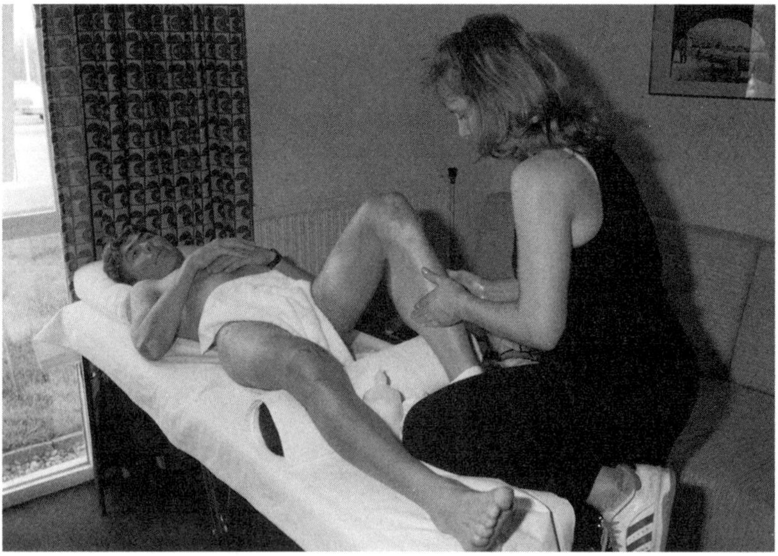

62. Davis Phinney struck his goalpost pose as he won a stage in the 1987 Tour de France. Reproduced by permission from Graham Watson Publishing.

63. Andy Hampsten leads Doug Shapiro in the Coors International Bicycle Classic. © Beth Schneider.

64. In 1989 Donald J. Trump put his name on the Tour de Trump, a ten-day international stage race from Albany, New York, to Atlantic City, New Jersey. Courtesy of the U.S. Bicycling Hall of Fame.

65. Jack Simes III, Oliver "Butch" Martin, and Fred Mengoni were optimistic about the prospects for American professional cycling in 1989. © Beth Schneider.

66. Greg LeMond wore the yellow jersey in the 1991 Tour de France prologue time trial in Lyon. © Beth Schneider.

67. Lance Armstrong, middle of the second row, recovered from cancer to win the Tour de France seven times, but was stripped of his titles for using banned pharmaceuticals. United States Postal Service Pro Cycling Team.

68. Marty Nothstein took home the silver medal in match sprints from the 1996 Atlanta Olympics. He had to wait four years to win the gold medal at the 2000 Sydney Olympics. Reproduced by permission from Graham Watson.

69. Marty Nothstein and Coach Gil Hatton discussed tactics and rivals between heats at the Sydney Olympics. Reproduced by permission from Graham Watson.

70. Evie Stevens left Wall Street to make her professional cycling debut in 2009 at the fiftieth annual Fitchburg-Longsjo Classic, which she won. Reproduced by permission from Mark Johnson.

71. Taylor Phinney, one of the most recognized faces in American cycling, was a crowd favorite in the 2015 Richmond worlds men's road race. Reproduced by permission from Mark Johnson.

72. Megan Guarnier sprints against breakaway partners to third place at the 2015 Richmond worlds women's road race. Reproduced by permission from Mark Johnson.

73. Her bronze medal around her neck, Megan Guarnier waved a bouquet to the home-crowd audience in Richmond. Reproduced by permission from Mark Johnson.

74. Kristin Armstrong winning a stage of the Cascade Cycling Classic in Oregon. Reproduced by permission from Mark Johnson.

75. James Armando pedaled his vintage three-speed Chemineau bicycle, which he imported from Saint-Étienne, France, almost one thousand miles from his home in Hartford to watch the 1930 nationals in Kenosha, Wisconsin. Photograph by Ed Bieber, courtesy of the U.S. Bicycling Hall of Fame.

THREE

"One Good American Rider"

15

The Awakening

There was the feeling that if the United States ever got into cycling at the international level, our country's wealth would provide a better future for the sport.

—JOHN ALLIS, after finishing the 1974 Tour of Britain

Health-conscious baby boomers took a fresh approach to exercise. All over the United States abandoned railroad tracks were converted to paved paths for walking, running, and cycling. Bicycles sold in unprecedented numbers. In 1971, a total of 8.9 million bicycles were purchased, twice the number in 1960. One-third of the bicycles were purchased by adults. They bought ten-speed bicycles for fitness and transportation.

The U.S. Olympic Committee introduced Olympic development grants, enabling ABLA officials to expand racing programs to better prepare cyclists for the Pan-Am Games and the Olympics. Top cyclists received modest financial support, although there still was more glory than money as they had no guarantee that expenses would be paid for portions of the thousands of miles they traveled each year. None of these matters concerned McElmury and Simes, racing in Europe.

McElmury and her husband, Scott, had divorced. She accepted an invitation to race the 1971 season in northern Italy for a women's team, Gruppo Sportivo CBM. It provided her with a racing bike, clothing, accommodations, and a stipend, along with a team car, mechanics, and a coach.

"The Italian experience was the highlight of my cycling career," she told me. "The Italians love cycling. Motorists would never dream of getting in your way when you were out training, even if you were taking up the whole road. I lived with a family in a villa that had a view of seven lakes. There was a wine cellar with five thousand bottles, all red. We raided it often."

The Italian Cycling Federation doled out cash to women, based on how they placed, what their appearance fee was, and how much sponsors paid. Racing and money didn't play well back home. ABLA officials tried to kick her out. "What I was getting was nice, but we were just getting by. I ignored the ABL."

She capped the season with a fourth place at the worlds road race in Mendrisio, Switzerland. There she met Michael Levonas, a New Yorker who had competed on the U.S. team in the 1971 Pan American Games road race. They stayed in Italy for the next season.

"Before each Italian race, Michael and I checked out the primes to decide which I would sprint for—like a case of wine or a brace of pheasants," she said.

At the 1972 worlds in Gap, France, Audrey was in the lead group at the end of the women's road race and again finished fourth. She and Levonas moved together to Boulder, Colorado, and married. She continued to race and took up coaching. In 1976 she spilled on a training ride and landed on her head, resulting in a concussion that left her with a permanent loss of smell.

"Frankly, I didn't have the nerve to race any more after so many accidents," she admitted. "You have to be fearless." She retired after eighteen years of competition to spend more time with her family and take up backpacking and running. She and her husband enrolled in a graduate program at the University of Denver and earned degrees in business management. In 1996 they retired to West Yellowstone, Montana, where Audrey died, aged seventy, in 2013.

• • •

When Audrey raced in Italy, Jack Simes competed on the Continent as a pro. After his release from the army early in 1970, he went to Europe. He made his debut into the cash ranks racing on the Antwerp Sportpaleis velodrome, a 250-meter tobacco-stained indoor board track.

His first big pro event on the Antwerp velodrome was a six-day with three-man teams. The program opened with a leg-ripping fast start featuring cyclists speeding in the slipstream of eight motorized dernys. Exclusive to Europe, dernys are equal parts bicycle and motorcycle, light for easy handling around the steeply banked turns and powered by gas engines. Dernys carry cylindrical gas tanks mounted in front of the handlebars; the vehicles resemble St. Bernard rescue dogs carrying a keg of medicinal whiskey around their neck. Derny drivers, using their motor-assisted pedals, sit upright to offer maximum shield for cyclists crouched behind. Dernys with cyclists in tow whizzing around the track create an impressive sight.

"I was pedaling so fast that my legs were like the blades of a fan," Simes said. "The opening chase was an hour and forty-five minutes, and I lost five laps on the leaders. I was really moving! But I never hurt like that before. Everything hurt from going so fast—my stomach, legs, everything. And I felt terrible that I lost five laps. After I got off the track, I saw that other guys in the race had lost twenty to twenty-five laps. Suddenly, my performance wasn't so bad, put in that perspective. You have to learn those things. I was thrown into brutal racing. Those guys were flying! Their season began in late September and they were in terrific shape by February. I was just out of the army. It was such an experience."

Simes established a residence in Rotterdam and joined the indoor velodrome circuit, thriving in the Netherlands and Belgium. He made a lot of friends and considered importing bicycles and clothing to America. In September he signed a contract for the Skol Six in London, a major event. There he made international sporting news, but not the way he intended.

On the first day, the pace was aggressive. Hours later, Simes and Dutchman Peter Post collided and slammed to the boards. Englishman Tony Gowland smashed into Post's back. No rider was badly hurt, but Post stood up in a rage. Nicknamed the Kaiser of the Six Days, Post was on his way to riding 154 sixes, ultimately achieving sixty-five victories. As a neo-pro, he had competed against Jack Heid in the Cleveland and Chicago Sixes. Now thirty-seven, the leg of his black wool shorts shredded, he angrily blamed Simes for deliberately causing the crash.

Simes politely apologized to Post. The Dutchman, considered tall for a cyclist, threw a few punches at Simes, who punched back. The next day, Simes packed his bags and quit. He was blackballed that season. The London-based *Cycling Weekly* lamented that a promising-looking bridgehead of American cycling on the Continent was lost. He returned to New Jersey.

• • •

Cycling in the United States was ratcheting up. The Olympic development funds were nurturing such projects as the Tour of Florida, an early spring event across the breadth of the Sunshine State, which helped riders get in shape early. Money remained small change, but college students flew on half-price plane tickets. Many races were designated as Olympic development events. That enabled ABLA officials to prevail on promoters to provide low-cost housing, which attracted a higher-quality field.

In international competition, American women led the way. In 1972, Sheila Young of Detroit dashed to a bronze medal at the world sprint championships in Marseille, France. The following year at the worlds in San Sebastian, Spain, she battled through days of qualifying heats to reach the final, matched against Czechoslovakia champion Iva Zajikova. Young got off to a nearly disastrous start. She and Zajikova were winding up their sprint when the Czech suddenly swerved in front of Young, causing the American to hit Zajikova's back wheel, flip through the air, and smack her head on the concrete. Young suffered a gash at the top of her scalp. The fork of her bike frame was badly twisted.

The judges ordered Young and Zajikova to re-ride the race after a twenty-minute intermission. Young's deep cut needed stitches, but she didn't have time to spare. A Dutch doctor at trackside closed the wound with two staples; they cut into unanesthetized flesh because Novocain is considered a banned drug in competition. Meanwhile, teammates removed the bent fork and replaced it with the fork from another bike.

Twenty minutes after falling, Young was back in action. She felt a little dizzy, but her adrenaline was pumping. She won her next two races decisively to clinch the match.

This time Union Cycliste Internationale officials had a recording on hand to play "The Star-Spangled Banner" in time for Sheila Young to step up to the top of the victory podium, the second American to pull on a world champion's rainbow jersey.

Young was introduced to cycling by her father, Clair, who had reigned as Michigan state ABLA champion for more than ten years. He had interrupted his cycling during World War II, fighting major battles in the South Pacific as a marine. His daughter's first bicycle race in 1965, at age fourteen, almost ended her career—she fell and broke her arm. Speed skating, which Young regarded as her primary sport, became both more important and more realistic.

She told me: "My dad used to say that if you want to be number one, you have to suffer. When I was an adolescent, I thought I was working hard and suffering. I kind of got a sweat going once in a while. I didn't know what he was talking about. I began to realize what he meant in the summer of 1972, when I was twenty-one. I got into cycling then to help me for skating, and I still remember distinctly when I realized the difference between sort of suffering and really suffering. But it paid off. One of the reasons I liked cycling was because of the travel. And when I got better, I did a lot of traveling."

Aficionados were surprised when eighteen-year-old Sue Novara dethroned Young in the 1974 Michigan state championship, and again at the nationals. Novara went to the world sprint championships in Montreal. She scored a silver medal, losing the final in a photo finish to Soviet rider Tamara Piltsikova.

Novara lived in Flint, an hour's drive from Detroit. Originally a speed skater, she had started cycling at age thirteen to keep in shape in the warm weather. She won her first national ABLA sprint championship in 1972, age sixteen. A little taller and more lithe than Sheila Young, Novara was known as Navajo Sue for the long ponytail she wore down the middle of her back.

Not only were the two Michigan cyclists so fast and lived near each other, they also were members of the same metro-Detroit cycling club, Wolverine-Schwinn, coached by Mike Walden, a bike-shop proprietor. "We influenced each other by being good competitors," Young said.

"We drove each other to win. You are only as good as your competition. We helped each other out competitively."

They took their rivalry overseas. At the 1975 worlds in Rocourt, Belgium, Novara defeated Iva Zajikova for the women's sprint championship, becoming the third U.S. cyclist to claim the rainbow jersey. Young took home the bronze medal. Both Americans stood together on the podium next to Zajikova for a rousing rendition of the American national anthem.

The following year, Young made even bigger sporting headlines when she speed skated at the Winter Olympics in Innsbruck, Austria, to a gold, a silver, and a bronze medal. Her complete set of medals set her apart as the first U.S. athlete to win three medals in one Winter Olympics. She was featured on skates for the cover of *Sports Illustrated.*

Young returned to cycling and led Novara to a one-two finish at the world championships in Monteroni di Lecce, Italy. Their rival, Zajikova, settled for bronze, the third time an American had foiled the Czech.

Young's cycling victory in addition to her Olympic gold medal, in the 500-meter sprint, meant she became the first athlete, man or woman, in the twentieth century to reign as world champion in two sports concurrently. Women still lacked their own category in cycling at the Summer Olympics. Young's feats and her cheerful personality contributed to lobbying toward introducing women's cycling in the Olympics.

• • •

Racing domestically proved successful for American women, less so for men. Yet geopolitics were unfolding in ways that raised cycling's profile and attracted more talent to the sport.

In late 1973 oil-exporting Middle East countries, led by Saudi Arabia, the largest oil exporter, quadrupled the price of oil shipped to the United States, forcing the price at the pump to jump more than a dollar a gallon. The price shock reverberated from coast to coast. Fuel shortages caused a crisis. Motorists lined up around the block and waited their turn to pull into local service stations. The stock market tumbled. Car sales languished. Consumers purchased bicycles in record numbers—15.2 million, including 5.1 million imports. They topped motor vehicle sales, something not seen since the turn of the century.

Raleigh Bicycles of Nottingham, England, had orders in America for 500,000 bicycles and opened a warehouse in New Jersey. Raleigh partnered with the Century Road Club of America to sponsor an elite team with a $10,000 package, a sum that when mentioned caused eyebrows to shoot up.

Around that time, the ABLA announced its first-ever national road and track cycling teams. The roster included many riders, including John Howard and Dave Chauner, now civilians, from the Army Cycling Team. John Allis, recently graduated with an MBA from Harvard, also was selected for the road team and worked as a publicist for Raleigh.

Raleigh also signed on as the title sponsor of the Tour of Ireland in mid-August. Its ten stages wended 740 miles from downtown Dublin, northwest to uppermost Ireland, then back to Dublin. Raleigh entered its American squad—the first time that a U.S. team ventured to a stage race across the Atlantic.

The Irish national tour drew teams from around the United Kingdom experienced in the rigors of daily stage racing. Most Irish, Welsh, Scottish, and English riders came from farms, factories, or service jobs. They were passionate about cycling and considered it as a possible opportunity to move up to the pro ranks and maybe a middle-class life. The Americans were expected to falter as "no-hopers" against tougher counterparts.

The Raleigh-CRCA team of John Howard, John Allis, Bill Humphreys, and strongman Stan Swaim arrived in Dublin during a heat wave with a sports director and a manager, provided by Raleigh. They traveled thousands of miles from home with little more than two sets of jerseys and shorts—one set they washed in the sink the evening before the race; the other set they wore the next day—along with a warm-up suit, a spoke wrench, and pocket change.

Three days into the tour the American team was holding its own. Howard moved into third in general classification, based on elapsed time, two spots ahead of Allis. Then Howard felt the luck of the Irish.

On stage 6, a rainy and chilly day in northwest Ireland, the course went ninety-five miles over the Iron Mountains to Athlone on the Shannon River. The rain stopped about halfway but left everyone soaked.

Howard saw three riders attack up a steep hill and joined them. Plunging down the other side, they accelerated to 60 mph on a narrow road bordered by sheep standing on both sides. On the road to the finish in Athlone, a city in the Lakelands region, the foursome worked in unison to maintain a short margin on the peloton. Spectators in sweaters and jackets crowded behind steel barricades to see if the breakaway could hold off the peloton, close behind.

"I picked the right wheel to follow and timed my sprint right—and won," Howard said. A photo showed him capturing the stage by a bike length as the pack, spread curb to curb, bore down a precious six bike lengths behind.

Phil Liggett, an Englishman serving as chief international commissaire, observed: "Winning the stage was a very big deal. John was a real novelty to us."

The Tour of Ireland concluded in Dublin with a thirty-mile criterium inside Phoenix Park. Howard's tires slipped on a slick turn. He fell and slid along the pavement, suffering cuts and abrasions. "But I managed to get back up and catch the field all right to stay in the action."

The American team finished, which earned respect. No longer were the Americans seen as "no-hopers." Chief Commissaire Liggett, also the new organizer of the Tour of Britain, the United Kingdom's biggest and most prestigious cycling event since the early 1950s, met with the Raleigh-CRCA team.

"I told them that what I saw of their riding in the Tour of Ireland indicated to me that they wouldn't disgrace themselves in the Tour of Britain," Liggett said. "I told them to bring their best six riders, and that we would pay their expenses."

• • •

A meaningful reform toward raising the racing standard and making larger fields safer was imposed by the ABLA in 1974, modeled after European cycling. The ABLA issued licenses that divided men into three categories. Category I was for national-class riders such as Howard. Cat II was for those making top-ten finishes in regional events. Cat III was for everybody else, intended to nurture novices to improve bike-handling skills—especially techniques for cornering and sprinting—and gain confidence. A similar system was imposed for women. The age for open men's and women's divisions rose from seventeen to eighteen.

The battle against advertising on jerseys and shorts in races ended with the soft scratching of pens signing checks. ABLA leaders were allowed to charge a commission for sponsorships. As a result, teams like Raleigh-CRCA were at liberty to splash the name Raleigh across jersey fronts and backs. French bicycle companies like Gitane and Peugeot and bike shops such as the Turin Bicycle Co-op of greater Chicago sponsored teams, and their riders carried their brand name everywhere they rolled.

With the advent of a national ABLA team, the organization needed a coach. Officials announced early in the 1974 season that the ABLA hired Butch Martin as the men's coach for the Montreal worlds that summer—a prelude to Montreal hosting the 1976 Summer Olympics. U.S. riders would ride the same roads where the Olympic races would be held.

Martin had wound down his racing after the 1971 Pan-Am Games. The two-time Olympian with experience racing in Italy, with his penchant for never riding harder than he needed to win, had a reputation as a rider's rider. He considered the best showing his team could make at the Montreal worlds lay in the four-rider 100-kilometer team time trial. It became the ABLA's Holy Grail.

A few months before the 1974 worlds came the two-week Tour of Britain. From the six riders on the U.S. team that flew to London would come the nucleus of Martin's team for the Montreal worlds.

Eleven national teams endowed with some of the greatest talent of their generation converged on Brighton on England's south coast for the May 26 start. World amateur road racing champion Ryszard Szurkowski wore the rainbow jersey as captain of the Polish squad. Future world pro champions Roy Schuiten and Jan Raas were on the Dutch national team. Seasoned teams from Czechoslovakia, West Germany, Sweden, and Norway joined the Irish and British teams.

Local reporters, who had made their bones on Fleet Street's cut-and-thrust journalism, predicted the U.S. team would quit before the

1,200-mile Tour ended in Blackpool, north of Liverpool, on the coast of the Irish Sea. "We were not taken seriously," John Allis said.

From the first day the American team suffered inopportune tire punctures, skin-ripping falls, and riders slipping off the back of the peloton up hills. The British press published betting odds daily on whether the U.S. team would survive. Despite the odds, all six finished. Howard was the best placed, in thirty-first; Rich Hammen of California persevered in last place, fifty-ninth overall, two hours and fifty minutes (about sixty miles) behind Tour winner Roy Schuiten. Hammen was awarded a red railroad lantern, signaling the caboose.

"We got some good press," said Allis, forty-third. "The tabloids gave us credit."

Phil Liggett thought well enough of what he saw to invite the team back for the next year.

The experience left Howard with no illusion about the state of American racing. He declared, "Compared to Europe, we are infantile."

• • •

Butch Martin kept close watch on national-level races he attended over the season to observe riders, talk with folks, and collect information to make his selection for who would represent the United States at the Montreal worlds road races. Milwaukee cyclist Jim Ochowicz, a speed skater–cyclist dating the indomitable Sheila Young, showed promise. Another rising star was Wayne Stetina of Indianapolis, a second-generation speed skater–cyclist winning criteriums with crowd-pleasing flair.

Martin waited till after the national road championships in Pontiac, Michigan, to see how the results shook out to pick his time-trial members: Howard, Ochowicz, Stetina, and Hammen—who had recovered from the Tour of Britain and won the Southern California road racing championship. For the road race, Martin entered Allis, Chauner, Mike Neel of Berkeley, California, and Marc Thompson of Kansas City.

Coach Martin appreciated that the road riders were strong but needed more speed. He had them pacing behind a motorcycle he drove. "My idea was to get them riding one or two miles an hour faster and doing it comfortably."

Ochowicz understood: "We had a lot of guys who could ride 25 mph or 26 mph all day, but they couldn't handle 28 mph very long. That difference might not sound like much, but it is. That is what separated us from competing against the big teams in Europe, who did race at 28 mph."

Martin's strength as a coach was motivating riders. "The key is to get them to see themselves as a winner," he said. "When you can finish in the top ten consistently, you can win. You are there in the action. Then it becomes a matter of honing physical abilities with a sense of tactics."

The day of the team time trial, August 21, was predictably hot, sunny, and humid—conditions difficult for northern Europeans accustomed to cooler temps and overcast skies. Each of the twenty-two teams departed at two-minute intervals over an undulating highway for twenty-five kilometers (15.6 miles) out to a traffic island where they turned around and went back, repeated again.

Each team rider took his turn leading so the others drafted in the envelope of wind protection before the leader swung out to the side and dropped back to the rear in a smooth rotation. Howard took double and triple pulls at the front before he dropped back to recover behind Stetina. Ochowicz, with his thick droopy mustache, took over, followed by Hammen. Martin kept track of the time as a passenger in the USA team car.

At fifty kilometers, the U.S. team clocked the twelfth fastest time, led by the Russians. Time trials, like eating oysters, are an acquired taste; this event drew only the press following in cars, team-support vehicles, and a swarm of motorcycle police roaring back and forth to keep traffic away.

The drama unfolded in the second half as some teams withered in the heat and humidity. The Czechs had charged through the first quarter in third place, but faltered and were overtaken by the U.S. team.

Martin's training his cyclists behind a motorcycle made a difference. In the final twenty-five miles, the U.S. foursome overtook the French and Italians. Ochowicz became the team's spark plug over the final six miles. The foursome finished together (the first three are timed) and beat the Belgians and West Germans. The U.S. team came in ninth place, with the Swedes winning.

"We didn't win a medal," Martin noted, acknowledging that the U.S. men continued their road worlds shutout. "But we were definitely closing the gap fast."

In 1976, the sport's national governing body changed its name from the Amateur Bicycle League of America to the U.S. Cycling Federation, a development that resolved long-standing friction with Latin American cycling organizations that complained the United States was not all of the Americas.

• • •

Northern California races offered matchless flourishes. One event that gained national attention was kicked off by a Grateful Dead rock concert, a scintillating parade of Playboy bunnies, and a bumper-to-bumper procession of throbbing, high-powered, metal-flaked Shelby Mustang GT350s.

Peter Rich, a Pedali Alpini veteran of Europe, had returned home to Berkeley to pass along what he learned. Rich, a former police officer, opened a bike shop, Velo-Sport. He imported high-end Masi bikes from Milan and sold the latest European equipment. He also produced the Berkeley Hills Road Race, founded in 1957 and now the second-oldest annual bike race in the country. In 1971, Rich had raised $50,000 by himself and organized the eight-day, ten-stage Tour of California, the first major stage race in the country. Regional U.S. teams competed against squads from Canada, Mexico, and Germany. From the back room of Velo-Sport, he published a newsletter on a mimeograph machine with tips on training, diet, and equipment; eventually his newsletter turned into *Bicycling* magazine.

Two Bay Area riders he sponsored became national forces in the early 1970s and rose to world class: Mike Neel and George Mount. Neel stood a slender six feet. He had light-colored hair and a quiet disposition, like a pensive James Dean. Neel had fended for himself at an early age. His first job was as a hot walker, holding the reins and walking sweaty racehorses after their workouts. Watching jockeys ride mounts impressed him how efficiency in motion and style figured in sustaining speed. He took up cycling under Peter Rich's tutelage and won the 1971 national pursuit title, which he reclaimed two years later.

George Lewis Mount, four years younger and a few inches shorter than Neel, had coal-black hair and brash self-confidence. Born in Princeton, New Jersey, he was descended from a long line of Princeton University grads; a relative was mayor of the borough of Princeton. His family moved to Northern California where he grew up. In high school he started cycling. At fifteen he made up his mind to compete in the Olympics and turn pro to race in Italy for *gran esperienza*, the "great experience." In races he charged ferociously up hills. Lesser-fit cyclists he dropped on climbs saw him turn and flash a crocodile smile. He turned eighteen in 1973 and refused to register for the military draft as his father insisted, although that year the draft was abolished in favor of all-volunteer armed forces. Father and son argued in a battle of wills until the son left home.

Mount and Neel lived the nomadic life of bike bums. They shared an outlaw ethos. Peter Rich let them sleep upstairs over his Velo-Sport shop.

In 1972 Neel traveled on his own to race in France. He won regional club races and made a name for himself abroad. At the end of the season he returned home to Berkeley. He subsequently was picked for the national ABLA team and accompanied John Howard and Dave Chauner to the 1975 Tour of Britain. Chauner won a stage and garnered headlines; the team finished a creditable fifth.

Neel also made forays to race in Italy. He preferred Italy over France. "In Italy you would never go hungry," he said. He joined an Italian squad.

Neel and Mount rode as the untouchables at the Olympic trials and went to the Montreal Olympics. Rain bucketed down in the 109-mile road race. Slick roads caused a pileup that eliminated Neel. Mount had kept at the front of the pack and finished sixth—only a few bike lengths out of third. For the first time in memory, the prospect of an Olympic cycling medal seemed a distinct possibility.

Days after the Olympics were over, Neel, twenty-four, flew to Italy and turned pro to compete in the 179-mile road race at the worlds in

Ostuni, Italy. He stayed near the head of the peloton, in the hunt yet shielded from the wind. The closer the finish loomed, the faster the pace. By the final miles all riders hunched low in a straight line, bright-colored jerseys close behind one another as train cars. Cheers from spectators five deep drowned out the sizzling of tires.

Neel drafted in the slipstream of Eddy Merckx, the Belgian called the Cannibal for his insatiable appetite to win all the races that counted. Merckx, six feet one, had a king-size heart, matching lungs, and beefy haunches to power his legs like a locomotive and feed his voracious hunger for victory. Merckx, like Fausto Coppi, was an all-rounder. He won pack sprints. He flew away from the peloton and won solo. He matched pedal strokes with smaller and lighter climbing specialists up steep, gravity-defying slopes in the Alps, Dolomites, and Pyrenees and beat them at their game. In time trials, he crushed everyone; on a velodrome in the rarified air of Mexico City—7,350 feet above sea level—he set the world hour record, reinforcing his stature as the defining cyclist of his generation.

"In the final kilometer I was well positioned in fifth place, behind the rear wheel of Eddy Merckx. Then I felt someone grip the back of my jersey," Neel told me. "We were flying single file and I was pulled out! I looked around. The guy grabbing my jersey was Felice Gimondi. He was the capo of the peloton, the enforcer. He said he didn't know me. Those guys had raced against one another all season and suddenly I came along. Gimondi told me I didn't earn my place behind Merckx. But he said that afterward he would get me good start money in races for the rest of the season. He did, too. Gimondi looked out for me. He got me into more races than I could have entered on my own. I made far more money than if I had stayed on Merckx's wheel."

Neel placed tenth. In American cycling, he catapulted to hero. Italian team Magniflex, sponsored by a mattress manufacturer, signed him to a contract. Magniflex was a low-budget outfit. Sometimes Neel joined his teammates waiting overnight in train stations and airports, sleeping on hard chairs, their feet on their luggage to ward off thieves. But he'd become the first U.S. rider since Joseph Magnani to reach the big leagues of European road racing.

• • •

Alarming concern over disadvantages that American amateurs had in Olympic competitions against state-supported Eastern bloc athletes galvanized the U.S. Congress to create the President's Commission on Olympic Sports, charged with conducting a comprehensive two-year study of the entire U.S. Olympic movement. All Winter and Summer Olympic sports were examined to see what reforms, which many observers felt were overdue, were needed to restructure amateur sports.

The President's Commission noted that bicycle racing was growing in popularity but the lack of money and bad administration hindered the development of domestic riders compared with cyclists in other countries. The Commission noted that until the sport overcame organizational deficiencies, attracted more cyclists to compete on a regular basis in Europe where the sport thrived, hired a permanent staff, and upgraded development programs, U.S. competitive cycling would fail to reach its full potential.

The Commission's findings and recommendations led the House and Senate to pass Public Law 95-606. President Jimmy Carter signed the legislation into law. The Amateur Sports Act of 1978 overhauled the U.S. Olympic Committee. The new law recognized each sport's national governing body and appropriated corporate funding for development and training grants—key to relieving athletes of the pressure to support themselves while training and traveling at home and abroad to competitions.

The U.S. Cycling Federation membership in 1976 topped ten thousand. Its budget shot up tenfold in five years. Corporate involvement and funds from the U.S. Olympic Committee pumped the USCF's budget to $235,000. Corporations like Exxon, Miller, Smirnoff, Pepsi, and Yamaha were sponsoring big-city clubs.

Conditions were improving rapidly, but an essential ingredient was still missing—a salaried full-time national coach. Martin, a paid consultant, proved he was a good coach, but politics intervened.

• • •

Eddie Borysewicz (pronounced Bor-SAY-vich) coached the Polish cycling team at the Montreal Olympics and immigrated to the United

States. He settled in New Jersey and painted bridges for the Garden State. While visiting friends he had raced with on the Polish national team, he met Mike Fraysse of Ridgefield Park, then serving as USCF competition committee chairman. Fraysse recommended him to the federation's board, which hired Borysewicz the next year as the United States' first full-time paid national cycling coach.

Martin resigned as coach and went home to New York. He managed a bike shop, Manhattan Express.

The Polish expat filled out forms to become a U.S. citizen. He and Fraysse got along speaking French, but he had to learn English. Americans called him Eddie B., easier than pronouncing his surname. In 1977 he began coaching at the Olympic Training Center in Squaw Valley, in Northern California. He relied on the twelve-year-old son of a former Polish teammate as translator. "It really cuts your authority," Borysewicz later said, "when you want to be commanding and you have to speak through a twelve-year-old."

He complained that Americans didn't sit on their bikes properly. Their saddles were set too low or too high, more forward or back than they should be for the best pedal stroke. Their weight wasn't distributed evenly along the frame, crucial when speeding downhill into turns where sand, gravel, or standing water can cause wheels to slide. He exclaimed that only one rider on the national team wasn't overweight. Eddie B. expected riders so lean he could count their ribs. Extra bodyweight when pedaling up hills amounted to unnecessary luggage.

"American cycling was incredibly empty," he contended. His approach was like that of a baseball or football manager taking over a major league team and building the future around youth. Veterans, like twenty-eight-year-old John Howard, found their days on the national team slipping into history.

Borysewicz's struggle with English helped him miss much of the criticism against him as he stressed that team members race together. American racing had been marked by rugged individuals going for the win rather than team tactics. In international events, tactics enable a team to best use an array of talents, from helping the climbing specialist to fly away up a hill, to snuffing breakaway attempts by chasing as a group from the front of the field and bringing everybody up to the breakaway, to positioning the best sprinter behind two or three teammates leading him like locomotives approaching the finish line.

At the Olympic Training Center in Squaw Valley, Eddie B. counted only one outstanding prospect—sixteen-year-old Greg LeMond from Carson City, Nevada. LeMond, a former national-class hot-dog skier (somersault flips in the air and other stunts), started racing two years earlier to keep his legs strong during warm weather.

LeMond stood five feet ten and weighed 150 pounds. Once he'd sought a challenge in the three-day Tour of Fresno for Category I men's open. He finished second, six seconds behind John Howard. Howard remarked that he had won but Greg showed class to become cycling's future.

LeMond won two of the three qualifier races determining selection of hopefuls going to the junior worlds road race. Although LeMond qualified for the first spot on the team, he was underage, thus ineligible to go.

When Borysewicz was asked what he saw in the blond, blue-eyed youth, he overlooked the pigeon-toed way LeMond's feet sat on the pedals—easily corrected. Eddie B. saw a special rider who was passionate about the sport, had quick recovery, and worked extremely hard. The coach replied in a heavy Polish accent: "A diamond, a clear diamond."

At the 1977 worlds in San Cristobal, Venezuela, U.S. women showed the men how to step up to the winner's podium. Sue Novara took a silver medal in the match sprints. Another speed-skater-turned-cyclist, Connie Carpenter of Madison, Wisconsin, snatched the silver medal in the women's road race.

Eddie B. planned to get his men and women ready for the 1980 Summer Olympics in Moscow—and then for the 1984 Olympics scheduled for Los Angeles. American cycling was awakening.

16

Breaking Away

When the cameras began shooting, the working title was *Bambino*. It wasn't long before this title changed to *Breaking Away*.

—STEVE TESICH, Academy Award winner for Best Original Screenplay

Through the late 1970s the U.S. Olympic Committee, one of America's most revered organizations, served as little more than a travel agency. It brought the best athletes together and sent them to the Pan American Games one year, the Olympic Games the next. All national governing bodies functioned as kitchen-table operations; officials volunteered their time. The Amateur Sports Act of 1978 transformed the entire Olympics program as methodically as the internet, laptop computers, and cell phones would later overhaul communications.

USOC executive director F. Don Miller oversaw the Olympic Committee's move in 1979 from a New York hotel suite to a decommissioned air force base in Colorado Springs, remodeled as the U.S. Olympic Training Center. The five Olympic rings were prominently displayed by the main parking lot and the International Olympic Committee flag's Olympic rings flew on a pole next to the American flag. Olympic emblems vied against the lingering military character of manicured lawns and sidewalks edged like high-and-tight haircuts.

The U.S. Cycling Federation moved into a four-room suite for administration and classes. The air force barracks were upgraded to dorm rooms for visiting cyclists. This represented a major advancement.

Revenue from growing corporate sponsorships, increasing USOC support, membership dues, and other sources by 1980 gave the federation a budget close to $500,000, a twelve-fold spike from $38,500 in 1973. Staff were hired to develop, train, and select amateurs to compete on national road and track teams.

The USCF's newly elected president Mike Fraysse and comptroller Howard Althoff shopped in Colorado Springs for furniture from Goodwill. "We bought a desk and chair," Fraysse recalled. "We also bought a couch seat with chrome arms that had come from a bus. That couch stayed at the USCF until about 1996."

After Eddie B. came on board as the first salaried national coaching director, Mike Neel joined as a coach. Neel had become the first U.S. rider in Spain's grand tour, the three-week Vuelta a España, where he scored top-four finishes. Neel ended his pro career on an Italian team after the 1977 season. He shifted to a support position to share his knowledge and fluency in Italian, French, and Spanish with the next generation of Americans competing abroad.

• • •

Two riders flying across the Atlantic frequently, sometimes on a USCF national team and often on their own, were the always-smiling George Mount and always-improving Greg LeMond, six years younger.

Mount achieved several victories in Italy in 1977, racing for a team that Neel had suggested, Castelfranco di Sopra, named after the locale midway between Florence and Arezzo in Tuscany. "The team, despite being small, was well connected," Mount told me.

The next spring he went back to Italy on the five-rider USCF national team managed by Neel, in an ambitious twelve-week campaign. "We were given round-trip [airline] tickets and a few hundred dollars to get by for three months," Mount said. The trip marked the first funded by the USCF, although their budget wouldn't last more than a few weeks. The team had to earn prize money to support themselves or go home early.

Mount won the first of what turned into a couple dozen races, which generated cash flow, supplemented by teammates scoring victories and placing in the top three. "We got on a roll," Mount said. "We often got start money. You have to remember that most American males going to Europe had virtually no success. We survived as a team primarily on my race winnings for all that time, which was considerable, plus Mike's amazing gift to make people do his bidding."

Neel, tall and narrow at the hips, stood with the upright bearing of a leader. Strangers could feel comfortable asking him for directions or offering help. "Neel not only could translate for us, he also negotiated lots of things, like meals, motel rooms, equipment that we needed to replace as things wore out or broke," Mount said. "He kept getting us lots of other stuff that kept us going."

In late May they crossed the Channel to England for the 1,200-mile Tour of Britain. Teams arrived from eleven nations across Great Britain, Europe, Scandinavia, and the Soviet Union to England's premier road race. East Europeans dominated most of the twelve daily stages, from Brighton on the south coast to Blackpool, the resort in northwest England on the Irish Sea. Polish rider Jan Brzeźny won from Sweden's Lennart Fagerlund and Britain's Bob Downs. Mount rode consistently well and claimed fourth place, the best U.S. finish there ever, only one second behind Downs.

The USCF team jetted back to Italy. They completed their itinerary as intended and returned home triumphant. "Eddie B. said that since we won so many races in Italy, it was too easy, so we should go to France," Mount said.

• • •

The summer of 1978 offered the country's de facto national grand tour, Colorado's weeklong Red Zinger Bicycle Classic, now in its fourth year. It radiated out of mile-high Boulder, on roads alternately slicing through open lowland prairie and scaling steep Rocky Mountain foothills. One stage took place around the many-storied Morgul-Bismarck loop—a thirteen-mile circuit south of Boulder featuring a mile-long uphill concluding up a summit so sharp it was dubbed "the wall." The eight-lap, 104-mile Morgul-Bismarck stage tested willpowers and muscles. The climbs shed weaker riders off the back of the peloton before it fractured into groups of varying fitness until only the strongest remained at the front—cycling's equivalent to Darwin's natural selection (big hills are known as "selections" in cycling terminology).

For eight laps under a burning sun and a cobalt sky, Mount showed his prowess around the Morgul-Bismarck circuit, capriciously named after a local race organizer's dog and cat. Mount shoved his arms into the race leader's red jersey. By the final stage, a circuit in North Boulder Park, crammed with thousands of enthusiastic fans, all he had to do was surf wheels in the peloton to add another victory.

Mount capped his season in New York at the highly publicized Apple Lap, a seventy-five-mile road race through New York's five boroughs. Riding on pavement cracked by winter freezes, buckled by summer heat, and mauled year-round by heavy traffic, he set a new national record for the distance on his way to victory. His prize was $4,000 cash (worth about $15,000 today) and allowable under revised amateur rules. (He could pocket $2,000 without jeopardizing his standing with the U.S. Olympic Committee or the U.S. Cycling Federation; the rest was deposited into a trust fund he could collect upon retirement.)

The next spring, as Eddie B. advised, Neel shepherded Mount and the USCF squad to France. Their 1979 campaign started in mid-April's four-day Circuit de la Sarthe, southwest of Paris. Organizers allowed the American and the Soviet state-sponsored amateurs to compete in a field of more than a hundred pros.

The opening stage of 110 miles ended in Allonnes, a suburb of Le Mans, on the banks of the Sarthe River. The peloton cruised briskly through rolling farm country for more than four hours and stayed intact. Over the closing miles, the tempo accelerated. The Soviets and pro teams jockeyed to set up their sprinters when Mount bulleted off the front, his legs spinning smooth as a sewing machine. The pack disregarded him, like a cat allowing a mouse to flee until the bigger animal decided to pounce on its tiny prey.

Mount had the energy of a fire truck. He tore open a minute's lead, then stretched his gap. Onlookers crowding the road heading into Le Mans applauded his valor. Motorcycle gendarmes clearing the road accelerated to protect him. The pack exploded into a frenzied burst from curb to curb to the finish, but he soloed over the line, arms raised overhead in a victory salute.

"George Mount is the first successful U.S. cyclist on the old continent," exclaimed the local newspaper. "This is historic."

The Russians and pros wised up. They prevented the Yanks from any further similar surprises. Mount became a marked man, his every move checked by the other teams. He started the second day in the leader's jersey. His team couldn't help him defend it, but they had made a big impression—and they bumped up their start money in future events.

After the Circuit de la Sarthe, Mount captured the high-profile Tour d'Auvergne. He and the national team returned to America in July. Mount was picked to ride in the 1979 Pan American Games in Puerto Rico. He powered the four-man squad in the 100-kilometer (62.5-mile) time trial to a gold medal. Next, he flew to Italy to race the rest of the season.

• • •

LeMond traveled with his Berkeley, California, friend Kent Gordis, fluent in French, to compete in Belgium and France, with forays into Switzerland. LeMond adjusted to faster speeds and longer distances than those that other junior riders had access to in the United States. In 1978, on the USCF national junior team, he won his first worlds medal. He led the junior worlds team to a bronze in the 70-kilometer (43.5-mile) four-man time trial, on the rolling hills of leafy Rock Creek Park in Washington DC. The junior worlds road races in the nation's capital and velodrome events at the Lehigh County Velodrome in eastern Pennsylvania marked the first worlds in this country in sixty-six years.

The next year at the junior worlds in Buenos Aires, Argentina, eighteen-year-old LeMond scored a bronze in the team 70-kilometer time trial, a silver in the individual 3,000-meter (1.9-mile) pursuit race on the velodrome, and a gold in the 120-kilometer (75-mile) road race—the first U.S. man to win a worlds road race.

As the 1980 Moscow Summer Olympics approached, the outlooks for the United States to win an Olympic cycling medal were brightening.

• • •

American moviegoers were introduced to bicycle racing in the 1979 Hollywood feature film, *Breaking Away*. Its engaging hero was based on the actual exploits of Indianapolis racer Dave Blase. *Breaking Away* wove two stories to give the movie universal appeal. Four adolescent boys, just out of high school in the early 1960s, were breaking away from adolescence and heading, bewildered and reluctantly, into adulthood, including the protagonist, played by actor Dennis Christopher, aspiring to race bicycles in Italy.

Film buffs watched the nineteen-year-old cyclist, living at home with his parents in Bloomington, south of Indianapolis, become Italian in his own mind. He emulated cycling legends like Fausto Coppi. Assuming imagined Neapolitan charm, he disconcerted his salt-of-the-earth parents by greeting them in lilting Italian: "Ciao, mamma, ciao, papà." He studied Italian phrases from a tourist guidebook and listened to Italian opera records. He renamed the family cat Fellini, after the Italian film director, and fed it from a Cinzano ashtray.

All this was a cultural leap for a midwesterner unable to tell an olive tree from a fig tree. Behind the reconstituted dots that filled the screen and told a story that went to the heart, the model for the movie's cyclist was Blase, called Dave Stoller in the movie. Blase's Italian persona cloaked adolescent shyness so he could talk to girls. At Indiana University his roommate and Phi Kappa Psi frat brother, Steve Tesich, took advantage of what he saw, a rider with Olympic aspirations also studying to become a biology teacher.

Tesich had gathered material from racing. He rode with Blase in 1962 on the Phi Kappa Psi team in the Little 500—a raucous April campus tradition of 200 laps around a 440-yard cinder track for fifty miles. After college, Tesich applied his experiences to make it in New York as a screenwriter. He wrote a script, "The Eagle from Naptown," about a cyclist from Naptown, a colloquial reference to Indianapolis, Blase's hometown. Tesich had emigrated at age fourteen with his parents from Serbia to a steel-mill community in Gary, Indiana. He wrote another script, about class conflict between rich and poor, then merged both stories. That script intrigued film director Peter Yates.

Blase even played the announcer in the movie, sporting a white short-sleeved shirt in the Little 500, serving as the movie's climax. His Phi Kappa Psi four-man team had been underdogs against thirty-two other squads. All teams received a sturdy one-speed, balloon-tired bike with a coaster brake, flat rubber pedals, and dropped handlebars. One rider from each team rode as fast as he could for as long as he could manage before pulling into the exchange zone on the home straight—slowing, hopping off, and handing the bike off to a teammate who took over. The Phi Kappa Psi team capitalized on Blase's cycling prowess. He churned the most laps. Phi Kappa Psi overcame the odds to win by a thirteen-second margin, although on screen the outcome comes down to a sprint.

The movie released by Twentieth Century Fox launched Tesich's career in screenwriting. *Breaking Away*, described by critic Roger Ebert as "a sunny, goofy, intelligent little film about coming of age," boosted the sport's profile.

• • •

Just when it appeared that the decades-long gap since the last Olympic cycling medals was to end for U.S. cyclists, and the public was ready to root for them, international politics intruded. In late 1979 the Soviet army invaded Afghanistan and ignited protests worldwide. Following the conclusion of the 1980 Winter Olympics in Lake Placid, New York, President Jimmy Carter announced a U.S. boycott of the Moscow Olympics. All U.S. medal hopes were quashed. The Olympic trials went ahead as scheduled; fifteen road and track cyclists and four support staff were selected. But the entire U.S. Olympic team stayed home.

• • •

Jonathan Swift Boyer in upscale Carmel-by-the-Sea, on Monterey Bay south of San Francisco, took up competitive cycling at age fifteen in 1970 as a member of the Velo Club Monterey. Through high school, he was mentored by Remo d'Agliano, a restaurateur with experience racing in France, and George Farrier, a cycling enthusiast and business success from his regional fast-food chain. D'Agliano and Farrier encouraged Boyer to set his sights on going to live in France, progress through the French amateur ranks, and turn pro.

Boyer won the 1973 Northern California district junior championship road race. That earned him a spot with two others to compete in July in the sixty-mile introductory European Junior Championships (predecessor to the junior worlds) in Munich, Germany. He and teammates stayed in the peloton until the final miles. "We got dusted on the final hill," he recalled.

The excursion to Germany entitled him to bragging rights for the rest of the summer in California. Instead of flying back to Carmel, he heeded his mentors and headed to the South of France. Boyer joined a small local cycling club. "I won six of my first twelve races," he said.

Victories drew the notice of d'Agliano's former team, Athletic Club Boulogne-Billancourt, a broad-based sports organization in suburban Paris. Known as ACBB, it has long developed world-class cyclists, notably France's five-time Tour de France winner Jacques Anquetil. ACBB features thirty-two disciplines, including judo, swimming, rugby, ice hockey, and figure skating. The next year, Boyer was accepted into ACBB.

Races in France thrust him into a diet of quicker average speeds, longer distances, larger pelotons. The fastest amateurs could make up to fifty dollars a race. Boyer picked up tricks of the trade: how to maneuver inside the peloton coursing along narrow country roads and pitching terrain, how to dash ahead to claim primes contested along the course, how to time his sprint approaching the finish to win.

Three years with the ACBB developed Boyer into one of France's top amateurs—outside the system developing in America. He turned pro at twenty-two in 1977 to ride with the French team, Lejeune-BP, sponsored by French bicycle company Lejeune and British Petroleum. Its sports director was Henri Anglade, gruff and imperious but respected as two-time French road champion and once the runner-up in the Tour de France. Lejeune-BP's star was 1976 Tour de France winner Lucien van Impe of Belgium.

Boyer's first-year contract paid about $650 a month, plus modest performance bonuses, altogether less than what he could earn stocking shelves in a Safeway store in Carmel. Yet he lived the life that other

American cyclists only dreamed about. "I was racing with Eddy Merckx," he said, adding he was unaware of what Americans thought of the famous Belgian.

He joined Lejeune's starting lineup for the 1977 Tour de France to support defending champion Van Impe—and a chance to make U.S. cycling history as the first to compete in the Tour since its introduction in 1903. Days before the Tour start, however, he fell on a training ride; injuries put him on the sidelines.

The next month he represented the USCF at the world pro road race championship in San Cristobal, Venezuela. His performance was impaired by an intestinal virus. It lingered for months. Boyer, six feet tall, dropped from a lean 150 pounds to an emaciated 125, accentuating his cheekbones and square jaw. His 1978 results were erratic. He missed getting picked for the Tour. He returned to Carmel for the first time in six years and competed in domestic races.

• • •

American cycling was emulating Europe. In Colorado the Red Zinger Classic had morphed into the nine-day Coors International Bicycle Classic, sponsored by the Coors Brewing Company. It was regarded as America's national tour and attracted teams from around the United States, Mexico, France, the Netherlands, Colombia, and Australia. Its route showcased ski resorts like Aspen and Vail. Fans lugged buckets of white paint and brushes to write the names of their favorites in big letters across the roads. The Coors Classic always concluded in a criterium in North Boulder Park, filled with a fervent crowd.

Boyer, back in Europe with French pro team Puch-Campagnolo-Sem, showed his return to health by placing twenty-fourth in June's Tour of Switzerland—including a top ten on the toughest mountain stage of almost eight hours over four peaks in the Swiss Alps. He returned to the U.S. as one of the favorites for the 1980 Coors Classic. Former USCF team member and winner of the 1977 Coors Classic Wayne Stetina praised Boyer's performance in the final stage, a sixty-nine mile circuit race in North Boulder Park, as one of Boyer's career best. Boyer had started the stage four minutes behind Colombia's Antonio Londoño.

"Jonathan and his teammates took off from the start and pulled right away," Stetina said. "They lapped the field three times. That moved Boyer into first to win the Coors Classic [by just nine seconds]. He was quite a character."

The Coors Classic added an American flair: the women's division. It was won by the world-champion-speed-skater-turned-cyclist Beth Heiden, grinning from the podium, her long hair braided in pigtails.

Boyer, his confidence restored, stayed at altitude to prepare for the upcoming world road championships, which were to take place at Sallanches, France, on the toughest course in worlds' history: twenty laps of a 14.4-kilometer (8.3-mile) circuit that included the 2.7-kilometer (1.7-mile) Domancy climb for a total of 4,600 meters (15,000 feet) of uphill. The course faced the majestic snow-covered Mont Blanc, the highest peak in the Alps. The Domancy hill was so steep that only 15 of the 107 starters in the pro road race managed to complete the twenty laps. Boyer, in his stars-and-stripes jersey, stayed in contention throughout the seven and half hours of racing to finish in a small group sprinting for third place. The solo winner was multi–Tour de France champion Bernard Hinault of France. Boyer finished an impressive fifth—the best since Joseph Magnani's seventh in 1947.

In the four-lap women's championship, Coors Classic winner Beth Heiden, a bronze medalist speed skater in the 1980 Lake Placid Winter Olympics, dashed to victory from the lead pack of four to become the second U.S. woman to claim the rainbow jersey as world road champion.

At the track worlds program in Besançon, Sue Novara dethroned three-time world sprint champion Galina Tsareva of the Soviet Union. Novara took home her second worlds gold—and her sixth consecutive worlds medal.

• • •

The world's fastest women on two wheels were Americans. Boyer was leading Greg LeMond, George Mount, and others to the sport's top echelon. And European cycling execs realized that Uncle Sam's cyclists had started to crash their domain.

The quickest to react was Cyrille Guimard, sports director of the French team Renault-Elf-Gitane. Its sponsors were the venerable

Renault Motor Company; Elf, the French oil company; and Gitane, the old French bicycle manufacturer—whose appellation translates as "a gypsy woman." Guimard was a retired pro. In a sport bound to tradition, he was an early advocate of converting his riders from wool jerseys and shorts to slicker Lycra outfits to reduce wind resistance. Other directors took their cues from him; and the entire peloton soon changed to Lycra.

Guimard's progressive approach and tactical brilliance contributed to his nickname, Napoléon. Impressed by Boyer's performance at the worlds, he signed the twenty-five-year-old American to a one-year contract for the next season on Renault-Elf-Gitane. Guimard also sought to recruit the amateur Greg LeMond, someone Boyer could guide like an older brother.

Pursuing LeMond set Guimard apart from other directors. LeMond lived six thousand miles away, in Nevada. The cost of transatlantic travel exceeded the salary he would offer the neo-pro, and the time involved to go out and come back bordered on recklessness. But Guimard saw the young American possessing the rare qualities of Eddy Merckx, now retired after a towering 525 victories, or Guimard's star of Renault-Elf-Gitane, Bernard Hinault.

The Napoléon of pro cycling was willing to bet that LeMond would win the Tour de France—and more than once. If that came to fruition, the American media would jet to France with a swarm of print, radio, and television newshounds toting cameras and microphones. The Fourth Estate would ask a barrage of questions to cover a topic about which they knew next to nothing. The costs of bringing LeMond onto the team would be negligible compared with the potential return.

• • •

LeMond, deprived of the chance to show his mettle in the Moscow Olympics, spent the summer competing in France and won often, notably the five-stage Circuit de la Sarthe. He also returned home to successfully defend his title at California's iconic Tour of Nevada City.

LeMond's stamina was widely regarded as astonishing. His sprint at the end of a road race stayed sharp and powerful as a boxer's knockout punch. He had a French-sounding name, approximating to Le Monde (the World), signifying his destiny—though the French pronounce his name as "Lemon." Off the bike, he was carefree, made friends easily.

LeMond raced with phenomenal intensity—as he exhibited when a squad of Soviet amateurs in solid red jerseys escaped from the front of a French race, the five-day Ruban Granitier Breton. LeMond chased alone, dangling in the no-man's-land between the red train and the peloton until one of his tires burst. He stopped, jumped off his bike, and yanked the useless wheel from the frame. He stood at the edge of the road and hoisted the wheel aloft to signal assistance from the USCF support car. He watched, helpless, as the peloton whooshed past, followed by the support caravan. Five minutes later, his support car came, the roof rack festooned with spare wheels and bicycles. Angry about waiting so long, he hoisted his bike overhead and smashed it against the vehicle.

Passion impressed Guimard. Now in his early thirties, he had won nearly a hundred road and track races in eight pro seasons. He achieved fame during the 1972 Tour de France for battling Eddy Merckx. Guimard wore the prized *maillot jaune*, "yellow jersey," as race leader, a point of pride for the French, tired of the Belgian ruling their national tour, on his way to winning it five times to tie Jacques Anquetil. But Guimard was straining his knees. Reports circulated that he had to be carried by two men to his bicycle to start daily stages. Pain in his knees caused him to lose the yellow jersey to the Belgian. He persisted in holding onto second place overall until two days from completing the three-week race when crippling pangs forced him to abandon.

Merckx in Paris on the winner's podium honored Guimard by giving him his green jersey for points awarded at designated sprint spots along the 2,500-mile route to keep the pace lively. The media voted Guimard as winner of the prized jersey for most combative rider. Even though he failed to pedal into Paris, he gave all he had—a moral victory.

Chronic knee agony contributed to Guimard retiring from competition. He embarked on a second career as team director. Hinault, friend and teammate, followed him to Renault-Elf-Gitane.

Hinault grew up on a farm in Brittany, in northwest France, near the English Channel, accustomed to working outdoors no matter the weather, the constant wind. As a young pro cyclist, he had overshot a bend on a descent in the Alps and fell into a ravine, buckling both wheels like potato chips. He climbed back onto the road, received another bike, pedaled away—and still won the stage. "Hinault had gone into that ravine as a rider," Dutch author Tim Krabbé wrote in his novel, *The Rider*, "but he came out a *vedette* [star], and the entire operation had lasted no more than fifteen seconds."

Victories in the 1978 and 1979 Tour de France and his 1980 Sallanches world road championship elevated him to one of Les Grands, "the Giants," of French cycling.

Pros raced without a helmet. Hinault favored a headband over his forehead to keep sweat from burning his eyes. The headband bulged up his dark hair, ruffling in the wind over his square face like a badger shaving brush. He was nicknamed le Blaireau, "the Badger," and he pedaled with the ferocity of a cornered badger, as though he turned the earth beneath his tires, his back flat enough to support a tray of wine glasses filled to the brim.

At the end of the summer, Guimard and Hinault flew to America to recruit LeMond.

• • •

Gregory James LeMond lived on the outskirts of Carson City, between Reno and Lake Tahoe, at 4,500 feet elevation in Nevada's high desert that leads to the Sierra Nevada mountain range. In 1975, he was fourteen when he saw his first bike race when one passed by his house. The circuit for the Northern California district championship—which includes Nevada—contained the country two-lane Franktown Road, home to the LeMond family. Greg and his father, Bob, stood on the front lawn of their two-story house and watched.

A few weeks later, father and son read in the local newspaper that riders selected for the U.S. cycling team to compete in the Pan American Games were entered in a program of races in Carson City. One event headed into the Sierra Nevada and climbed to the Mount Rose ski resort, at 8,260 feet elevation.

The peloton of about fifty riders pedaled out of Carson City into the country. Bob LeMond drove his white Dodge van with Greg in the passenger seat to watch. They saw John Howard and George Mount break away on the first big hill. Bob drove behind the breakaway.

"My dad couldn't keep up with Howard and Mount down the descents," Greg recalled in our interview, noting the country roads twisted like coils. "They passed us, and we would try to stay with them. But my dad wasn't used to the speed they went. They were hitting 60 mph. That was the first time I saw all-out racing. After watching John Howard and George Mount riding all out up and down the mountains, I wanted to be a bike racer."

Father and son bought new bikes and raced to strengthen their legs. Bob, thirty-eight, bypassed veterans' events (over thirty-five) for open-division competition and progressed from entry-level Category IV to elite Category I. He raced everything he could drive to and competed in the Red Zinger Classic, the stage race in Colorado that evolved into the Coors Classic.

Racing captured Greg's imagination. He drew notice right away in the cycling community for the commanding way he won junior races.

Ever since Greg could remember he heard stories over the dinner table from his great-grandmother Nellie Mae, a native of Newark, about an uncle who trained cyclists on the Newark Velodrome. Arthur LeMond, Greg's grandfather, told me when he was in his late seventies that he used to go often to the velodrome with his mother to watch races.

"My uncle [Fred] Bullivant took care of the riders and their bikes. That was how he made his living," recalled Arthur LeMond. "I remember hearing about the big names of the sport, like Frank Kramer."

Bullivant earned respect on the six-day circuit as a crackerjack trainer. He coached a half-dozen national champions, including Donald McDougall, twice national champion, who won the 1912 world amateur sprint championship on the Newark Velodrome. The trainer's son Cliff Bullivant came of age competing on the Nutley Velodrome and turned pro in the late 1930s to race sixes.

Arthur LeMond had the bluest of blue eyes, a gene he passed to son, Bob, and grandson Greg, along with a deeply furrowed forehead, which Greg acquired when he filled out in his forties. It took me a while to relax during my interview with the elder LeMond. The way he held his head and shoulders, raised his eyebrows in conversation, and walked like his grandson reminded me of Victorian authors referring to offspring as "copies."

Arthur worked retail sales in New York, on Manhattan's East Side, for Armour & Company, a leader in the meatpacking industry, to support his wife, Edna, their son, Bob, and three daughters. In 1947 Arthur was transferred across the country to Southern California. He moved his family to Long Beach, where Bob LeMond grew up.

Guimard and Hinault flew to Carson City and signed up LeMond for the Renault-Elf-Gitane team. Then they climbed aboard a jet to New York City to announce that LeMond would be riding for the French team. Guimard arrived in New York wearing a bolo shoestring tie with a turquoise ornamental clasp, the kind sold in the Las Vegas airport gift shop, and blue jeans held up with a big buckle suitable for rodeo.

LeMond spoke no French; the Frenchmen knew only a smattering of English. Corporate suits at Gitane's headquarters in eastern France hired its U.S. importer, Mel Pinto, as translator. "We spent a few days together in New York, dealing with the press, dining in fine restaurants," said Pinto, a dapper dresser, thick hair swept back. Reared in Casablanca, Morocco, he spoke four languages, including French and English. He lived in Arlington, Virginia, across the Potomac River from Washington DC. Pinto was one of the biggest Gitane importers in America and a leading importer of cycle-racing clothes and bicycle components. "Greg LeMond still looked like a boy, with long curly hair."

Bernard Hinault expressed his unabashed faith in LeMond. He told reporters, "Greg will be the next champion after me."

• • •

George Mount turned pro in Italy after President Carter's Olympics boycott. Mount entered the cash ranks on the San Giacomo–Benotto squadra, sponsored by home furnishings company San Giacomo and Giacinto Benotto, a craftsman manufacturing bicycles. Belgian's flamboyant ace Freddy Maertens, renowned for winning fifty races in a season and two world road championships, was on the twenty-rider team in 1980. “For me, it was a real treat as he had a wonderful personality and was a great champion,” Mount recalled.

The American gained respect for helping the team leader, cycling’s equivalent to an NFL quarterback, and the designated sprinter. “I was called l’Americano,” Mount said. “Heck, I have a picture somewhere where that was painted on the road.”

In April 1981, when the team’s title sponsor had changed to Sammontana, an ice cream producer, he rode to support team leader Roberto Visentini’s victory in the Giro del Trentino, a four-day battle in mountainous northern Italy. It served as a tune-up for Italy’s three-week grand tour, the Giro d’Italia, in May. Italy’s Giro ranks second in prestige to the Tour de France.

Visentini’s triumph assured Mount’s place on the team to ride the Giro d’Italia. Mount had reached big-time Italian cycling, as remarkable as it would be for an Italian to go to America and play for the Boston Red Sox. His role was to keep Visentini and designated sprinter Moreno Argentin in the action. That meant chasing down breakaways with teammates to protect Visentini’s overall daily standing and, especially, sheltering the leader from the wind—every exposure to the wind blunts a little physical energy and shaves speed. Mount had the same duties for the squad’s designated sprinter, former national track champion Argentin, to win stages—essential to publicize their team sponsors.

“I was close in size to both of them, so they could take my bike when they crashed and needed a replacement right away,” Mount said. “I often gave my wheel, and food, to Roberto. Then I had to wait for the team car. All in a day’s work.”

Visentini completed the Giro sixth overall; Argentin won two stages. Mount wound up a respectable twenty-fifth—third best of his team and the first U.S. rider to complete Italy’s grand tour (Joseph Magnani in 1946 crashed out). “While I got no coverage in the United States, it was pretty extensive in Italy, with interviews in *Gazzetta dello Sport* and other Italian journals.”

• • •

The next month, Jonathan Boyer broke into the Tour de France peloton. His debut on the ten-member Renault-Elf-Gitane team was so special that Tour organizers suggested he wear a red-white-and-blue jersey with stars rather than his trade team's yellow-black-and-white colors so onlookers could spot him in the peloton.

The Tour de France debuted in July 1903 as a desperate, backs-against-the-wall, Hail Mary pass to keep the money-losing Paris sports newspaper, *L'Auto*, from failing and throwing its staff onto the street. *L'Auto*, published on yellow newsprint to stand out from other journals in kiosks, challenged riders to compete over three weeks around the inside circumference of France, shaped like an irregular hexagon. Le Tour started and finished in Paris.

L'Auto devoted oceans of ink to promoting and covering the inaugural contest on one-speed bikes and published a map of France for readers to follow progress. *L'Auto*'s circulation soared. Ad revenue jumped. The next July, Le Tour continued, and has ever since. *L'Auto* continues today as *L'Équipe*.

The Great War (renamed World War I) cancelled Le Tour between 1915 and 1918. France and its economy suffered massive destruction—including the slaughter of 1.5 million troops. Le Tour resumed in 1919. Until then, the leader in overall standings wore his regular team jersey. It's said that inspiration struck *L'Auto* editor and race director Henri Desgrange during a stage at the end of the first week. He realized the crowds standing roadside couldn't spot the leader in the peloton. He cabled *L'Auto*'s Paris office and ordered some *maillots jaunes* (yellow jerseys), matching the paper's newsprint. It took a week before they were made and sent to his hotel in Grenoble.

Before starting stage 11 in Grenoble, Desgrange handed out the first *maillot jaune* to the overall leader, Eugène Christophe, a Paris locksmith turned cyclist and winner of a few stages. Christophe subsequently surrendered the lead to another rider, who pushed his arms into his own *maillot jaune*. Christophe, third overall in Paris, gained immortality as the first to wear the *maillot jaune*.

Today the Tour draws an estimated fourteen million roadside spectators, a majority of them waiting for hours to watch the peloton sweep past like a sparkling meteor. About a thousand vehicles—a mobile caravan almost ten miles long including journalists, visiting dignitaries, and support vehicles for the riders—accompany the race.

So strong was Le Tour's hold on the French that in 1960 *New York Herald-Tribune* syndicated sports columnist Red Smith explained: "There is a saying here that an army from Mars could invade France, that the government could fall, and even the recipe for sauce béarnaise could be lost, but if it happened during the Tour de France, nobody would notice."

Smith was intrigued by the throngs standing for hours on roads to see the peloton whiz past in less than a minute. He captured the essence of Tour fever on the Col de Perty, a long climb in the Alps near Gap, "a barren knob not close to anything or anybody, yet it looked like the bleachers in Yankee Stadium on a good day with the White Sox."

Boyer, scarcely known in the United States, was well established in France. The French press called him Jacques (translated to "Jock" in America) or, sometimes, Le Cowboy. His role, like Mount's in the Giro, was dedicated to support the team leader, a job the French call *domestique*, essentially a drone in the team's beehive. Boyer's personal best stage performance was ninth on the longest day, 165 miles.

After three weeks of pedaling on roads winding around France and into adjoining Switzerland and Belgium, Boyer on the final day tucked inside the peloton charging up the Champs-Élysées in Paris for the finish line near the Arc de Triomphe. He completed the event in a respectable thirty-second-place. Boyer had fulfilled his duties in helping team leader Hinault win his third Tour, elevating the Frenchman to one of cycling's greats.

• • •

LeMond was still nineteen in May 1981 when he recorded his first pro victory—the sixty-five-mile stage of the Tour de l'Oise in France. He had earned his bona fides in the pro peloton.

Team director Guimard had a different philosophy than his counterparts, tradition-bound to keep pros racing from February through October. He put LeMond on a light racing schedule in his first year as a pro. When Boyer rode the Tour de France, LeMond left with a team to compete against a tough Soviet squad at the Coors Classic in Colorado. The nine-stage event culminated in a showdown between LeMond and the Soviets, with LeMond triumphing.

• • •

At summer's end, LeMond and Boyer went to the worlds in Prague, Czechoslovakia, for the pro road race. Mount joined them, making three American pros in the peloton. Mount, LeMond, and Boyer rode the rolling 175-mile road race but finished together in the main peloton in forty-sixth, forty-seventh, and forty-eighth places respectively.

They were upstaged at the worlds by Sheila Young-Ochowicz. Back in 1976 after winning the world sprint championship in Italy, she married two-time Olympic cyclist Jim Ochowicz and retired from competition. Later she gave birth to a daughter, Kate.

When Kate began nursery school, the athlete in Young-Ochowicz hungered for a new challenge. She got back into shape and won the 1981 national women's sprint championship. Sheila Young-Ochowicz made headlines at the worlds in Brno, Czechoslovakia, by winning her third gold medal in the women's match race.

The next year on the velodrome at the worlds in Leicester, England, Young-Ochowicz faced her Michigan clubmate and future sister-in-law Connie Paraskevin in the match-sprint final. The family battle ended with Paraskevin defeating Young-Ochowicz and embarking on a three-year winning streak. The track pursuit final was also an all-American affair, with the favored Connie Carpenter being upstaged by newcomer Rebecca Twigg. These two gifted athletes were preparing for the introduction of women's racing at the 1984 Olympic Games.

• • •

The Olympics were still strictly for amateurs, the branch of the sport in America overseen by the U.S. Cycling Federation. There were still no fully professional races in the country, but when amateurs turned professional to race abroad, they had to apply for an international license from the Professional Racing Organization of America (PRO). That was the case with Jack Simes III, who said, "When I went to Europe in December 1969, four days after I got out of the army, I got my U.S. PRO license from Chris van Ghent in January 1970."

Van Ghent had immigrated from the Netherlands in 1948 to ride the sixes in Washington and New York. He settled in Denver and opened a bike shop. In the mid-1960s, after the National Cycling Association went defunct following the 1961 Madison Square Garden six-day fiasco, Van Ghent founded PRO as a nonprofit. "Van Ghent paid affiliation dues to the UCI for years," Simes said. "He saw U.S. PRO as the beacon of light into the future—he knew pro cycling would come back."

That comeback began in 1976, after *Bicycling* magazine owner Bob Rodale financed construction of a velodrome at Trexlertown, Pennsylvania. On being asked to be the track director, Simes contacted the just-retired Dave Chauner; they formed a company, Omni-Sports, to promote racing at the velodrome. To include international pro races, they needed approval from the governing body. This resulted in Omni-Sports acquiring PRO from Van Ghent, with Simes as its new executive director.

At the same time, an Italian American, Fred Mengoni, was helping the sport develop in New York City. Mengoni had raced in his native Italy during the frugal postwar years. Short in stature suitable for a climber, he kept trim when he left racing for a career in business. He profited from selling musical instruments and cars before immigrating in the late 1950s to Manhattan, where he earned a fortune in real estate. In 1979 he spotted Greg LeMond racing around Central Park and recognized talent worthy of investment. The two became friends and Mengoni funded a team, Gruppo Sportivo Mengoni, hiring Butch Martin as the coach. Mengoni often wrote checks to pay travel expenses for LeMond and other North American racers.

• • •

After LeMond turned pro with Renault-Gitane, there were expectations that he and new teammate Jonathan Boyer would form a firm connection. Instead, they drifted apart. Although Boyer was the first American to ride the Tour de France with Renault, in 1982, he signed for another French team, Sem-France-Loire, with fellow American John Eustice to ride for the team's Irish star Sean Kelly.

Boyer's season included placing eighteenth at the grueling cobblestone classic Paris–Roubaix and an improved twenty-third at the Tour. After getting podium finishes at three European stage races, including a stage win at Italy's Tirreno–Adriatico, LeMond was slated to lead the Renault team at the Tour de l'Avenir—considered the young riders' Tour de France—that he would start right after the world championships in Great Britain.

A nine-man U.S. team was named by PRO for the road race at southeast England's Goodwood. Only six showed up because riders had to pay their own way. No one expected LeMond and Boyer to race as true teammates. Boyer could rely on Eustice, while LeMond was aligned with Italian-based George Mount and U.S.-based David Mayer-Oakes and Eric Heiden (testing himself in pro cycling after his 1980 Olympic gold-medal rampage in speed skating).

On the last of eighteen laps of the rolling 9.5-mile circuit, with more than six hours of racing in their legs, only 35 of the 136 starters remained as contenders. The fast pace was set by six Italians preparing the ground for their sprinter Giuseppe Saronni on the uphill finish. LeMond and Boyer were still there, while Kelly had support from Irish teammate Stephen Roche. With about two kilometers remaining, Spain's Marino Lejarreta sped away from the peloton. Boyer raced after him, accelerated past as the finishing climb began, and established a lead of about seventy-five yards.

This was new: an American attacking in the finale of the world pro championship. But the best racers in the world were just behind. Unfortunately, from a U.S. angle, it was LeMond who chased after Boyer on the hill's steepest grades. He was towing a handful of others, including Saronni, whose fresher legs helped him burst clear with 300 yards remaining to take the title, followed by LeMond in second, and Kelly third.

As the Americans celebrated their first-ever pro worlds medal, Boyer was almost in tears as he crossed the line in tenth place, feeling he'd been betrayed by his young "teammate." Boyer's fans, in the belief that he could have won, stirred up a considerable controversy in the following days. They couldn't change the result, but their passion showed that American pros were truly breaking in to the European hierarchy.

• • •

Despite LeMond's silver medal and his subsequent domination of the Tour de l'Avenir in the French Alps (he won three of the twelve stages and took the final victory by ten minutes over the runner-up, Robert Millar of Scotland), American pro cycling was facing a crisis in the summer of 1983 when all international governing bodies were required to select riders for the worlds. The U.S. Cycling Federation in Colorado Springs picked amateur track and road entrants and arranged their travel and accommodations. Simes, who was running PRO out of his house in New Tripoli, Pennsylvania, had no income to send LeMond, Boyer, and four others to the UCI's pro road race in Altenrhein, Switzerland.

"Just when I needed it, the phone rang," Simes recalled. "Fred [Mengoni] was calling to ask what he could do to help. That really got us over the hump. He helped financially with accommodations and paying expenses of riders to the worlds. Fred stepped forward when no one else would. He saw the light at the end of the tunnel for pro cycling, [which] hadn't been accepted in this country. It was like an orphan sport, and Fred said, 'Let me help.'"

Mengoni became president of the rebranded USPRO, as American pro cycling's *patron*, one who provides. When I asked him what motivated his generous commitment, he replied in an accent blending Italy and Manhattan: "I like to give something back to the country that has been so good to me." Friends described him as demanding and temperamental, but loyal to those who appreciated his help.

Mengoni was in the U.S. contingent that traveled to the Swiss worlds, hoping that LeMond could go one better than his silver twelve months earlier. Still only twenty-two, LeMond had grown in stature with fourth place in the Tour of Switzerland and overall victory at the prestigious, weeklong Dauphiné-Libéré. He knew he wouldn't get any help from Boyer, while his other teammates had dropped out by halfway through the eighteen-lap, 270-kilometer (167.5-mile) race. He just had moral support from his Australian friend Phil Anderson, who took some pressure off of LeMond by making it into two long breakaways.

Just 46 of the 117 starters were left when LeMond's wiry Tour de l'Avenir rival, Robert Millar, attacked up the longest hill with two and a half laps (about twenty-four miles) to go. LeMond immediately counterattacked. Out of the saddle and dancing powerfully on his pedals up the grade, he escaped. Only Italy's Moreno Argentin and Spain's Faustino Ruperez could catch him.

The one hundred thousand paying spectators packing the course applauded and cheered as LeMond kept charging. Behind the trio, the Italian team in azure-blue jerseys sought to protect Argentin in the breakaway by riding interference with the chasers. With two laps to go, the gap was almost a half minute. Then, on the steep hill where the breakaway had sprung, Argentin suddenly faded, taking with him Italy's chance of winning. The crowd went wild seeing that the rest of the Italian team—without the radio communications available today—continued to stall the peloton and protect their rider—but he was no longer in the breakaway. Only when the pack overtook Argentin did the Italian squadra realize LeMond's strategy, too late for a successful chase.

LeMond maintained a blistering tempo and on the shorter climb starting the final lap, with about seven miles left, he dropped the Spaniard. For the first time, the red-white-and-blue U.S. jersey was clear, alone, in the sport's most grueling pro road race. LeMond's brilliant tactics and skillful execution appealed to savvy spectators as he pedaled the race's fastest lap to win by more than a minute.

When he crossed the finish line, thousands of people jumped over barricades, ignored police blowing whistles and waving hands to hold the crowd back, and swarmed all over the road. Four chasers sprinting for second place, closely followed by the thirty-strong pack, rushed headlong toward a wall of humanity. Several riders crashed into the mob. LeMond's mom, Bertha, was almost flattened. After Greg emerged from the melee to mount the podium, his dad, Bob, said, "Now I know what it's like to be a rock star."

So, at the end of seven hours of racing, America, in the figure of Greg LeMond, reigned supreme at the worlds.

17

The Drought Finally Ends

I love racing. Your mind is so tuned in.
Your senses seem to be enhanced.
—PATTY PEOPLES

The 1984 Los Angeles Olympics opened with the first-ever women's cycling event—a fifty-mile road race. Many of the forty-five entrants from sixteen countries were national champions and worlds medalists. Under a searing July sun and over a hilly and arduous 9.9-mile course in suburban Mission Viejo, the race for medals turned highly tactical. On the fifth and final lap, two U.S. riders—Connie Carpenter and Rebecca Twigg—had broken away with four others representing West Germany, France, Norway, and Italy.

An estimated two hundred thousand enthusiastic spectators lined the route. In the crowd was Victor Fraysse, seventy-two, and his adult son Mike. "My father finally made it to the LA Olympics, just fifty-two years after when he might have been on the cycling team," Mike Fraysse said. "My father wanted to buy one of the souvenir T-shirts, but they were selling for twenty dollars. He remembered when he couldn't afford to go to the 1932 Olympic cycling trials because he would have to leave his nine-dollars-a-week job at Hornblower & Weeks on Wall Street during the Depression. He refused to pay twenty dollars for a T-shirt."

The unrestrained audience created a solid wall of shouting and clapping that followed the cyclists like a soundtrack. The odds against both Americans winning medals seemed immense. Their expected strategy called for one to pace her teammate through the final stretch to ensure a podium result rather than each trying independently, only to bungle and come up empty. Taking home a medal would finally relieve the drought in U.S. Olympic cycling going back to 1912.

The media had picked Carpenter as a pre-race favorite. She and her husband, Davis Phinney, winner of so many races with his flamboyant, muscular sprint that he picked up the nickname Cash Register, were subjected to high expectations. The couple was besieged at their home in Boulder, Colorado, for interview requests, especially Carpenter.

Now twenty-seven, she had twelve years of competing internationally. At fourteen, she speed skated in the 1972 Winter Olympics in Sapporo, Japan, finishing seventh in the 1,500-meter event. In 1976, she won the women's national outdoor title at that distance. While training for the Olympic trials, however, she injured an ankle. A friend in her native Madison, Wisconsin, suggested she try cycling, which she immediately enjoyed.

In her first season of racing bicycles Carpenter scored two national titles—the road race and, on the track, the 3,000-meter pursuit. She emerged as queen of American women's racing in 1977. She capped the season with a silver medal at the worlds road race in Venezuela.

Early in the 1978 season, she fell heavily. She was rushed to the hospital emergency room for stitches to close a cut to her scalp and was treated for concussion. She quit cycling to resume studies at the University of California, Berkeley. There she rowed on the crew team. Five feet ten and 130 pounds, Carpenter was well proportioned to row; her long torso and arms gave her extra reach for powerful strokes. She earned a seat on the UC Berkeley women's varsity shell her first year. In 1980 she rowed on the coxed-four shell to victory in the women's national collegiate championships in Oak Ridge, Tennessee.

Carpenter might have stayed away from cycling forever if she hadn't met her future husband, Davis Phinney, from Boulder. His outgoing personality lit up any room he entered; she preferred to avoid attention. Phinney was unabashed about admiring her talents. When he first heard that the International Olympic Committee announced women's cycling would debut in a road race at the LA Games, he encouraged her to resume cycling and aim for the Olympics.

Corporate sponsorships had greatly improved by 1981, the year she graduated with a degree in physical education. She rode for Puch bicycles, imported from Austria for the U.S. market. Puch provided a stipend to help meet living expenses, crucial because upper-level racing imposes traveling for up to two hundred days between February and September.

The next year a new star cropped up: Rebecca Twigg of Seattle. Shorter than Carpenter by three inches, lighter by five pounds, and younger by six years, Twigg developed as the only woman capable of beating Carpenter. Twigg had streaked through grade school as spectacularly precocious; upon completing the eighth grade, she enrolled at fourteen in the University of Washington to study biology. She also became intrigued in cycling on the Marymoor Velodrome in Redmond. Twigg won the 1982 national road race as well as the pursuit title. At the 1982 worlds in Leicester, England, Twigg and Carpenter battled in the pursuit final. Twigg defeated Carpenter for the gold medal.

Twigg suspended college to prepare full-time for the Olympics. She moved to the Olympic Training Center in Colorado Springs and became a resident under coaching director Eddie B. To focus on road racing, she skipped defending her pursuit title at the 1983 track worlds in Zürich, Switzerland.

Carpenter, on the U.S. Cycling Federation team headed by Eddie B., flew to Zürich to compete in the pursuit. Her two previous silver medals in the worlds gnawed at her. She had claimed twelve national titles, but they were junior varsity compared with the worlds. Winning is everything. Winners get their names written in record books for posterity. Second-placers are forgotten like the names of Einstein's children. The difference between first and second depends on who thinks most clearly under duress.

She had never spent much time with Eddie B. One day at the Zürich velodrome he gave her his full attention. Carpenter spoke to me about his advice. She learned more from him in fifty minutes than over the last twelve years combined, mostly about self-confidence. She won the 1983 world pursuit title.

Grateful about what he instilled in her, she soon invited Eddie to lunch and gave him a gold watch. (In 2016, when they met again at the USA Olympian Reunion in Las Vegas, he was still wearing the watch.)

Carpenter catapulted to an international favorite for the inaugural women's Olympics road race. Print and television newshounds pestered her for interviews. Photographers wouldn't let her out of their lens.

"Davis and I kept a low profile when we weren't racing," she said. "We focused on our training regimen. Kept our focus. Took it one day at a time."

The Olympics road race course wending through Mission Viejo, fifty miles southeast of downtown Los Angeles, turned into a big party scene. Hundreds of people had set up camps the day before and held overnight barbecue parties to keep their places to watch. On race day, hundreds climbed up trees for a better view. Some shimmied up street-lights. Groups waved American flags and chanted "U! S! A! U! S! A!"

Rubberneckers recognized Carpenter's angular face, her leather helmet hiding long, curly, strawberry-blonde hair, and Twigg's cherubic visage from a cascade of newspaper and magazine articles. Fans shouted their names.

"It definitely made a big difference," Carpenter pointed out. "What made the Olympics special was that a number of us had raced in the world championships several times where the support wasn't there, so we appreciated the support in the Olympics."

The pack of fifteen trailing the breakaway on the final lap included two teammates of Carpenter and Twigg. They dutifully chased down attempts by others to charge away and bridge the gap to the leaders. Occasionally the teammates went to the front and held the pace in check.

On the final lap, Carpenter and Twigg looked confident. Their movements were sure and smooth. Now and then they reached a hand down to pull a water bottle from the bicycle frame to drink and keep hydrated from a little more than two hours of sustained exertion. Five weeks earlier at the Olympic trials, Twigg had won the road race to show she had the edge. Since then, Carpenter focused to hone her sprint. Husband Davis Phinney taught her to approach the finish by rising up off her saddle and straightening her arms to throw her bike forward—a cyclist's spurt for the line the way a runner leans at the tape.

After scaling the last steep slope, up a road named Vista del Lago, and plunging down the other side, the six leaders eyed one another like cardsharps. Over the final mile, thousands along the route and tens of millions watching the television broadcast—many seeing cycling for the first time—were wondering whether Carpenter or Twigg would capture a medal.

With 500 yards left, Maria Canins of Italy popped off her saddle, heaved her body over the pedals, and surged into the lead on the blacktop. She was too far from the finish to sustain her effort, but the gap she opened forced others to chase. Sandra Schumacher of Germany caught Canins and dashed ahead.

In the last 200 yards, Carpenter and Twigg boiled past Schumacher. Twigg rushed into the lead. Carpenter caught her slipstream. With each quick pedal stroke carrying her closer to the gold medal, Twigg rode with poise, legs churning faster and faster, almost blurring.

In the final fifty yards the thought flitted into Carpenter's mind that she was losing. She had planned to retire on the awards podium. The realization that time was running out roused her to accelerate and move up on Twigg's right. Three yards before the line, Twigg was leading. Both women grimaced and dug deeper than ever.

A few lengths behind, Schumacher held off Canins and a Norwegian.

One yard from the grandstand finish, where flags representing dozens of countries fluttered in the breeze and the crowd was screaming, Carpenter drew even with Twigg and executed her bike-throw. She squeezed her eyes shut. Then opened them. She shot a glance at Twigg to her left. As they coasted, breathless, past the finish, they veered closer together. Carpenter leaned over and kissed Twigg on the cheek. They overcame the odds and grabbed the top two medals.

The judges had to examine photos. Officials ruled Carpenter the winner by the width of a tire.

Nobody could take anything away from the American victory, even though the Communist countries boycotted the LA Olympics in retaliation for President Carter's boycott of the Moscow Games. Los Angeles boasted 7,800 athletes from a record 140 countries. The women's cycling race was fundamentally unaffected by the boycott: Eastern-bloc countries did not excel in women's road races the way they did in track cycling or track and field.

On the steamy late morning of July 29 in Los Angeles, women pedaled into the Olympics and pulled the United States out of cycling medal poverty. Carpenter made U.S. cycling history by scoring the first gold medal in the LA Olympics. She stood on the podium, one step higher than Twigg and Schumacher. All three bowed heads, one at a time, for an official to drape an Olympic medal on a ribbon over her head. They held heads high as the American national anthem played.

Carpenter stepped down and strode purposefully to the start-finish line where her husband and his team were staging among 135 men representing forty-three nations for the start of the 119-mile road race.

She held her gold medal to her chin. "Here's what it looks like, boys. It's your turn to win yours."

• • •

Less than 7 miles remained in the men's 118-mile road race when the leader, Alexi Grewal of Aspen, Colorado, seemed shattered. Six miles earlier he had burst courageously from the breakaway of seven, including Phinney, and forged a twenty-four-second margin, pedaling strongly like a sure winner. Now, however, after 111 miles of racing under a burning sun, his energy flagged. When he hit the steep pitch of Vista del Lago, the last major climb, ascending 920 feet above sea level, he looked exhausted. The gangly six-foot-two, twenty-three-year-old who had earned his reputation by riding fast up the Rocky Mountains was so fatigued that he had to zig and zag across the width of the road, inching his way a little higher, as though he chopped the hill into bite-sized pieces.

His solo gamble for a gold medal appeared all but over. If Grewal could reach the summit before the other six, he had a chance to recover on the descent and hammer to the finish. Yet cheering for Grewal from spectators lining both sides of the road seemed pathetic. Guts and determination he had in abundance. But he appeared to have spent his energy too soon, just as he had at the amateur worlds road race the previous September, where he ended up fourteenth.

From behind came Canadian Steve Bauer. In his light-blue jersey with the red maple leaf across his chest and back, Bauer caught Grewal on the second half of the hill and whipped past. Grewal panicked but regained his composure in time to take advantage of Bauer's rear wheel and draft. That reduced wind resistance, but didn't make the hill any less steep. Yet every turn of the pedals that Grewal took with the seemingly fresh Canadian meant their pursuers were held at bay that much longer. Grewal still had a chance for a medal.

Still out of sight but moving quickly to catch up were the five chasers; behind them lurked the peloton of fifty, whittled down from the original 135 starters.

Bauer pulled Grewal over the crest. They dropped down the other side like a waterfall. Bauer, from Fenton, Ontario, was renowned for his explosive finishing kick. He appeared headed for Canada's first cycling medal. The blond, chesty Bauer won many pack sprints, but occasionally lost. Two years earlier, he was beaten at the finish of the Commonwealth Games road race in Australia.

Grewal, the son of a Sikh father from India and a British mother, was a naturalized U.S. citizen. He was one of the most flamboyant yet temperamental cyclists. The year before, he had led all alone the last miles of a grueling ninety-two-mile race in Colorado's Rocky Mountains. Approaching the finish, he jammed his brakes to halt in front of the line, stopped, dismounted, and shouldered his bike so he could step casually over the line. Then he collapsed to the ground with leg cramps. Once on a European tour with the U.S. Cycling Federation team, he quit and flew home.

Until just days before the Olympics, nobody was sure he would compete. He had been leading the Coors Classic stage race a few weeks earlier when he tested positive for traces of ephedrine, an alkaloid found in many over-the-counter cold remedies as well as in Dr Pepper and some herbal teas. The USCF slapped him with a thirty-day suspension, which included the Olympics. Less than a week before the Olympic torch was lit, the test was ruled to have been administered improperly and he was reinstated. His chances restored, a grateful and stoked-up Grewal vowed to win the Olympic gold medal.

Now late-afternoon inky-black shadows lengthened over the final mile. Bauer steadily increased the pace as Grewal surfed behind. At one point, both looked over their shoulders—not at each other but to check their margin. Two Norwegians from the breakaway were closing in.

With 300 yards to go, Grewal and Bauer were far enough ahead so that after almost five hours of racing they had a match sprint. Bauer had beaten Grewal in the past. One hundred yards from the finish, the Canadian jumped away. Grewal drafted snugly as Bauer pedaled faster, harder, his level back unmoving without betraying the intensity of his effort. Fifty yards from the line, Grewal stood off his saddle to unleash everything he had. Bauer dug down and pedaled harder. But Grewal out-accelerated him as the gradient tipped upward and flew past to win by a wheel.

Grewal's victory was stunning. Here was a second gold for the United States on opening day of the Olympics.

Twenty-one seconds later, Norwegian Dag Otto Lauritzen claimed the bronze medal. Phinney was the next U.S. rider in, taking fifth place.

A week later, Phinney doubled in the four-man 100-kilometer team time trial on what was called the most lackluster venue in the Olympics—back and forth on a 15.5-mile slab of concrete called the Artesia Freeway. With Ron Kiefel, Roy Knickman, and Andrew Weaver, Phinney helped power the U.S. team to take home the bronze medal. They finished behind the Italian and Swiss teams, and ahead of stalwarts such as the Netherlands, Sweden, France, Denmark, and Great Britain.

Olympic track racing on the outdoor velodrome at Dominguez Hills yielded other successes. The match sprints turned into an all-American final of Mark Gorski, a graduate of the University of Michigan, versus Nelson Vails, a former New York City bike messenger, with Gorski winning the gold.

Former downhill ski champion Steve Hegg, an obscure contestant in the lung-bursting 4,000-meter individual pursuit, stunned his thirty-two opponents to claim another gold medal.

At the conclusion of the Games, U.S. cyclists took home nine medals—including four golds. The seventy-two-year dry spell finally was over. American riders asserted themselves among European countries that had long dominated.

• • •

While American cyclists took turns stepping onto the Olympic awards podium, another woman continued to lead the men to the top of the sport in Europe. Just as Audrey McElmury was the first to wear the rainbow jersey and Connie Carpenter the first to win an Olympic gold medal, Marianne Martin of Boulder became the first to wear the *maillot jaune*.

In 1984 Tour organizers introduced the inaugural edition for women, the Tour de France Féminin. The United States nearly went unrepresented. The U.S. Cycling Federation announced it declined to send a team because its best women cyclists were participating in the Olympics, which began a week after the Tour de France concluded. The North Jersey Women's Bicycle Club organized a six-rider team for the Tour de France Féminin. Its members wore jerseys supplied by a French company because they could not wear USCF jerseys, and Peugeot Cycles of France supplied bicycles. Team selection was determined only two weeks before the riders boarded an Air France jet. The last picked was Marianne Martin.

"I begged and pleaded to get on the team," she said. "I hadn't been riding all that well in February and March. I was over-trained and anemic. It was April before I could really train to turn my condition around. I got back into form in early June. I knew I was a good climber. I really do like to climb. I just made it on the team."

Martin joined five compatriots for the rolling start of the eighteen-stage race against teams from the Netherlands, Great Britain, Canada, and two squads from France. Women raced the last thirty-five to fifty miles of the men's stages, ending two hours before the nearly two hundred men charged in as the main attraction.

From the start near Paris, Dutch women ruled the Tour de France Féminin's early flat stages, marked by pack sprints. Martin stayed in the peloton to record the same time as the stage winners.

Teammate Betsy King rode as the designated leader. She'd moved from Farmington, Connecticut, to France four years earlier and joined the Paris amateur club, Antony Berny Cycliste. A month before the women's Tour began, King gained acclaim as the first woman to complete the 560-kilometer (350-mile) Bordeaux–Paris, a strenuous one-day grind from Bordeaux, in France's wine region, to Paris. Bordeaux–Paris had been held annually since 1891—a classic for pros. She started two hours before the men and completed the course an hour after the last man had finished. The *New York Times* praised her for blazing a first for women and called her eighteen-hour effort "a great triumph."

After the Tour Féminin race got underway, Martin found she was ignored by teammates when they planned each morning's strategy. Four stages into the event, she felt like abandoning. But she was encouraged to continue by Patty Peoples of Silver Spring, Maryland. "Racing the Tour was like living a fantasy," Peoples told me. "Everybody gave us a lot of support. People gave us sponges. They gave us water. It really increased our morale."

Martin raced into shape. By the time they reached the Alps at the end of the second week, she was strong, unlike King, still fatigued from her Bordeaux–Paris slog—a distance equivalent to thirteen consecutive Boston Marathons.

The fourteenth stage went only twenty miles but climbed nearly a mile in altitude to La Plagne, a tony ski resort. Martin smiles so sweetly she could do television weather reports. Her wholesomeness distracts from powerful yet slim arms developed as a white-water rafting guide in the Colorado Rockies.

On the ascent to La Plagne, she rode off the front and won by nearly four minutes, a decisive victory that thrust her into first place overall. Martin became the first U.S. rider to win a Tour stage and to pull on the *maillot jaune*. (Greg LeMond, riding his first Tour that year, won the white jersey, the *maillot blanc*, as top rookie, finishing third overall.)

Peoples called the three days of riding in the French Alps, up and down steep mountains, her hardest experience. "We would climb for an hour, an hour and a half—all at once. The descents were scary. We would go 60 mph down gnarly, narrow roads. I would rather climb than go down the descents."

She and her teammates supported Martin. They took over the team competition, based on each squad's total elapsed time. The Dutch team attacked repeatedly in attempts to displace Martin as race leader. Dutch team leader Heleen Hage and her teammates won fifteen of the eighteen stages over the 620 miles and twenty-two days. The Americans reeled in all breakaway attempts and defended Martin's *maillot jaune*.

The final stage was fifty miles long and finished in Paris with eight laps on a circuit up and down the celebrated, tree-lined Champs-Élysées, in sight of the Arc de Triomphe. Thousands of spectators ten deep on the streets watched. As the peloton sped in a tight bunch, Martin was surprised to hear a familiar voice call her name from behind a street barricade.

On the next lap, she looked at the place where she had heard her name and spotted her dad. He had flown in from his home in Fenton, Michigan, to watch his daughter in the *maillot jaune* win the inaugural Tour de France Féminin.

18

The Americans Are Coming, the Americans Are Coming

The years are passing, my dear, and presently
nobody will know what you and I know.
—VLADIMIR NABOKOV, *Speak, Memory*

After the LA Olympics flame was extinguished, American pro cycling appeared phoenix-like. The fledgling generation differed from its forgotten Jazz Age predecessors. Young pros on twelve-speed road bikes picked up the dazzling heritage of charging in vibrant-colored packs like shooting stars along straights and leaning in ballet precision through turns.

The four-year build-up to the LA Games saw corporations sponsoring amateur teams like never before. Company logos bloomed on jerseys and shorts. Among them were the 7-Eleven convenience-store chain, car companies Alfa Romeo and Plymouth, along with Campbell's soups, Lowrey's meat products, Weight Watchers, Wheaties, and Schwinn. Brands as diverse as Pepsi, Ore-Ida potatoes, Prince pasta, Subaru, and breweries such as Coors, Molson, Budweiser, and Miller underwrote races with budgets challenging events on the Continent.

Among the new pros was Tom Broznowski, national road champion and a University of Washington mechanical engineering graduate. He signed a contract in 1985 to ride for the Schwinn-Wheaties Cycling Team. "I could make as much money racing bicycles as I could working for an engineering company," he said.

Broznowski and others looked up to Greg LeMond, who had left Cyrille Guimard and Renault-Elf-Gitane for the French team La Vie

Claire (the Healthy Life), named after a chain of French health-food stores. He signed a three-year contract paying him a million dollars to become the first cyclist ever to command that much money. His contract stunned European cycling.

LeMond thought big. European pros accepted one-year contracts—two years at most. Their career plan was to save enough so when they hung up their racing wheels they could purchase a house and open a bike shop. When LeMond wasn't racing or training, he confounded traditionalists by grabbing a bag of golf clubs and playing on the links, or loading a shotgun to go hunting. His realtor father had funded his forays to Belgium, Switzerland, and France. As a pro, LeMond intended to build a golf course and surround it with houses he could sell.

America's foremost cycling team was sponsored by 7-Eleven. Over five years its men and women in outfits pitching the stores' logo and red-green-and-white colors raced in more than six hundred races in venues from coast to coast. They boasted more than four hundred victories, a 64 percent victory rate. The gush of print and television coverage impressed parent company, Southland Corporation in Dallas. Southland steadily upped the team's budget from $250,000 to $3.5 million.

Directing the 7-Eleven Cycling Team was Jim Ochowicz, a two-time Olympian from the twilight era of the Amateur Bicycle League of America. After the 1984 Olympics he converted his team from amateur to professional to create America's first pro squad and hired Mike Neel as sports director. They shared a vision to make the 7-Eleven Cycling Team a powerhouse like the New York Yankees in baseball.

Major League Baseball culminates every autumn, with the top division teams in each league competing in playoff series to decide which two advance to the World Series in October, which crowns baseball's season in the sun. Cycling operates on a different timetable. The premier cycling event on the globe is the Tour de France in July. The winner and top finishers cash in on greater appearance fees for a year.

Pro cycling teams compete to qualify for the Tour de France as fiercely as ball teams play to reach the division playoffs. The upstart 7-Eleven squad faced a daunting task. Ochowicz and Neel had no playbook to follow. They recalled when the New York Mets had formed in 1962 as part of the National League's expansion. The Mets posted MLB's worst-ever first season—40 wins and 120 losses. Yet the Mets became the "Miracle Mets" and won the 1969 World Series.

Ochowicz and Neel recruited a deep bench of the country's best talents. In 1983, George Mount came home from Italy and rode on the 7-Eleven team before retiring at the end of the year to coach. Ochowicz and Neel created a two-part, three-year strategy to get into Le Tour. Neel had contacts in Italy for the first part, entering Italy's 1985 Giro d'Italia, a notch less demanding than the Tour.

Och (rhymes with coach), as he's called, grew up in Milwaukee and played little league baseball. The fattest on the team, he became catcher because he had the best chance to stop the ball. Five feet eight, dark hair combed neat as an altar boy, he had the face of a cherub.

He slimmed down through cycling. Inspired by his dad's ABLA state championship medals, he joined the Milwaukee Wheelmen. He won most junior races on the local Brown Deer asphalt track and counterparts in Northbrook, Illinois, and Kenosha, Wisconsin—within a hundred-mile radius.

He lived to race. After graduating from Pope Pius XI High School, he supported his passion by working construction in the off-season, enduring Wisconsin's bitter-cold winters. The only days he missed laboring outside were when the temperature plunged below zero. "Too cold to pour cement," he said.

Och competed in the 1972 Munich Olympics on the track pursuit team, eliminated in the first round. He went home and changed to road racing. Butch Martin picked him for the break-through ninth place in the 100-kilometer team time trial at the Montreal 1974 worlds. Och was selected for a second Olympics in 1976. When Eddie B. was hired as USCF head coach, he dismissed Och as too old, at twenty-six, for another national team. Disappointed, Och quit cycling.

Along the way he married Sheila Young, two-time world sprint champion and speed skater extraordinaire. Och also speed skated. His first managerial employment was with the national speed skating team in 1979. He coached skaters including Beth and Eric Heiden, who led the USA team to a conquest of seventeen of the twenty world championship gold medals.

The next year Eric Heiden captivated the sports world for nine days at the Lake Placid Winter Olympics. He swept all five of the long-track speed skating events—from the 500-meter sprint to 10,000 meters (6.2 miles). His haul of five golds exceeded those won by Finland, Norway, the Netherlands, Switzerland, West Germany, Italy, Canada, Hungary, Japan, Bulgaria, Czechoslovakia, and France combined. Heiden set four Olympic records and one world record.

Despite speed skating's obscurity in the United States, Heiden catapulted to America's superstar. *Time* magazine featured him and sister Beth in head-to-toe skating tights on the cover, recognition usually reserved for heads of state, Hollywood stars, or famous artists.

Twenty-one-year-old Eric Heiden sported a Prince Valiant haircut and flashed a searchlight of a smile. The son of an orthopedic surgeon father and homemaker mother in Madison, Wisconsin, he intended to retire from skating after the Olympics and complete studies in biology at the University of Wisconsin. Instead, he was deluged with offers for appearances like a rock star.

Dutch sports agent George Taylor took him on as a client. Taylor had brokered Southland Corporation's agreement with the Los Angeles Olympic Organizing Committee to sponsor the cycling venue for the LA Games. Taylor, soft-spoken and a model listener, had a relaxed cosmopolitan air. He grew up in the Netherlands watching bike races. He earned a business degree there, studied at Bowdoin College in Brunswick, Maine, and graduated with a master in business and management from Kent State in Ohio. He flew to Dallas and suggested that Southland officials start a men's cycling team of five, built around Heiden.

"George was the agent who sold sponsorship to the Southland Corporation in 1980 to form the 7-Eleven team with Eric Heiden and me," Och said. Och confidently guaranteed that one of the 7-Eleven cyclists would win an Olympic medal.

Heiden adapted easily to bike racing. Crowds—and the media—flocked in unprecedented numbers to see him race. His bulging 185 pounds of muscles on a six-foot-one frame strained the Lycra sheath of his 7-Eleven jersey and shorts, unlike skinny cyclists. He was legendary for torquing bicycle frames like potato chips from the force he exerted when driving pedals down so hard from mighty twenty-seven-inch thighs, almost the size of his waist. Teammates nicknamed him Gomer, like a kindly, simple-minded guy unaware of his strength.

Och poached Mike Neel from Eddie B. at the USCF and expanded 7-Eleven to sixteen men, six women, and fourteen juniors supported by fourteen full- and part-time mechanics, coaches, and masseurs. Och was regarded as a stern taskmaster. Yet he relaxed over meals or behind the steering wheel of the team vehicle and told laugh-out-loud stories. His riders called him Sergeant Rock, as much for leading them into battle as for his midwestern calm under pressure. Davis Phinney said to me that if he ever had trouble with the law and was allowed to make just one phone call, he would call Och.

Phinney noted that he and others had accomplished their Olympic goals. They looked for new objectives. Och and Neel agreed: 7-Eleven had to go to Europe in 1985 and subsequently enter the Tour de France. The CBS television network covered Le Tour to follow LeMond and broadcast coverage to America. Och wanted his team to win and get airtime on CBS for invaluable publicity.

Och flew to Europe to beat the drum for a major sponsor there and to secure his team's place in the Giro. In 1985 he made twelve round trips across the Atlantic. Relentless travel and eighty-hour workweeks turned him into another business guy in a tweed jacket. He found a warm reception from Erminio Dall'Oglio, an inventor. That year Dall'Oglio opened a manufacturing plant in Switzerland. Dall'Oglio was middle-aged, his hair thinning as his midsection widened, fond of cigars, and passionate about pro cycling. He presided over Hoonved, a manufacturing company producing industrial dishwashing machines for restaurants, bakeries, and hospitals. He co-sponsored the American team.

• • •

In March 1985 Neel led the 7-Eleven-Hoonved pros to Europe. His cyclists, mechanics, and masseurs were thrown into the illustrious spring classics, a series of revered one-day road events, some held since the 1890s, and short stage races on the pro circuit in France, Belgium, Italy, and Germany.

The pace of classics like Paris–Roubaix was breakneck, the courses pitiless. After a rolling start on a wide boulevard, some two hundred riders went all-out to get the best position before the first turn, which led to a pinched country lane. Blustery rural landscapes were littered with farm-to-market cobblestone roads, the stone edges round as babies' heads.

None of the 7-Eleven riders had served in the military, but they were tossed into a severe boot camp. Neel counted on the rigors of the hallowed classics to toughen his bunch for the Giro, starting May 16 in Verona, Italy.

• • •

Davis Phinney, 7-Eleven's star sprinter, described the Giro as an exclusive Italian men's domain. He and his eight American teammates were treated like caddies in a golf tournament. While the sponsors of the other teams were household names in the host country, not so with 7-Eleven. It had grown from a small business in Dallas selling ice, insulated with sawdust before the advent of refrigerators, open daily 7 a.m. to 11 p.m.

Most of the twenty teams, nine riders each, were Italian and included cyclists from all over the Continent. "The Italians wanted us to go to the back of the pack and basically stay out of their way while they did the men's work," Phinney explained later. "They would point to the 7-Eleven logo on our jerseys, shake their head, and ask what *sette-undici* [Italian for 7-Eleven] meant."

Word caromed around Verona before the start that 7-Eleven upset the taboo against women working in the Giro—or any pro race in Europe. Shelley Verses of Santa Barbara, California, accompanied the team as one of four *soigneurs*, French for "one who cares for others." Soigneurs take care of riders like mechanics maintain bikes. Soigneurs do everything from massaging weary muscles to cleaning wounds, from buying food in local shops to preparing custom meals for cyclists to eat at breakfast, from providing finger food to refuel on the bike during the race to washing clothes. Daily racing in the Giro typically lasted four to six hours, but soigneurs travailed fifteen-hour days. *USA Today* in 2005 rated soigneur as the ninth-worst job—behind horse-racing groom, boxing sparring partner, rodeo bullfighter, and Iditarod sled dog.

"Our team was looked upon as something from out of America's

Wild West," Verses told me. "We looked different, acted different, and there was me. I was twenty-five."

Blue-eyed, with sunflower-blonde hair, and five feet four on tiptoes, for all the commotion she caused upon arrival in Verona she might have been nine feet tall. "People at the race immediately started asking me: Was I somebody's girlfriend? Who was I having sex with? Did I have sex with somebody to get the job? These questions came at me so fast, I didn't know what hit me."

Growing up in a sports-oriented family in Stamford, Connecticut, she competed on the YMCA swim team, played street hockey as an equal among boys, and participated in school basketball and field hockey. Instead of sitting in typing class, she went to the gym and cleaned basketballs. "I was kicked out of the Girl Scouts for wearing pants under my uniform."

Verses studied physical education at Springfield College, where basketball was invented. She came of age when Title IX of the 1972 Education Amendment Act cracked open opportunities for women. Thanks to Title IX requiring two women to work at every beach in Stamford, she had a job as a lifeguard.

"I used to be a little angry at society for holding women back, not allowing us to play sports with the boys," she said. "That made me an activist. I felt my grit, my perseverance. I was more or less thrown into the pot to fight for women's rights because I was in the right place at the right time. Title IX was changing things. Eddie B. had seen me working as a masseuse at bike races around Santa Barbara, California, rubbing riders' legs at the curb before races and later out on the course, at the side of the road, handing up bags of food in the feed zones. One day Eddie B. said to me, in his thick Polish accent, that under Title IX he had to pick three men and two women masseuses for the U.S. Cycling Federation. He provided me with expenses to go to the U.S. Olympic Training Center in Colorado Springs. There was no pay. But I lived for free at the OTC."

Neel heard from riders about her as diligent and one of the best soigneurs caring for the 1984 Olympic cycling team. He recruited her for the 7-Eleven pro team. Now in Verona with the Giro to start in a couple of days, Italy had nothing like Title IX to protect her. Neel had to manage a team trying to prove its worth in the 2,400-mile grand tour. He listened to Verses's sexual harassment onslaught and counseled her to give up wearing her 7-Eleven T-shirt and shorts in public. He left her alone briefly and came back with a long-sleeved, full-length doctor's white coat and told her to put it on. It went past her knees.

"I looked like an infirmary worker," she recalled. "Mike wanted to send a silent message that I wasn't somebody's girlfriend. When I said the lab coat wasn't *me*, he said I couldn't be *me* anymore. No more going out in a tank top. He had too many unexpected fires to put out. I had to face the issue of decorum."

Verses could have quit. "I had that feeling come over me, *I'll show them*. It's like a secret inside me. I had it in Stamford when I played street hockey with the boys, getting pushed around and pushing right back, and just as hard. At the Giro, I was willing to stick it out for the full twenty-two days."

The Giro opened in central Verona with a four-mile prologue—a short, individual time trial that sorted out the 180 starters. Riders whipped through streets bordered by raucous *tifosi* before heading into the Verona Arena, a Roman amphitheater built in the first century and famous today for international large-scale opera performances, the filming of an *Inspector Morse* episode, and rock concerts by icons like Alicia Keys, Pearl Jam, and Sir Paul McCartney. Giro riders one at a time charged to the finish line at the rear of the theater—and quickly had to slam on the brakes to avoid smashing into the audience.

The next day the field rolled out of Verona for stage 1, a 135-mile jaunt to Busto Arsizio, north of Milan. Jonathan Boyer had been hired by 7-Eleven to share his continental experience. He imparted invaluable insight into the personalities and physical strengths and weaknesses of players he knew for years but were strangers to his countrymen. "It was great," Boyer exclaimed. "Something I always dreamed of—riding in Europe with an American team."

Five hours later and thirty miles from the finish, the pace ramped up. Phinney found Boyer in the pack. Boyer guided him, diving through openings between riders that only Boyer spotted, protecting Phinney from the wind as they sliced to the front. In Busto Arsizio with about a thousand yards to go, Phinney locked on Boyer's rear wheel rocketing at the nose of the peloton, rivals knocking Phinney's elbows to usurp Boyer's shelter.

The serious high-end speed launched in the final 400 yards. Boyer peeled off, his labor done. Phinney caught the slipstream of an Italian sprinter hunched in a tight ball over his frame and pedaling madly at 40 mph. In the last 100 yards Phinney blasted ahead. Behind him all 179 others spread out across the road, the shouting of the enormous crowd echoing off buildings. Phinney noticed from the corner of an eye that a rider pipped him, another adversary slid by, followed by one more. At the finish, he threw his bike to the line—fourth place!

Day after day in pack sprints, Phinney finished eight times in the top ten. For two weeks, he and teammates who had excelled in America were reduced to toiling like the hapless old New York Mets.

Each night nine teams or so stayed in the same hotel. "Our team dressed casually for dinner," Verses said. "We showed up wearing different T-shirts, shorts, and flip-flops. The Italian teams all came to dinner looking sharp in their warm-up suits. The director, soigneurs, and mechanics wore beautiful sweaters. We were laughed at for looking different, laughed at for our riders crashing, laughed at for not doing so well."

Shelley Verses bridled against Old World chauvinism from team soigneurs. "I think the biggest thing that I represented to them was change. That women could do just as good what they were doing."

Every morning when the peloton spun away for the next stage, she and another 7-Eleven soigneur loaded seventy pieces of team luggage into an oversized van and a station wagon and drove to their destination hotel; two other 7-Eleven soigneurs drove another vehicle to the feed zones along the route. When Verses and her colleague arrived to their hotel, they carried the luggage inside and delivered each piece to riders' assigned rooms.

"So I was carrying two big pieces of luggage across the parking lot to the hotel glass entrance door," Verses recalled. "Sometimes you use two bags to hold the door open for the next soigneur while you continue to your next room. The other soigneurs *never* did that to hold the door open for me. In the evenings I saw the other soigneurs and mechanics sitting together for a glass of beer or wine or a cup of coffee. When I showed up, they made fun of me. One of the mechanics told me they had a bet going that I wouldn't get past ten days. I felt so angry that I wanted so bad to quit."

Sharing her frustration with any of the 7-Eleven riders was off limits for a soigneur. Early on Neel had cautioned her from his familiarity with racehorses how important it was to keep them quiet in the stables so they could reserve their energy for the turf. He had lots of stress handling his stallions.

Frustrated and incensed, Verses phoned her father at home in Connecticut. He listened patiently to her venting. He advised that in a man's world, she had to work harder than them—a magnitude of two or three times greater. If the hotel door was closed when she unloaded luggage, she had to put the bags down, pull the door open, go through, leave bags to keep it propped open for the next soigneur, go about her duties, and later retrieve the bags she'd left behind.

As the days unfolded and her luggage ordeal continued, she persevered like Sisyphus. She ensured that the soigneur behind her could follow straight through. Then one by one soigneurs asked her for small favors. Once a soigneur ran out of water bottles and sought her to lend him some; he returned the bottles the next day and they established a friendship. Another soigneur agreed to sell her a special rubbing oil, exclusive to Europe, that warmed up leg muscles before the day's rollout start. European cyclists asked her how Eric Heiden was feeling.

"I started making friends with riders and other soigneurs," she said. "We were swapping favors to help one another. I was being accepted."

She breezed through the Giro's first ten days. The mechanics who had a bet she wouldn't last that long gave in to acknowledge her.

In the final week, on the 127-mile stage 15 from L'Aquila to Perugia, 7-Eleven's fortune changed. Soon after leaving L'Aquila, Ron Kiefel of Denver joined twenty men storming off the front. His breakaway group over the next five hours dwindled to him and three others. Kiefel, an all-round rider with a silky pedal style that appears effortless, stealthily surged away. He crossed the line first, the first American to claim a

Giro stage, two seconds ahead of two former world champions, Dutchman Gerrie Knetemann and Italian Francesco Moser.

"By the time Kiefel won the stage, we were getting straightened out as a team and wore our warm-up suits to dinner," Verses said. "The other teams no longer laughed at us."

Five days later, stage 20 was the shortest massed-start leg, thirty-six miles, in northwest Italy's picturesque deep valleys and snowcapped mountains. The course featured an eleven-mile ascent to the finish in mile-high Valnontey di Cogne, in the Gran Paradiso National Park. The uphill finish motivated Andy Hampsten of Grand Forks, North Dakota. He was twenty-three, a new pro. Neel signed him to a thirty-day contract from the American team sponsored by Levi's jeans. Hampsten had challenged pros riding up the Rockies in the Coors Classic, which mixed amateurs and pros. He had an ideal physique, five feet nine and 140 pounds, for scaling mountains—all-round slim with legs that curved and tapered thin as baseball bats.

Stage 20 took place in the late afternoon. That morning Hampsten and Jonathan Boyer pedaled from the start in Saint-Vincent to the end to check out the route. Mike Neel drove them back. "I was disappointed that the climb wasn't steeper or longer," Hampsten told me. "But driving back with Neel and Boyer, Neel suggested I should attack on a particular curve."

To anyone else, the curve seemed nothing special. Neel spotted it as tactical. Hampsten's teammates would roll to the head of the pack before the curve. He would spring ahead out of the bend as teammates eased the pace. Most of the peloton flowing softer into the arc—and all the media back in the support caravan—would miss seeing him go. Hampsten, in a sleek one-piece Lycra skinsuit rather than a road jersey with back pockets bulging with food, would capitalize on the element of surprise and play his uphill strength.

From the start, La Vie Claire with Greg LeMond swarmed to the front and set a punishing pace. Team captain Bernard Hinault wore the leader's *maglia rosa* (pink jersey), matching the sponsoring newspaper, *La Gazzetta dello Sport*. La Vie Claire laid down the law to discourage any challenges. The peloton fractured into small groups trailing behind. At the base of the final climb on Neel's designated curve, Hampsten flew ahead. He soloed eleven uphill miles to win by a full minute. He snatched 7-Eleven's second stage win.

"Each night at dinner the Italians drank wine, but our team never did," Verses said. "After Andy's stage victory, we celebrated, and the wine flowed."

By the conclusion of the Giro in Lucca, in Tuscany, Eric Heiden came through as another 7-Eleven surprise for winning the "Catch sprints" prize of $5,000—for designated sprints within flat stages to spur the peloton.

LeMond, dutifully helping Hinault win, finished third. LeMond joined his team leader on the podium—the first American on the Giro podium.

7-Eleven's Giro success opened opportunities. Ochowicz and Neel advanced to the second part of their plan. Och met with Tour officials in Paris and successfully persuaded them to admit 7-Eleven to the following year's race. Le Tour charged an entry fee of $35,000—extravagant compared with chump-change Och paid in his ABLA days. The enormous difference was a measure of Le Tour's high stakes. He didn't hesitate to write a check for 7-Eleven's entry into the 1986 Tour de France.

• • •

The CoreStates USPRO Championship, a 156-mile road race, debuted in June 1985 in Philadelphia. Its $20,000 first prize and $105,000 purse topped anything in Europe. (Paris–Roubaix, the greatest one-day classic in France, offered a $43,000 purse.) And the City of Brotherly Love welcomed foreign riders.

The championship was created by Dave Chauner. He had traded his racing togs for a three-piece suit to promote races with Jack Simes III. In 1976 they began programs at the new Lehigh County Velodrome in eastern Pennsylvania, and headed PRO, the Professional Racing Organization, governing U.S. pro cycling. Since 1980 Simes had presided as executive director of PRO.

Chauner founded International Cycling Productions to put on professional races sanctioned by PRO. His CoreStates USPRO Championship, sponsored by the CoreStates Financial Corporation (now part of Wells Fargo), was audacious. He convinced Philadelphia city officials to close fifteen miles of major streets for seven hours on the first Sunday in June. The race started and finished downtown, on the Benjamin Franklin Parkway near the Philadelphia Art Museum.

The course showcased Fairmount Park, Lemon Hill, Kelly Drive with its bronze statue of Olympic champion John B. Kelly Sr. rowing his single scull, and, at the far end in northwest Philadelphia's working-class neighborhood of Manayunk, a diabolical hill two-thirds of a mile long that humps up a steep 17 percent grade soaring 285 feet tall—Chauner christened it the Manayunk Wall.

KLM Royal Dutch Airlines jumped aboard as a sponsor to fly riders from the Continent. Another two dozen companies supplied everything from mineral water to portable toilets. The year before in Rome, Simes had presented a plan for the race to the Union Cycliste Internationale and persuaded it to put the event on its international schedule.

The CoreStates USPRO Championship drew more than a hundred pros from a dozen nations. The championship had a charmed ending as Eric Heiden won a sprint from his breakaway partners, two Danes and American Tom Broznowski, crossing the finish line with his arms raised straight overhead, displaying his 7-Eleven jersey.

The media loved Heiden and lavished enormous publicity on his triumph. What was good for 7-Eleven was good for American cycling—and Philadelphia.

• • •

In July at the Tour de France, LeMond supported Hinault to win his fifth Tour. He equaled France's Jacques Anquetil and Belgium's Eddy Merckx.

LeMond had won an individual time trial, a show of strength and finesse without challenging team leader Hinault. LeMond finished second.

On the awards podium on the Champs-Élysées in Paris, Hinault announced to the international press corps that the next Tour would be his last. He intended to retire on his thirty-second birthday. He promised to help his protégé LeMond win in 1986.

But bicycle racing is unpredictable. And Hinault could be contradictory.

• • •

The 1986 Tour de France was hyped in U.S. newspapers, magazines, and weekly CBS television specials. Superlatives described the Tour: a record 210 racers from fifteen nations faced the arduous 2,543-mile contest over one of the most mountainous courses in Tour history. Americans were proud. For the first time, an all-American team entered; the 7-Eleven squad was composed of eight cyclists from the United States, a Canadian, and a Mexican. Americans were prouder still because LeMond was a pre-race favorite.

On the second day, July 5, Le Tour offered surprises. 7-Eleven's Alex Stieda of Vancouver, Canada, who placed twenty-first in the previous day's prologue, twelve seconds behind the winner, realized he could take the yellow jersey if he broke clear in search of time bonuses of twelve seconds each at three intermediate sprints. Wearing a skinsuit, he attacked solo on the fifty-three-mile stage 1 morning run in suburban Paris. He netted all thirty-six seconds of those precious time bonuses; so, despite being caught by five chasers and crossing the finish line in fifth, his time bonuses catapulted him to race leader. Stieda stepped up to the podium and pulled on the race leader's yellow jersey.

Three hours later in the stage 2 thirty-five-mile team time trial, Stieda was so knackered that he couldn't stay with his team and dropped behind. Two teammates went back to pace him so he could make the time limit and stay in the race. The pacers saved him, but he no longer wore the yellow jersey.

Stage 3 rolled from the outskirts of Paris north for 133 miles to the old mining town of Liévin. Davis Phinney took off in the day's decisive breakaway. In the closing miles he didn't see that a rider who attacked had stopped with a mechanical, and he thought he was sprinting for second place. Phinney narrowly took the sprint, and then learned from reporters that he had won the stage. On the awards podium, he received a silver hexagon statute shaped like France, five inches tall, etched with the Tour route, marked by two tiny diamonds—signifying the day's start in Levallois-Perret and the finish in Liévin. Americans saw television footage of his victory.

The presence of Hollywood star Dustin Hoffman and a film crew shooting footage for a movie, *The Yellow Jersey*, starring Hoffman, revved up the peloton for stage 11. It was the Tour's longest day, 160 miles of rolling farmland through southwestern France's wine country to Bordeaux. (The movie script, based on the novel of the same title by Englishman Ralph Hurne, centered on the first non-European to win Le Tour; the project tanked.)

The following day, the route ascended into the Pyrenees where an epic battle erupted. LeMond expected support from the man he had helped the previous year, only to find his greatest rival was that very man—Bernard Hinault, desperate to claim a record sixth Tour victory.

On stage 12, Hinault sprinted off the front at the foot of the long steep climb that the local Basques call the Cross of Iron. Only the light climbing specialist Spaniard Pedro Delgado could go with him. Delgado shared the drafting as the two stretched their lead to a hefty five minutes. Hinault rewarded Delgado by easing up near the finish, in the city of Pau, for the Spaniard to claim the stage. Hinault gladly gave up the day's victory to take over the lead—more than five minutes ahead of LeMond, second overall. Midway through Le Tour, Hinault was in the yellow jersey. LeMond was in distress.

Hinault's derring-do, like a high-wire performer, encouraged fans to paint his name large on the pavement. When he spun by, crowds chanted his name. Only a few years before, the French had scorned him. He'd won Tours, but without trouncing the competition like the public expected. Then he endured knee surgery. The Renault-Elf-Gitane team dismissed him as a has-been.

In 1984 he formed La Vie Claire, wearing colorful jerseys in the distinct red, yellow, white, and blue rectangular pattern of Dutch painter Piet Mondrian. Hinault as an underdog had ended Le Tour in second. The next year he won—and became more popular yet.

In 1986, the French did not perceive that he betrayed LeMond. They saw Hinault's swagger as welcomed flamboyance. His flying up mountains opened up a game of catch-me-if-you-can. And the throngs loved him.

LeMond, for all his talent, was criticized for not showing more of it. In the recent Giro d'Italia, he'd finished fourth—unlike his second-place to Hinault the year before. LeMond also recently rode the Tour of Switzerland, but came in third, and he had been equally close in a few major one-day classics. The French public thought he didn't take the risks he should to assert himself and win.

Hinault counted more than two hundred victories, including ten grand tours, a worlds road race, and a dozen or so classics. Devotees felt he had earned the license to change his mind and go for the immortal sixth Tour victory.

On stage 13, with three monster climbs under a relentless sun up and down the rugged Pyrenees for 115 miles, Hinault brazenly fled from the lead group of sixteen, including LeMond and La Vie Claire teammates Andy Hampsten and Steve Bauer. Hinault gained two minutes. If he held that lead over the next two climbs before the uphill finish in the ski resort of Superbagnères, he would have forged a decisive lead over LeMond and the Tour would be all his.

LeMond's group included several of the best climbers from other teams with their own motives to catch Hinault. They cut the Frenchman's advantage to twenty-five seconds by the time he crested the next-to-last mountain. After a long downhill loomed the last ascent to the finish banner arching over the road ten miles away. LeMond's group bridged to Hinault at the base of the climb.

Hinault would have to drop everyone again. Instead, he thrashed up the slope, slipped off the rear of the group, and faded. Hampsten, the wiry teammate LeMond had recruited, proved himself more of a force than anyone expected and led LeMond at a brisk tempo. He set LeMond up for the final heave to win the stage. When LeMond crossed the line after six hours of toil, the audience studied wrist watches to see how much time passed before Hinault arrived. More than four minutes passed; his overall lead narrowed to forty seconds over LeMond.

It was headline sports. Three stages later, Hinault escaped again in a mountainous stretch in a small group that LeMond missed. All politics are local, and La Vie Claire had become embroiled in a contentious split—his French teammates backed Hinault while Hampsten and Bauer supported LeMond. Hinault failed to gain time on LeMond on that stage. But the tension within La Vie Claire made Le Tour as dramatic off the bikes as it was on them.

Within the team, the North Americans and French were sometimes as different as chalk and cheese. LeMond pronounced *France* the American way, rhyming with *pants*, unlike the French back-of-the-throat elocution. Moreover, he ate ice cream, causing French teammates to recoil in alarm at the fat he licked into his high-performance body. He was amused that in France nobody seemed to consider the fat they consumed from the cheese board laden with Brie, Camembert, Gruyère, and other varieties passed around as a savory after meals.

By stage 17, more than a quarter of the Tour starters had abandoned. Eight more were to quit in this alpine leg. LeMond fled in a group that left Hinault behind. The American challenger forced the tempo with others to rip the peloton apart. By the time he crossed the line atop the Tour's highest-ever finish line, at 7,917 feet above sea level, after nearly six hours of racing, he had stretched a lead of more than three minutes over Hinault. LeMond leapfrogged to first place.

LeMond at last stood on the podium at the daily ceremony and pulled on the yellow jersey. Six stages remained. Anxious, he openly complained that he hoped Hinault would work for him.

The next day, in the central French Alps, the two giants of the race broke away together, to the delight of masses standing along most of the 101-mile route. Up climbs, fans crowded the roads to cheer, leaving only a narrow path for cyclists to cut through. Sometimes admirers pushed slow riders strung out at the end of the pack. Down descents, the roads were vacant as riders hit 66 mph.

The day turned momentous. The road to the finish atop the Alpe d'Huez ski resort at an altitude of 6,100 feet was packed with humanity. Thousands of people spent the previous night camping along the famous twenty-one hairpin turns leading to the resort. Devotees spilled onto roads and partied.

LeMond and Hinault gained an incredible five-minute lead by the time they had the finish banner in sight. The road widened as barriers held back the crowd. The two rivals acted like playmates—patting each other on the back, smiling, waving to jubilant fans. Hinault took the stage.

When LeMond dismounted, he nervously looked toward victory in Paris.

So far the 7-Eleven team had lost five members to crashes or fatigue: two in the Pyrenees, one in the plains, and two in the Alps. That day, Heiden was so fatigued he missed a turn down a fast descent, flew off the road into trees, and suffered a concussion; a helicopter rushed him to a hospital. Another casualty was Phinney (crash, broken wrist). By Paris the team's top rider would be Bob Roll in sixty-third overall.

Shelley Verses had been working with other soigneurs on the side of roads in the feed zones—the first for a woman. "When it was go-time and the riders swept into the feed zones, there was no messing around," she said. "I was treated like one of the other soigneurs. But away from the public, the other soigneurs made sarcastic comments and innuendo. They had a gang mentality."

Part of what kept her going was witnessing the great drama. "Every day I was there seeing Greg LeMond and Bernard Hinault and other greats—Jean-François Bernard, Charly Mottet, and others. I felt like I was in a Hall of Kings."

When the 7-Eleven team roster dropped to five riders, Mike Neel dismissed two soigneurs but kept Verses. She stayed all the way to Paris.

Five stages remained, but after Alpe d'Huez came the only rest day. For riders in grand tours, a rest day typically means pedaling for two to three hours to keep leg muscles flexed and tuned.

The rest day was followed by another mountain stage of 112 miles, which had no effect on overall standings.

The following day proved crucial. It was the last individual test—a thirty-six-mile time trial over a hilly and twisting course in Saint-Étienne, a city of 170,000 in east-central France. Hinault, a time trial specialist, boasted he was feeling super and could win the stage and reclaim the yellow jersey.

Excitement focused on the LeMond-Hinault duel. LeMond led overall by two minutes, forty-three seconds, a margin that could evaporate in a time trial on a tricky course like in Saint-Étienne. If the American won the time trial he would silence critics claiming he wasn't worthy of winning Le Tour. As the younger challenger, LeMond had to show more fortitude, greater courage.

Just past the twenty-three-mile point, LeMond rounded a sharp right turn too fast and fell. Suffering abrasions to his legs and arms, he quickly jumped back on his bike and resumed. Then he discovered that his front brake was rubbing against the rim. That forced him to stop and replace the bicycle with one from his support car trailing close behind.

Hinault had no complications and won, his third stage of his swan-song Tour. The Badger outrode LeMond, in second, but only by twenty-five seconds, about the same amount of time he lost in his fall and bike change. He kept his yellow jersey and, important to the French, showed character worthy of a winner.

After a summit finish on Le Puy de Dôme, where LeMond pushed his winning margin over Hinault to three minutes, the remaining stages were flat, the providence of sprinters banging elbows and rubbing wheels in mass pack sprints. The battle between the two rivals had been decided: Hinault failed in his bid for a sixth Tour; LeMond took Hinault's best shots and beat him.

The final day turned into the traditional ceremonial ride into Paris, up the famous Champs-Élysées. LeMond became the first non-European to win the eighty-three-year-old show. His performance and personality showcased he had the right stuff to win this and, potentially, even more Tours to surpass even Hinault, Merckx, and Anquetil.

Andy Hampsten claimed fourth overall. He was awarded the white jersey for top rookie, like LeMond in his first Tour.

Hinault told reporters that he had pushed LeMond to the limit so that later he would know how far he could go. He tried, but failed to get the record sixth victory—nevertheless, to the French, he retired as a hero.

Jacques Goddet, the Tour co-director, wrote in the newspaper *L'Équipe*, "This was a Tour unquestionably won without complicity by Greg LeMond, a champion representative of his generation, a very nice young fellow who leaves the hope that there are more like him on the other side of the Atlantic."

Goddet called LeMond "a champion representative." Frank Kramer would have called him the "one good American rider" to help bring cycling back as a popular spectator sport in the United States.

After a frantic week of media demands in Paris and his home base in Kortrijk, Belgium, LeMond flew across the Atlantic. He stopped in Washington DC for a private meeting with President Reagan in the Oval Office. Accompanied by his wife, Kathy, carrying son Geoffrey in her arms, LeMond walked up the White House entrance. He presented the president with a yellow jersey. President Reagan awarded him with a clear glass jar of jelly beans and two silver cups, boxed and wrapped in gold embossed with the presidential seal.

As soon as LeMond emerged from the Oval Office, he was asked over to a forest of microphones from the White House press corps. He took questions at the impromptu press conference and replied with the poise of any member of the Senate or Congress, but with more exuberance and a deeper tan.

"I think that meeting with the president is my highest award. It is probably the biggest honor in my life to be invited to the White House."

His remarks echoed what Fred Spencer had said sixty-one years earlier, when he and Bobby Walthour II met President Coolidge: "It was a greater thrill than winning the bicycle championship of America," Spencer said. "I never thought I would be able to shake hands with President Coolidge. I told the president I considered it a great honor, and I will never forget it."

When LeMond was asked if there was any ill will between him and Hinault, he grinned like a Cheshire cat. "Things are all right between us. I have been riding with Bernard for six years. We get along well, and he is coming over here to ride in the Coors Classic."

LeMond was asked if he had a political preference for Republican or Democratic presidents. "I am an athlete. I am not a politician. My job is to race bicycles. But I am glad to see the recognition that cycling is getting now. I think my future in cycling is in America."

• • •

The variety of road and track events for amateur and professional men and women put the U.S. Cycling Federation and USPRO in the global arena. Colorado Springs hosted the worlds late in the summer of 1986—the first in America since 1912 in Newark. More than seven hundred men and women cyclists from fifty-five countries converged on Colorado Springs. Big things were expected. The worlds marked the first time since 1980 that Russian and American athletes competed against one another in a major international sporting event.

Hopes were high for U.S. riders to build upon their LA Olympics medal harvest, that spectators would flock to the races, and the eleven days of events would produce fulsome media. Instead, no U.S. rider won any of the sixteen events. Attendance was disappointingly light. Media coverage fizzled.

Nevertheless, some U.S. riders turned in scintillating performances. On the 7-Eleven Velodrome in Memorial Park, Leonard "Harvey" Nitz pulled off a brilliant effort at the end of the thirty-one-mile points race to snatch a bronze medal. Tandem sprint riders David Lindsey and Kit Kyle scored a silver medal. Two women took home medals—Rebecca Twigg claimed a silver in the 3,000-meter women's pursuit race, and match-race sprinter Connie Paraskevin scored a bronze.

Some events at the velodrome—which sat 8,200—were sold out, but most racing took place before vacant seats. Even when the velodrome seats were filled, attendance amounted to only two-thirds of Newark's 1912 worlds, when the U.S. population was less than half than in 1986.

Domestic television network coverage was limited to the local affiliate as a result of an impasse in negotiations with the major networks. Advertising painted on the 7-Eleven Velodrome surface became the irreconcilable issue. Network executives nixed coverage, complaining they would give away free advertising each time a rider was shown passing the ads.

The road races on the Air Force Academy grounds had a smaller audience. I walked with English journalist John Wilcockson around the 9.3-mile course on a chilly day. Most of the sparse attendance gathered at the start/finish.

On a chilly day in the women's thirty-eight-mile road race Janelle Parks rode through a Rocky Mountain mist to finish strong and claim a silver medal.

• • •

The cascade of developments in 1985–86 created a fault line in American cycling. Before 1985, the grand tours functioned as the domain of Europeans, as exclusive to men as Greco-Roman wrestling. The 7-Eleven team barged into the Giro, then thrust itself into the 1986 Tour de France.

U.S.-based teams were seen as regulars on the international pro calendar. Shelley Verses jostled the male establishment as the first woman soigneur on the Continent. La Vie Claire hired her away from 7-Eleven with a bigger salary. She would work a decade on other French and U.S. teams and lead generations of women soigneurs such as Julie Wells, Monica Van Haute, Trudi Rebsamen, and April Neel. American pro cycling had returned to the world stage.

19

"The Day the Big Men Cried"

Jamais deux sans trois

(Never two without three *or* Three's a charm).

—Old French proverb

Nine months after ruling as king of the Tour de France, Greg LeMond lay crumpled and bleeding on the ground, in the weeds and bushes of bucolic California, blood soaking his clothes and turning sticky as he gasped, one hoarse and painful shallow breath after another, from dozens of shotgun pellets that tore into his lower back and right side.

He should not have been there. In March 1987 he was competing in the black-and-white colors of the Dutch team PDM, one of Europe's top squads, when he fell and broke his left wrist. He was racing in Tirreno–Adriatico, a stage race across central Italy, from the Tyrrhenian Sea on the west to the Adriatic Sea on the east. His wrist immobilized in a cast, he flew home.

On April 20, LeMond joined his brother-in-law Patrick Blades and uncle Rod Barber at his uncle's ranch to hunt wild turkeys in the foothills of the Sierra Nevada. They pulled on camo garb, loaded shotguns, and tramped through open ranch country, a hundred miles east of San Francisco. At eight thirty that Monday morning LeMond and his companions became separated. LeMond stepped around a hedge about thirty yards from Blades and galumphed through the undergrowth. Blades confused the rustling for a turkey, pointed his rifle in the direction of what he heard, and fired.

Lead pellets ripped at 150 mph into LeMond's right side, shoulder, leg, arm, and back. Two ribs were broken, his right lung collapsed. He was miles from civilization. His uncle ran in panic back to his house to call 911, but help was a long time coming. By chance, a California Highway Patrol helicopter, dispatched from McClellan Air Force Base in Sacramento, was in the area for a traffic accident and it was diverted to Barber's ranch.

An hour after the shooting—and with nearly half of LeMond's blood lost—the chopper landed. Flying to the University Medical Center at the University of California–Davis School of Medicine took only a dozen minutes. Bloody and filthy in ragged clothes, he could have been mistaken for a homeless derelict.

"I was semiconscious and was lying on my back on the stretcher," he told me. "As they took me into the hospital, a nurse kept asking me to say my name and spell it out. Over and over. She was trying to keep me from losing consciousness. Then they gave me a local anesthetic on my side, slit it open, and jammed a tube between my ribs to drain my chest—to suck out the blood and get my lung to open again. When they jammed that tube in me, I arched up and almost fell off the stretcher. That really *hurt*! It was one of the most painful things you can imagine. The pain was such a *shock*!"

A surgical team in a brightly lit operating theater sliced open his abdomen and operated for the next two hours, picking dozens of round lead balls the size of BBs threatening vital organs. Two lead balls lodged in the lining of his heart; a few in his liver: they were left there rather than endanger his life attempting to remove them. Others that eluded detection later wended their way to his skin.

Brother-in-law Blades grew hysterical. He was taken to Roseville Community Hospital for observation.

Journalists from around the world flew into Davis to cover LeMond's misfortune. For two weeks he lay on his back in a hospital bed in critical condition, fed by intravenous-drip bags. He lost fifteen pounds, mostly muscle. "I realized how fragile life is. You can be at the top and then *boom!* You're *down*!"

Five weeks passed before he could breathe deeply enough to fill his chest. "All that time, I just had shallow breathing. Little breaths. That was all I could do. I think it was after I got out of the hospital and started riding my mountain bike that I started to recover faster and breathe normally. Then I began to recover more quickly."

He plotted his return to the peloton. "When cycling was taken away, I wanted to get back in it again." His troubles, however, weren't over—in July he underwent emergency surgery to repair an intestine.

• • •

LeMond's absence from the sport coupled with Hinault's retirement set off a reordering of the European peloton.

The 7-Eleven-Hoonved team prepped for the 1987 Tour de France in a spring campaign on the Continent. Climbing ace Andy Hampsten, hired away from La Vie Claire, won the ten-day Tour of Switzerland—for the second time. He drew lavish press coverage in Europe but little in America. If pro cycling was to make an impression in 7-Eleven's homeland, its squad had to get noticed by the CBS film crew following Le Tour.

Team members had been grumbling about grossly overcooked pasta. To boost morale and improve cuisine, 7-Eleven hired a chef, Willy Balmat, a former Swiss Air flight attendant. Balmat drove a camper trailer equipped with a kitchen for cooking fresh pasta and sauces.

The 1987 Tour offered a prize list of 6.3 million French francs, worth $1.5 million, including a shiny new Peugeot awarded to the winner of each stage. Le Tour boasted twenty-five stages (plus the short opening prologue time trial), more than ever before, covering 2,630 miles—farther than the distance from Los Angeles to Buffalo. To allow two more teams, to twenty-three, each squad had a roster of nine cyclists instead of the usual ten, for 207 starters. The race started on July 1 in West Berlin to celebrate the former Prussian capital's 750th anniversary.

Davis Phinney had his eye on winning a Peugeot. He'd spent the winter in a gym lifting weights and cross-country skiing in the Rockies. He was renowned for smiling ear to ear on awards podiums, hands hoisting up an oversized check for photo ops.

Boulder High sports came easy to him, especially wrestling, which favored his fast-twitch muscles. When he joined some scrawny cyclists he could have pinned to the mat in seconds without breaking a sweat, they left him behind, to his chagrin. Cycling intrigued him—not just the requisite fitness but also the range of skills in negotiating hills, drafting, and timing jumps.

He applied himself more to extracurricular cycling than school sports. Phinney became admired for his finishing speed, but he never was picked for a U.S. Cycling Federation team sent to the junior worlds. "I worked out in the gym in the winter and skied to come back for the next season a percent or two stronger than the previous year," he said. "After several years, the improvements can add up. I was counting on that."

His persistence paid off. He was selected for the LA Olympics and scored a bronze medal in the four-man 100-kilometer team trial. Davis and wife, Connie Carpenter, attended a special reception for medalists and donors to the LA Olympics Organizing Committee. Guests swarmed around Connie like butterflies, gushing over the gold medalist. A perfectly coiffed matron noticed Davis standing beside his wife. He was asked what he did. He replied he was a cyclist. Asked if he was in the Olympics like his wife, he proudly mentioned his bronze medal. He received advice to do better next time.

As the 1987 Tour traveled across Germany before reaching northeast France, Phinney felt better with the aggressive pace than the year before. Day after day in pack sprints he came close to victory, only to get pipped in the crucial last fifty yards by flying Dutchman Jean-Paul van Poppel or tall Belgian ace Eric Vanderaerden. On the twelfth stage, 142 miles of hilly terrain from Brive southwest to Bordeaux, he felt self-assured.

The day was baking hot. A big group that had sailed away early was chased down, like sacrificed chess pieces, as the peloton neared Bordeaux. Phinney knew the finishing circuit—a lap and a half around a 1.9-mile downtown course lined with tens of thousands of passionate onlookers. The pack flew into the circuit, topping 35 mph. Phinney slotted fifth in the front line.

In the last 400 yards, Dutchmen Van Poppel and Teun van Vliet were up front shoulder-bumping and elbowing each other on the finishing straight. Phinney drafted. In the last fifty yards, he swung to the side and scorched ahead. He crossed the line sitting up, flashing a master of ceremonies broad smile, arms overhead like goal posts. He won the stage—and the keys to a new Peugeot.

Two days later, July 14, came Bastille Day, France's national holiday. The route headed up the Pyrenees on the Spanish border. The 7-Eleven-Hoonved team's Dag Otto Lauritzen, a Norwegian, won the stage.

On the final day, from Créteil to the finish 119 miles away on the Champs-Élysées in Paris, Jeff Pierce also scored for the team. A graduate of Michigan State University, Pierce skillfully maneuvered into a nine-man breakaway before attacking two miles from the finish. He timed his move flawlessly—an American in Paris crossing the line one second ahead of Canadian Steve Bauer, arms up in triumph to the roar of thousands of spectators.

The U.S. team earned CBS-TV coverage broadcast stateside. Ochowicz sold the cars they won and pooled the money among riders and support crew.

Stephen Roche of Ireland, on the Italian team Carrera, won Le Tour, the second English-speaking victor.

• • •

LeMond slowly recovered from his appendectomy. By late August he was taking part in criteriums in Belgium and France, but he was only a shadow of his normal self.

"Everybody was glad to see me," he recounted. "The first two weeks they said: No, I wouldn't make it back racing. But after that they saw I was starting to improve. My big problem with the Europeans is that they want me to be like them. They don't understand that during the season I want to play golf and hunt."

I caught up with him in October at a media gathering over drinks in the lobby of the posh Coral Gables Biltmore near Miami. He looked fit, gestured with gusto, and grinned. He had competed in some thirty races on the Continent. He finished forty-fourth of 120 starters in the Tour of Ireland. He was fresh from a ninety-four-mile downtown Atlanta race and sounded like Eddie B., saying, "Ninety percent of the riders in the race sat in bad positions on their bikes."

When we shook hands, he expressed delight in his firm grip. A shotgun pellet that struck his upper arm had caused numbness in three fingers and nearly total loss of strength in his hand. Recently the feeling and strength returned, a sign he took as cause for optimism.

Like most others, I was aware of his misfortune. Reports indicated an upbeat prognosis, then the story vanished. I asked about his wound. He promptly yanked up the front of his polo shirt. Surgical cuts usually leave sharp scars—straight lines or crescents. He showed me a jagged, smudge-like pink streak, thick as his little finger, running from his sternum and to below the belt line.

"The whole thing was a lot more serious than what the journalists were saying," he declared, face flushing with restrained anger. "They were saying that I was out of the Tour de France and wouldn't be able to defend my win last year. The truth was, if I had been another five meters closer to the shotgun blast, or had to wait another thirty minutes for help to arrive, I would have died."

He expressed confidence about winning another Tour de France. "But let's face it. Maybe I don't know how much this shooting affected me. Maybe I will not be ready in 1988, but in 1989. But there is no reason I can't come back. There is no reason I can't win the Tour again. Maybe not win five Tours like Bernard Hinault, but win two, three, or four Tours."

• • •

That spring Phinney's 1988 season was almost cut short. Sixty miles into one of Belgium's April classics, the 169-mile Liège-Bastogne-Liège, a long trench sliced across a narrow road. The first ten cyclists at the front bunny-hopped their bikes over the gap, a couple feet across. Phinney and dozens more fell like bowling pins.

"It was such a ridiculous scene," he told me. "I wrecked my wheels. It seemed like everybody wrecked something. The mechanics ran out of extra wheels and had to get more. When we finally got going again, I figured we were out of the race, but at that point we had nothing to lose and I wanted to finish. Two days before, I had a fourth in a semi-classic race in Belgium. I had won the field sprint, and I felt I was going well."

He and teammate Alex Stieda finally inserted new wheels in their frames and dashed away. They overtook other survivors, who joined their pace line. The fast speed burned Stieda off the back. Phinney reached the tail end of the caravan of vehicles carrying team support, commissaires, and journalists. He surfed up the line and spotted bright jerseys of the peloton ahead.

"The riders were bunched up," Phinney related, indicating the group was cruising at a conversation tempo. "I was within about 200 meters of the peloton, in the gap between the peloton and most of the support cars. I put my head down to really go for it, to regain contact. At that point, though, I was really tired. I had been hammering for quite a while."

A team car had parked in the middle of the road—breaching race etiquette of pulling over on the right side—for a mechanic to service a rider. Phinney, in a full-out effort, pedaling 30 mph, looked up and saw the car in front of him.

"I was a little too tired," he said. "There was no way that I could do anything to avoid what was going to happen. My front wheel hit the rear bumper of the car—a European station wagon, which didn't have safety glass on the rear window. I flew over the front of the bike and hit the rear windshield, dead on, with the left side of my face. I completely shattered the window. Then I slid down the back of the car and fell on the street."

A doctor responded quickly and slapped a compress on the left side of Phinney's face. Stieda found his teammate sitting in a pool of blood and accompanied him in the ambulance to the hospital. By coincidence, it was three days from the anniversary of LeMond's shooting.

"I spent about two hours in surgery," Phinney said. "I had a good surgeon. He reconstructed my face. He broke my nose and put everything back together. I don't know what the count was on the stitches in my face—between 120 and 150—plus another 30 stitches in my arm."

He left the hospital with his face heavily bandaged and a plaster cast on his right arm. Ten days later the bandages, sutures, and cast were cut away. Phinney was back racing. He smeared a gob of white zinc oxide cream over fresh scars to protect the skin from sun exposure. Ten days later, he scored third in the final stage of the Tour of Trentino in Italy.

On May 8 Phinney flew to Washington DC, a twenty-four-hour excursion for a thirty-eight-mile criterium, the fifty-two-year-old National Capital Open. It was part of the festivities honoring his wife. The National Capital Open was held on the Ellipse, the circular road behind the White House.

He coated zinc oxide over his facial scars and joined teammate Doug Shapiro, a veteran of 7-Eleven-Hoonved's Tour de France the previous year. They soon took off with two others and lapped the field. On the bell lap, Phinney at the front of the pack with Shapiro sheltered on his rear wheel revved the speed from 28 mph to 36 mph. The peloton stretched like chewing gum into a line of backs and wheels snaking halfway around the Ellipse. Near the finish, Shapiro sprang ahead. He won the $1,500 cash prize.

Afterward I interviewed Phinney about his Belgian accident. Pink scars shined bright as minted coins. "A crash like that really takes it out of you," he admitted. "It had a big effect on me. I had a tremendous fear of riding again. In the first several races I was really nervous. But that was something I had to face, and I wanted to start back racing as soon as I could." He gestured as though pushing fear aside. "After a while you get back where you want to be."

Phinney left for Dulles International Airport to catch a jet winging across the Atlantic. Two days later he started the Tour de Romandie in Switzerland, where he won the sixth and final stage in a big-bunch sprint. Then to the 1988 Giro d'Italia, starting May 23 in Urbino, a small walled city near the Adriatic Sea.

• • •

Freezing rain kept drumming on hotel roofs and woke everybody up on Sunday morning, June 5, in Chiesa Valmalenco, a ski-resort in the Italian Alps. Officials of the Giro and representatives of all twenty teams huddled in a hotel conference room to discuss the start of the day's stage 14, seventy-five miles, mostly uphill, including the brutal climb over the Gavia Pass, one of Italy's highest summits. Rumors swirled of a snowstorm on the Gavia Pass. Some riders complained that if snow made the road impassable, they would stop in protest.

A phone call to the restaurant atop the Gavia confirmed snow was falling, but a plow was promised to keep the road clear to the finish in a ski village sixteen miles away. Jim Ochowicz and Mike Neel marshaled their 7-Eleven squad to scour local ski shops to purchase wool hats, gloves, balaclavas, and jackets. Riders returned to the hotel and each filled a musette bag with new clothes to pull on at the top of the pass before descending the other side.

It was the end of the second week of the 2,224-mile Giro. Two days earlier Andy Hampsten, in the 7-Eleven-Hoonved colors, won stage 12 and moved up to fifth overall, one minute, eighteen seconds down on the overall race leader, Franco Chioccioli, a hatchet-faced Italian.

Mountain climbs are regarded as a contest apart, calling for incredible physical ability to scale steep grades up dizzying heights. A single day in mountains often completely changes the standings.

"We were targeting me to take over the race," Hampsten recalled. "The weather had raised the stakes. We held a team meeting. Och would stand one kilometer from the top of Gavia with our bag of gear for the descent to the finish, twenty-five kilometers away in Bormio. Also, one of the soigneurs would be waiting for us with a thermos of hot sweet tea, four kilometers from the top."

Neel ordered the four soigneurs to lather all nine riders in lanolin—the fat from wool, which seals water from entering the skin. "We had lanolin smeared not just on our legs and arms but also our chests, our complete trunks, our faces," Hampsten said. They greased up like English Channel swimmers.

Snow and bone-chilling winds were familiar to Hampsten, who grew up in Fargo, North Dakota, playing outdoors every winter. "I was very good at dressing for extreme conditions. I used to ride my bike where I wanted to go. I didn't drive. I wouldn't go on a training ride unless it was above twenty degrees [Fahrenheit]. My bike rides would be to see friends ten to fifteen minutes away. Sometimes my ear lobes would get frostbite, but they healed in the spring."

On the day of the Gavia Pass, he pulled on neoprene gloves, stuffed arms through an orange long-sleeved polypropylene shirt under a short-sleeved wool jersey, and donned 7-Eleven shorts.

The first test came around ten miles, up a 6.4 percent grade—comparable to most of Colorado's Rocky Mountains—to Il Passo dell'Aprica, a modest 3,550 feet above sea level and home to a ski resort. Hampsten sat relaxed in the saddle, hands curled, like he was holding eggs, on the handlebars. Franco Chioccioli, wearing the leader's *maglia rosa*, drafted behind. After cresting the Aprica, the road swooped down 1,500 feet to the town of Edolo before climbing steadily toward the foot of the Gavia.

Drenching rain and stinging sleet incited talk in the peloton of a slowdown. Johan van der Velde of the Netherlands and a dozen allies capitalized on the squabbling and scampered away.

Hampsten shook his head at the talk of slowing. "I couldn't understand all the Italian. I'm a bike racer. We knew the road was open. The race was on."

The road tilted up at 7.9 percent and coiled in a series of hairpin turns, narrow through the bends and long in the straights, twisting skyward to the Passo di Gavia, peaking at 8,609 feet altitude. Phinney and teammates charged to the head of the pack. They paced Hampsten into the first bend, where he surged away. Phinney and the rest watched him go; then they prepared to survive.

"The switchbacks were tight and the road was steep," Hampsten said. "I could look down and see everyone behind me. Everybody was on his own. Everyone was terrified. Everyone was cold. I thought it was great—a guy from North Dakota pulling ahead in the Giro."

Hampsten, twenty-six, had been racing since he was thirteen—owning an Amateur Bicycle League of America license in Fargo. His parents taught in the English department at the University of North Dakota. He is soft-spoken, confident, reserved.

When he turned fifteen, his family spent the summer in England. He competed in more English road races and individual time trials than ever before. He also devoured *Cycling Weekly*, chocked with coverage of events around the United Kingdom and the Continent, and he studied French cycling publications. They fortified his cycling passion.

He developed through U.S. Cycling Federation teams. His remarkable back-to-back victories in the ten-day Tour of Switzerland, the fourth most prestigious national tour, earned him recognition as a top climber. To train for the 1988 season, he lifted weights, skied cross-country, took long walks.

About eight miles from the top of Gavia Pass, rain turned to snow, the two-lane asphalt road pinched into one lane of hard-packed dirt, and the grade reared up to a muscle-straining 16 percent. Despite snow a couple of inches deep, the dirt gave his narrow tires traction. "There was definite drag in the surface. My tires never slipped."

He overtook the earlier breakaway riders, one by one, except for Dutchman Van der Velde. A few miles from the summit, the road cut through a jagged opening dynamited out of rock. There a 7-Eleven soigneur handed Hampsten a welcomed thermos of hot tea.

He knew that Och was waiting less than a mile from the top with a bag containing a wool cap, a neck warmer, and a rain jacket. "I thought I would wipe the snow out of my hair before putting on the cap," he said. "I was flipping my fingers through my hair and felt snow—I wasn't creating enough heat from the top of my head to make snow melt."

He snatched the bag from Och and kept pedaling. It was convenient to sit up and free his hands to pull on the wool cap, don the neck warmer, and thrust arms through the jacket sleeves. But howling wind whipped the ends of his jacket. Struggling to zip it closed, he slalomed back and forth across the road.

"I didn't stop, out of foolish pride, for the fifteen seconds it would take to set my foot on the road and zip my jacket. In a race, cyclists just don't stop. I was so cold I told myself that when I saw Och I wasn't going to stop and get into a discussion. I was on the uphill and very, very cold. I was looking at the spectators. They were so cold, yet so phenomenally excited. They were creating the feeling of an incredible event happening. The energy from the sides of the road was great. People were shivering. They were jumping up and down in excitement. I was not their favorite rider—they were fans of Italian riders. But they were excited that we were going through the Gavia, just like previous generations. We were all going through great hardships."

By the time Hampsten finally zipped his jacket, Erik Breukink, a tall Dutchman riding his third grand tour, caught him. Breukink, riding for Panasonic, had started the day seventh overall, a precious twenty-seven seconds behind Hampsten overall. They pedaled together across the flat section, the road congested from a multitude of cars parked by *tifosi* (fans) and team support vehicles, all hidden under a blanket of blizzard snow.

One of the parked team vehicles kept its engine running, the heater blowing full blast to warm Johan van der Velde, the first up the Gavia. But his short-sleeve jersey, intended for spring weather, was frozen stiff and he suffered hypothermia—body shivering uncontrollably, teeth chattering. He stopped at the summit, abandoned his bicycle, and climbed into his support vehicle. A soigneur supplied him with a new jersey and shorts as Van der Velde sipped thermoses of cognac and hot tea. Nearly an hour passed before he remounted his bike to finish.

From the great pass, all that remained were sixteen downhill miles to the village of Bormio, nearly a mile in elevation below the Gavia. Ordinarily throngs of tifosi lined the road offering newspapers for riders to tuck under their jersey fronts to blunt the wind chill on the descent. But the road was eerily deserted.

"Visibility was about one hundred yards," Hampsten said. "Riding in the slushy snow was tricky."

Plunging down the mountain, he and bareheaded Breukink could have let gravity pull them to Bormio. But the wind chill dipped to fifteen degrees Fahrenheit. They pedaled to keep their bare legs moving and feathered the brakes to keep ice from forming on the rims. Hampsten's rear derailleur froze.

"I didn't see any race officials all the way down the mountain," he said. "There was a mechanic walking with a wheel in each hand down the middle of the road. He was in an anorak [ski jacket]. He appeared out of the snow. I pedaled around him. He thought he was the only one on the road. There was no race radio. Usually there's a helicopter flying overhead, radioing the race report, but no helicopter was flying."

Phinney in his memoir, *The Happiness of Pursuit*, describes his terror going down the narrow, twisting road with few guardrails overlooking deep valleys. He worried if he went off a cliff, his body wouldn't be found till spring.

Near Bormio, the road widened to two paved lanes. The snow turned to rain. Hampsten's derailleur thawed. In the last five miles, the downhill steepened. Breukink pulled ahead. His team director, former six-day rider Peter Post, driving a Panasonic team car, was screaming nonstop in Dutch at Breukink to keep going, he could win. Neel drove behind Hampsten, ready to provide support.

"I had some hypothermia," Hampsten said. "I'm going about sixty kilometers per hour [38 mph] in a driving rain. It's a much faster descent on the second half. I was pedaling and tucking, pedaling and tucking. I used Breukink as a rabbit. He won by seven seconds."

Behind them, dozens of riders discarded their bikes on the Gavia. None of the other nineteen teams made provisions to supply dry winter gear. The road was choked with men who jogged, slipping in cycling shoes, seeking refuge in team vehicles. Or they rapped knuckles on car windows of tifosi and begged to sit in a warm car. English journalist John Wilcockson, on the Gavia summit, reported in *VeloNews* that previous Giro winners Roberto Visentini and Giuseppe Saronni "were reduced to tears." Wilcockson's reportage was repeated. The Gavia Pass stage went down in Giro history as "the Day the Big Men Cried."

The day's desertions were compared to the 1956 Giro's penultimate stage, through the Dolomites. Horrific hail, rain, and snow had forced nearly half of the starters to quit. Charly Gaul of Luxembourg, about Hampsten's size, won the stage and vaulted from eleventh place to take over as leader and lock up victory.

Breukink, winner of stage 14, jumped up from seventh overall to second. Race leader Franco Chioccioli lost more than five minutes and fell to fifth place.

Hampsten achieved Giro history as the first American to pull on the *maglia rosa*. He was a marked man over the final week. Italians sought every opportunity to win back the *maglia rosa*, although teams had lost an average of two riders each, which diminished their firepower. The 7-Eleven-Hoonved squad remained in full force to counter daily challenges.

"It was the most I have ever been pushed," Hampsten said. "My teammates and I knew we had a huge task. Nobody ever held back."

On stage 18's individual time trial, a taxing eleven miles uphill, from Levico Terme to Valico del Vetriolo, Hampsten won the stage to gain a minute on Breukink.

Hampsten wore the *maglia rosa* the rest of the way to the finish in Vittorio Veneto. Only 124 of the 180 starters finished.

Images of Hampsten in the pink jersey circulated in news stories on the Continent and in America. Admirers in Boulder where he lived collected all the pink plastic flamingo yard ornaments they could find. When he arrived at Denver Airport, he was greeted by a legion of well-wishers in pink shirts. They accompanied him in a motorcade to his log-cabin house (purchased from Olympic marathoner Frank Shorter). The front yard overflowed with pink flamingos.

• • •

Billy Packer, familiar to millions of basketball fans for commentary on network television college basketball, had an idea to share with New York real estate developer Donald J. Trump. Through business contacts, Packer wrangled a two-minute meeting in Trump Tower on Fifth Avenue to make a pitch.

Hampsten's Giro victory following LeMond's Tour de France triumph impressed Packer. Phinney had recently won the 1988 Coors International Bicycle Classic, America's national tour in Colorado and western states. The Coors Brewing Company announced it withdrew title sponsorship for 1989, to fund a new Coors Light Cycling Team. Packer sought to create a new national tour. He called it the Tour of New Jersey.

Ushered into Trump's inner sanctum high up in Trump Tower, he asked what the property developer thought about promoting an international bicycle race that could grow to rival the Tour de France. "I said it could start at one of his properties in New York City and end at one of his casinos in Atlantic City," Packer recalled in a press conference before the race. Aware that Trump's name adorned everything from a six-level yacht, *Trump Princess*, almost as long as a football field, to the 566-luxury-room Trump Plaza Casino and Hotel in Atlantic City, Packer said: "I told him we could call it the Tour de Trump."

Trump winced. "You've got to be kidding," he said. He paused and gazed out his office window, offering a spectacular view of Manhattan Island. Five years earlier he had spent more than $10 million for the New Jersey Generals football team and players in the short-lived United States Football League. He garnered more publicity in the USFL's single season than a decade in real estate. Ten seconds after Packer's offer, he said: "It's so wild, it's got to work."

Eight months later, on May 4, 1989, Trump sat at a table in a hotel conference room in Albany, New York, alongside LeMond and a half-dozen other cyclists as brilliant and high-priced as the crystal, marble, and brass adorning Trump's four-star Atlantic City hotel. He faced more than a hundred media professionals filling the room to standing room only from around the United States, Australia, and Europe.

The developer had allowed his name to be used in the Tour de Trump without his organization investing, unlike other sponsors, from Gatorade to Proctor & Gamble, from Oldsmobile to BMW, that wrote six-figure checks. As a result, the Tour de Trump offered a purse topping $200,000, with $50,000 to the winner. The 837-mile itinerary over eleven days, from May 5 to 14, began in Albany, wended south to Richmond, Virginia, then turned north to Atlantic City and concluded on the boardwalk in front of the Trump Plaza.

A glossy seventy-two-page Tour de Trump souvenir program featured bright cover art by pop artist Leroy Neiman. It depicted a cyclist modeled after Davis Phinney, arms thrust skyward like goalposts in front of a towering hotel and casino. The glitzy publication featured a welcome from Trump, his portrait photo and signature writ in a broad nib, vertical strokes sharp like shark teeth.

Asked in the press conference if he would consider changing the name to Tour d'Amérique, Trump smiled and shook his chestnut-brown mane combed in a 1950s Tab Hunter style. "We could if we wanted to have a less successful race," he replied, igniting a burst of laughter from the exuberant Fourth Estate.

Trump grinned around the room, relishing the attention. Unlike cyclists and managers in team warm-ups or sports journalists dressed like they were washing clothes, he stood out in a white shirt with a point collar, gold cufflinks, a pink tie, and a boxy dark pinstripe suit. At six feet one and age forty-three, he carried himself like a former first baseman.

"My name has turned out to be a great asset," he declared as cameras flashed like an electrical storm. Trump sat by Belgian sprinter Eric Vanderaerden of Panasonic, a team directed by former six-day star Peter Post. Jan Gisbers, director of the Dutch PDM squad, announced that he skipped the Four Days of Dunkirk in France for the Tour de Trump: "We knew this would be a really professional race. In Holland we saw a documentary on television about Donald Trump."

Trump and Trump Plaza partnered with NBC Sports and Packer's Jefferson Pilot Productions to produce the event. "The Trump Plaza casino is the number-one casino in Atlantic City," Trump boasted. "Trump Apartments in Manhattan have the highest rental rate per square foot in New York City. I don't want to have a race with my name on it that is not a success."

He waved a manicured hand to the scrum of reporters, photographers, and network camera crews. "My name is the difference between a press conference like this and holding a press conference and speaking to only one reporter." He admitted surprise when Packer proposed the name Tour de Trump. "Truthfully, I almost fell out of my seat when I heard it."

The Coors Light team, captained by LeMond, on a special arrangement for U.S. racing when not in Europe competing for a Belgian team, was among the eight pro squads and eleven amateur crews of six riders each. They composed a field of 114 starters from fifteen countries. A pro team from Italy had racers from the Soviet Union, marking the first time that a Soviet professional squad in any sport competed in the United States. The U.S. Cycling Federation fielded two USA teams—one included a triathlete from Texas, Lance Armstrong.

New York governor Mario Cuomo had the honor of official starter before the peloton in front of the nineteenth-century gray-stone Empire State Capitol. He set the riders and race followers off for the Tour de Trump stage 1 road race, on their way to a serpentine route through five states.

NBC Sports dispatched a crew of seven to program two-hour Tour de Trump specials on the two Sunday afternoons, supplemented by ESPN coverage Monday through Friday. The 7.5 hours of national TV topped what CBS had beamed of the Tour de France. NBC hired LeMond, in a blue-and-white Coors Light jersey, to record fifty spots for NBC affiliates.

In the race, flu hampered LeMond.

The Tour de Trump rolled over undulating and twisting secondary roads between cities, where crowds were consistently large. Bystanders held up cardboard posters. One said: "Welcome bikers, welcome Donald Trump, welcome NBC." Another read, "Send money, Donald." Giggling school children stood in a line facing the street and held posters, each with one letter, that spelled: "WE ARE OUT STANDING IN OUR FIELD."

Phinney burst ahead of the galloping pack to sit up, face beaming, arms high in the air, before enthusiastic throngs in Baltimore's Inner Harbor and near the Pentagon in the office enclave of Crystal City, Arlington, Virginia.

The event drew an audience of more than a million, doubling all cycling events at the LA Olympics combined, and generated unprecedented Northeast and Mid-Atlantic local coverage. Winner of the Tour de Trump was Dag Otto Lauritzen of Norway on the 7-Eleven team, which snatched five places in the top ten. For brass of the Southland Corporation in Dallas, parent company of 7-Eleven, the media splurge of their brand justified eight years of sponsorship.

Trump in his suit joined Lauritzen in a red-green-and-white 7-Eleven jersey on the winner's podium in front of the Trump Plaza. Mogul and cyclist waved to the crowd. Newshounds concluded the event exceeded all expectations. Plans were underway for a bigger Tour de Trump.

I was walking with an aide from the Trump Organization in the Trump Plaza and Hotel down a crowded carpeted hall when the aide spotted The Donald walking toward us. The aide called to him and made introductions. I was wearing the money-green Tour de Trump media badge around my neck. The instant our palms touched, he pulled me close and asked in a soft voice, "What do you do?"

"I'm a writer, Donald."

The future forty-fifth president of the United States threw my hand down, hard enough to bounce off the carpet if it weren't attached to my arm, and he walked away.

• • •

LeMond finished in a disconsolate twenty-seventh place. He flew to Italy to join his Belgian-based team to ride the Giro d'Italia, starting on June 11 in Taormina, on the island of Sicily. Over the last two years he had endured a shooting accident, an emergency appendectomy, and surgery to repair an ankle lacerated in a 1988 crash racing in Belgium. His winning form appeared elusive. Yet he remained confident and kept trying.

Also in the Giro and striving to put health problems behind him was former Renault-Elf-Gitane teammate Laurent Fignon. A native of Paris and a year older than LeMond, Fignon was nicknamed the Professor for his round wire-rimmed eyeglasses and having quit studies in veterinary school to race pro. In 1983 team leader Bernard Hinault was sidelined with a knee injury. Twenty-two-year-old Fignon, in his first Tour, won, the youngest Tour winner in a half-century. His love of nightclubbing, dancing in discos with chichi like Brit film star and Bond girl Jane Seymour, attending celebrity ski weekends, and his long blond locks pulled into a ponytail contrasted with Hinault's hard-headed persona. Fignon had won the 1984 Tour, ten minutes ahead of runner-up Hinault, on La Vie Claire. The Professor ascended to France's latest superstar.

A knee injury and two Achilles tendon operations in 1985 knocked his career sideways. Comeback attempts turned into media gossip. He turned inward, became remote, brusque, stopped smiling for photographers. Not until the spring of 1989 did Fignon finally return to full strength, winning the Milan–San Remo classic.

He dominated the 1989 Giro. Over the highest peaks that strung out the field of 198 starters, he gamboled as though riding for fun. Fignon took possession of the *maglia rosa* at the end of the second week. He won the mountainous 137-mile stage 20 in a drag race against a dozen others to the line. The Frenchman ruled the final week to win the Giro overall. Defending champion Andy Hampsten came in third.

The muscular and seemingly carefree style of Fignon in the 2,130-mile Giro boldly signified he was once again the world's top road racer. He was a heavy favorite to win the Tour de France, starting in less than three weeks. Another Tour favorite was defending champion Pedro Delgado of Spain.

While Fignon capitalized on Italy's majestic mountains, LeMond labored among second-raters. Stage 2 finished at 6,000 feet elevation near the top of Mount Etna in Sicily. LeMond lost eight minutes to the winner. "I felt as bad that day as I'd ever felt on my bike," he said. "I was so disappointed. I really lost a lot of morale. I questioned how long I could stay in the sport."

Teammates and friends encouraged him to keep pushing, to ride back into top shape. Yet he struggled. On stage 13 he barely could pedal up to a mountaintop finish in the Dolomites. He had nothing in his legs. In his room at the economy hotel where his team stayed, he cried in rage and frustration. He telephoned his wife that he would quit the sport if he didn't improve.

His soigneur and confidant Otto Jacome, a Mexican conspicuous on the European pro cycling circuit for wearing a ten-gallon hat and pointy-toed cowboy boots, noticed his friend's hard-tanned face looked bleached—a symptom of anemia. Jacome prescribed a vitamin injection containing iron. Grand tour cyclists burn up to ten thousand calories daily, five times greater than normal; such injections were allowed under the rules (since amended to prohibit injections).

"I asked a doctor about it and he said it was worth a try, so I did," LeMond wrote in a column, "Turning Things Around at Last," for *Winning* magazine. "From that point on, I was fine."

On the final day, a thirty-three mile individual time trial from Prato to Florence, a rejuvenated LeMond turned in the second-fastest time among the 141 riders. He blasted the course a minute quicker than Fignon. LeMond's rally came too late to make a difference overall and drew scant attention. Cyrille Guimard, director of Fignon's team, noticed. He forecast that his two protégés were going to battle one another to win the 1989 Tour de France.

• • •

The 1989 Tour coincided with the bicentenary of the French Revolution as well as the centenary of Paris's iconic Eiffel Tower. National sentiment was high for Fignon to win for the glory—*La Gloire!*—of the Republic.

Le Tour began on Saturday, July 1, in Luxembourg, a grand duchy stocked with castles and bordered on the south by France. The race opened with a blunder that threw the twenty-three-day race wide open. Defending champion Pedro Delgado reported nearly three minutes late for his turn in the small portable start house for the prologue time trial. He had been warming up and lost track of the time. He ended the first day in last place, 198th.

Dutchman Erik Breukink won the 4.8-mile prologue. Fignon came in a close second, followed by Irish strongman Sean Kelly, and LeMond fourth—all within six seconds. Breukink on the awards podium pulled on the *maillot jaune*.

The stage 2 team time trial pitted all twenty-two squads of nine riders each against the clock over a twenty-nine-mile route in Luxembourg. The fifth rider of each team over the line scored the time that counted for the team's overall time.

Fignon's Système U team, sponsored by a French grocery chain and directed by Guimard, was the fastest. LeMond rode for ADR-Agrigel-Bottecchia, representing three countries: ADR, a Belgian car-rental company; Agrigel, a South African fertilizer company; and Bottecchia, an Italian bicycle maker. His team finished fifth, fifty-one seconds behind Système U. LeMond trailed Fignon in the general classification by fifty-one seconds.

The course rolled west through Belgium. Then all riders boarded a plane flying to northwest France for stage 5, an elongated forty-five-mile individual time trial, "the race of truth," from Dinard to the two-thousand-year-old city of Rennes.

Just as the French created high fashion, elevated cuisine to fine dining, and set the standard for glamour, the Tour de France established the grand tour format devotedly followed by the Giro d'Italia, Spain's Vuelta a España, and most multiday races worldwide.

Le Tour's autocratic founder Henri Desgrange added a pair of innovations to energize the three-week contest. He devised a separate category for the majestic Alps and beauteous Pyrenees, called King of the Mountains. It awarded points to the best climbers counting toward cash prizes—in addition to money awarded for daily stages and overall general classification. He also introduced individual time trials. The many-time 1920s Tour stage winner and Paris native Francis Pélissier loathed time trials for their brutal demands; he caustically called them "go-the-whole-way-racing." These disciplines create subplots in the Tour's narrative.

LeMond caused a sensation in the stage 5 time trial. He used aerodynamic equipment favored by triathletes in America but scorned in tradition-bound Europe. His time-trial bike had handlebars fitted with a U-shaped bar, wrapped in white tape, which angled up from the middle to pull him in a low ski-tuck crouch, hands close together to part the air. Tri-bars were revolutionary. Race commissaires, known for dedication to the machines of riders in the first Tour, in 1903, tut-tutted before they shrugged and allowed them.

Instead of riding bareheaded like other pros, LeMond strapped on a prototype tear-shaped helmet, not yet available for sale, featuring a smooth plastic outside shell, yellow with white trim down the center, to cut wind resistance. His solid-disc rear wheel lessened drag compared with standard, spoked wheels.

LeMond won the time trial. He beat Fignon—blasé, like many, to gadgetry—by fifty-six seconds and gained a five-second overall lead. After missing the Tour in 1987 and 1988, LeMond took back the yellow jersey.

As Guimard had forecast, Le Tour turned into a two-man contest. The peloton continued in supporting roles, fighting for stage victories and media attention. Pedro Delgado, runner-up to LeMond in the time trial, was levitating in general classification like a helium balloon.

For five days LeMond owned the yellow jersey. Fignon snatched it back in the Pyrenees. Guimard had stocked the Système U squad with climbers to pace Fignon in the mountains. LeMond's teammates were prepared for rigorous spring classics but none excelled up hills. Fignon eked out a lead of seven seconds.

LeMond capitalized on another individual time trial on stage 15, twenty-four miles in southeast France from Gap to the ski resort of Orcières-Merlette. He rode faster than Fignon to regain the yellow jersey and lead by forty seconds.

Two days later, up the twenty-one hairpin turns to the mountain-top finish at L'Alpe d'Huez, Fignon stole time on LeMond. Again the Frenchman stood on the podium and shoved his arms into the yellow jersey. He led by twenty-six seconds. The next day, July 20, was stage 18 and went fifty-six miles to the ski village of Villard-de-Lans. Fignon won and extended his lead over LeMond to fifty seconds.

On July 21 LeMond's New York benefactor and friend Fred Mengoni celebrated his sixty-fifth birthday, LeMond wanted to do him proud. Stage 19 went seventy-eight miles over three mountain passes in the Chartreuse to Aix-Les-Bains. LeMond, Fignon, Delgado—all previous Tour winners—and the skeletal Dutchman Gert-Jan Theunisse in the polka-dotted King of the Mountains jersey, broke away over the three peaks. LeMond outsprinted his rivals, shooting his arms to the sky in triumph, a couple lengths on Fignon, second. LeMond dedicated his victory to Mengoni.

The Tour descended for an eighty-mile cruise to L'Isle-d'Abeau in eastern France. The cyclists then took a TGV express train three hundred miles northwest to Versailles for the final act—a fifteen-mile individual time trial from Versailles into Paris, up the Champs-Élysées to the Arc de Triomphe, and back down the avenue to the finish.

LeMond and Fignon would duel against the clock. The Tour winner would receive a cash prize of 1.5 million French francs, worth $250,000.

Fignon's fifty-second margin over LeMond influenced some Paris editors to prepare special editions of the Frenchman in his yellow jersey on the cover. They may have been swayed by the maxim from France's Antonin Magne, Tour winner twice in the 1930s: "Wearing the yellow jersey doubles your strength."

LeMond reckoned he had to ride fifty-one seconds faster than

Fignon—a daunting gain of nearly four seconds each mile. “I had to go all-out every second and told my team I didn’t want anybody to give me time splits,” he said. “I couldn’t think about anything else except to give every last ounce of effort.”

Individual time trials favor cyclists endowed with a deep understanding of their physical capabilities to apply even exertion from start to finish and better than the competition. Time trialists contrast to the climbers—tough characters fighting gravity up mountains that day-trippers pay good money to ski down. Both categories differ from sprinters—aristocrats gifted with high-end speed over the final yards that allow them to show off at the finish line.

Time-trial protocol calls for riders to roll out of the start house at one-minute intervals, in reverse order of general classification—the last one first, the yellow jersey last. More than a million people lined the route from Versailles to Paris, with thousands packed along the Champs-Élysées.

If Fignon won this third Tour, he would enter France’s pantheon of immortals. It was a sunny, sultry Sunday afternoon. His compatriot and teammate Thierry Marie, down in the standings, completed his time trail around the Champs-Élysées in the fastest early time: 27 minutes, 27 seconds.

LeMond had a passion for big gears. “Pro cycling is all about pushing big gears,” he said often, smiling. The bigger the gear, the farther he went with every pedal turn, but big gears are harder to pedal, like lifting heavy weights. Big gears separated amateurs from pros, and singled out the strongest pros.

Alexi Grewal described LeMond’s appetite for big gears, when joining the new Coors Light team for a training ride prior to the Tour de Trump. “Greg led us out of the parking lot where we had met up and we heard the *clunk, clunk, clunk* of his chain shifting in his biggest gear,” Grewal said. The team followed his example, shifting into their smallest rear sprocket and the large chainring as though they were descending a long hill. LeMond muscled the gear and led the Coors Light squad for two hours out and two hours back. The next day, young pros who had drafted the whole ride moaned about sore legs.

Second overall, LeMond was the penultimate rider down the start house's short ramp to the street. He rose off his saddle and leveraged ferocious strength to spin his legs as fast as he could. Then he sat in his aero tuck, sleek and low. He pedaled with smooth ease.

Crowds yelled for him all the way from Versailles to Paris, but he paid no attention. Nearing the finish, he sped up the famed tree-lined Champs-Élysées, home to world-class shops, restaurants, and offices, made a U-turn below the Arc de Triomphe, and sprinted back down to the finish.

LeMond flew over the line completely spent, gasping for breath. His time—26 minutes, 57 seconds—beat Thierry Marie's by 33 seconds.

As soon as LeMond could, he stopped and studied the digital clock over the finish line, flashing each second Fignon was taking on the road. LeMond watched, a nervous expression on his face, a fountain of gushing sweat. His soigneur Otto Jacome kept toweling his face like a cutman in a boxer's corner.

Fignon stormed the course in old school, bareheaded style, the ponytail between his shoulders. A painful saddle sore had interfered with his sleep the previous night. Pedaling made him grimace. When he reached the top of the Champs-Élysées in sight of the finish line, he had lost forty-nine seconds to LeMond—chipping his overall lead to one second.

Before Fignon hit the line, he had lost the Tour. The announcer boomed that LeMond won the time trial, beating Fignon by fifty-eight seconds.

So the American won the Tour de France by eight seconds—the closest-ever margin in history. He also rode the Tour's fastest time trial, averaging a fierce 34.5 mph.

His winning time after 2,041 miles was 87 hours, 38 minutes, and 35 seconds. The eight-second victory margin measured less than the length of a football field.

When Fignon heard he lost, he groaned and collapsed to the street.

LeMond radiated with happiness and screamed exuberantly.

The French press called him Le Roi Soleil, "the Sun King," after charismatic King Louis XIV, who redefined France with a grand sense of style, and because the king's Palace of Versailles was where this Tour time trial started.

With his aero bars, LeMond heralded a new era in time trialing—the sport's biggest change since 1933 when Tour riders began fitting derailleurs to their frames.

• • •

LeMond and Fignon battled again the next month at the world pro road race championship in Chambéry, nestled in a valley on the edge of the French Alps. They were among 190 contestants over a twisting, hilly 7.7-mile circuit lapped twenty-one times, a total of 162 miles.

Heavy dark clouds hovered until the race was underway and rain poured. Aggressive riding each lap up the Côte de Montagnole, a strenuous 7.25 percent incline 2.5 miles long in the middle of the circuit, compounded by slick conditions at speed downhill through a chicane and hairpin turns, eliminated nearly everyone by the final lap. After six hours of attacks and counterattacks, LeMond, Fignon, and four others were the leaders.

In the final two-thirds of a mile, Fignon, in the French national tricolore jersey with bands of blue, white, and red, ripped open a gap. He was chased by LeMond in a stars-and-stripes USPRO jersey, Dmitri Konyshev of the Soviet Union, in solid red, Sean Kelly, in the green jersey of Ireland, and Steven Rooks in Dutch orange. They stormed past Fignon with 400 yards to go, too fast for him to tack on.

The worlds came down to a four-man match sprint along the final straight, bordered by a vast crowd defying heavy rain. With 100 yards to go, LeMond, back low, legs pumping feverishly, edged ahead. He grinned and punched the air with his right fist after the line, winner by a bike's length over Konyshev, inches ahead of Kelly, with Rooks in fourth.

Fignon freewheeled in three seconds later for sixth.

LeMond had clinched his second world road racing title.

• • •

From lying in an intensive care unit at a hospital two years earlier, LeMond became only one of five men in history to win the Tour and the worlds in the same season—and the only American to win both.

The White House staff had issued him an invitation after his Tour victory for President George H. W. Bush to congratulate him in the Oval Office. But the cyclist was inundated with offers from around Europe to race on the cash-rich criterium circuit, deliver keynote speeches, and present awards at corporate galas. He promised to visit the White House when his schedule slowed.

When LeMond finally landed in Washington, he strolled on a sunny Wednesday morning, September 27, up the sidewalk bordering the iron fence on 1600 Pennsylvania Avenue to the White House gate. He was accompanied by Fred Mengoni; LeMond's father-in-law, Dr. David Morris; and Jean-Yves Haberer, president of Crédit Lyonnais, the Tour's principal sponsor. (Wife Kathy was at home in Wayzata, Minnesota, preparing for the birth of their third child, daughter Simone.)

A uniformed Secret Service officer at the gatehouse read LeMond's name on a piece of paper and waved him inside the compound.

The world champion cyclist could pass as an intern in a dark-blue plaid jacket, gray trousers, and a blue tie on a white shirt, accentuating his deep tan. His Oval Office visit went as scheduled—a photo op, a brief exchange of cordialities. He gave President Bush a yellow jersey and other Tour jerseys for grandchildren. The President doled out little navy boxes of cuff links with the Presidential Seal, the backs engraved with his name.

"It was very quick," LeMond told me, one of a few of the Fourth Estate to interview him. White House staff thought the meeting went too quickly. They lobbied the president, a former captain of the Yale baseball team, to spend time with his guest. He hosted LeMond and companions to a private lunch.

"This was a lot nicer visit than the past," he said, referring to meetings with President Reagan and President Carter—who invited Olympians to the Oval Office as consolation for the 1980 Moscow Olympics boycott.

LeMond left the White House to take advantage of favorable weather for a ride with local cyclists out of the city into the rolling Maryland countryside. He wore his white world champion rainbow jersey bearing bands of blue, red, black, yellow, and green over his chest and back. He drew no notice as other cyclists he encountered wore jerseys of their favorite pro teams.

• • •

LeMond successfully defended his yellow jersey in the 1990 Tour. His three Tour victories created critical mass that propelled him into mainstream media. Like country songwriter Willie Nelson and gothic novelist Anne Rice, he was so successful in his field that he crossed over to the general culture.

The *New York Times*, *USA Today*, and other publications hawked his image on page 1 above the fold, riding to victory on the Champs-Élysées or grinning over a bouquet he was holding on the podium. *Sports Illustrated* made him its exalted Sportsman of the Year. The cover featured LeMond looking happy in a tux, shouldering his Greg LeMond brand of bicycle. The American public took notice of this millionaire who shaved his legs.

"It was only after I won the Tour that strangers recognized me on the street," LeMond said.

Once in a generation comes a distinct figure whose name readily evokes recognition among the general public—like Miles Davis in jazz, I. M. Pei in architecture, Steve Jobs and Bill Gates in computers, Mark Zuckerberg in social media. LeMond fulfilled former world champion sprinter Frank Kramer's forecast a half-century earlier that to revive the sport in this country it would take "only one good American rider."

Yet sports figures are vulnerable. Lead pellets lodged in his body from the hunting accident sapped LeMond's Herculean stamina. In the 1991 Tour, he managed seventh place. His recovery lagged; performances plummeted from brilliant to lackluster. He dropped out of races, including the 1992 Tour—something he admitted was "devastating to [him], because [he] never imagined losing the Tour de France, let alone stopping the Tour de France."

He hired a personal trainer to boost his strength. He followed a strict diet. Nothing helped. He abandoned the 1994 Tour and flew home to Minneapolis and took a battery of medical tests at the University of Minnesota. Researchers examined the relationship of lead in his body to his energy level. Tests indicated the more he exercised, the higher his lead level rose.

"When I am in a totally rested state, I have no lead level in my blood," he explained. "But when I exercise, my lead level goes up and up. This shows I have mobilized my lead." When his muscles flexed and relaxed during exercise, tests showed that his blood picked up lead. "Slowly I will get more run down."

At the end of 1994, LeMond reluctantly announced his retirement from racing. He was thirty-three. He looked forward to spending more time with his family, recreation mountain bike riding, and pursuing business ventures.

• • •

One of LeMond's regrets was never competing in the Olympics. In cycling, the Games were still restricted to amateurs when he retired. The International Olympic Committee in 1981 had struck the word *amateur* from the Olympic Charter to open the Olympics to professionals, beginning with tennis and hockey. And in a momentous development, the IOC voted overwhelmingly in 1986 to split the Winter and Summer Olympics into alternating two-year Games, beginning in 1994 with the Winter Olympics in Lillehammer, Norway, followed by the 1996 Summer Olympics in Atlanta.

This change enhanced marketing opportunities for television networks, paying billions for broadcast rights; the Olympics were thrust before the public and media every other year rather than every four years. Opening the Olympics to pros attracted the best competitors from 180 nations to the Olympics.

The Union Cycliste Internationale called for one organization in each country to oversee all amateur and professional cycling disciplines. The U.S. Cycling Federation in Colorado Springs, overseeing amateur road and track, sued to take over USPRO, affiliated with the UCI in Geneva. The UCI ruled USPRO was the exclusive body governing American pro cycling.

The USCF offered a full-time staff coaching men and women, sanctioning races, administering records. The USCF held training camps, offered assistance to grassroots affiliates, and provided other services.

"Anyone who attends a USCF training camp improves at least 25 percent," said four-time national champion Nancy Neiman Baranet.

"They learned more at the camp than they would on their own, and they go back home to pass on what they've learned. This helps raise the standards for everyone."

The USCF presided over almost all cycling in America, including the more recent National Off-Road Bicycle Association (NORBA) governing mountain biking. In 1995 the USCF presented Simes an offer he couldn't refuse.

"We had a meeting of myself representing USPRO and representatives of the USCF and NORBA at the Broadmoor Hotel in Colorado Springs," said Simes. As a result, USPRO and the USCF merged. That cleared the way for founding USA Cycling on July 1, 1995, as the sport's umbrella organization, incorporated in Colorado, to direct the future of American cycling.

20

Liars Club

The world of elite cycling management was as small and interrelated as the characters in a Jane Austen novel.

—MARK JOHNSON, *Spitting in the Soup: Inside the Dirty Game of Doping in Sports*

Nothing protects us against practiced liars and hucksters; nothing ever will.

—MARY KARR, *The Art of Memoir*

In December 1996 Lance Armstrong stepped onto the Paramount Studios theater stage in Hollywood and faced two hundred cycling and media luminaries in black tie attending the Korbel Night of Champions. USA Cycling hosted the gala to hail the year's achievements and medalists at the Atlanta Olympics. Armstrong, twelfth in the road race, weeks later began vomiting blood, suffering severe headaches and blurry vision. By October he could no longer ignore groin pain. Doctors diagnosed testicular cancer. It spread up his body—tumors infested his abdomen, lungs, and brain. He was told he had stage 4 cancer and had a 20 percent chance of surviving.

Many in the audience had watched him barge into the sport, all brashness and swagger, as though he burst from a Bruce Springsteen ballad. From a brazen teen triathlete out of Plano, Texas, he developed through U.S. Cycling Federation teams. He won the 1993 USPRO Championship road race in Philadelphia, followed by a stage victory in the Tour de France, then capped the season by soloing to the world pro road championship in Oslo, Norway.

When he showed up to the Korbel Night of Champions, Armstrong had endured two aggressive chemo blasts. They destroyed cancer cells but burned swatches of skin from the soles of his feet to forehead. All hair, even eyelashes, fell out. Brain surgery left a pair of pink polka-dot scars shining bright as neon lights on the top of his bare scalp. Hidden was a stainless-steel plate over the back crown of his skull where brain tumors had been removed. Chemotherapy forced him to sleep up to twenty hours a day; yet chemo didn't scar his lungs the way radiation treatment would: if he toughed out the regimen, he had a second chance at life—and his cycling career. He still faced another chemo round.

He escorted Lisa Shiels, a blue-eyed blonde resembling his mother twenty years younger and thin as a Giacometti sculpture. Conscious of stares, he alternated wearing a black beret to cover the pink scars and removing the beret.

After dinner everyone filled the Paramount Studios theater seats to watch awards presented on the stage. Honored were Olympic silver medalists on the track: Marty Nothstein in the match sprints, Erin Hartwell in the men's 1,000-meter time trial; and, in the women's inaugural mountain bike cross-country event, bronze medalist Susan DeMattei.

Armstrong stood on the middle of the stage. "What do you think?" he asked, pointing a finger to the beret on his head. "With?" He paused a couple of beats before tugging it off. "Or without?"

The room fell silent. Unseen ventilation fans hummed. Here was a twenty-five-year-old who had ridden against the biggest names of cycling on five continents. As a rookie pro in the 1993 Tour de France, he scored an audacious 115-mile stage victory to Verdun by going into a rage-like, eye-bulging sprint in the last yards against five seasoned breakaway partners. Weeks later near the end of the 161-mile Oslo worlds road race over rain-slick streets, he fell twice and chased to catch the pack of international stars, then charged up the final hill in a shocking display of power. Over the final six miles he opened a big enough gap on the peloton to sit up straight on the saddle and cheerfully blow kisses with both hands to the crowd as he cruised to the line. Now in the spotlight on a Hollywood stage, he appeared shorter than his five feet ten, his complexion white as gauze. You could feel his defiance.

"What do you think?" he repeated. He donned the beret and pointed at it again. "With?" He tugged it off. "Or without?"

The audience spontaneously shouted in unison: "Take it off! You don't have to wear it!"

Armstrong smiled and stuffed the beret in a back pocket.

Through the happy confluence of modern medicine, his positive attitude, and encouragement from family, friends, and fans he outrode death. By January 1997 his cancer was pronounced in complete remission. Doctors declared he was free to train again and compete.

Until cancer had disrupted Armstrong's career, he showed potential to succeed Greg LeMond, ten years older. Some reporters praised him as the next Greg LeMond. Armstrong argued: "I'm the next Lance Armstrong."

Within a few years I would put my trust in Armstrong and write a book for him and his coach Chris Carmichael. I watched Armstrong embark on one of the most heroic comebacks in sports. Like in a fairy tale, he turned into a multi-million-dollar global superstar—unprecedented for a cyclist.

• • •

A few days before the 1998 Tour de France began on July 11, customs agents in northern France, near the Belgian border, shortly after dawn stopped a car of the Festina Pro Cycling Team, sponsored by the Festina watch company and among the sport's most successful squads. Agents found the vehicle loaded with enough pharmaceuticals to supply a hospital for three weeks.

Police arrested Willy Voet, the driver and a team soigneur, for possession of large amounts of banned substances: tinkling glass vials of EPO (erythropoietin, a synthetic hormone that boosts red blood cells and enhances stamina), vials of human growth hormone to speed up cell reproduction, red capsules of testosterone, amphetamine tablets, and other meds for thinning blood to prevent side-effects such as clots from EPO, which thickens blood density. There were boxes of needles and syringes.

Seizing the contraband, the biggest drug bust in Tour history, set off shock waves worldwide. Such a scandal confirmed suspicions that pro cycling was infested with doping. Leadership at the International Olympic Committee in Lausanne, Switzerland, saw a threat that could sour public interest in cycling and discourage corporate contributions. IOC leadership insisted that representatives of all Olympic sports create an independent World Anti-Doping Agency before the 2000 Sydney Olympics to combat sports fraud.

The upshot was reminiscent of the response Major League Baseball team owners took after the 1919 Black Sox Scandal over Chicago White Sox players throwing the World Series to the Cincinnati Reds. Team owners established a commissioner granted with full authority to act in the best interests of all organized baseball.

Voet, a fifty-three-year-old Belgian and former amateur racer, had no formal medical training. The team's doctor and its director also were arrested and questioned by police. Gendarmes searched the Festina team headquarters office in Lyon, France, and found the names of riders on labels of refrigerated EPO drug vials. The evidence pointed to a sophisticated doping program. Tour organizers kicked out the team.

At the Tour French police raided team hotels and rousted riders and staff from sleep to search luggage and personal belongings. Uncovering contraband drugs led to a Dutch team's hasty departure. All four Spanish squads and one Italian team quit. Of the 189 starters, only 96 finished, the fewest in memory. Journalists called it the Tour of Shame.

Voet stood trial, was convicted, handed a ten-month suspended sentence, and left cycling to become a bus driver. Several riders and staff on other teams were prosecuted in an attempt to rid cycling of abusers.

French rider Christophe Bassons of the Festina team had not been picked to ride the 1998 Tour and missed the police raid. Nevertheless, he was ordered to report to police headquarters in Lille for interrogation. All twenty-four team riders had to provide blood and urine samples, even undergo a rectal inspection to check for whether they took suppositories. Bassons emerged as Festina's only cyclist to test drug-free. He was nicknamed Monsieur Propre, or "Mister Clean."

He was unusual in another way—a college grad, with a civil engineering degree from the University of Toulouse. He discloses in his frank 2014 memoir, *A Clean Break: My Story*, that he had adamantly refused peer pressure to take performance-enhancing drugs. Bassons considered drug taking as cheating.

At the end of the season, Monsieur Propre left Festina to join La Française des Jeux, a team supported by the French lottery. He looked ahead to realize his potential in a clean peloton.

Officials of the Tour and Union Cycliste Internationale promised more frequent and advanced tests. Tour organizers marketed the 1999 edition as the Tour of Renewal.

• • •

In April 1999 Chris Carmichael, former USA Cycling national coaching director, phoned me to say that he and Armstrong had a contract offer from Rodale Books. Carmichael put Armstrong, leader of the U.S. Postal Service Pro Cycling Team, on a strict regime for the Tour in July. He explained that Armstrong hoped to finish in the top ten, maybe top five. Over the next year he could improve for a podium finish, then possibly win in 2001 or 2002.

Carmichael expressed doubt about what lingering effects chemo might have on Armstrong's liver, a vital source of producing red blood cells, and other organs. Of the thousands of road, track, mountain biking, and BMX races every year, the three-week Tour towers like Mount Everest. Only a dozen Americans ever completed La Grande Boucle (the Big Lap), as the French call it.

I had last seen Armstrong at the Korbel Night of Champions. He appeared so debilitated that I felt if he recovered and drove a car to the store for a quart of milk that that would be a huge accomplishment. Now Carmichael asked me to write a book about Armstrong and himself as coach.

Rodale Inc., publisher of Rodale Books, in Emmaus, Pennsylvania, promoted health and wellness through magazines such as *Bicycling*,

Runner's World, *Women's Health*, *Men's Health*, and *Prevention*. Armstrong's story and Carmichael's coaching were a natural fit.

Carmichael acknowledged the extreme odds for Lance's Tour scenario. He poured out a torrent of exceptional numbers Armstrong registered for watts pedaled, oxygen intake, and more wonky measures. Armstrong, fanatical about preparation, was weighing the food he prepared for meals—lots of pasta, fresh veggies, and fruit smoothies—to maintain his low 4 percent body fat.

Before cancer, Armstrong distinguished himself in one-day events. His combative weapon had been bursting away up sharp hills. But the Alps and Pyrenees in every Tour are as panoramic as they are brutal. Legendary climbs like Col du Galibier, 8,678 feet above sea level; Col du Tourmalet, 6,939 feet; and Col de la Madeleine, 6,539 feet, go higher in altitude than the distance of the Kentucky Derby, which is flat. Tour cyclists sweat and gasp as long as twenty-miles up those mountainsides, then fly down at 60-plus mph through terrible twisting roads to the next climb, and one or two more, for three or four consecutive days—in each mountain range. A contender doesn't win the Tour in one day, but can lose it in just one bad day.

In the 1993 Tour, Armstrong had won stage 8 to Verdun, passing farm fields and grazing cattle over an undulating plain. The Tour soon headed into the Alps of southeast France. On the first day, he lost twenty-one minutes to the stage winner; on the second day he gave up twenty-eight minutes more. As a neo-pro, he went home. He later started three other Tours, completed one: 1995, thirty-sixth place, almost ninety minutes behind winner Miguel Induráin of Spain, in his record fifth consecutive Tour victory.

To the sports world, Armstrong would enter the 1999 Tour as a no-hoper.

Carmichael stressed that Armstrong's illness had reduced his bulky torso muscles, built from years as a competitive swimmer and fitness weight lifter, while still retaining a high strength-to-weight ratio. When Armstrong received the medical all clear to resume training, Carmichael devised a two-part strategy.

First, riding a mountain bike while seated, rather than rising from the saddle to leverage body weight on the pedals, over rough trails and loose sand to boost his pedaling efficiency on paved roads.

Second, since he'd lost muscle mass in his butt and quads, he depended on smaller gears. Carmichael prescribed upping pedal cadence from the usual 70 to 90 rpm to 110 to 120 rpm. His road bike had a small gear for steep grades—like insurance for clapped-out cyclists to reach the summit. He spun through Texas Hill Country at 110 or more rpm for hours. Pedaling faster shifts some exertion from muscles to the heart, lungs, and blood; it also raises heart rate and burns extra carbohydrates. His body took some nine months in 1997 to adapt.

Armstrong's chronic back pain diminished as he recovered from cancer, possibly from muscle loss. He had a congenital fracture at the base of his spine, called spondylolisthesis, splitting the vertebrae around the belt line into two or three pieces. It prevented him from bending from the waist; he set his handlebars higher and rode with a hump behind his shoulders.

He consulted John Cobb of Baton Rouge, Louisiana, a pioneer in the science of reducing aerodynamic drag, to try more radical time trial positions in tests at the Texas A&M University low-speed wind tunnel near Houston.

Those improvements aided Armstrong in September 1998 as team leader of the U.S. Postal Service squad to finish fourth overall in Spain's three-week grand tour, the Vuelta a España. He appeared ready for Le Tour.

The day after Carmichael called, Bill Stapleton, agent of Carmichael and Armstrong, phoned from Austin to discuss the book, my fee, contract terms, and the deadline. Rodale had a working title: *A Perfect Ride: Lance Armstrong's Secrets to Successful Cycling*. Intended for a general audience, it delved into his sports background, how he coped with cancer, and his comeback. The book also provided tips on cycling skills, training principles, and nutrition.

Stapleton, in an expansive mood, ended sentences by calling me "brother." He grew up in St. Louis and attended the University of Texas at Austin on a swim scholarship. He competed in the 1988 Seoul Olympics, in the 200-meter individual medley, sixteenth fastest time. He earned a bachelor's degree in biology, a master in business administration, and a law degree. He joined the Texas bar and served on the board of the U.S. Olympic Committee.

An Austin law firm welcomed him on board. A career relying on legal precedents, however, paled compared with the money—and the action—of sports agents. He left to launch Capital Sports Ventures Inc. and represent Olympic-medal swimmers. One recommended Armstrong, who also lived in Austin. The two men became friends.

Stapleton explained he submitted proposals to corporate marketers. Proposals included photos, column inches of print, radio and TV airtime clients accrued—measures of publicity that would promote products. For Lance, Stapleton secured modest year-to-year sponsorships with Nike sportswear, Oakley sunglasses, which provided health insurance, and the Japanese bicycle components manufacturer Shimano. Stapleton took his 15 percent commission off the top, including the Rodale advance and any future royalties.

No matter how Armstrong fared in Le Tour, the book was intended to help promote more sponsors, bigger contracts.

If I accepted, I would have to quit my editorial job in Washington DC, giving up health insurance and a regular paycheck. My portion of the book advance would almost keep my income even to meet the deadline.

Armstrong's racing had impressed me. Time after time he audaciously bolted from the pack to create a new act—the getaway and the chase.

We first met in 1992. He rode on the U.S. Cycling Federation national team and put on a show for a hundred thousand spectators in the 120-mile Atlanta Grand Prix, a serpentine route from Peachtree Street downtown out over the hilly Piedmont plateau circuit and back. On each of the ten laps up a 1,000-foot-tall climb, clusters from the hundred starters fell behind like debris scattered from a highballing eighteen-wheeler. The finish straight was packed with people screaming. Armstrong drafted behind a seasoned U.S. pro toward the grandstand, filled to standing room only. He jackrabbited ahead in the last yards for victory—and a $10,000 payday.

In our post-race interview, we sat on folding chairs in a high school gym. I clutched my notebook and pen as he scrutinized me like a security guard. He came across as intense, confident bordering on cockiness. He relaxed at my questions. In our exchange he met me more than halfway.

Most riders scrunch up race faces under physical strain. He rode with a stare that could burn eyeholes through steel-reinforced concrete. He had bought his first bicycle after selling a drum set, giving up music for sports. A favorite band was Metallica. He listened to loud, emphatic beats and massive sound pouring from his mom's car radio as she drove alongside him. When swimming laps, Metallica songs played in his head.

His reputed aggression shaped a race even when he took it easy, such as in the 1994 USPRO Championship in Philadelphia. Early in that 156-mile event, a group of twenty-five fled while defending champion Armstrong stayed in the bunch, cruising on the 15-mile route around the City of Brotherly Love. Everyone in the pack eyed him, but they were sucker-punched. Halfway through, he veered off course to take a shower in his motel. A teammate in the breakaway won.

Armstrong's Tour de France dream sounded fascinating, bold, brave. Theater impresario William A. Brady, once Major Taylor's agent, manager of two world heavyweight boxing champions, and producer of more than two hundred Broadway plays, wrote in his memoir, *The Fighting Man*, that if you're going to fail, do it big because no one notices small failure. I accepted Carmichael's invitation.

• • •

Carmichael grew up privileged in suburban Miami and circulated in the right places at the right time. His father, Lynn P. Carmichael, was a prominent medical doctor, a clinical professor, and chairman of the University of Miami Department of Family Medicine & Community Health; his mother, Joan, earned a PhD in medical research. He might have followed his parents into medicine, like his siblings, except that at age ten in 1970 he was excited by South Florida's dynamic bicycle racing community. Expats from Cuba and Colombia brought their cycling culture. As the youngest in group rides and races, he was nicknamed Kid, a handle that stayed with him.

The Kid's easygoing personality, strength up hills, and classy finishing kick earned him a spot on an early U.S. Cycling Federation team for juniors. He was picked for the 1977 and 1978 USCF junior worlds teams with LeMond.

In the early 1980s Carmichael posted consistent wins: criteriums in venues from St. Petersburg, Florida, to Montreal, stage victories in the Tour of Mexico and the Coors Classic in Colorado, and scorching-fast crits in the Netherlands and Belgium. He was a shoo-in for the 1984 Olympic cycling team.

Carmichael worked a stint as apprentice chef at Le Chateau restaurant in New York. The restaurant's loss was cycling's gain—after the Olympics he joined the 7-Eleven team that turned pro. He went to Europe with Eric Heiden and Davis Phinney for the spring classics, Giro d'Italia, and 1986 Tour de France.

A broken leg suffered while skiing in the off-season shortened his racing career. In 1990 the USCF hired him as men's road coach. He had a role developing the next generation, among them Armstrong and George Hincapie, a tough New Yorker who started racing at age eight. Armstrong, Hincapie, and other juniors under Carmichael raced in the 1992 Barcelona Olympics.

"Lance and George and the rest on USCF teams that went to Europe to race season after season stayed in the same hotels and raced on the same roads as the pros," Carmichael told me. "By the time they turned pro, they already were familiar with the hotels and courses so they could concentrate better on racing."

After the Barcelona Olympics, Armstrong and Hincapie turned pro and joined the Motorola Cycling Team, sponsored by the electronics company.

Carmichael became director of USA Cycling's athlete and coaching programs before taking over as national coaching director. He knew the sport's ins and outs. By 1998 he left USAC to found Carmichael Training Systems and offer coaching, training camps, and nutritional services.

His client list comprised a dream team, topped by Armstrong.

• • •

One of the first things Armstrong did as his cancer treatments wound down in early 1997 was to found the Lance Armstrong Foundation in Austin, a not-for-profit to serve people affected by cancer. The foundation introduced an online community for cancer survivors to share their stories and raised money for testicular cancer research.

The foundation held a high-profile fundraiser the week before Memorial Day 1999. Armstrong jetted into Austin with wife, Kristin, from Nice, France, to deliver the keynote address and court donors. Carmichael came from Colorado Springs. Rodale arranged my flight and reserved a hotel.

We three met one afternoon in late May, our bikes leaning on the wraparound porch of a house serving as the foundation's office. Armstrong wore a blue U.S. Postal Service jersey. His dark hair had grown back, clipped close. He had a preoccupied look in steel-blue eyes like he was thinking of where he was going next. His tanned face was rawboned, cheeks concave like Nureyev at the same age. Carmichael appeared at ease, as slightly overweight as a weekend softball player, sideburns stylishly long.

We pedaled to a forty-mile evening pickup race outside Austin, on back-road loops through the Hill Country. The contest capped Armstrong's eighty-mile morning sally. He tucked into the pack of sixty or so, surfed wheels, didn't contest the sprint, and promptly departed for a dinner planned with his wife and friends. While Carmichael and I discussed where to meet after we cleaned up for dinner, we heard others say they heard a rumor that Armstrong would ride and were disappointed they hadn't seen him.

The next morning, Armstrong and I were scheduled to discuss the book, but Carmichael phoned to cancel. He planned to drive a motorcycle for Armstrong to pace behind and sharpen his legs.

In my motel room on the tenth floor I read magazines as a thunderstorm blew in heavy rain. A couple hours later the sky cleared, and I went for a ride. As I strained to pedal near the top of the mile-long Balcones Fault hill, near Lake Austin where Armstrong lived, he popped on his bicycle over the crest in the opposite lane and zoomed down.

Traffic clogged my lane before I could turn around and chase. The road ahead had nobody on a bicycle, but at the bottom of the hill the road divided with a sweeping right turn. It took me into the countryside, grassland to the horizon, trees here and there. In the distance I saw a dot gliding along the blacktop.

I couldn't see if it was Armstrong. I pursued, figuring I was good for fifteen minutes of intense chase. Maybe I could get close enough to shout and get his attention, or he could check over his shoulder and spy me and slow down. I hadn't counted on the blasting headwind, like a nightclub bouncer's hand pressing against my chest.

How ridiculous I felt, chasing a world champion dedicated to winning the Tour. My legs burned like wildfires when I could see the dot materialized into a cyclist in the blue USPS team jersey. Armstrong turned his head in my direction without a hint of slowing. I felt on the verge of blowing up and falling behind.

A red light at an intersection forced him to stop. The light turned green and he started to continue when I pulled alongside him. My chest was heaving. I couldn't speak. He grinned at me.

We soft-pedaled under shade trees bordering the road, a welcome windbreak. He said he couldn't start the motorcycle—gas in the line had turned gummy while he was out of the country. Then came the storm. I finally caught my breath and asked if he had anything in mind for the book. No reply. I wondered if the wind swallowed my words. I suggested he might have read something that inspired him as a model.

He stared at me and said he didn't read books—he browsed the internet and leafed magazines. He suggested I should talk to his mother, Linda Armstrong Walling, and Ironman triathlete Hall of Famer Scott Tinley.

Armstrong said that when his oncologist had finally given him the all clear to train hard and race, Stapleton sent letters to all the European teams to let them know he was available. Stapleton's fax machine spewed out rejection letters that covered the office floor.

"I was turned down by every team in Europe. They thought I was damaged goods."

His single offer came from U.S. Postal Service Pro Cycling. His salary was a fraction of his last million-dollar agreement. "My new contract is stacked with performance bonuses. They could bring me back up to what I was paid before. I don't owe anyone on those other teams anything."

That afternoon Carmichael and I convened in Stapleton's office, an alcove on the ground floor off the front door of his Spanish-style house where he ran Capital Sports Ventures. Stapleton, in a polo shirt and loafers, greeted us. I had earlier signed a representation agreement with CSV. In his office I signed a contract with Armstrong and another with Rodale Books. The wall phone was on speaker. Calls went unanswered as we discussed Armstrong's prospects.

• • •

The evening fundraiser attracted hundreds into a conference center. There was a mix of Austin business leaders, philanthropists, cancer survivors, cycling industry honchos, and cycling and swimming Olympians. Former Texas governor Ann Richards, in her pouf of white hair and bright-red lipstick, seemed to know everybody. Jim Ochowicz in a tux worked the room like a politician. Five-time Tour de France winner Miguel Induráin came from Spain to show support.

A wing of the floor was given to the silent auction—cases of fine wines from Texas and California, Dell laptops and accessories donated by Austin's eponymous magnate Michael Dell, Oakley sunglasses, Nike sportswear, Trek bicycles, and expensive swag.

Armstrong introduced me to his wife, Kristin, a willowy champagne-blonde, blue eyed. I met his mother, Linda, five feet two and ninety-five pounds, golden-haired. She addressed her son in a soft two-beat accent: *Suh-on*. She doted over Kristin, pregnant with the couple's first child, Luke—her first grandchild.

Armstrong at the lectern gave an impassioned talk about the importance of the Lance Armstrong Foundation—raising money for cancer research and educating awareness for early detection. He spoke without a Texan drawl, like a network news commentator, although he tossed in the occasional *y'all*. His passion and authenticity connected with the audience. They laughed at his light humor. Occasionally they interrupted him with applause.

Cancer is America's second most deadly disease, behind heart disease, and kills more than half a million Americans a year, twenty-eight million people worldwide. He discussed visiting cancer patients at their hospital beds and talking with them, listening to what they're going through. A cancer survivor and celebrity, he brought hope and encouragement—what he called pixie dust. The man who showed no mercy to beat everyone showed a softer side.

• • •

I resumed my writing job on the banks of the Potomac. Stapleton was negotiating with a Rodale vice president and assured me by email they were close to a final contract. He suggested I turn in my resignation and get cracking on the manuscript. I believed in the project and submitted my two-week notice.

• • •

Armstrong was brought up by a single mother. Linda Mooneyham was a seventeen-year-old high school junior in Dallas when he was born. "I thought I was blessed with him," she told me. She worked as a project manager at Ericsson, the Swedish telecommunications company with a division in Plano.

Lance said several times that he never met his biological father, his mother's first husband, Eddie Gunderson. "His name never came up."

Her second husband, Terry Armstrong, legally adopted Lance and gave him his surname, but the couple divorced and he remarried. Her third marriage, to John Walling, ended in divorce. She worked two jobs, sometimes three, to make ends meet before joining Ericsson in 1987 as a temp.

Like Carmichael, Armstrong began his trajectory at age ten, without any hint where it would lead. "He started out running, in the fifth grade in 1982 at Dooley Elementary School in Plano," his mother said. "He came home from school one day and said he was going to run in a race on Physical Education Day. He told me he was going to win. I reached for my purse and pulled out a shiny half-dollar. I said, 'Son, here's a silver half-dollar. Keep it for good luck.' He won the race."

Americans of all fitness levels were running and walking in weekend ten-kilometer (6.2-mile) fundraisers for all manner of causes. They drew hundreds of participants competing in age-graded categories awarding trophies or medals to the top three. Armstrong entered some and was hooked.

"Lance and I have the same psychological makeup," his mother said. "When we want to do something, we really focus on it. We don't understand the word *No*. That is not in our vocabulary. We have run into *No* so often. We learned to overcome it with confidence, by working hard, and believing in ourselves."

In the seventh grade, he joined the City of Plano Swimmers. "He didn't have a good stroke like others who already had been swimming with a team," she said. "So he started with a team of third-graders, half his size. To face up to the fact that he was in the seventh grade and swimming on a third-grade level, he had to swallow his pride and choke back some tears of humiliation. But he made that choice to join the swim team and work his way up. I told him, 'Son, all you have to do is beat that clock, swim a little bit faster in every competition. Don't let anything distract you.'

"He worked so hard at beating that clock. I'll never forget the day he tried out and finally got in the group with his peers. He was so proud. And so was I."

Armstrong swam in all competitions—butterfly, backstroke, crawl, breaststroke. He excelled at the mile. "He developed an incredible swimmer's build—strong across the shoulders," his mother recalled. "From behind, he was built with a swimmer's V-shaped back. He had such great lung capacity."

By thirteen he acquired a bicycle to pedal to swim practice from the apartment on the east side of town to the Plano Aquatics Center, ten miles away. Individual sports appealed to him, rather than team sports, to succeed on his own.

An over-the-top contest called the Ironman in Kona, Hawaii, leapt to the mainland. Ironman started on February 18, 1978, with fifteen men, including a former Navy SEAL, standing on Waikiki Beach near Honolulu in the dark. At first light, they splashed into the surf—and created sports history. They swam 2.4-miles through ocean swells, scrambled up the beach to hop on bikes for a 112-mile time trial around the island, then laced up running shoes to trot a 26.2-mile marathon—composing what they dubbed a triathlon. Twelve hours later, Gordon Haller, holding a college degree in physics, won the inaugural Ironman.

The next year, *Sports Illustrated* dispatched a writer and a photographer to Ironman II. The magazine's ten-page spread served as a birth announcement. Its dramatic story and images of athletes swimming, cycling, and running thrust this novel endurance ordeal upon the world.

Ironman spoke in a dog-whistle way to hard-core jocks. Promoters and sponsors saw opportunities. Three-time Olympic cyclist John Howard won the fourth edition, validating Ironman's credibility. Short triathlons pared down to a one-mile swim, twenty-five-mile cycling time trial, and a ten-kilometer run proliferated. Top finishers qualified for the next full Hawaii Ironman.

Fourteen-year-old Armstrong entered the short yet arduous triathlons and placed well against the emerging sport's big names, like Scott Tinley, winner of the 1982 Hawaii Ironman and again in 1985. A new U.S. Triathlon Series of short triathlons cropped up in Dallas, Miami, Atlanta, Los Angeles, Phoenix, and Bermuda. Winners took home up to $2,500—decent money at the time.

"I first encountered Lance in 1983, [Lance was born September 17, 1971]" Tinley said. "I thought Lance was a better swimmer than me—we were coming out of the water at the same time in 1984, when Lance was twelve and I was twenty-seven. I thought he had great potential."

One Sunday morning in June 1988 Tinley and his wife heard a knock on the front door of their home near San Diego. "It was Lance, standing there with one of his buddies. They drove in his buddy's car from Plano after the school year ended. Lance said he was in San Diego to train with us triathletes. He had rented an apartment about a hundred yards from my wife and me."

That summer Armstrong worked out with Tinley and other triathletes—including Mark Allen, a former All American swimmer and six-time Hawaii Ironman winner, and Scott Molina, winner of a hundred triathlons worldwide and nicknamed the Terminator.

"We were fifteen years older than Lance," Tinley said. "So we called him Junior. In some ways, he got a bad rap early on because people thought he was cocky. And he *was*! But when you got to know him, he was very confident of his abilities. He also had a rough time at home. He told me he had to throw his stepfather out of the house when he was twelve or fourteen years old. We cut him a lot of slack because under the show of cockiness, he was a good-hearted guy."

Armstrong won the 1989 National Sprint Triathlon Championship. *Triathlete* magazine named him Rookie of the Year.

• • •

In the spring of 1989 U.S. Cycling Federation coaches invited Armstrong and others under age nineteen from around the country to the Olympic Training Center in Colorado Springs to try out for the USCF national junior team. Those selected would go to the junior worlds road race in Russia in mid-July. Going to Colorado meant Armstrong missed a few weeks of classes from school.

In Colorado Springs he broke away in a circuit race and lapped the field for a solo victory. That landed him on the USCF national junior team. He was set to race for the squad that summer and go to Moscow, Russia. But when he returned to Plano East Senior High the principal said he had too many absences to graduate with his class. He had to take summer classes.

"Lance came home from school infuriated," his mother remembered. "I told him to go to school the next day. I said I would figure a way out of this."

He was seventeen, the same age she had been when, pregnant, she dropped out of high school. Later she earned a GED, but without a college degree she was limited to the ghetto of hourly paid jobs. Resolute about her son graduating on time and still going on the USCF team to the worlds, she phoned schools and explained that her son had good grades in Plano East but wasn't allowed to graduate because he missed classes while at the Olympic Training Center trying out for the national cycling team. Several schools turned down her request. But she finally found interest at Bending Oaks, a private high school in Dallas, which offered flexible approaches to teaching.

"I told them that I didn't have the money to pay tuition," she told me. "But if they accepted my son for the last six weeks of the semester and he graduated, he would ride in the Olympics and win a medal. One day the school could claim him as one of theirs. They accepted him without my paying tuition."

Faculty at Bending Oaks, about twenty miles away, created a program fulfilling his academic requirements in time for commencement. Armstrong graduated from Bending Oaks high, class of '89.

He competed in the junior worlds road race outside Moscow. "He broke away early so he could pass the grandstand giving the Texas hook 'em horns," Carmichael said, wangling his hand, pinkie and thumb sticking out. Armstrong was caught by the pack and finished seventy-third. "If he had waited till later to do that, he probably could have had a podium finish," Carmichael suggested.

• • •

The July 3 start of the 1999 Tour de France was approaching when I emailed Stapleton for an update on contract negotiations. I'd left my day job to work full time on interviewing and writing *A Perfect Ride* with Carmichael. Our timeline called for submitting half the manuscript by mid-July.

"We're still dotting i's and crossing t's," Stapleton said. "Keep writing."

• • •

Armstrong and the U.S. Postal Service Pro Cycling team went to the Tour as low-budget ugly ducklings. Nineteen other squads converged at the start in Le Puy du Fou, a medieval theme park in western France, pulling up in luxury buses for all nine riders and support crew. The Posties had two camper vans like vacationers.

Armstrong pinned on humble number 181, designating him as leader of the bottom-ranked team. He was among the first down the portable start-house ramp to the street for the 4.2-mile prologue individual time trial. Wearing a teardrop helmet covering his ears to reduce drag, he crouched low and gripped his aero handlebars in a ski-tuck position. He needed only eight minutes, two seconds to smoke the course. One by one the other 188 cyclists aimed to beat his time. By the end, Armstrong pulled off an upset win. He nipped runner-up Alex Zülle, a Swiss and the world time trial champion, by seven seconds.

The Texan stood triumphant on the podium and pulled on the yellow jersey. His trajectory from bed-bound cancer patient to the cycling summit in France created spectacular news worldwide. He pumped up the Tour of Renewal.

Armstrong held the lead only for a day, then reclaimed it on stage 8 when he won the 35.1-mile individual time trial in Metz, in northeast France, defeating runner-up Zülle by a minute. Critics questioned whether the Texan or his teammates would bear up under severe pressure over the 2,300-mile gauntlet to the finish in Paris. Millions lined the roads for a glimpse of Armstrong in the yellow jersey among cyclists whooshing past, and millions more followed Le Tour on television and the internet around the world.

While Armstrong's celebrity brightened daily, Christophe Bassons's standing in the peloton diminished. He was participating in his first Tour, on the Française des Jeux squad. The Paris newspaper *Le Parisien* retained him to contribute a daily column. Each evening he shared observations with a staff journalist ghosting his columns. They began with the kicker informing readers that Bassons was racing *à l'eau claire* (on fresh water), without doping products.

Bassons stated that inside the peloton, the majority of cyclists were pedaling on illegal pharmaceuticals. A minority riding *à l'eau claire* couldn't recover as soon or pedal hard for as long as dopers. He declared in print that it was impossible for someone to win a stage simply by being strong without doping. Bassons told readers the peloton was racing "as if the roads of France are nothing more than one gigantic descent."

The drug that most transformed cycling was synthetic erythropoietin, nicknamed EPO. Introduced in the late 1980s, EPO was an artificial hormone approved by the Food & Drug Administration to save the lives of patients whose kidneys don't produce enough natural erythropoietin hormone to make red blood cells delivering oxygen from the lungs to muscles. Athletes injected with EPO benefited from more oxygen to their muscles, boosting performance capacity up to 10 percent—a major increase when road races can be won by the width of a tire and time trials are sometimes decided by thousandths of a second. Cyclists on EPO rode like they had a motor on their bicycle. EPO was prohibited by the International Olympic Committee and other sports governing bodies.

Pharmacies sell synthetic EPO by prescription in clear-glass vials containing one-milliliter (about 0.3 ounce) doses. EPO requires refrigeration until injected, usually inside the upper forearm near the elbow. Besides raising an athlete's aerobic threshold, the point when muscles begin to burn from oxygen debt, EPO hastens recovery, like recharging batteries sooner.

Three other outlawed meds that aid riders by reducing pain, speeding recovery, and packing more muscle mass are cortisone, human growth hormone (designed in labs to treat dwarfism), and testosterone. These pharmaceuticals came after amphetamines, standbys for World War II fighter pilots, long-haul truckers, and pro cyclists.

A group of hormones that strengthen and bulk muscles are anabolic steroids. At the 1988 Seoul Olympics, Canadian runner Ben Johnson had tested positive for steroids after winning the showcase 100-meter dash. The International Olympic Committee stripped him of his gold medal and banned him as a cheater.

Bassons in *A Clean Break* writes that during the 1999 Tour his columns turned him into a pariah in the peloton. He violated pro cycling's self-imposed *omertà*, Italian for "code of silence," associated with the Mafia. Riders cruising in the peloton for six hours a day in the saddle usually talked about money, women, and cars. Bassons was subjected to radio silence, not even a simple *bonjour*. Teammates turned on him as a troublemaker. After each stage, journalists clustered around Bassons for interviews. In the second week, the cold-shoulder shunning that surrounded him advanced to open hostility. Riders sidled up, one after another like vigilantes, to scold him for talking to reporters on the lookout for dirt that would sabotage the sport.

Stage 10 on July 14, Bastille Day, marked a turning point in Bassons's career—and later affected Armstrong. The 137-mile route was fraught with pitiless climbs between the start high up in the Italian Alpine village of Sestriere, 6,700 feet altitude, dropping into a deep valley, then soaring again to finish atop the ski village of Alpe d'Huez.

Armstrong created welcome attention to the Tour of Renewal. Before the start of stage 10, he decreed as overall leader that the pack would ride easy for most of the day until in view of the final strength-sapping climb so the lesser talents could better ride through a hard workday.

Bassons retaliated against the dictate. At the first opportunity, he attacked. He ranked low in general classification based on total elapsed time, no threat to the leaders, and sought to score victory on Bastille Day, France's national holiday. The pack quickly overtook him and he sat up, caught like a fish in a net. Armstrong slipped next to him and put a hand on his shoulder.

"We are essentially the same size and exactly the same weight," Bassons writes in his memoir, adding that they also have matching oxygen-consumption rates. The physical similarities would suggest close results in individual time trials. Yet Armstrong dominated while the Frenchman seemed an also-ran.

Armstrong had a potential disgrace after testing positive for cortisone after his prologue time trial victory. But he was quickly cleared by a doctor's signed certificate claiming he was being treated with a topical ointment containing a trace of cortisone for a saddle sore, an occupational hazard.

"The yellow jersey stared into my face," Bassons recounts in *A Clean Break*. Armstrong said in English that what Bassons had been telling journalists was bad for cycling. Bassons replied in English that he was saying what he thought—there was doping in the peloton.

"If you're here to do that, it would be better for you to go home and find another job," Armstrong retorted, according to Bassons.

Bassons defended his right to say what he thought was true.

"Then get the hell out!" Armstrong exclaimed, sweeping a hand through the air in contempt as he swerved away.

The contretemps lasted about ninety seconds. Gossips in the peloton spoke for hours about it in the slipstream and later over dinner. Irish journalist David Walsh, following in the press caravan, subsequently heard of the quarrel. He suspected Armstrong was hiding a secret.

Bassons writes that his team director reprimanded him for sabotaging their team's prospects—nobody would cooperate with Monsieur

Propre or his teammates. Under normal circumstances, riders selected to ride the Tour keep going until they give their all and can no longer turn the pedals. Bassons found the antagonism against him infuriating. He packed his suitcase and abandoned Le Tour a week before the finish on the Champs-Élysées.

The day he departed, he'd missed finishing in Saint-Flour, in south-central France. Walsh wrote about a banner that fans erected over the road that read: FOR A CLEAN TOUR, YOU MUST HAVE BASSONS.

• • •

When I phoned my Rodale editor to tell him I was emailing a file with the manuscript in progress, he laughed like I told a joke. He said G. P. Putnam's Sons signed a contract with Stapleton for Armstrong's story. My editor referred me to Stapleton. I had signed three contracts, but Putnam's outdid Rodale.

Days ticked past before Stapleton responded to my phone call. He was under a tsunami of over a hundred offers a day—coming by phone, fax, email, special delivery mail. He hired staff from his previous law firm to sort requests.

Stapleton said he would get back to Carmichael and me with a different book deal from Rodale. We revised our chapters for a training book.

After stage 8 in Metz, where Armstrong regained the overall Tour lead, he stepped up to the top of the podium every day for the next two weeks, a smile creasing his face. He stuffed his arms into another new yellow jersey and shot his arms in triumph overhead. He was a conquering cyclist, the world's most famous cancer survivor. His former goal of a top-ten place, or a podium finish a year later, blew away with hurricane force.

Stapleton later told me, the last time we talked on the phone, that on the Tour's final day in Paris, he spotted a Shimano vice president strolling toward him through the raucous crowd on the wide sidewalk near the Arc de Triomphe. In the peloton zooming around the short finishing circuit leading to the final sprint up the Champs-Élysées, Armstrong in the yellow jersey was surrounded by teammates in matching yellow helmets and gloves. The Posties delivered their team leader to Paris—ugly ducklings transformed into swans.

Stapleton related that he figured he and the Shimano veep would discuss extending Armstrong's sponsorship. So Stapleton came up with a magic number that was outrageous. He would say the number, the veep would laugh, and they would haggle. When asked what he wanted, he was ready.

"I told him, 'Ten million dollars!' The next thing I knew, we're shaking hands and grinning at each other. I *never, ever* should have said my number first. You never swing at the first pitch. But I thought it was so shocking he would blow it off. He said they could do ten million, for five years. I thought I need to take a step back, go on a retreat, assess where we are now. Everything has become so wild."

• • •

Armstrong not only won the 1999 Tour and its $400,000 grand prize, he also set the record for the fastest speed in its ninety-six years, topping an average of 25 mph for the first time.

The worldwide media drove his life into hyperdrive. He received jackpots of appearance money to ride one-day races in France, Germany, and Switzerland before jetting to New York City for a press conference hosted by Nike. He was interviewed on the *Late Show with David Letterman*, followed by Fox cable television. He posed for photos featured in *Vanity Fair*. The press corps anointed him spokesman for American cycling and cancer survivors.

A private jet flew him to Austin for a parade in his honor. Then with wife, Kristin, and agent Stapleton in matching yellow polo shirts, he swooped into Washington. At a National Press Club luncheon, he received a standing ovation from the Fourth Estate, the U.S. Postal Service national headquarters staff, and the local cycling community.

Armstrong, in a blue blazer, beamed at the audience. "I feel a little funny standing up here because I think you guys are used to hearing from politicians, the military, people from foreign countries who are diplomats, and well-known people, but not necessarily professional cyclists."

His twenty-minute talk was followed by softball questions. He departed with his wife, agent, and Postmaster General William J. Henderson to the White House by limo two blocks away to meet President Bill Clinton. In the Oval Office Armstrong presented the president with a yellow jersey.

• • •

Carmichael was invited to Washington DC for the U.S. Olympic Committee black-tie awards banquet on September 18 at the Ronald Reagan Building and International Trade Center on Pennsylvania Avenue. He was called to the stage with four other finalists for the USOC Coach of the Year Award for Olympic and Pan American Games Sports.

After videos showed performance highlights and testimonies praising each finalist, USOC executive director Richard Schultz opened an envelope. He pulled out the paper with the name of the winner selected by a special committee from each of forty-five governing bodies. A hush fell like Oscars night. Schultz broke the silence by announcing the winner: Chris Carmichael.

"This is a shock," he told the audience of four hundred eminent athletes, corporate sponsors, and the media. "I think that the greatest thing that a coach can give an athlete is inspiration and motivation. And an athlete can give a coach inspiration and motivation. Lance has given me that gift of inspiration."

• • •

Stapleton at last closed a deal with Rodale. Carmichael and I co-wrote: *The Lance Armstrong Performance Program: The Training, Strengthening, and Eating Plan behind the World's Greatest Cycling Victory*, by Armstrong and Carmichael, written with me.

The material was based on Carmichael's experience coaching Armstrong and USCF riders. Carmichael prescribed setting short-term objectives as stepping stones toward medium- and long-term goals, training schedules, taking mental breaks by doing something different, evaluating the strengths and weaknesses of rivals, and remaining receptive to new workouts and different challenges. He also provided nutritional guidance.

In 2000 Rodale published *The Lance Armstrong Performance Program*. By then I had joined a magazine staff and fell out of Armstrong's orbit.

• • •

For seven straight years, Armstrong enjoyed the good luck of his mother's silver half-dollar, bearing the profile of President Kennedy. Every July from 1999 to 2005, the Texan planted the American flag on the Champs-Élysées. *Sports Illustrated* called him "the most dominant cyclist in history."

He topped LeMond's three Tour triumphs and the five each of immortals Miguel Induráin, Bernard Hinault, Eddy Merckx, and Jacques Anquetil. Yet the Texan's career lacked the depth of LeMond's achievements, such as two world titles, a Giro stage victory plus top-five Giro finishes, and nothing like the Europeans for victories in the two other grand tours and numerous classics.

Armstrong became one of the world's most recognized athletes when he retired from racing at thirty-four in July 2005. He was featured on the cover of *Outside* magazine ten times and on eleven covers of *Sports Illustrated*. He held multi-year, million-dollar endorsement contracts with Nike, Shimano, Oakley, Anheuser-Busch, Bristol-Myers Squibb, and more. *Forbes* magazine estimated he was worth $125 million—plus endorsements worth $15 million a year.

His divorce from Kristin, mother of their son, Luke, and twin daughters, Grace and Isabelle, was national news. So were liaisons with rocker Sheryl Crow, actress Kate Hudson, and a bevy of blue-eyed blondes.

Armstrong campaigned with a politician's flair on the stump to increase attention for cancer treatments and research. In eight years, the Lance Armstrong Foundation raised $75 million from corporate sponsors, individual contributors, marketing and licensing, merchandise sales, and other sources for cancer survivorship programs, research grants, and helped thousands of people with cancer. He served on the foundation and the board for gratis.

He was too busy to attend his mother's 2002 marriage to Ed Kelly, an IBM executive. Linda Armstrong Kelly published her 2005 memoir, *No Mountain High Enough*, coauthored with Joni Rodgers. She recounts rearing her son while learning on the job about emerging wireless technology at Ericsson. Corporate policy required its management team to have a college degree. She was granted a waiver to move up to project manager.

She describes persuading Bending Oaks school officials to accept her son. "And when I got them to agree to that," she writes, "I had to mention the additional fact that I couldn't afford to pay tuition."

Stapleton expanded his operation into event and music production. His agency was renamed Capital Sports & Entertainment, LLC.

Carmichael's Carmichael Training Systems offered coaching and nutrition programs to more than ten thousand men and women cyclists, triathletes, and ultra-distance runners.

• • •

Yet from across the Atlantic allegations swirled about Armstrong's use of illegal performance-enhancing drugs. He passionately denied every accusation, insisting he had never failed any of the more than five hundred drug tests he took.

Nike, one of the biggest names in athletic shoes and sportswear, put its reputation for quality behind Armstrong in a thirty-second documentary-style TV spot, "What Am I On?" The ad broadcast in 2001 over American television networks. The camera showed him in a USPS team jersey having blood drawn from his arm by someone in a white lab coat, followed by jump-cuts of him riding on the road and pedaling on a stationary trainer while breathing into a clear mask covering his mouth and nose as he intoned in voice-over: "*This is my body, and I can do whatever I want to it. I can push it, study it, tweak it, listen to it. Everybody wants to know what I'm on. What am I on? I'm on my bike busting my ass six hours a day. What are you on?*"

The message intended to dispel doubts and convey that he won because he trained harder than everyone and applied the latest science. This jibed with the Lance I knew. Over the years, riders who rode against him in Dallas told how he seriously he treated racing—firing off the front of the pack up hills, into the wind, out of tight turns to open gaps and break legs.

Irish journalist David Walsh of the London *Sunday Times* had been a fan of the young Texan's rebelling against the peloton's old-world pecking order. After Armstrong bullied Christophe Bassons in the 1999 Tour de France, however, the newshound began snooping.

In 2004 Walsh and French journalist Pierre Ballester coauthored a book, *L.A. Confidentiel: Les Secrets de Lance Armstrong*, published in Paris, contending he won the 1999 Tour on EPO.

Armstrong's lawyers sued to block publication in the United States. Under Britain's libel law for publishing an article that referred to the book, he sued the *Sunday Times*. He won a $1.5 million settlement out of court and received from the newspaper a written apology. The resolution tarnished the reputations of Walsh and Ballester and protected Armstrong.

I read news reports that doping suspicions dogged him in Europe. He heatedly denied accusations. I believed that a former stage 4 cancer patient who beat 5-to-1 odds against him wouldn't roll the dice with performance-enhancing drugs. Dr. Lawrence Einhorn, Armstrong's chief oncologist at the Indiana University School of Medicine in Indianapolis told me: "I gave him a 20 percent chance of surviving. His cancer had metastasized. The number was more to give him the feeling he had a chance."

Some athletes have inimitable makeups. Davis Phinney slowed down in his mind the furious action surrounding him, while thrashing all-out at top speed, bumping elbows with rivals closing in on the finish line as crowds screamed, and he chose the exact moment to shoot ahead and win three hundred races. LeMond figured strategies unfolding on the road like a CEO doing cost-benefit analyses to execute the move that miles, and hours, later would score victory.

I believed in Armstrong.

• • •

Bob Hamman, chief executive officer of SCA Promotions, a Dallas-based insurance company, seemed an unlikely adversary for Armstrong. White-haired, heavyset, midsixties, Hamman read *L.A. Confidentiel*. He contacted Walsh at the *Sunday Times* and paid to fly him to Dallas to share what he knew.

Hamman has always been unconventional. He founded SCA Promotions to offer insurance policies subsidizing flashy casino advertisings, consumer sweepstakes, and million-dollar challenges of sports events on national television. He saw opportunity in hooking audiences and inspiring fans to take a shot at winning a shiny new car or a pile of money if they sank a hole-in-one, threw a half-court shot, or got lucky at something else. In 2019 SCA boasted on its website that over twenty-seven years it charged fees on $10 billion worth of risky ventures and paid out $170 million. SCA determined the odds involved and charged event sponsors a premium based on the probability of someone winning the prize value and the number of contestants. In the glamorous promotional industry, he became a game-changer. ESPN labeled Hamman, the Stunt Man.

In 2001 SCA had sold a $420,000 insurance contract to Tailwind Sports, which owned and managed the U.S. Postal Service Pro Cycling team, offering Armstrong a $1.5 million bonus for winning his fourth Tour de France, $3 million for a fifth Tour, and $5 million for an unprecedented sixth. Hamman set the premium based on his trust that a cancer survivor who nearly died wouldn't risk his health using drugs, and on cycling's international governing body enforcing its rules against banned pharmaceuticals.

When Armstrong won the 2002 and 2003 Tours, SCA wrote checks for $4.5 million—greater than the Tour winner's $852,000 prize total for those years. After reading *L.A. Confidentiel*, Hamman refused to pay the $5 million bonus for Armstrong winning his sixth Tour.

A California native, Hamman had dropped out of the University of California, Los Angeles, in the 1950s, too engrossed in playing bridge in the student center. For five semesters he studied probabilities, watched how people behaved, and honed a knack to calculate the moves of opponents. He founded an insurance company and steadily ascended in the niche game of bridge. Over fifty years he won fifty national titles and twelve world championships.

In the autumn of 2004 Armstrong sued SCA Promotions to get his bonus. The case of *Lance Armstrong et al. v. SCA Promotions* went to a three-member Texas Arbitration Panel.

The case crawled on through Armstrong's unmatched seventh Tour victory and retirement from cycling. On August 23, 2005, in Paris *L'Équipe* published a cover story, "Le Mensonge Armstrong" (The Armstrong lie). An eye-catching color photo filled the front page of Armstrong in the yellow jersey at the 1999 Tour. The article by Damien Ressiot of *L'Équipe* was based on scientific analysis of urine samples tested at the National Laboratory of Anti-Doping outside Paris. Ressiot wrote that Armstrong had won his 1999 Tour on EPO.

There had been no test for EPO until 2000 when the French Laboratory of Anti-Doping, an independent agency, discovered how to detect EPO in urine. The 1999 urine samples were re-examined exclusively for research purposes. Samples were numbered to identify donors in one set of documents; separate papers identified cyclists by numbers. In 2005 Ressiot obtained a form with numbers that labeled six 1999 urine samples that belonged to Armstrong and tested positive in 2000 for EPO. The study's results were unofficial, but *L'Équipe* in 2005 contended they showed that Armstrong had lied.

Instead of seeking legal recourse, Armstrong played the American media. He appeared in an hour-long television appearance on *Larry King Live*. "This thing stinks," he said to King and co-host and sportscaster Bob Costas. "I've said it for seven years—I have never doped. I can say it again. But I've said it for seven years. It doesn't help. But the fact of the matter is that I haven't."

He referred to his cancer recovery. He said he had no reason to jeopardize his health with dope: "That's crazy. I would never do that. No. No way."

Armstrong touted the good work of his cancer foundation. The conversation shifted to whether he and Grammy Award–winning singer-songwriter Sheryl Crow would wed. The hour concluded with smiles thin as paper cuts from Costas, King, and Armstrong.

L'Équipe wielded influence on the Continent but didn't publish a U.S. edition. The paper's scoop remained quarantined in France.

A chorus of U.S. Olympic and cycling officials defended Armstrong in the media. Television producers, enthralled with his star power, booked him as a celebrity for appearances that allowed him to repeat that he never doped.

Millions of Americans saw him host *Saturday Night Live*, featuring Sheryl Crow as musical guest. In a public relations coup, he announced his foundation was establishing a chair in oncology at Indiana University, funded through a $1.5 million endowment for the Indiana University Cancer Center.

Armstrong had trumped Hamman's hand.

• • •

Hamman launched his own private investigation. He created a defense from sworn testimonies obtained under subpoena from witnesses giving confidential depositions under oath before a camera recording the proceedings.

Witnesses included Irish soigneur Emma O'Reilly, an employee of the 1999 U.S. Postal Service Pro Cycling team. She testified she'd helped Armstrong cover up drug use when he tested positive for cortisone after winning the Tour prologue time trial. O'Reilly said she was massaging him on a table when the team director joined them and discussed how to take care of this potential disaster. He and the director decided the team doctor would write him a prescription, backdated to before the Tour start, for a cream containing a trace of cortisone for a saddle sore. O'Reilly testified he didn't have a saddle sore and had a cortisone injection a week earlier to hasten muscle recovery.

The backdated prescription breached Union Cycliste International protocol requiring that any rider using outlawed medication first submit a doctor's prescription for exceptions to race organizers before the Tour commenced. UCI and Tour officials bent the rules for Armstrong.

The arbitration board, without ruling on the testimony, found that SCA Promotions were in the insurance business for the purpose of that wager. Since Tour officials had declared Armstrong the victor of the 2004 Tour, SCA Promotions paid him the $5 million bonus, plus $2.5 million in interest.

Armstrong claimed vindication. *New York Times* sports columnist George Vecsey wrote Hamman was "doomed to be remembered as the businessman who lost a $7.5 settlement to Lance Armstrong."

Hamman played a long game. He held his testimonies as aces in the hole.

• • •

In May 2006 Spain's Guardia Civil raided the Madrid office of Dr. Eufemiano Fuentes, a tall and flamboyant physician to highly paid sports figures. Authorities seized caches of EPO, steroids, human growth hormone, and diaries of doping schedules for sixty top-ranked cyclists on a half-dozen teams. Fuentes said that pro soccer and tennis players were also among his clients.

The Guardia Civil confiscated two hundred frozen blood bags—a blood bank from cyclists who visited Fuentes's office to have a needle stuck in their arm to make an IV transfusion into a bag to store for future re-transfusions prior to major races. The practice, called blood doping, is banned by the International Olympic Committee and the Union Cycliste Internationale, but difficult to detect.

News of the raid, called Operación Puerto, caromed like a cue ball striking two other balls on the pool table. The World Anti-Doping Agency, in Montreal, Canada, rallied more than six hundred sports federations—including the U.S. Anti-Doping Agency in Colorado Springs—to adopt the World Anti-Doping Code to fight against performance-enhancing drugs in sports.

The International Olympic Committee took the unusual step of threatening to bar cycling from the Olympics if the Union Cycliste Internationale didn't reform its sport. The UCI increased out-of-competition testing, stiffened penalties, and adopted a no-needle policy that prohibited injections of recovery-boosting vitamins, enzymes, and sugars.

Dr. Fuentes was arrested and later sentenced to one year in prison for breaking public health laws.

• • •

Weeks later at the 2006 Tour de France, pro cycling's doping problem finally reached America, thanks to Floyd Landis.

He seemed an improbable outlaw. Brought up in a sect of Mennonites on an eastern Pennsylvania farm, he had toiled as support rider on three of Armstrong's Tour-winning teams. Landis, four years younger than Armstrong, had wide-set eyes and red hair snipped short. He jumped from the Posties to lead a Swiss-based squad. In the 2006 Tour, on a day of brutal climbs he powered to a dazzling stage 17 victory in the Alps and moved up to second overall, thirty seconds behind the leader. Two days later, in the last individual time trial, he seized the overall lead and kept it into Paris.

Instead of gaining international recognition, he set a notorious record for brevity as Tour champion. Before he started the post-tour circuit, his urine tested positive for synthetic testosterone on stage 17. His team immediately sacked him.

Prolonged court appeals cost him $2 million, mostly paid for by donations he solicited from supporters believing his fervent claims of innocence. He later confessed to taking performance enhancers. The U.S. Anti-Doping Agency thumped him with a two-year suspension.

• • •

Armstrong's wealth, fame, power, philanthropic publicity, and seven Tours weren't enough for him. In early 2009 he announced he was coming out of retirement in an attempt to win yet another Tour before his thirty-eighth birthday in September. He signed with Astana Pro Team, based in Astana, the capital of oil-rich Kazakhstan, a former state of the Soviet Union. Nike launched print ads featuring his snarling, feel-the-burn race face, captioned: "Hope Rides Again."

Like former heavyweight boxing champion Muhammad Ali coming out of retirement at thirty-eight to challenge champion Larry Holmes for the title, Armstrong came up short. Five minutes down on winner Alberto Contador of Spain, Armstrong finish third. He announced he would lead a new team, sponsored by RadioShack, the chain of electronic stores, for the 2010 season.

Landis was racing again. Spurned as toxic by European teams, he was back where he'd started—on a low-budget American team. He'd disgraced his family, his marriage was ruined. He and Armstrong overlapped wheels in the spring of 2009 in the eight-day Amgen Tour of California. He resented crowds cheering Armstrong as an idol but taunting himself as a doper.

Landis grew up with a contrary streak. His father considered cycling as frivolous and kept him busy with farm chores. From dawn to dusk every day but Sunday, he lugged big feed bags, threw hay bales, dug postholes to maintain miles of fences. When evening came, he joined the family for dinner. Afterward, instead of relaxing, he jumped on his mountain bike and rode dirt trails; in the dark, he wore a helmet light.

His strong back and arms eased his rise among mountain bikers. He entered road races, gained national recognition, and turned pro for an underfunded team. The Posties snapped him up and took him to Europe. One rainy day in Girona, Spain, he persuaded a teammate to cut their daily training ride and relax in a café. Landis became a minor legend for downing thirteen cappuccinos, enough caffeine to kill a litter of kittens; his teammate quit at five.

It helped that he and Armstrong were the same height. For three years, Armstrong slipped behind his rear wheel in races, especially during the Tour up torturously steep, snaking, and elongated mountain climbs where Landis excelled and sacrificed his chances for Armstrong.

Landis begrudged Armstrong for earning millions to his $60,000 salary. More stinging was watching him travel by private jet or chopper instead of the team bus. Millions of fans, the insatiable media, industry chieftains, and the devoted cancer community all insisted on face time with Armstrong. Landis labored anonymously.

Since sitting out his doping sentence, he longed for something in return after all he had done for his leader. He agonized over injustices. As a neo-pro in 2002 he took performance enhancers like winners and most support riders alike. Headline cyclists, aided by support staff and supervised by a majority of the team managers, colluded in a pharmaceutical war to score the best results for sponsors. The press corps following races and fans waiting for hours in roadside tailgate parties to cheer riders swiftly passing by contributed to winner fever.

The 1998 Festina scandal only briefly exposed pro cycling's drug problem. But doping continued, the liar's club guarded by insiders enforcing a code of silence as vigilantly as lawyers guarding the formula for Coca-Cola.

Landis attempted to clear his name in 2007 with Loren Mooney, executive editor at *Bicycling* magazine, writing his memoir, *Positively*

False: The Real Story of How I Won the Tour de France. It was discredited. Mooney wrote a mea culpa, "The Lies I Told," on the magazine's website, saying their book was "based on all the lies Landis pathologically told."

An outraged Landis decided to blow the whistle on the sport, Postal Service teammates, even Armstrong.

In May 2010, while Armstrong and his RadioShack team competed in the Amgen Tour of California, Landis went public. The sullied 2006 Tour winner sent emails to USA Cycling officials and Postal Service Pro Cycling Team sponsors claiming that Armstrong had taught him and other Posties how to use drugs, game the system, and beat detection. He told the *Wall Street Journal* that the expensive drugs were purchased with money from selling team bikes. The *Journal*'s article ignited a media firestorm.

Landis confessed on national television to using EPO, human growth hormone, and testosterone. He said his whole team did blood transfusions in buses and motel rooms. He cited names, even Armstrong loyalist George Hincapie.

As soon as Armstrong completed that day's stage, he organized an impromptu press conference to retaliate. He angrily refuted Landis's accusations and insisted he never doped.

Around this time, I read an Armstrong biography by English journalist John Wilcockson, *Lance: The Making of the World's Greatest Athlete*. Wilcockson quoted Terry Armstrong, second husband to Lance's mother, about how he'd paid Lance's tuition to Bending Oaks high school. He told Wilcockson that his ex-wife sent him a letter asking him to pay thousands of dollars to the private school; he claimed to still have the cancelled check.

Terry Armstrong's account indicated that Lance's mother was misleading in what she'd told me and wrote in her memoir, *No Mountain High Enough*, about not having the money to pay tuition for her son to attend Bending Oaks.

In the meantime, the U.S. Food & Drug Administration opened an inquiry into the distribution and sale of EPO, human growth hormone

(HGH), and other performance enhancers among a list of more than 180 cyclists, triathletes, swimmers, and others in the agency's crackdown on drugs in sports.

The U.S. Anti-Doping Agency in Colorado Springs, under chief executive officer Travis Tygart, opened an arbitration case against Landis's protest that he was unfairly prosecuted by USA Cycling. Landis lost the arbitration. Tour de France organizers stripped him of his 2006 victory.

In the spring of 2010 the U.S. Food & Drug Administration, prosecutors from the FBI, the Drug Enforcement Agency, and the U.S. Postal Service delved into possible money laundering, drug trafficking, tax evasion, and bribing of foreign officials in pro cycling. Federal prosecutors impaneled a grand jury in a Los Angeles federal courthouse to look into the criminal investigation.

Landis shared personal details of the witches' brew of drugs he and USPS Pro Cycling teammates took. He handed over a diary of his doping schedule to the U.S. Food & Drug Administration and the U.S. Anti-Doping Agency. He declared that Armstrong and their team director had paid an international cycling official in 2002 to cover up Armstrong's positive test result for EPO.

Landis also filed a federal whistleblower lawsuit under the False Claims Act, signed into law by President Lincoln during the Civil War. Congress had passed the legislation in response to civilian contractors swindling the federal government. The act grants private citizens the right to sue on behalf of Uncle Sam. Landis cited Armstrong, Bill Stapleton, Stapleton's Capital Sports & Entertainment, and Tailwind Sports, owner of the USPS Pro Team.

His suit claimed the team had defrauded the USPS, which paid $32.3 million from 1998 through 2004 as title sponsor. Under the False Claims Act, the government could win triple the amount—almost $100 million. Landis as whistleblower could collect up to 25 percent.

• • •

U.S. Food & Drug Administration prosecutors subpoenaed and solicited testimony from more than a dozen minor players, then widened the probe with a grand jury impaneled in Los Angeles. Testimonies came from Armstrong's USPS teammates, including Tyler Hamilton, who helped him win his first three Tours. George Hincapie, who assisted Armstrong in all seven Tour victories, gave a separate deposition. Each cyclist testified alone, in closed sessions.

Prosecutors upped the tempo like French composer Maurice Ravel's *Boléro* by informing officials at team sponsors Trek, Nike, and Oakley about the probe. Prosecutors flew overseas to meet with officers at the headquarters of the international police agency Interpol in Lyon, France, consulted with French and Italian prosecutors conducting their own investigations, and conferred with leaders of other national anti-doping powers.

By 2009, the cancer foundation's tenth anniversary, officials and staff dropped using Armstrong's name, referring to the organization as the Livestrong Foundation. It raised a hefty $50.4 million from individuals, marketing and licensing, and merchandise sales and distributed $30 million (81 percent of expenditures) on education and policy, advocacy and government relations, and research grants. The foundation served 260,000 visitors through online support services. It disseminated 19,200 cancer guidebooks and planners to help patients and families better cope with the disease and treatments.

Armstrong's 2010 Tour de France brought him more problems than all his previous campaigns combined. Tires punctured. Pileups in the peloton cost him time. He fell off his bike at 40 mph, shredding his RadioShack jersey and tearing skin from his back, elbows, and legs.

He couldn't avoid news from Los Angeles about subpoenas issued to witnesses who financed the Postal Service team to testify before the grand jury. In Paris he finished twenty-third overall, thirty-nine minutes behind winner Alberto Contador—who was later disqualified for using a banned substance, clenbuterol, with the Tour going to runner-up Andy Schleck of Luxembourg.

• • •

Armstrong retired again from cycling. He resumed competing in triathlons. Accusations of performance-enhancing drugs shadowed him.

Yet the cancer community, influential politicians, and international corporate sponsors backed Armstrong. He seemed too big to fail.

In May 2011 the balance of power between Armstrong and the investigation to clean up the sport changed. CBS's weekly news magazine *60 Minutes* aired an interview with Tyler Hamilton. He'd been busted twice for blood doping; he served two suspensions between 2005 and 2008, then in the spring of 2009 he failed another drug test, for an illegal steroid, and retired. Like Landis, he'd spent his savings defending himself unsuccessfully in litigation, and his marriage hit the rocks. But he witnessed cycling's underworld and agreed to talk.

"He took what we all took," Hamilton said of Armstrong. "There was EPO, there was testosterone. And I did see a transfusion, a blood transfusion." He said Armstrong and team leaders pushed a doping schedule to win Tours.

Armstrong the next day in a press conference angrily denied the accusations. He persisted he was "the most tested athlete on the planet," claiming to have been tested five hundred times. His attorneys sent a letter to the CBS chairman and the *60 Minutes* executive producer, accusing the segment of building on falsehoods. The letter demanded that *60 Minutes* give Armstrong an on-air apology for the charge that he had used EPO. CBS stood by its story.

Hours later, *CBS Evening News* broke the story that George Hincapie, one of the most respected pro cyclists, told federal investigators in a deposition that he and Armstrong supplied each other with EPO and took testosterone for races.

Armstrong and Hincapie had been together since trying out as teens for the USCF national junior team in Colorado Springs. In contrast to Armstrong's brusque disposition and raptor stare, Hincapie, two years younger, had a Buddha-like calm, his dark eyes expressing warmth. For his congeniality and six-foot-three stature, he was nicknamed Big George.

Hincapie, from the New York borough of Queens, learned how to ride a bike from his big sister, Clara. He followed older brother, Rich, and their father, Ricardo, into racing. From an early age pedaling in the onslaught of car and truck traffic that turned roads into pocked, rutted, and corduroy pavement, Hincapie developed a keen sense of where he was at all times in the flowing river of steel. He served as Armstrong's lead-out man in the peloton in daily elbow-bumping, wheel-rubbing wind-ups of Tour de France stage finishes.

Hincapie never tested positive. His revelations in the CBS *Evening News* disclosure came from a leaked confidential deposition. Upon learning of the news report, like millions of viewers across America and around the world, I thought Hincapie told the truth.

The *60 Minutes* broadcast and CBS *Evening News* report struck a one-two punch that cracked Armstrong's saintly image. Nevertheless, a grassroots legion of cancer survivors from coast to coast rallied behind him. The Associated Press quoted cancer survivor Raifie Bass of Aspen, Colorado: "What Lance has done for the global message of cancer and awareness, it's unstoppable."

The federal criminal investigation continued for the rest of the year without handing down an indictment.

• • •

On the Friday of the February 2012 Super Bowl weekend, the U.S. Attorney's Office for the Central District of California, investigating Armstrong, loaded a notice on its website titled: "U.S. Attorney Closes Investigation of Professional Cycling Team."

The two-year probe cost taxpayers millions and shut down without explanation. The grand jury was disbanded. Prosecutors expressed shock.

Juliet Macur of the *New York Times* covered Armstrong's Tour victories and subsequent investigations into doping allegation. She writes in her book, *Cycle of Lies: The Fall of Lance Armstrong*, that André Birotte Jr., the U.S. attorney for the Central District of California, dropped the case due to pressure from Armstrong supporters on Capitol Hill. Members of Congress submitted more than twenty pages of letters to the U.S. Department of Justice opposing the federal investigation—letters never released to the public.

Armstrong maneuvered national lawmakers to win the public's opinion.

Travis Tygart, a lawyer and chief executive officer of the U.S. Anti-Doping Agency, however, plotted a chess move to capture the king.

• • •

The Justice Department, studying whether to join Landis's False Claims Act lawsuit, declined to hand over case files to Tygart, so he couldn't resume the federal case against Armstrong. Over the spring Tygart contacted former Armstrong teammates, most still competing. The key witness would be Hincapie. He felt burned when his confidential deposition about Armstrong leaked to CBS *Evening News*. Big George abhorred the notion of testifying again. But USADA governed all U.S. Olympic athletes; if he wanted to keep racing, he had to cooperate.

Hincapie in his memoir, *The Loyal Lieutenant: My Story, Leading Out Lance and Pushing Through the Pain on the Rocky Road to Paris*, written with NBC sportscaster Craig Hummer, tells how he took performance-enhancing drugs as a young pro in 1993. He saw seasoned teammates swallowing and injecting a variety of pharmaceuticals in apartments, hotel rooms, and on the team bus as casually as construction workers donning hard hats.

"The thought of cheating never crossed my mind," he wrote. "It was the thought of not letting myself get cheated that drove me." In 2006, as out-of-competition drug tests ramped up, he went clean.

Big George won national road and time trial titles. He competed in five Olympics. What he was most proud of was his sixteen Tour de France finishes, the most by far of any American. He aspired to entering the 2012 Tour for his seventeenth Tour to tie the all-time record held by Dutch legend Joop Zoetemelk.

If Hincapie testified against Armstrong and the U.S. Postal Service team, Tygart could offer him a delayed six-month suspension, starting in September. If he didn't cooperate, he faced an immediate lifetime ban. It was the hardest decision of his career. He finally acquiesced.

Tygart and his USADA staff of almost fifty at their Colorado Springs headquarters collected evidence for a report based on sworn testimonies from eleven former teammates, who received delayed suspensions, like Hincapie, if they were still competing; support employees against Armstrong; the team manager, team trainer, two team medical doctors, and Armstrong's personal coach in Italy, Dr. Michele Ferrari, an outspoken advocate of improving performances through pharmaceuticals.

On June 28, USADA charged Armstrong for acting as the center of an elaborate doping ring in all seven Tour victories. The charges were based on a mass of lab results and financial transactions to purchase outlawed drugs. Armstrong was accused of breaking anti-doping rules by using EPO, cortisone, testosterone, human growth hormone, blood transfusions, and saline injections to dilute blood levels of EPO for unplanned drug tests, from 1996 through 2010.

• • •

On August 20, Armstrong sued USADA and Tygart in federal court in Washington DC to stop its investigation on the grounds it was unconstitutional.

The lawsuit ignited dismissals and counter-suits that concluded with U.S. district court judge Sam Sparks declaring that USADA had the authority to pursue its case.

Tygart and USADA won in federal court to set up his endgame.

Three days later came the unexpected. "Enough is enough," Armstrong said through lawyers. He accepted USADA's sanctions barring him from competing. He insisted his decision did not mean he was admitting guilt—he wanted to spend more time with his family and his foundation. He and lawyers reasoned that without a public hearing, USADA's evidence would stay confidential; he could say there was no evidence against him.

That changed at 10 a.m. on October 10, 2012. Tygart played his chess move. He went public with USADA's "Reasoned Decision." USADA released a report, "Statement from USADA CEO Travis T. Tygart Regarding the U.S. Postal Service Pro Cycling Team Doping Conspiracy," on its website for all the world to read.

Tygart appeared on the local ESPN station to discuss the team's doping conspiracy in a national broadcast.

The report and support material topped a thousand pages and delivered an overwhelming argument that Armstrong had lied for years about taking performance-enhancing drugs. Testimonies from former teammates and staff were listed in alpha order, including Hincapie. There were incriminating photos and video. USADA said the USPS Pro Cycling team operated "the most sophisticated professional and successful doping program that sport has ever seen." Results of blood tests indicated that Armstrong had failed twice, including testing positive for cortisone after winning the 1999 Tour prologue time trial. Evidence indicated the number of tests he passed was about three hundred rather than the five hundred he claimed.

The case proved beyond the shadow of a doubt that Armstrong had taken performance-enhanced drugs and blood-doped, and he lied about it.

• • •

Armstrong's honor, power, and fame evaporated. Nike terminated its contract, worth millions. The Trek Bicycle Corporation bailed. RadioShack dropped him. Ditto Oakley, despite having created national news for fighting successfully with its insurance carrier on his behalf during cancer treatments when the insurer wanted to drop him to avoid huge medical bills. He lost $15 million in cash flow.

Rodale Books discontinued *The Lance Armstrong Performance Program*. His two tomes written with Sally Jenkins at Putnam's were pulped.

His mother's *No Mountain High Enough* also disappeared.

The *Sunday Times* of London sued Armstrong and won back its earlier $1.5 million settlement, plus interest.

David Walsh regained credibility. His book, *Seven Deadly Sins: My Pursuit of Lance Armstrong*, was adapted into a feature film by English director Stephen Frears, *The Program*, alluding to the doping protocol.

In the movie, Bob Hamman was portrayed by Dustin Hoffman. Hamman and SCA Promotions sued to recover $12.1 million plus interest the company paid Armstrong; they settled out of court for an undisclosed sum.

Chris Carmichael turned away from his former protégé.

Tour de France organizers scrubbed Armstrong's name from Le Tour's records. The only years in Tour history where no winners are listed are during World War I, World War II, and from 1999 to 2005.

The International Olympic Committee revoked the bronze medal he was awarded in the individual time trial at the 2000 Sydney Olympics.

Armstrong's hardest personal blow came from the foundation he founded. Its board ousted him as chairman and renamed it the Livestrong Foundation.

• • •

The U.S. Justice Department joined Landis in 2013 in the whistleblower lawsuit, which Armstrong said could leave him bankrupt. He spent his days consulting with a team of high-priced lawyers.

On April 19, 2018—weeks before the case was scheduled for a jury trial in the Federal District Court in Washington, where he risked paying the federal government nearly $100 million if he lost—Armstrong agreed to pay $5 million to the federal government.

A total of $1.1 million of the government's payment went to Landis. In addition, Armstrong paid him $1.65 million to cover legal costs, according to lawyers for both Landis and Armstrong.

The eight-year case ended and left him, age forty-six, with a fortune worth north of $25 million.

• • •

Armstrong's story of the man who fought stage 4 cancer, regained his health, and won the most grueling sports event in the world for an unprecedented seven years seemed like a fairy tale, which calls for a happy ending. In truth, it was a tragedy, ending in disgrace.

If Armstrong had stayed retired after 2005, he may have escaped detection: the statute of limitations on blood samples was running out, and he may have avoided infuriating Landis.

Mary Karr in *The Art of Memoir* relates she wrote a blurb in 1996 praising Binjamin Wilkomirski's childhood recollection of the Nazi concentration camp at Auschwitz, *Fragments*, winner of international literary prizes but subsequently exposed as a fraud. The *New Yorker* writer Philip Gourevitch outed author Wilkomirski, born Bruno Dössekker, a Christian who spent the war years as a child living in Switzerland, a haven for refugees.

We all know that if something sounds too good to be true, it's probably not true. Lance Armstrong seemed so exceptional. I wanted to believe his story. I never suspected his secret. He didn't know there's no such thing as a secret—only a head start.

21

Queen of the Oval Hour

The artist is nothing without the gift,
but the gift is nothing without work.
—ÉMILE ZOLA

Evelyn "Evie" Stevens wanted to fly. On February 27, 2016, she swooped on an aero bicycle through sloping turns and skimmed the straights of the 7-Eleven Velodrome in Colorado Springs. Sheathed in a long-sleeved skinsuit, back flat, arms extended, she sliced through the air like Superwoman. Stevens, a Dartmouth grad who had chucked a Wall Street investment banking career to race bikes, focused on breaking the Union Cycliste Internationale women's world hour record—to pedal farther from a standing start in sixty minutes than any woman ever. She chased the record of 46.882 kilometers (29.1 miles) set a month earlier in Adelaide, Australia.

Conditions at the velodrome in Memorial Park near the Olympic Training Center were near perfect. The mile-high, open-air facility offered thin air and had recently been upgraded with a white acrylic dome to allow the oval to operate through the winter. The dome cupped eighty-five feet tall. (It could be removed in warm weather.) Almost a hundred electric lights suspended from the ceiling illuminated the interior. There was no wind and the temperature was controlled.

The interior white polyester canopy lining blocked out the grandstand and surrounding seats, lending a laboratory atmosphere and heightening sounds. About two hundred people packed the infield: officials, media, sponsor reps, and those lucky enough to purchase a limited number of tickets, snapped up within minutes after USA Cycling announced their sale on its website. About fifty thousand viewers and media worldwide watched Stevens in a livestream internet broadcast.

To casual observers, even most of the cycling community, the hour record appears like a regular time trial. Yet the differences are stark. Time trials take place on roads with hills and corners. Riders shift gears, lean through turns, rise off the saddle up inclines, and have the liberty to swig from a bottle carried on the frame. The hour-record ride has no second place—either you set a new record or you don't. Charging from a standing start to quickly reach a record-breaking pace, Stevens had locked into the position she would hold for the duration. She turned over the same gear. She fired the same muscles every pedal stroke. If she crossed the start-finish line off record pace for one lap, she had fallen behind schedule, difficult to make up; two tardy laps could mean she was burnt toast.

After forty-five minutes of unwavering world-record speed, her body cried out for relief, the pain unlike any she'd ever felt in her thirty-two years.

Dan Lee, author of *The Belgian Hammer: Forging Young Americans into Professional Cyclists*, stood on the home straight watching. "I could tell from the look of her face that she was in pain," he said.

• • •

Stevens's ability to sustain world-record pace goes back to college days, a scrappy underdog vying against other high achievers for the last spot on the Dartmouth women's varsity tennis team. Once she'd earned her place, she never let up her competitive drive while majoring in government and women's studies. The fourth of five siblings growing up in the Boston suburb of Acton, her ambitions at age nine were to become a reporter, an Olympian, and the president.

Upon graduating from Dartmouth, class of 2005, she moved to New York City. Work as a reporter lost appeal as the internet blew up the communications industry. Striving grads went to Wall Street for big money. Lehman Brothers, one of the largest investment banks, holding assets of more than $600 billion, hired her with a signing bonus (unheard of for cub reporters).

On workday mornings she pulled on a business suit, grabbed a cup of coffee, and left her small apartment for Lehman's high-rise glass-and-steel world headquarters. She was partial to wearing pearl earrings. A curling iron disciplined her brunette hair to cascade shoulder-length. She applied makeup sparingly. She shouldered a duffle bag. More than a fashion item, the bag doubled as a portable desk holding shoes for the office, documents, a new book or magazine she was into—reading is one of her hobbies. "I love to read all types of books and genres," she told me. "I just enjoy learning."

The job consumed her life. Stevens sat at her desk in a cubicle and slogged through twelve-hour workdays. She studied vast amounts of financial information and trade reports on computer screens to mine data for spreadsheets. During one three-month stretch she worked ninety consecutive days. Occasionally she pulled all-nighters to meet deadlines. She sipped Diet Coke, snacked on vending-machine food. "I had no idea about nutrition," she said.

Two years of beavering away led to a gnawing thought that she was missing her life. "I was kind of doing what I was expected to be doing," she said. "I was making good money, but something else was calling me to do something different." Attending meetings in Lehman's posh conference room on the penthouse floor, she gazed out high windows at the sky and felt a restless yearning: "I wished I could just fly out of here."

She left Lehman in the summer of 2007 for the investment fund, Gleacher Mezzanine, which would prove well timed. Over the Thanksgiving holiday she vacationed with an older sister, Angela, in San Francisco. Angela had signed her up for a cyclocross event in Golden Gate Park near the iconic Golden Gate Bridge.

When autumn rains fall, tree leaves and cyclocross riders turn brown as cyclists get caked with mud, often from helmet to shoes, from competing in a discipline that combines cycling with cross-country running, often during foul weather. Participants confront all kinds of obstacles—man-made and natural. Cyclists alight from bikes and run holding them over and through whatever lies in their way, then jump back on and pedal to the next hazard. Rudyard Kipling could have described the sport when he wrote about "where the best is like the worst."

Angela entered her sister in the novice category and loaned her a bike. Evie hadn't ridden since childhood. During the cyclocross she fell repeatedly, ripped clothes, got filthy. Still she finished—and was enthralled.

Back in New York, she purchased a bicycle. "I started riding and fell in love with the sport," she said. "I honestly thought I would take a year off, just ride my bike some, see the world a little bit, go back to work again." She participated in evening group rides in New York's leafy Central Park: "On the bike, I felt like I was flying."

Stevens's slender, fawn-like arms and legs could pass her for younger than her age. Years of tennis practice and tournaments, swinging her racket forehand and backhand to smash the ball to upwards of 100 mph, then running fast spurts on the court, had strengthened most muscles. Her passion for tennis transferred to cycling. She raised eyebrows for dropping racers up hills. "Everything felt right when I was on the bike."

In June 2008 she attended a Century Road Club Association women's cycling clinic in Central Park and met like-minded enthusiasts. She found a bridge of her own and crossed it when she joined the CRCA. She registered with USA Cycling, which issued her an entry-level Category 4 racing license (Roman numerals are not used anymore for racer categories). Stevens entered high-spirited early-morning spring and summer weekend contests around Central Park. "Racing was such an adventure," she said.

Her boss at Gleacher & Co., Phil Krall, had attended summer cycling camps that Davis Phinney and Connie Carpenter Phinney held at Colorado ski resorts. Krall suggested that she call Connie for information.

"She was very eager to improve and wondered if it was worth it to quit her day job to pursue cycling," Connie Carpenter said. "I remember telling her that it wasn't going to be lucrative, but it was time sensitive, so if she wanted to try it and could afford to try it, that she should go for it."

Their conversation energized Stevens, and they started a friendship.

• • •

Over Labor Day weekend Stevens won the women's rookie Cat. 3/4 Green Mountain Stage Race in Vermont, a small state so hilly that

New Englanders joke if the Green Mountain State were rolled out flat, it would exceed Maine in landmass. Her aptitude up mountains created buzz at the event.

Days after she returned, clutching her winner's trophy, to the Big Apple, Lehman filed for bankruptcy—the largest in history and unfathomable to many, including Stevens. America's $8 trillion housing bubble had burst under the weight of toxic mortgages. Lehman's twenty-five thousand employees counted among the more than 8.4 million workers tossed from jobs, the most since the Great Depression.

The ensuing stock market collapse and the vacant Lehman building prompted Stevens to think about doing something else. Some colleagues were applying to graduate schools to earn an MBA. She hired Matt Koschara as coach to learn from his experiences winning more than a hundred amateur and professional races.

"She was very quiet when we first met through mutual friends on a ride in Central Park in August 2008," he told me. "The next month we started working together. Evie had been in a few races and wanted to know more about the basics. Like different approaches to cornering—in the rain, through gravel or sand or standing water, going fast at the bottom of a downhill. She was quick to realize there was no one right answer, that a cyclist constantly makes micro-changes to her approach."

Stevens trained fourteen to twenty-two hours a week. She pedaled around Central Park and sometimes rolled across the George Washington Bridge into northern New Jersey; indoors, her bike clamped to a stationary trainer. Koschara had her warm up easy before alternating between intense intervals and recovery. He helped her select a pricey top-of-the-line carbon-fiber racing bike.

"It was clear immediately that she had incredible physiology," he said. "Her background was playing tennis in high school and college, but no real cycling. Through the winter we kept upping the lengths of intensity and recovery—from three minutes on and three minutes off to five-minute sessions, then ten minutes. I kept scratching my head at her incredible rate of improvement. You could chart it in a steady rise. Lots of other people improve and reach a plateau for a while, but she just got better and better."

On about a dozen occasions Koschara took Stevens to a gym stocked with free weights. He taught her strength-training fundamentals specific to cycling for upper body, back, and legs. She shouldered 135 pounds for deep squats, greater than her 120 pounds on a compact five-feet-five build. She holds her back so straight that friends recall her as taller.

Koschara said she lived a monastic lifestyle: "Her days were spent either working full time, training, or sleeping."

He praised her organizational skills: "Evie has a very good mind and is process driven—always looking for ways to improve. To come across an athlete like her is rare. She had great physiology matched with the right competitive temperament. You can coach someone to be stronger, faster. But you can't teach how to be competitive. She quickly took her work ethic, her hunger for success, and her flair for competition to become one of the most break-out athletes."

• • •

One day at work in the spring of 2009 Stevens received an email from John Eustice, twice USPRO criterium champion and a veteran of the European peloton, including the Giro d'Italia. He knew her from riding in Central Park. He sent a news photo of Dutch cyclist Marianne Vos winning the women's Flèche Wallonne, a major international event in Belgium's rugged Ardennes, for the third straight year. Eustice urged Stevens to study her.

Vos, aged twenty-two to Stevens's twenty-six, had short dark hair, a pinched-lean face, and a beaky nose while Stevens had the soft features of an ingénue. Vos crossed the finish line at La Flèche Wallonne Féminine sitting up, arms out wide, exulting. Behind her, a rival frowned as runner-up, another adversary rested her hands on the tops of her handlebars, resigned to third. Vos had surged in time to showboat for the raucous audience.

Eustice told Stevens, similar in size to Vos, that she had the potential to beat her and win the Flèche Wallonne (which translates to the "Wallonia Arrow" for Belgium's French-speaking southern region). Vos and Stevens lived worlds apart. Vos, an elite pro, competed worldwide—even in China, where she seized a gold medal in the women's points race on the velodrome at the 2008 Beijing Olympics. She won numerous world titles on the road, cyclocross, velodromes, and ruled off-road races. Vos earned comparisons with Eddy Merckx as the finest, hardest-working cyclist of her generation. She has been the subject of global media attention. Throngs besieged her for autographs. Stevens, an anonymous novice rider, was trapped in grinding workdays, in a cubicle, inside a Manhattan high-rise office building like a caged eagle. She taped Vos's picture to her computer and scrutinized the Dutch queen of the road.

Vos had a decade of development in the vigorous Dutch cycling tradition. A savvy natural, she mastered how to read a race, jump off a wheel to pop ahead, coax partners on a breakaway to share the workload and keep their lead, rocket down hills, and flawlessly win sprints.

Eustice told me that he knew Stevens had what it took to win La Flèche Wallonne Féminine: "It finishes at the top of one of the steepest hills in the sport. Evie likes to achieve. She possesses the intellectual disposition—a super high-achieving, educated person with experience working on Wall Street, which requires a tough mentality to survive brutal workday pressures. I rode with her a few times and saw she was a diamond in the rough, more an athlete on a bike than a cyclist. But she was developing into one of the strongest women in cycling. As long as Evie arrived with Marianne at the bottom of that hill, Evie could out-power Marianne to the top and win."

Stevens also had backing from CRCA clubmates in their blue-and-white jerseys. They supported Project Evie, fortifying her motivation. That spring Stevens won four national-level events. Among them Arizona's three-day Valley of the Sun in and around Phoenix, and upstate New York's Tour of the Battenkill, where she outsprinted six breakaway partners in a sixty-two-mile race abounding in hills.

"After each event she was in, we spent a lot of time talking about tactics, on the phone for three or four hours," said Koschara, an avid chess enthusiast. "What had happened? Why? How could she do better next time?"

Her early-season results earned points to upgrade her racing license in record time to women's elite. "I decided in the spring of 2009 that I was going to quit my job and leave Wall Street," she said.

Stevens informed her parents that she intended to swap her desk and spreadsheets for a bike and road racing. Right away her mother, a special education teacher, gave her full endorsement. She knew Evie as inner-directed, self-reliant, like her namesake, her father's mother, Evelyn. Quitting her day job, without any assurance she would ever earn money in cycling, amounted to a career gamble. Yet she was single and ready to act on her dream rather than later look back and wonder if she had what it took to be a contender. She resigned from Gleacher & Co. at the end of June.

"Her decision to leave a corporate job was very bold," Koschara said. "She left for the vicissitudes of pro cycling—one of many privateers on their own, guest-riding as a temp on local teams rounding out their roster at big races. Team directors saw she had ability, but she had been racing less than a year. It was unheard of to offer a one-year contract to someone so new to the sport."

Four years after she had arrived in New York, she gave away her bed, what meager pieces of furniture she had, and struck out for pro cycling: "Everything I do I do intensely if I like it."

Once she had packed her suitcase, however, she stood alone in her empty apartment. The shock of leaving corporate Wall Street, its culture, energy, and money collided with an uncertain future. "I just burst into tears."

Koschara used connections to land her a guest slot on Team Lip Smacker for a race over the long July 4 weekend in the Fitchburg-Longsjo Classic. Near her hometown of Acton, Fitchburg hosted the fiftieth anniversary of its memorial race to Art Longsjo. Stevens walked out of her apartment for the last time and left for Fitchburg, her debut as a full-time pro cyclist.

• • •

Hundreds of men and women from around North America and ten countries converged on Fitchburg. Its program offered eight categories in four events: a time trial, circuit race, road race, and crit.

"The racing at Fitchburg was always very competitive," said Canadian racer Anne Samplonius, captain of Team Lip Smacker, sponsored by the manufacturer of flavored lip balms and glosses. She added that "2009 was one of the better fields."

The women's Cat. 1/2 event drew 110 contenders. The local press picked Samplonius as a pre-race favorite. Others included French star Jeannie Longo, still a force at age fifty-one with a thousand career victories and thirteen world titles, and Alison Powers from Grand Junction, Colorado, national time trial champion and Pan-Am Games gold medalist in the time trial.

Stevens joined Samplonius and six more on Team Lip Smacker. They included red-haired Carla Swart of South Africa, a cycling scholarship racer for Lees-McRae College in North Carolina and winner of a string of national collegiate titles, and national road champion Jessica Phillips of Aspen, Colorado.

Samplonius, forty-one, had the most experience on the squad. She had played ice hockey in college at the University of Alberta before she found cycling and quickly emerged as one of Canada's best. At the women's inaugural world time trial championship in 1994, thirty kilometers (18.8 miles), in Catania, Italy, she scored a silver medal, behind winner Karen Kurreck of the United States, and ahead of France's Longo. Samplonius excelled at time trials. She twice won Canada's national title and took home a gold medal at the 2007 Pan-Am Games in Rio de Janeiro, Brazil.

She captained Team Lip Smacker. "We knew Evie had won—dominated, actually—enough races around the East to register on everyone's radar," she told me. "So she was good. But she had no pack skills or bike-handling skills."

As guest, Stevens was lent a team jersey, shorts, and gloves. The squad lacked extra bicycles so she brought her own road and time trial bikes. Everybody met in Fitchburg two days before the race began, on Thursday, July 2, to rest up from travel. Team members stayed in private housing; Stevens commuted from her parents' home in Acton, a thirty-mile drive in light traffic.

Samplonius said the outcome of the opening day time trial, 8.9 miles over a flat course on the edge of town, would sort out the team: its fastest finisher would ride as leader.

"Alison Powers was one of the strongest time trialers in the country,"

Samplonius said. Longo arrived fresh from winning her fifty-seventh French national title, in the time trial. "Evie was an unknown."

Powers smoked the time trial for victory. She donned the leader's yellow jersey, bearing Art Longsjo's visage. Stevens finished four seconds behind for second, and four seconds ahead of Samplonius, third. Next came Longo, fourth. Swart arrived in seventh; Phillips was eleventh.

"Evie pushed monster gears," Samplonius said. "She could have been much better if she knew what she was doing. But Evie rode the strongest among us. That settled it for our team. She was our leader."

The next day came the circuit race around the Fitchburg State University campus. Samplonius led the team pre-race strategy meeting. "Evie's weakness was that she had no clue about what she was doing," Samplonius said. "She had a fear of cornering in the pack, common to those who start racing as older. We had a team of riders who had good experience, especially Jessica Phillips."

Stevens was eager to take directions, Samplonius said. "She was easy to get along with. She really listened, took everything in. She was so good, so strong."

Lip Smackers guided their leader around the campus circuit, with just a hundred feet of elevation difference. The aggressive pace whittled down the peloton on each of eleven laps. Stevens turned heads with aggressive, smart riding under Samplonius's direction and support from her Lip Smacker sisters. After thirty-four miles, Stevens galloped in third. That netted her a time bonus, which put her ahead of Powers in overall standings to take over the yellow jersey.

On Saturday, July 4, Independence Day, the penultimate stage was a sixty-five-mile road race—six times around a circuit up and over Longsjo's favorite Wachusett Mountain. A breakaway fled out of sight.

"Evie was antsy to get up there," Samplonius said. "But I held her back to let the team do the work. I told her we had to use team tactics. Our team did a lot of chasing. The break dwindled down to a couple riders who weren't a factor in the overall classification. Evie finally tore it apart on the mountain. Nobody could stay with her. She won the pack sprint for second place and picked up a time bonus. That added to her overall lead."

On the last day Lip Smackers kept their leader out of trouble through the finale, a downtown crit, starting and finishing in front of city hall. The one-mile grid of streets featured right-angle corners and a tight 180-degree turn that led to the long final straight. A throng filled the sidewalks embracing the course. Stevens crossed the finish line in the pack as the overall winner.

"I thought that was a breakthrough race for Evie," said Samplonius, fifth overall, twenty-four seconds down. "When you have a big engine, which she did, she had that raw talent, that can get you far."

Stevens stood on the top podium step, above runners-up Powers and Longo. They smiled and waved to the crowd.

"I'm not sure what my specialty is yet," Stevens told reporters. "It's all exciting and surprising and being in the yellow jersey has given me a lot of confidence."

Her victory paralleled Longsjo's trajectory from unknown outsider to Massachusetts state champion on his fast rise to national class. She handed back her Team Lip Smacker kit. Koschara lined her up with another guest spot, on the better-funded Webcor Builders Cycling Team for the Cascade Cycling Classic, July 21 to 26, radiating out of Bend, Oregon. The event boasted its status of longest-running stage race in North America. Stevens flew west.

• • •

The plan among the six-rider Webcor Builders squad going into the seventy-one-mile stage 1 was for Stevens to lead out Gina Grain in the final kilometer. Stevens would pace Grain, Canadian national champion and one of the world's top road sprinters, up to the last 200 meters, then swing aside for Grain to take over and win for the team.

As expected, a series of attacks livened the pace without any of the 110 starters getting away. That set up a big pack sprint. In the final miles the speed went up and the peloton snaked toward the end. Stevens moved to the front, towing Grain. When Stevens spotted the final kilometer sign on a side of the road up ahead, she jumped. Grain, a silver medalist at the 2006 track worlds in the ten-kilometer scratch race, couldn't stay in her draft. At the 200-meter marker, Stevens glanced over her shoulder and saw she had a gap on the peloton. She kicked it in for victory.

"No one could hang on Evie's wheel in the lead-out and she won," recalled Samplonius. "Yeah, she was that strong!"

Stevens cheerfully told *Cycling News* reporter Kristen Frattini that nobody had ever taught her how to do a lead-out. Grain came in fourth.

Stevens pushed her arms into a new yellow jersey. The next day's seventy-eight-mile stage 2 played to her strengths. At around forty miles, Samplonius and six others escaped. They formed a pace line and built up a three-minute lead at the base of the ten-mile climb to the finish at the summit of Three Creeks Mountain. Stevens exploited the steep gradient to catch the leaders and surge past for a second triumph.

Two days later, Stevens soloed to her third stage triumph, a seventy-mile road race that finished at the 5,700-foot-high Mount Bachelor Ski Resort.

Her Webcor Builders partners battled to protect her lead over the last two days. Stevens clinched victory in another stage race. Standing on the podium she credited her five teammates for riding with the strength of twenty-five.

She was riding for prize money while riding out the recession.

• • •

That month she and Koschara talked on the phone in post-race assessments after each stage in Fitchburg and Oregon. "Sometimes she handed her phone around to teammates so I could hear what they had to say," he recalled. "Evie learned rapidly. She rarely made the same mistake twice."

Stevens and Koschara had been operating outside of USA Cycling's development programs. As the racing season went into full swing, word of her achievements circulated among racers, team directors, journalists, and promoters. The USAC coaching staff vigilantly scoured the country for emerging talent, seeking the next LeMond, another Connie Carpenter. Now came Evie Stevens.

After the Cascade Cycling Classic, she finished second in the USA Cycling national time trial championship in Bend, Oregon.

The USAC recruited her to join the national team flying across the

Atlantic for the weeklong Route de France Féminin Internationale in central France. La Route de France was the country's only major stage race for women (the Tour de France Féminin had folded). It attracted national and trade teams from around the Continent.

Stevens received a full kit with jerseys inscribed USA in large letters across the front and back, on T-shirts, the side panel of shorts, and gloves. She supported team leader Kim Anderson of suburban Chicago. Anderson captured the overall race. Stevens won a stage and finished second in general classification—a remarkable overseas debut.

While in France she was recruited by management of Team HTC-Columbia, which employed Anderson. Sponsored by the Taiwan consumer electronics company HTC and the Columbia Sportswear Company in Cedar Mill, Oregon, it was the biggest U.S. pro cycling team: twenty-eight men and thirteen women. It was a major league Union Cycliste Internationale organization and participated in top-tier UCI events, including the men's squad in the Tour de France (including Britain's Mark Cavendish, on his way to winning thirty Tour stages) and the most important women's events on the UCI calendar. In U.S. cycling, Team HTC-Columbia was the New York Yankees baseball team. Stevens signed on to race in the team's distinctive black-yellow-green colors in 2010 and 2011.

When she flew back to America, she entered the USAC national time trial championship in Greenville, South Carolina. She wore her Century Road Club Association jersey for the last time. She took home a silver medal, behind winner Jessica Phillips and ahead of defending champ Alison Powers.

More foreign excursions followed. In late September USAC made her flight and travel arrangements to the road worlds in Mendrisio, Switzerland. She accompanied six other women including Phillips, defending world time trial champion Amber Neben, and Kristin Armstrong (no relation to Lance's ex-wife), the 2008 Olympic time trial gold medalist. Armstrong won the time trial title against women from sixty nations; Neben finished sixth; Phillips was fourteenth.

Days later in the road race Stevens rode support to lead Armstrong up hills after Neben and Anderson dropped out. Armstrong finished fourth. Stevens, fourteenth, gained recognition as a new force in American elite road racing.

• • •

Stevens earned her place among high-profile women. They were as slender as Degas ballerinas. And tougher than they looked—as competitive, gritty, and determined as any men. USAC women were hauling home more medals than men from the worlds and Olympics. Marquee events were broadcast into tens of millions of households around the world. As America's governing body for cycling, USAC depends on winners to generate media coverage. Corporate marketing mavens directed sponsorship money to winning teams. The sport had been stained by a steady barrage of reports about banned drug use among men pros. These women provided wholesome success.

Also in contrast to male counterparts, leading women riders often had college educations and occupational skills. A standout was Kristin Armstrong, a graduate of the University of Idaho, in exercise physiology. She worked as a project manager at an ad agency with clients including Hewlett-Packard. (Since 2017 she has worked in communications for a community hospital in Boise.) Her 2009 time trial gold in Switzerland came after winning the 2006 world time trial in Salzburg, Austria, along with previous silvers and bronzes. Other victories included the Tour of Holland, stages on the other side of the world in the Tour of New Zealand, and a half-dozen U.S. road and time trial titles.

Kristin Armstrong had been a professional triathlete and competed in the Hawaii Ironman World Championship. But she suffered leg pain that kept getting worse. Medical tests indicated she had osteoarthritis in her hips; bone chips floated in her hip capsule. Running was out of the question.

Her doctor recommended cycling for therapy. Armstrong joined a local cycling club. In 2002 she received a contract to turn pro. She won the 2004 national road title and competed in the Athens Olympics.

Nicola Cranmer, the director of the professional Twenty16 Ridebiker Team, picked Armstrong for her squad in 2016. "I like persistence," Cranmer told me. "And I look for someone who is detail oriented. Kristin Armstrong is the queen of details. We call her Miss Millimeter. She knows how to prepare well for a race. She works super-hard. I'm not into supporting people who do it just for fun. I look for people who really put a lot of effort into their craft."

That means facing tough choices. "Kristin makes incredible sacrifices," Cranmer said. "That's what it takes to be a champion. She's a mother. She has a career in communications. A lot of athletes don't understand what it takes to make a champion. Sometimes your best friend has a wedding on a weekend when you have a stage race that week. So you have to choose which to sacrifice."

Another high-performer was Amber Neben. A college-scholarship runner at the University of Nebraska, she began cycling after graduating with a biology degree. She earned a master's in biology at the University of California, Irvine, and was in a PhD program when she withdrew to focus on cycling. Neben, a national road champion, won the 2008 world time trial title in Varese, Italy.

Mari Holden, a philosophy major at the University of Colorado, won six national time trial and road championships as well as the 2000 world time trial in Plouay, France, and a silver medal in the 2000 Sydney Olympics.

Photographers snapped Kristin Armstrong, Amber Neben, Mari Holden, and other women in action shots and smiling radiantly on awards podiums, medals draped around their neck—refreshing images gracing sports pages, magazine covers, websites, and internet streaming.

Stevens, a photogenic rising star, brought a new dimension to the sport.

"Evie has a charisma that I have seen in very few pro cyclists I've met," observed author Dan Lee. "Sort of like Davis Phinney or Belgian superstar Tom Boonen. They all give off a sense of confidence that's also friendly, almost a twinkle in their eye."

• • •

In 2010 Stevens joined ten world-class cyclists on Team HTC-Columbia. Some had been titleholders in running and speed skating before cycling. Among them were German national road champions Judith Arndt and Ina-Yoko Teutenberg, and more from Australia, the Netherlands, New Zealand, and Sweden.

The team alternated competing on both sides of the Atlantic. Their continental base during the season was Girona, Spain. Stevens's cycling sisters could switch without missing a beat to chatting in different tongues, although English was their common language.

A crucial difference between racing in America and in Europe—for women and men—was greater depth in the peloton. Women's races in the United States typically attracted around a hundred on the start line; about twenty to thirty were capable of winning. In Europe there might be up to two hundred in the peloton and half could win. Moreover, formation of the European Union in 1993 eased travel across borders of twenty-eight nations, which expanded access to more races. Most EU nations replaced ancient money systems with the euro. That eliminated the inconvenience of converting French or Belgian francs, German deutsche marks, or Spanish pesetas. The EU had a greater talent pool—a 510 million population compared with some 330 million in the United States.

Cycling is a much bigger sport in Europe, with support in schools and deep grassroots communities. The media routinely covers the sport and cyclists. Riders grow up training and racing in large pelotons coursing along narrow farm-to-market roads, many paved by stretches of cobblestones. Americans race mostly on asphalt roads. U.S. cyclists go to Europe and face a steep learning curve to adjust to different conditions.

Just one year after studying Vos's photo taped to her computer, Stevens entered the 2010 Flèche Wallonne Féminine with HTC-Columbia teammates. The race took place on the same day and on the same strenuous course as the men's event, which had been drawing enormous crowds since 1936. The Flèche Wallonne had been held midweek in mid-April, falling between the Amstel Gold Race in the Netherlands and Belgium's monument classic, since 1892, from Liège to Bastogne and back. The three events created an extravaganza and always drew the best teams. The backlists of winners included Eddy Merckx and other giants. In 1998 the Flèche Wallonne organizers introduced its women's edition.

In 2010 the women's peloton set out from the ceremonial start in the industrial city of Charleroi through Wallonia, passing quaint windmills, abandoned industrial buildings, and deep crowds on the hilly seventy-five-mile route (fifty miles shorter than the men's event). Stevens stayed in the front group and maintained good position for the finish up the notorious brutal climb in the ancient Roman city of Huy, on the Meuse River. The precipitous mile-long uphill begins on a substantial 10 percent grade and rears up to a muscle-burning 26 percent before the summit. It is called the Mur de Huy, "the Wall of Huy," far steeper than the Boston Marathon's Heartbreak Hill.

In the last 100 yards, Stevens held second place, behind Britain's world champion Emma Pooley (an engineering graduate of the University of Cambridge). But Stevens had misjudged the pitch and faded to fifth.

Although Stevens possessed phenomenal physical and mental abilities, she was cautious in road races. Anne Samplonius remembered riding with her at the back of the pack in the Holland Ladies Tour late in the summer of 2010, when Samplonius was on the Canadian national team.

"The narrow roads and no wind made it impossible to get to the front unless you were willing to push your way through, taking risks," Samplonius said. "I didn't have that desire any more, late in my career, to put things on the line to fight for position. Evie and I were at the back, out of trouble, laughing and surfing wheels. We got in some of the best motor pacing you could ask for." (A week later, Samplonius won a European time trial, Chrono Champenois, in France's Champagne region.)

Stevens was spooked by how fast European pelotons schussed down hills. She had skied but was risk averse and stayed in her comfort zone. As a cyclist, she had a new skill to learn. Between races, a teammate tutored her in the art of descending—leading her down steep grades faster than 50 mph, carving turns, leaning through them, to the bottom. A driver in the team vehicle took them back up for another go, a routine repeated for three days.

Evie's best results came on courses loaded with tough hills that chopped the field to pieces. She captured stage 7 of the 2010 Giro Donne in Italy, a rigorous eight-day, rain-or-shine contest through mountains, regarded as one of the toughest and most prestigious stage races on the women's UCI calendar. Confident in time trials, she won the U.S. title in 2010, edging Amber Neben.

The year concluded with the Columbia Sportswear Company ending its sponsorship. In 2011 the team was renamed HTC-High Road, emphasizing its dedication to racing without performance-enhancing drugs. That spring Stevens took advantage of her time trialing strength at La Flèche Wallonne Féminine. She attacked off the front after forty-three miles. Her solo failed to attract anyone willing to join forces. She struggled and flamed out by the time the pack overtook her. Vos won a record fourth victory.

Stevens won her second national time trial title, again eclipsing Neben, and seemed ready to fulfill her childhood ambition to become an Olympian. She set her sights on competing in the 2012 London Olympics.

Then in the summer of 2011 on a training ride she received a cell-phone call from a journalist who said HTC-High Road was folding. The report came as unexpected as Lehman's bankruptcy. She and teammates would have to fend for themselves, jeopardizing chances to prep for the Olympic trials.

Weeks of heady negotiations followed. Finally a deal was struck to keep Stevens and most teammates together on a new all-women squad: Specialized-Lululemon. Registered in Germany as a UCI team, it was sponsored by California-based Specialized Bicycle Components and the sportswear manufacturer Lululemon Athletica, headquartered in Vancouver, Canada, and renowned for upscale yoga pants. Specialized, under founder and chairman Mike Sinyard, one of the industry's foremost innovators, stepped up its involvement with the new team by supplying more bicycles and helmets than it had for Team HTC-Columbia. The roster of thirteen women constituted a foreign legion: Australia, Canada, Germany, Great Britain, the Netherlands, Sweden, and the United States.

All this time, Stevens and Koschara often talked on Skype and cell phones and exchanged emails. In October 2011 they amiably concluded their arrangement. "She was one in a million when I started working with her," Koschara said. "Three years later, she was one in ten million."

• • •

Stevens got along well enough with Connie Carpenter and Davis Phinney that in the off-season Stevens moved to Boulder, Colorado, home to the Phinneys, their grown son, Taylor, and daughter, Kelsey, and a robust community of pro cyclists and triathletes. The Phinneys saw she had the potential to become one of America's greatest women cyclists.

"We started spending more time together," Connie said of Stevens. "She has become a close member of our extended family. It was really a lot of fun to witness her journey. As with any cycling journey, it was full of ups and downs. She is an amazing person. A truly talented rider who represented women's cycling with class and a big smile."

Over home-cooked dinners, Connie shared lessons about coping with competitive pressure and controlling as many variables in life as possible—emphasizing healthy food, reducing distractions, and getting proper sleep.

Stevens rented an apartment with twenty-two-year-old Taylor Phinney. He became like her taller, six-feet-five, younger brother. Following his mother and father, he was national road champion and an Olympian—at eighteen he'd competed in the 2008 Beijing Olympics. He trained to compete in the 2012 London Games, and so did Stevens. She accompanied him on mountain bike rides. He led her down winding single-track descents on uneven, gravely paths, and through open countryside in sight of the scenic Front Range of the Rockies. Months of off-road riding quickened her steering reflexes and sharpened eye-hand coordination.

Stevens consulted with a sports psychologist, standard practice for Taylor Phinney and modern athletes. They seek an edge on keeping focus during exhausting competition fraught with distractions, coping with everyday stresses from their own expectations and those of teammates and managers, and boosting motivation to keep a hectic routine of training, traveling, and competing.

Taylor introduced her to his first coach, Neal Henderson. A former professional triathlete, Henderson had graduated from Penn State and served as strength and conditioning coach for the Hershey Bears pro ice hockey team. He moved to Boulder for grad studies at the University of Colorado and coached USA Cycling riders. He was named 2009 USAC National Coach of the Year. In 2010 he tutored Taylor Phinney to win the 2010 world individual pursuit championship at the velodrome in Ballerup, Denmark, adding to his previous gold in that event the year before in Pruszków, Poland.

Henderson took over as her coach. He did preliminary tests for watts pedaled and oxygen consumption. He joined the chorus of praising her as "a really big engine."

At his urging she tried another discipline—riding on the 250-meter outdoor Boulder Valley Velodrome with USAC development teams under age twenty-three. Pedaling laps in the group, she let the bike lean through banked turns while she held the bottoms of her handlebars and whipped onto the straights.

• • •

Mountain bike and track riding broadened Stevens's repertoire. She launched her 2012 season in February on the other side of the world, in the five-day Women's Tour of New Zealand. She felt comfortable in the flowing peloton and won. When she returned to Europe the next month for a crit in Italy, she flew in and out of turns with ease.

Everything came together in April at La Flèche Wallonne Féminine. On a chilly, sunny Wednesday Stevens lined up with five Specialized-Lululemon teammates, distinguished in chic black outfits trimmed in arty white. Marianne Vos was back as four-time champion, favored to win yet again.

The three-hour race over a gauntlet of sharp climbs tattered the field of about two hundred starters to a handful at the base of the Mur de Huy. The former Danish national champion Linda Villumsen, now a citizen of New Zealand, led Stevens and Vos up the climb. At the 500-meter sign, Stevens surged ahead, then recognized she'd made her move too soon.

"I realized I had to get off the front," she said. "So I actually stopped pedaling. I was thinking it was the dumbest or smartest thing I ever did in my life. It was pretty steep so I just stopped. It looked like I blew up."

Vos counterattacked. She sat poised in the saddle and set a pace that only Stevens, up dancing on her pedals, could match as Villumsen slipped behind.

Stevens paced on Vos's rear wheel—saving the element of surprise. Vos rose off her saddle to close in on a record fifth conquest. Both women were gripping their brake hoods, standing on the pedals, grimacing as they squeezed the last of their energy. Motorcycles puttered a few feet away, carrying cameramen beaming television images.

Stevens focused so intently on each pedal stroke that she blocked out screaming spectators creating a tunnel of humanity standing against steel barriers. She missed seeing any of the prayer chapels that every other day of the year gave the street its nickname, *le chemin des chapelles*, "the way of the chapels."

"I was just telling myself, 'This is now, this is when you do it,' and just going, digging deeper than I've ever dug," she said.

She jigged around the left side of Vos: "I just went as hard as I could."

Stevens drew even with Vos before gaining a bike length, two lengths, three. At the line she punched her right fist in the air. She sat up and put her hands over her heart and smiled. Vos, vanquished by the newcomer, scowled.

Stevens became the first American woman to win the Flèche Wallonne Féminine. "And it was the most, yeah, the most exhilarating feeling and experience I've ever had."

She and the Specialized-Lululemon crew soon ventured to the Czech Republic, in its coal-mining region, for the twenty-sixth annual Gracia-Orlová five-day stage race for women. It drew national teams representing Australia, Austria, Russia, and Ukraine, and trade teams from Belarus, France, Germany, Great Britain, the Netherlands, and Poland.

Late in the sixty-five-mile stage 1 road race from the village of Dětmarovice to the town of Štramberk, renowned for its castle tower, Stevens dashed off the front with Belarus national road champion Alena Amialiusik and British national time trial champion Sharon Laws. Stevens won the sprint and took over as race leader. Two days later, she captured the 220-mile event.

Stevens flew over the Atlantic for America's biggest road race for women, the five-day Exergy Tour in Idaho. She and her squad dominated. On the last day, she and one other surged away together up a long punishing climb. At the summit stood her sister Angela. When Angela spotted her, she yelled like a maniac and ran alongside.

Stevens won the overall Exergy Tour. Points she had earned from recent triumphs earned her automatic selection by USA Cycling officials determining the four-woman London Olympics road team.

Her season continued rolling in high gear under Neal Henderson's coaching. She flew back to Europe and captured the seventy-eight-mile stage 3 of the Giro d'Italia Femminile in Italy. She finished third overall, standing on the podium with winner Marianne Vos and runner-up Emma Pooley. In France's major stage race, La Route de France, Stevens claimed two stages and the overall title, leading Specialized-Lululemon to team victory.

ESPN journalist Bonnie Ford wrote that Stevens had the potential to become a transformative athlete in her sport, capable of broadening the American fan base like Mia Hamm had done for soccer and Cammi Granato in ice hockey.

• • •

Stevens fulfilled her dream of competing in the Olympics—in the eighty-eight-mile road race. On race day, rain bucketed down, creating slick streets and interfering with brakes. Both Stevens and Kristin Armstrong fell, but they got back up and chased together to regain the peloton. Teammate Shelley Olds, former captain of the Roanoke College women's soccer team, joined a breakaway with Marianne Vos, English star Lizzie Armitstead, and Olga Zabelinskaya of Russia. A puncture in the final miles blew Olds's chance for a medal. Vos outsprinted Armitstead for the gold.

Olds had a fast wheel change and finished seventh, followed by Stevens, twenty-fourth, Armstrong and Neben thirty-fifth and thirty-sixth.

Armstrong came through with a gold medal in the time trial, the only U.S. cycling gold.

American women scored three more medals. On the track, Sarah

Hammer of Temecula, California, scored a silver in the women's omnium, based on points to the top finishers in six short events. Hammer took another silver in the team pursuit with Dotsie Bausch of Lexington, Kentucky; Jennie Reed of Kirkland, Washington; and Lauren Tamayo of Ashville, North Carolina. And Georgia Gould of Baltimore captured bronze in cross-country mountain biking.

The best of USA Cycling's men was Taylor Phinney, fourth in both the individual time trial and the road race. A survey among athletes worldwide asked what they considered the worst place to finish agreed that fourth place in the Olympics was the worst. He looked ahead to improve at the next Olympics.

For Stevens and teammates, the season's main goal was the new women's elite team time trial at the road worlds in Valkenburg, the Netherlands. The long tradition at Union Cycliste Internationale worlds programs called for riders to wear jerseys carrying national colors, as was the custom in the Olympics, rather than wearing sponsor names, logos, and brand tints. In 2012, the UCI inaugurated an exception with six-rider team time trials for elite men and women—recognizing the importance of corporate patronage that funded pro cycling. For all the other UCI worlds events, riders competed in national team jerseys.

Taylor Phinney scored two silver medals: one riding in his red-white-and-blue USA Cycling jersey in the twenty-nine-mile individual time trial; another in the red-and-black of his U.S.-based BMC Racing Team, with Colorado-based Tejay van Garderen, three Italians, and a Belgian in the thirty-three-mile team time trial.

Stevens won the gold medal in the 21.5-mile elite women's team trial with Specialized-Lululemon teammates Amber Neben, Ellen "the Animal" van Dijk of the Netherlands, and Germans Ina-Yoko Teutenberg, Trixi Worrack, and Charlotte Becker.

Stevens took home a silver medal for USA Cycling in the 15.2-mile individual time trial. Standing twice in three days on the worlds podium signified a heroic makeover. She concluded the season ranked as fourth best in the world, based on UCI race results. Stevens soared to America's top road cyclist.

"What she did was like someone who takes up baseball at age twenty-six and in four years plays in the World Series," said John Eustice. "She overcame a tremendous development shortage to attain astounding accomplishments."

• • •

Stevens set high expectations for 2013. Applying her investment-banker skills, she created a spreadsheet with race dates, locations, and plans for her racing calendar. She added fancy hot-keys with photos and personal comments and shared her art with family and friends. Among priorities were returning as defending champion to two events: La Flèche Wallonne Féminine, to square off against Olympic gold medalist Marianne Vos, and to defend at Gracia-Orlová in the Czech Republic.

But cycling, like horse racing and presidential elections, is unpredictable.

In mid-March she and teammates competed in the Classica Città di Padova, a seventy-eight-mile contest in northeastern Italy, an early-season tune-up. It had been ruled by Italians until the year before when it was won by Carmen Small of Durango, Colorado, a new addition to Specialized-Lululemon.

Stevens was clocked at a speedy 35 mph on a roundabout when she fell face-first onto the asphalt and was knocked unconscious. She woke up strapped to a gurney inside an ambulance, siren screaming. Her neck was immobilized in a brace. An IV line was sticking in an arm. She couldn't speak—her lips were lacerated. The blunt force of her fall broke all front teeth. The left side of her face was scraped raw by the pavement. Her left eye was swollen and blackened.

Cuts to her lips and face required forty stitches. She was pushed in a wheelchair for excruciating dental surgery. She slept eighteen hours a day for a week. When finally released from the hospital, she appeared like a mummy—white bandages taped over her chin, under her nose, crossing in an X over her nose to her forehead. She pulled on a dark-blue ball cap and peered under the bill through oversized sunglasses to walk out of the building.

"The worst part was that my lips were so cut up that I couldn't smile, which made me feel sort of trapped," she said. "As a female, to have your face deformed, it was really quite a blow."

Stevens jetted to Boston to recover with her parents on the Massachusetts shore of Cape Cod. Her black eye healed. The bandages were removed, exposing neon-pink scars. She avoided looking at her face in the mirror for a week. She had lost two teeth. Dental surgery restored her smile, a little wider. Her strength returned. She resumed riding to relax her restless mind, up to five-hour cruises.

"Riding the bike is kind of my therapy," she said. "When something you love is taken away, you realize how much you love it."

Later in a television interview she reflected that racing bicycles at elite level and working on Wall Street shared similar all-encompassing lifestyles marked by unpredictable crashes. One big difference is that bicycle crashes can put you in a hospital.

She flew to Europe and visited the Phinneys at their second home in Italy, offering a panoramic view. Davis Phinney's facial scars, from his disastrous 1988 Liège-Bastogne-Liège smash-up, aged into thin tracks of normal skin color. He shared with her what the accident had taken from him mentally and physically, how he willed himself to race again soon.

As hungry as she was to compete, she was forced to sit out the 2013 Flèche Wallonne Féminine, won by Marianne Vos for the fifth time.

On April 24 Stevens rejoined teammates in the Czech Republic for Gracia-Orlová. Five weeks had done no damage. In the opening-day 1.4-mile prologue time trial, on a Tuesday in the coal-mining town of Havirov, she finished fourth.

The next day, in a hilly stage 1 sixty-five-mile road race, Stevens felt anxious in the peloton. When she struggled for position in the pack sweeping along narrow roads, she calmed down by recalling the coffee she drank with her parents on Cape Cod, the views of the Italian countryside with the Phinneys, the support she received from friends and teammates.

The stage concluded at the top of a long steep hill bordered by boisterous fans. She and Dutch teammate Ellen van Dijk surged ahead.

They banged elbows and matched pedal strokes as rivals from Belarus, Germany, and Russia bore down on them before Stevens surged to pip Van Dijk.

On Sunday, the last day, Van Dijk as team leader won the overall tour. Stevens finished runner-up, ahead of Emma Pooley of Britain (nearly done with her PhD in geotechnical engineering). Stevens stood on the awards stage with Van Dijk and Pooley. Stevens's lips had healed. She smiled full wattage for the cameras.

The season turned out differently from what Stevens had planned. In May she turned thirty. She had endured numerous falls, but the seriousness of her latest galvanized her to set an expiration date. She wanted a shot at the 2016 Rio Olympics—and afterward a return to banking.

In the meantime, she added impressive victories, including the time trial in the Amgen Tour of California, a successor to the Tour de Trump as America's top international stage race. At the worlds in Tuscany, she took home another gold medal in the women's team time trial with Ellen van Dijk, Carmen Small, and four others from Great Britain and Germany. Stevens scored fourth in the individual time trial (new national champion Small beat her for the bronze), and fifth in the road race (won by Marianne Vos).

Tuscany held something else for her. In July she had flown to Sun Valley, Idaho, for a friend's wedding. There Stevens met Brett Baker, a California native who had captained the tennis team at Occidental College; he was selected for the Southern California Intercollegiate Athletic Conference All Conference Team. "I learned how vibrant and fun she was," Baker recalled.

They went their separate ways: to San Francisco for him, employed in brand partnerships at Twitter; to Europe for her. Many Skype calls later, he traveled to Tuscany in September to take her out for their first date.

To carry on their romance and live near her sister Angela, Stevens moved in the off-season to San Francisco. The City by the Bay suited her. It operated as the financial center in a state with an economy that has surpassed France as the world's sixth-largest gross domestic product. San Francisco offered a golden career bridge to the Wall Street alumnus.

• • •

Her original intention to take a year off, ride her bike, and see the world had extended to four years. A high-flying athlete, she lived out of a suitcase to race worldwide while she and Brett Baker kept their romance blooming.

By then Stevens acquired what the French call *souplesse*—that quality of sitting as one with the bike, pedaling fluidly, flowing along the road as smooth and efficient as a pro golfer's swing, an Olympic swimmer's stroke. She took her place as a contender at the head of the peloton forcing the tempo, shaping the race. She added the Holland Ladies Tour to her growing list of triumphs. Like Greg LeMond, most of her racing took place in Europe.

Other victories included the Thüringen Rundfahrt der Frauen in Germany; the Giro del Trentino Alto Adige in Italy; a stage across the International Date Line at the Women's Tour of New Zealand; and the time trial in the Amgen Tour of California.

She scored back-to-back triumphs in the sixty-mile Philly Cycling Classic in Philadelphia, America's only UCI women's road race. It drew 140 women from fifteen countries. They whipped five times around a twelve-mile circuit, which capitalized on the landmark Manayunk Wall. Over twenty-five years of Dave Chauner's USPRO championships, the Manayunk Wall gained fame. His protégé, Robin Morton, organized the Philly Classic and featured the Wall as the route's centerpiece—starting the race at the top and ultimately finishing there as multitudes jammed the street to party and cheer cyclists up the climb. Morton also split the $60,000 purse equally between men and women.

In September Stevens took home a third UCI gold medal for winning the team time trial at the 2014 road worlds in the ancient city of Ponferrada, Spain. In the individual time trial for USA Cycling, she claimed a bronze medal.

Tejay van Garderen of BMC Racing Team also won a gold medal at the worlds in the team time trial with colleagues from Australia, Italy, Slovenia, and Switzerland. (Taylor Phinney was recovering from a disastrous crash after colliding with a motorcycle while descending Lookout Mountain in Tennessee during the national road championship; a compound fracture of the tibia and a severed knee tendon threatened his career.)

The next week, Stevens climbed aboard an airliner to Boston, near her parents' house on Cape Cod. She and Baker announced their engagement.

• • •

Stevens switched in 2015 to the top-ranked Boels-Dolmans Cycling Team in the Netherlands, sponsored by a Dutch global construction-equipment rental company and a landscaping business. She joined compatriot Megan Guarnier, a national road champion and former All-American swimmer at Middlebury College. Also on the squad were England's road and track champion Lizzie Armitstead and eight headliners from the Netherlands, Denmark, Germany, Luxembourg, and Poland.

Guarnier, two years younger than Stevens, had more cycling experience. Guarnier's thirteen years of competitive swimming ended after her first year at Middlebury College due to shoulder problems. She tried some triathlons; cycling was her weakness. To improve, she trained with classmates on the Middlebury cycling team. Collegiate cycling turned into a good fit. Points that both men and women earned in collegiate race results were tallied together by USA Cycling to determine national college team rankings.

Guarnier percolated up the amateur ranks while majoring in neuroscience. She intended to become a medical doctor. After graduating in 2007, she postponed medical school to race full-time. She scored international acclaim in the summer of 2011 for winning the Giro della Toscana Internationale Femminile stage race in Italy.

The next year she spent much of her season racing in Europe, including seventh place in La Flèche Wallonne Féminine. She returned to America to win her first national road championship. Guarnier became a player on the European circuit, with consistent top-ten finishes. Boels-Dolman hired her in 2014.

Guarnier scored a major international victory in March 2015 in Italy's Strade Bianche women's road race. Fifty miles after the start in San Gimignano, she attacked and opened a gap of forty seconds on a field of a hundred. She toughed out her narrow margin for the last ten miles, ending in a solo triumph before a huge crowd in picturesque Siena. A month later, Guarnier claimed a podium finish with third place at the Flèche Wallonne Féminine.

Stevens, sixth in the Flèche Wallonne, flew back to America to win the time trial in the Amgen Tour of California. She finished the Amgen Tour with a podium spot. She also won a stage in the Women's Tour of New Zealand.

• • •

Stevens and Guarnier were among thirty men and women selected for the USAC delegation at the 2015 worlds road races and time trials in Richmond, Virginia, September 19 to 27. The best talents on the globe flocked to battle for medals, rainbow jerseys, and cash. Richmond, a two-hour drive south from Washington DC, offered far more spectators and news outlets than the worlds twenty-nine years earlier in Colorado Springs.

(Track races had taken place in February near Paris in the Vélodrome de Saint-Quentin. Jennifer Valente of San Diego took home a silver medal in the individual pursuit; Bobby Lea of Easton, Maryland, scored a bronze in the scratch race.)

Some eight hundred men and women cyclists came together in Richmond, the state capital (and the capital of the Confederacy during the Civil War). Flags representing seventy-six nations flew from flagpoles along downtown streets. The sun would shine for most of the nine days on the twelve men's and women's events. Crowds exceeded expectations, reaching about seven hundred thousand. More than five hundred international media covered the program; broadcasts reached an estimated three hundred million people.

Taylor Phinney arrived after months of agonizing rehab for his mended tibia. His missing most of the racing season led to speculation that he could be a liability on the BMC Racing Team in the six-rider team time trial. On opening day, he joined an Aussie, two Italians, and two Swiss teammates. They blitzed the course and won the gold medal—a charming comeback for Phinney.

Stevens, in the orange-and-black Boels-Dolmans colors, claimed a silver in the team time trial with English ace Lizzie Armitstead and *consoeurs* from the Netherlands, Luxembourg, and Poland.

Two USAC eighteen-year-olds—Chloé Dygert of Indianapolis and Emma White of Delanson, New York—snatched the top two places in both the junior women's road race and the individual time trial: Dygert won two golds; White carried home two silvers.

Two more USAC teens claimed medals in the men's junior time trial—Adrian Costa of Stanford, California, copped the silver medal, and Brandon McNulty of Phoenix earned the bronze.

Forty-four women from thirty-three countries contested the individual time trial. Stevens rode on medal pace through the first half of the nineteen miles. A photographer snapped her in full flight, dried salt on grimacing lips, gold-capped back teeth shining. She finished sixth, twenty-five seconds from the gold medal and one spot behind Kristin Armstrong, ten years older.

The last medal USAC claimed came on the penultimate day, in the women's road race, on the same course as the men's road race held on the final day. The course began and finished in a canyon of downtown office buildings, restaurants, and shops. It looped around a ten-mile circuit punctuated by sharp turns and two punishing climbs in quick succession up cobblestone roads in the historic colonial-era neighborhood of Libby Hill Park.

Stevens and Guarnier lined up for the eighty-mile road race with two teammates: Shelley Olds, who had studied health and human performance at nearby Roanoke College, and Lauren Stephens, a former schoolteacher. They straddled their bikes on the front line of 135 women from forty-six countries. When they saw a UCI official on the sideline wave the UCI flag in a down stroke, everyone clicked into her pedals at the same time and hurried away.

The U.S. foursome showed USA jerseys at the front of the peloton to the home crowd. Then a flurry of individuals and small groups fled off the front to keep the tempo aggressive. By forty miles a small group pulled away and threatened to steal the show without a USA Cycling rider in the mix. Shelley Olds and Lauren Stephens had pulled out: Olds fell, Stephens punctured. Stevens surged to the front. She set a brutal tempo that stretched the bunch snaking through Richmond in a chase that caught the escapees while burning off dozens.

The closing miles featured attacks that split up the field. Stevens missed the decisive break. But Megan Guarnier went with the leaders, among them Lizzie Armitstead, her dark hair in a braid down her back. Guarnier was followed everywhere by spectators chanting "USA! USA!"

After three and a half hours, Armitstead blasted in the last mile up the final hill, igniting cheers from a wall of spectators bordering the road. Guarnier and six others stayed with her. The main pack pursued, ten seconds behind—about two hundred yards. Down the hill on the level street, Armitstead faked a surge to bait someone else to lead. She kept glancing over her shoulder to monitor her opponents. In the last sixty yards, Anna van der Breggen in the Dutch orange jersey shot ahead at top speed, Guarnier sticking to her rear wheel, Armitstead drafting. Then Armitstead, formerly a track racer, zipped around to win by a half-length for the gold medal.

Guarnier, one length behind, claimed the bronze.

Nineteen seconds later Stevens came in, twenty-fourth.

• • •

In Richmond, Stevens and Neal Henderson had coffee together. "I failed with sixth in the time trial," she said. "I like to win."

She was twenty-five seconds from gold in the time trial—tantalizingly close. Now thirty-two, the eldest of eleven on Boels-Dolmans, she had one last Olympics, in eleven months in Rio de Janeiro, Brazil. She wanted to medal.

Stevens was entering her seventh year as a pro and looked to go beyond what she had done before. The UCI women's world hour record was still fresh in her mind. Two weeks earlier, Molly Shaffer Van Houweling, a Harvard Law School grad and professor at UC Berkeley School of Law, had improved the twelve-year-old mark by about two hundred yards established by Dutch woman Leontien van Moorsel. Van Houweling covered 46.273 kilometers (28.75 miles) on a velodrome in the rarified atmosphere of Aguascalientes, Mexico.

Stevens proposed going after the women's hour record in early 2016. Preparing for the attempt required her to increase power. If successful, she would launch the next season stronger than ever.

Henderson had successfully trained Rohan Dennis, a road and track pro from Adelaide, Australia, in his world hour record ride in February 2015. Dennis pedaled 52.491 kilometers (32.3 miles) around a track in Grenchen, Switzerland. Months later Dennis, a BMC Cycling teammate of Taylor Phinney, capitalized on the power in his legs. After earlier failures to win Australia's national time trial title, he finally captured the 2015 championship. Extra strength propelled him to win the Tour de France opening time trial, which netted him the coveted yellow jersey.

Henderson and Stevens were hoping she would have a similar performance upgrade on her road to Rio.

Since 1893 most UCI world hour records belonged to Europeans. The rare American was William W. Hamilton, on July 3, 1898. He first put his name in the record books on March 2, 1896, setting the national record for one-third of a mile in Coronado, California, in 34⅓ seconds. During his 1898 hour record ride, around a track in Denver, he established U.S. marks for ten miles, twenty miles, and twenty-five miles en route to pedaling twenty-five miles, 600 yards (40.781 kilometers). He was the fourth to hold the world hour record, the first to break twenty-five miles. It lasted seven years, broken by Lucien Petit-Breton, later twice winner of the Tour de France.

The women's hour record dates back to the evening of Friday July 7, 1893, in Paris when a light-opera singer named Antoinette Marie Edmonde de Rafélis Saint-Sauveur on the popular Vélodrome Buffalo pedaled sixteen miles, 287 yards (26.012 kilometers). In the fashion of that mauve decade, she wore a white flannel suit with billowy leggings and a small-brimmed straw hat.

Dublin journalist Feargal McKay has written about Saint-Sauveur, and notes her record was soon improved by a succession of other women entertainers as audiences paid to watch women time trial farther. Unofficial hour records continued to be set, notably by French woman Jeanine Lemaire, who topped 39 kilometers in 1952. But the

UCI did not recognize world records for women until 1955. On July 7 that year Tamara Novikhova spun into cycling history for the Soviet Union. She set the first official UCI women's world hour record around a velodrome in Irkutsk, Siberia: 38.473 kilometers (23.9 miles). She remains the only Russian to claim the hour mark.

Stevens and Henderson agreed they would initiate her preparation in early November. They would shoot for an assault on Van Houweling's record in February 2016. Colorado Springs would be the ideal venue. The 7-Eleven Velodrome there would be capped by a new dome, co-funded by USA Cycling and the U.S. Olympic Committee.

Before gearing up for the campaign, Stevens took a vacation. She and fiancé, Brett Baker, married on October 3 in San Francisco.

• • •

Henderson coached Stevens for four years. Now he created a regimen to boost her world-class performance without straining tendons, muscles, or overloading her immune system. With the same attention to detail as a bespoke tailor, he scrutinized key performance measures: max oxygen consumption, watts pedaled, how big a gear she could manage, the rpm she could sustain. He declined to disclose workouts, but allowed that he designed one to increase her pedal cadence from 70 to 90 rpm to 102 rpm.

He focused on boosting her power from a standing start. Stevens practiced reaching the record-setting pace of 30 mph in less than twenty seconds—exerting several hundred pounds of torque on the pedals. The plan was for her to fly through turn four on record pace, tucked aero down the home straight. Her hour assault would take her twice as far as she had ever time trialed.

Henderson mounted a video camera on a motorbike and drove around the track at exactly 30 mph to document what the two straights and four turns looked like at that speed. She watched his video and visualized her performance.

Stevens had a custom aero carbon-fiber bike, midnight-black, designed by Specialized Bicycle Components. She drove to Specialized's headquarters in swanky Morgan Hill, California, to consult with experts. They meticulously refined her streamlined position in a wind tunnel and the bike-fit studio, where experienced staff used video cameras and metric rulers to dial in details.

To take mental breaks, she frequented one of the Reboot Float Spas popular in the Bay Area. They offered enclosed egg-shaped pod tanks filled with warm water saturated with Epsom salt. Floating face-up in a womb-like temperature for sixty minutes relaxed muscles and joints. The silence eliminated distractions, diminished stress. Spa soaks in a gravity-free environment freed her to visualize what she would do on her hour-record attempt—pushing herself to pedal farther than any woman in one hour.

Runners talk about how the 26.2-mile marathon breaks down to two parts: the first 20 miles and the last 6.2 miles. Stevens knew her final fifteen minutes were going to build increasingly harder, more painful.

Legendary Eddy Merckx has compared the fierce agony of his 1972 world hour record set in Mexico City with compressing into sixty minutes all the suffering he had felt in the hundred or so hours he exerted over three weeks to win each of his five Tours de France. He ranked the hour record with a Tour victory. He called the last minutes of his record the most painful of his career.

Stevens explained she took a two-part approach to dealing with the pain ahead. First, avoid thinking about it. "Second is to know it's going to be terribly painful. And that's one of the reasons I'm doing it—to push beyond that pain. If it was going to be easy, then what would be the point of doing it?"

• • •

On January 22, 2016, Stevens and Henderson were counting down the days and adjusting workouts when news came from Adelaide, Australia, that Bridie O'Donnell, an Aussie cyclist-turned-orthopedic-surgeon, had smashed Van Houweling's record by 609 meters—more than a quarter mile—stretching the distance to 46.882 kilometers (29.13 miles).

O'Donnell toughened Stevens's determination.

• • •

Stevens prepared more intensely for her hour record attempt than any race. A couple weeks before her scheduled ride, she relocated to Colorado Springs. She practiced taking off from standing starts to 30 mph on the 7-Eleven Velodrome. She worked out pedaling laps at record speed for short sets, which were repeated, while growing intimate with every aspect of the aging, imperfect concrete, the sloping turns connected to straights. She hugged the black perimeter line, where distances are measured around the 333-meter oval (1,093.5 feet). Three feet away was a parallel red line. The black and red lines defined the sprinters' lane—the leading rider entering it is limited to staying in the boundaries when a competitor tries to fly by. She stayed inside the lane.

The middle of the home straight featured the black start-finish line. It spanned the track width, from the black perimeter border through the red line, the five vibrant-colored Olympic rings painted on the surface, the large likeness of the American flag, and ended at the track's edge abutting the blocked-off grandstand. On the flat infield apron inside the black line was a Tiffany-Blue band. On it were foam bollards, resembling tightly rolled spa towels, set every few feet around the turns to alert her if she strayed out of bounds.

Davis Phinney came regularly as friend and supporter. One afternoon following a workout, Stevens sat on a metal infield bench with him. She wore her red-white-and-blue Captain America USA Cycling skinsuit. She unstrapped her helmet, placed it upside-down like a tortoise at her side, and talked with *VeloNews* journalist Caley Fretz. She comically impersonated a stoner discussing the existential questions of what is time and what is the length of an hour.

Fretz prodded her about how she would handle pain in the final minutes. When he mentioned Merckx's name, Phinney interrupted. "Some things are better left unsaid," Phinney told the scribe. "She doesn't want to think about it."

• • •

On Saturday morning February 27, some two hundred ticket-holders strode into the velodrome infield to watch from inside a waist-tall pen of plexiglass boards. Guests included Van Houweling and Stevens's husband, Brett Baker.

Neal Henderson held a small computer and hovered on the home straight. Behind him UCI and USAC officials sat at a long table holding computers—witnesses recording for accuracy and posterity.

"The care in preparation for Evie's ride was meticulous," said Dan Lee, on the premises as content manager for SRAM Road and Zipp wheels, the Chicago-headquartered sponsor of all Stevens's pro teams. "Cycling is a team effort—involving coaches, mechanics, soigneurs. The mechanic carried her bike across the velodrome infield and set it carefully on the concrete to avoid any debris getting on the tires. The mechanic carefully aired the tires for the final time. Everything had to go perfect, or near perfect."

Shortly before noon, everyone stood for "The Star-Spangled Banner."

"When Evie sat on a chair near her bike to put on her shoes and helmet, I saw her face grow serious," Lee said. "There was tension on her face."

At twelve o'clock, she approached her bike in a gray stand behind the start-finish line. She swung a leg over the top tube, clicked into the pedals, set her feet at eleven and five o'clock, and raised off the saddle. She gripped the wide part of the handlebars, launched away, and accelerated swiftly like a plane on the runway. Before leaning into the first turn she moved her hands to the close-set aero bar extensions and leaned into her Superwoman pose. The bike stand was removed before she flew down the home straight and whooshed past Henderson.

He bellowed encouragement, his voice resounding in the dome as the whirr of tires and the whoosh of solid-disc front and rear wheels came and went.

About halfway through her ordeal, Stevens got a taste of what Merckx meant. "I almost puked, so I backed off a bit," she later said.

For the first forty-five minutes, she piloted a smooth flight. Her laps around the track surpassed one hundred: "I was just in the zone saying, 'Pedal, push, pedal, push.'"

In the final ten minutes, her shoulders betrayed her. She veered through a turn and crossed the black line onto the blue apron. Her front wheel thumped against a foam cushion. She overcorrected and careened across the red line, then straightened up back in the lane and flew right.

Her face tightened from grimace to snarl, then deepened to rictus as minutes ticked down.

Fans on the infield screamed and smacked palms against the plexiglass.

A UCI official fired a blank handgun to end her hour ride.

She had completed her 144th lap. Stevens set a new world hour record: 47.980 kilometers (29.813 miles), more than a kilometer, or five-eighths of a mile, farther than O'Donnell.

Her face relaxed. She broke into a broad smile.

Caley Fretz asked her if it was the longest hour as Merckx had declared. "There was one moment when I thought about Merckx, how he said it was the worst sensation ever. Oh, yes, he was *right*!"

She set her hour record in an all-American way: near the U.S. Olympic Training Center, on a bike designed in California, with wheels manufactured in Indianapolis, and her ride livestreamed worldwide from start to finish over the internet created by California universities and the Pentagon.

Dan Lee remarked that her women's hour record made a big impression. "As someone who grew up in road cycling as a teenager in the 1980s, when cycling was a cult sport here, watching Evie circling the track in front of two hundred people, a small audience, what really connected to me was that this is what American cycling is all about—plucky upstarts, doing things our way."

After going almost 48 kilometers in an hour, Stevens had reason to be hopeful to win a medal in the Rio Olympics. Its time trial was only 29.8 kilometers.

22

The Match Sprinters

The past is never dead. It isn't even past.

—WILLIAM FAULKNER

Like musicians endowed with perfect pitch and math whizzes mastering calculus without breaking a sweat, match sprinters live in a rarified milieu. Much remains to polish natural gifts. Even more, the art of winning involves an edgy mix of physical strength, intuition, and audacity. The difference between the almost-right move that loses and the right move that wins looms as large as what Mark Twain described as the difference between lightning bugs and lightning.

When Marty Nothstein defeated brawny Australian national champion Darryn Hill in the 1994 elite match sprint at the world track championships in Palermo, Italy, Nothstein fans rejoiced at the Lehigh County Velodrome in Pennsylvania, near his hometown. Journalists consulted record books. Eighty-two years had passed since Frank Kramer and Donald McDougall had won world match sprint titles—Kramer as pro, McDougall as amateur.

Nothstein (pronounced NOTE-stine, rhymes with gold mine) followed three sprinters who had turned to coaching. Each imparted lessons, refinements, and ideas and held his successor on a bike to push him from start lines.

This succession spanned the twentieth century. It began unassumingly with Jack Disney, a distant relative of cartoon animator Walt Disney. Born in Topeka, Kansas, Jack Disney came of age in 1940s suburban

Los Angeles. He starred in high school football when coaches toughened players with push-ups, pull-ups, and in gyms climbing hand over hand up thirty-foot ropes to touch the ceiling.

Disney stood five feet eight, weighed 160 pounds in his prime, and had thick dark hair, clipped in a crew cut. After high school graduation in 1948 he worked as a draftsman and, on his own time, speed skated on indoor rinks trendy in Southern California. A fellow skater lent him a Red Devil bicycle for a three-mile contest hosted by a Pasadena cycling club around the Rose Bowl Stadium.

"I was into boxing and wore boxing shorts," he recalled. "The club president told me to just get in front of everybody and when someone comes up, to wind it up faster. So I did that and won my first race."

In 1949 he finished second in the Amateur Bicycle League of America state championship. He qualified for the ABLA nationals in San Diego, a weekend series of four events. "They were on a high school quarter-mile dirt track. There were a lot of crashes because the turns had no banking and riders ganged together around turns. In my heat, I was leading and crashed, landing on my head. The doctor said I had a concussion. I went home."

Disney didn't race for four years. He served two years in the army and married his fiancée, Alice. They had a daughter, Jacqueline. He resumed racing in 1954, under the guidance of Albert "Musty" Crebs. In 1911 on the board velodrome in Salt Lake City, Crebs bulleted one lap around the oval and set the world record for one-sixth of a mile (293 yards). A native of Jersey City, New Jersey, Crebs lived the itinerant life of a professional cyclist and settled in Long Beach, outside LA, in 1945. He operated a tiny bike shop, repaired push lawnmowers, and sharpened blades.

He also coached locals. They called themselves the Crebs Wheelmen. Among them were 1932 Olympian Russell Allen, 1936 Olympian Charles Morton, and Don Hester, 1946 national ABLA champion.

"Musty was a nice person," Disney said. "He got the nickname because he rode scrunched up on the bike. There were twenty or more of us in the Crebs Wheelmen club. We got together on Sunday mornings in Long Beach when the weather was good. We rode straight half-mile stretches, sprinting to the end, then turned around and did the same back. We did that six times. Musty kept score about who finished first, second, and third."

Disney said Crebs had mystique for his uncanny way of straightening steel frames that lost alignment after a crash. Riders took their bent frames to his shop. "He took the frame, told the customer to wait, and disappeared in the back. After a while he returned with the frame, all fixed. Customers wondered what he did when he disappeared with their frame. One day a rider took his damaged frame to Crebs while a buddy waited out back to see where Crebs went. Crebs walked out the rear door, stepped over to a tree, and put the frame into the crook of a limb, bent it this way and that, eyeballing the frame till he got it right."

The old pro shared a trade secret: winning was less about strength and more about timing. He came from the tradition of hanging back until the final turn, then uncorking his energy. All that mattered was putting your front wheel over the line first. Winning by the width of a tire counted the same as two or more bike lengths; the difference was that spectators felt they got their money's worth from watching tight battles. Pros took pride on giving close shaves.

Disney drove to the 1954 ABLA nationals in Minneapolis, on a quarter-mile asphalt running track. "It was slightly banked, but the wrong way to let rain water drain off the outside surface. Everybody was crashing. I didn't do any good on the track in my first race. But then the races went to the road. My confidence level went way up. A highlight of my career was crossing the finish line in both the one-mile and five-mile finals and no one was ahead of me."

Points in both races resulted in winning his first national championship.

• • •

Disney was picked for the 1955 Pan-Am Games team that March in Mexico City. U.S. athletes dominated track and field, gymnastics, and swimming, but cyclists were shut out of medals. Nevertheless, Disney impressed a promoter who offered him an opportunity to race on tracks in Europe.

"I declined," he said. "Cycling was my hobby. There wasn't enough in it to leave my job in California."

Disney trained more miles to bolster stamina on top of a natural jackrabbit jump. He relied on both qualities at the 1956 Olympic match sprint trials in San Jose. "I raced thirteen sprints in various heats to get to the final. We were riding on an asphalt midget-car track, a quarter-miler. Only one sprinter was going to the Olympics. I won the final to be that sprinter."

He flew with the U.S. cycling team to the Games in Melbourne, Australia. "It was a big moment when we marched into the stadium, hearing the band and the roar of the spectators," he said. He was eliminated in the quarterfinals. The experience impressed him to raise standards back home.

Jack Simes was fifteen when he met Disney at the 1958 nationals in Newark, New Jersey, on the one-mile dirt Weequahic Park horse track. Disney had won his fifth consecutive title. "I thought he was the best in the country," Simes said. "I hoped he would keep going long enough that I could race against him."

They never squared off, but they shared a room at the 1964 Tokyo Olympics—Simes as match sprinter, Disney in the tandem sprint with his protégé Tim Mountford. "Disney was quiet, but he could be a bundle of nerves. When we traveled out of the country, he seemed to miss being away from Southern California. He was uncomfortable with the weather, the motels, the food."

Disney was regarded as the next Jack Heid as the top U.S. sprinter. But the two men had vastly different outlooks.

"Heid was tough," Simes said. "Nothing affected him—he was like a blunt instrument. Disney was not cast in that mold. Except for going abroad for three Olympics, he stayed in America. Disney won a lot of races, competed much longer than Heid, and inspired more people. That made him good for the sport. He definitely took sprinting here to a new level."

Al Stiller, Heid's teammate at the 1948 London Olympics and Disney's teammate at the 1955 Pan-Am Games, told me he considered Disney the more consistent sprinter. "As much as I liked Jack Heid, he was not as consistent as Disney. Occasionally I could beat Heid—although when he was on, his performance couldn't be touched."

Disney's best sprint against foreign riders took place at the 1959

Pan-Am Games in Chicago. On a 250-meter board saucer he reached the final against Juan Canto of Argentina. "In the first round, I let him get way too far out there. Going into the last two hundred meters, he had thirty meters on me when I poured it on. At the finish, I was drawing even, but too late. I did the same thing in the next match."

His silver medal marked a 1950s milestone.

• • •

The 1966 ABLA nationals on the Ed Rudolph Velodrome in Northbrook, Illinois, introduced the match sprint championship. Match sprints had been a mainstay from the 1890s but disappeared after 1941 with track cycling's collapse. At the new ABLA match sprint championship, Disney triumphed.

He went as defending champion to the 1967 nationals in Portland, Oregon. Thousands of spectators filled the Alpenrose Velodrome bleachers, despite a heat wave pushing the temperature to a sultry 100 degrees. Flags hung limp on poles. Simes and Disney joined dozens vying for bragging rights. Disney, thirty-seven, lost a qualifying round to his pupil, California state sprint champion Tim Mountford. The aging lion ended up fourth as Simes won.

Another winner in Portland was ten-year-old Gil Hatton Jr. He seized the gold medal in the midget division, age thirteen and younger.

The next year at the nationals on the Encino Velodrome, Disney roared back to capture the match sprint, his seventh national title.

He coached daughter Jacqueline to three national championships, 1969 to 1971, and taught fellow members of the Paramount Cycling Club. Gary Campbell claimed national match sprint titles in 1971 and 1972. The club impressed the West Coast distributor of Peugeot Cycles to provide bikes, jerseys, and shorts.

The 1973 nationals, again in Northbrook, marked nineteen years since Disney's first championship. Now forty-three, he combed his silver hair back like a statesman. He reached the final against Roger Young, whose father, Clair Young, had for years failed to beat Disney.

"People called him the Gray Ghost because he was always ready,"

Roger said. He nipped Disney by a half-wheel in two matches. Those who saw their duel talked about it for years.

Northbrook's 1973 nationals witnessed a rare family double: Roger and sister Sheila Young won both men's and women's match sprints.

Winner of the junior men's national championship was sixteen-year-old Gil Hatton.

Disney retired from racing and coached Hatton.

• • •

Hatton, a Los Angeles native, discovered cycling through his father, Gilbert Hatton Sr., an aerospace company machinist, motorcycle racer, and cyclist. Hatton senior took his nine-year-old son to watch track races. Father and son were called Big H and Little Gil.

Little Gil won his first race at ten in 1966, on Catalina Island. "I loved scratch racing—everybody starting together and racing to cross the line first," he said. "I saw Disney win the national match sprint in 1968 and heard about his three Olympics. I thought he was one of the fastest guys in the world."

Twelve-year-old Gil was taken by his mother, Eva, to meet Simes. "I was on the Army Special Services cycling team, training for the 1968 Olympic trials," Simes said. "The team relaxed after workouts at a place near Long Beach. Little Gil was shy and quiet. One rider had a big raspberry bruise on his thigh from a fall. Little Gil spotted it and got a serious look on his face. His mother gasped in shock."

Little Gil trained and raced on the concrete Encino Velodrome. On summer weekday evenings he encountered an elderly gent on a vintage bike. He noted the outdated long wheelbase and wooden rims. Someone identified him as Bill Honeman. The old national champion, pulling the fluttering ghost of Frank Kramer, and Hatton were overlapping past and future champions.

"I was young and didn't know much about him," Hatton said. "Later, I thought it was pretty cool that I rode on the same track as Willie Honeman."

Little Gil enjoyed the track's sense of community. "Training was bland. No technique. There was no national team. Just a group of guys training and racing together. Working out with older guys like Jack Disney, Skip Cutting, Chuck Pranke, watching them win national championships and go on to compete on Olympic teams encouraged me. I didn't train with other kids. I was surrounded with great men. I was sincere about cycling and learned a lot fast."

He was fifteen when his mother moved out with both his younger sisters. "I took cycling seriously when I was a kid. When I looked at photos of myself from back then, I realized I didn't smile much. I raced hard and seriously. I was an angry rider. That made me a better athlete."

He played high school football and baseball and ran sprints on the track team, but favored cycling. "On a team, you can have a great performance but still lose. I prefer to win or lose based on how I did. Unlike football and baseball, cycling was an Olympic sport. I liked winning. That set me apart from others."

Hatton was drawn to the informal Paramount Cycle Club. Disney saw him as a younger version of himself—almost the same height, eager to learn. "Gibby had good finishing speed and a good kick at the end of the sprint," Disney said.

"Disney's expertise was hanging back on a guy's rear wheel and whipping around off the last turn," Hatton said. "That was Disney's forte. I was taught that as my tactical weapon."

On the 250-meter Encino Velodrome, about half the size of a high school running track, the finish line was only sixty yards off the last turn. That played to Hatton's fast-twitch jump. "That was my favorite move."

He practiced with Disney, Cutting, Pranke, and others. Each took a turn at the front of the cruising pace line, pedaling 90 rpm on their fixed gears. The last rider accelerated into the final turn and snapped the pedals around at 120 to 130 rpm. That launched him in a 200-yard anaerobic effort, lasting some ten seconds and taking him past everyone to the line. The exercises came naturally to Hatton.

In 1972 Disney moved with wife, Alice, and their daughter Jacqueline to San Jose for a job designing semi-conductors for new-fangled computers. In the summer of 1974 Hatton stayed as their guest. Disney also volunteered as an ABLA coach. He and Hatton traveled to Detroit where trials were held for the European junior cycling championships in Warsaw, Poland.

Hatton outclassed match sprint rivals, including Leslie Barczewski of West Allis, Wisconsin. They flew to Warsaw with Disney and nine road riders.

"It was a great adventure, my first time out of the country, and Poland was communist then." Hatton remembered. "We had an all-star team, maybe one of the greatest of all time." It included future Olympians Harvey Nitz and the brothers Wayne and Dale Stetina.

• • •

More than twenty governing bodies sent their best junior cyclists to Warsaw, Poland's capital. Teams arrived with masseurs, mechanics, medical doctors, and gofers—support unknown to the ABLA crew. Warsaw's outdoor 333-meter concrete track was shaped like a football; the straights and corners had been resurfaced with different compounds. "The turns were smooth, the straights were rough," Hatton said. "Took some getting used to them."

He progressed through knockout rounds against rivals from across Europe and the Eastern Bloc to reach the final match against Italy's Giuseppe Saronni.

Thousands of spectators filled the grandstand and bleacher seats. They watched Hatton, in a jersey with USA inscribed on the front and back. He sat composed on his bike behind the start-finish line, staring straight ahead. He was held by Disney, bent at the waist, a hand gripping the frame head, the other on the seat post, like Musty Crebs did for him. The crowd saw Saronni, in Italy's azure-blue jersey, looking to the horizon while his handler supported him.

Both seventeen-year-olds had dark hair poking through slatted leather hairnet helmets. Both were medium height, although Hatton had a few more pounds. Both were unassuming. They preferred to express themselves with their legs. Both were addicted to winning. Since Italy counted nine world pro sprint champions, Saronni, national junior track champion, was the odds-on favorite.

Hatton preferred match sprints to anything else. "They are like boxing. You're head-to-head, one rider versus the other, always close together. If you're confident, that's half the battle."

In the first match Saronni led, controlling the tempo, turning his head to check on Hatton, a stranger. Through the final turn Saronni bulleted onto the straight, head down, legs spinning like a locomotive.

Hatton bent his elbows out, pulled hard on the handlebars, and made his move. "I came around from the rear position and won by three-quarters of a length. For the second match, I rode from the front and kept it slow. My idea was to use my jump and take it to the line."

Hatton won from behind and off the front. In boxing parlance, he punched above his weight and KO'd the Italian stallion.

"I felt like I was in a dream when I got off my bike," he told me. "I was somewhat in shock. I think if it was not for my teammates shouting and cheering there may have been a stunned silence over the whole track. They brought me to realize what I had just accomplished. The awards ceremony was delayed because officials didn't have a recording of our national anthem. Officials had to search around Warsaw. Hah!"

His conquest marked the high point for the ABLA squad. Barczewski lost a qualifying round but fought back in a repechage (a run-off for those who had failed to win a heat) and claimed fifth.

The team flew home for the U.S. track nationals, again in Northbrook. Hatton captured his second sprint title in the same month. He also won his second junior ABLA title—fifty years after Bill Honeman's ABLA junior victory.

• • •

In the summer of 1976 Hatton moved to Trexlertown, locally called T-town, near Allentown in eastern Pennsylvania, for the Lehigh County Velodrome, a 333-meter concrete track. It opened under management of Jack Simes and Dave Chauner. They invited world-class competitors to train and race there. "I wanted to be where Jack Simes was doing something new. Pennsylvania became my home. I put down roots."

Simes said Hatton was a popular attraction. "Gil was very colorful to watch in action," Simes said. "He had spectacular moves. He could thread the needle—passing between riders bunched close together, like he was invisible. And he was really fast."

Hatton was hired as one of the original coaches in the Air Products Developmental Program. Created by Simes and Chauner, it promoted competitive cycling and offered fitness plans for youth and adults by loaning bikes, equipment, and paid coaches who gave free advice. The program has steadily attracted upward of four hundred people a year. It remains funded by Air Products & Chemicals, an international corporation headquartered in Allentown. "Back then I was just teaching basic skills and general riding," Hatton said.

Simes described him as a natural coach. "Gil is one of those guys who has a coaching genius, like someone who can sit down and play the piano without any music lessons."

Coaching paid a modest bread-and-butter income. Not enough for foreign travel necessary to compete at the highest levels of the sport. American track racing was eclipsed by road racing in prestige and number of events.

Leigh "the Tree" Barczewski, Leslie's older brother, beat Hatton in the 1976 national match sprint championship, which landed Barczewski on the team that went to the Montreal Olympics.

The ABLA was succeeded that year by the U.S. Cycling Federation. Hatton was selected for the USCF national squad, which boarded airliners for the track worlds in Monteroni, Italy, and the next year in San Cristobal, Venezuela. On both occasions he competed in the tandem sprint with the tall Californian Jerry Ash, known as the Gentle Giant, and endowed with dry humor. In Venezuela they rode their best performance together, fifth place.

Hatton grew restless. "My career dipped. I wasn't fitting in with the amateur thing." He retreated to Los Angeles.

In late 1978 during a harsh winter freeze gripping Pennsylvania he returned in a car without a windshield. Simes advised him to go to Montreal for an international program on the indoor board track. "In Montreal Gil started his comeback," Simes said.

Hatton also founded the American Cycling Academy to provide private coaching. He had filled out and gained a new nickname, the Bear. He married a Pennsylvania native, Terri. She said he was like a teddy bear. Rivals said he competed like a hungry grizzly.

The United States' boycott of the 1980 Moscow Olympics changed Hatton's perspective. Leigh Barczewski had won five national match sprint titles, twice defeating Hatton, yet Barczewski quit racing at age twenty-four for a day job. Hatton's vanquished European championship foe Giuseppe Saronni had turned pro and switched to road racing—winning the 1980 Flèche Wallonne and Giro d'Italia.

Hatton didn't care for road racing. He turned pro and captured the national match sprint title. The Union Cycliste Internationale had upgraded the European junior championship to the UCI junior worlds. Simes presided over USPRO and pulled strings for the UCI to recognize Hatton's victory. During a summer program at the Lehigh County Velodrome, Simes presented him with a delayed UCI world's gold medal and rainbow jersey.

Then from the Orient came the *keirin*, an event created for pure sprinters.

• • •

The UCI introduced the *keirin*, Japanese for "racing cycle," at the 1980 worlds in Besançon, France. Keirin racing had flourished for three decades in Japan. Featuring pari-mutuel betting, it generated unparalleled incomes for sprinters but remained unknown to Westerners until Koichi Nakano and Yoshi Sugata shocked the 1977 worlds in Venezuela. Nakano and Sugata breezed through heats in the pro match sprints like they had an extra gear. They faced off in the final, which Nakano captured.

Two-time defending champion John Nicholson, an Aussie, managed third. Humiliated, he went home to Melbourne and retired.

At the 1978 worlds in Munich, Germany, and the next year in Amsterdam, the Netherlands, Nakano crushed all-comers. UCI officials realized they witnessed a big change. The UCI and Japanese Keirin Association negotiated a deal to add keirin racing to the UCI worlds program, beginning in 1980 in Besançon, France. Danny Clark, an Aussie popular with Lehigh County Velodrome audiences and a rival of Hatton, won the inaugural UCI keirin title.

Nakano romped again in Besançon for his fourth straight world match sprint title. Twenty-five-year-old Nakano stood a well-proportioned five feet eight, small compared with the more muscular Eastern Bloc sprinters. What distinguished him were sharper reflexes, better-timed moves, and punchier jumps—all skills he honed over seven years on Japan's keirin circuit.

The emperor of match sprints perplexed the cycling media at a press conference. Nakano said through an interpreter that the hallowed UCI worlds took him away from the lucrative keirin circuit, which meant he lost money—a drawback that discouraged keirin riders. Nakano attended the UCI worlds as Japan's volunteer cycling ambassador.

In 1981 the Japanese Keirin Association announced it would invite foreigners, like Danny Clark, to Japan. Hatton set his sights on going to the East.

• • •

Keirin racing grew out of desperation. After Japan's unconditional surrender finally ended World War II, the Land of the Rising Sun struggled to rebuild cities bombed to ruins and to restore its devastated economy. Years of grim food shortages caused the slaughter of horses for meat.

The Danish cycling federation offered a creative solution to Japan's dire straits. Denmark had a tradition of pari-mutuel betting on bicycle races over short distances on tracks for fast, lively action. Representatives of the Danish cycling federation visited Japan to share how to build concrete velodromes inside full-size stadiums. The Danes advised establishing pari-mutuel betting, which puts betting revenue into a pool, takes all taxes and the house's percentage off the top, and calculates payoffs from the money left to pay bets that win, place, and show.

Substituting two-wheelers for four-legged beasts created high-speed, crowd-pleasing keirin racing over about two kilometers (1.2 miles). It debuted in 1949 in Kitakyushu, now home to a million residents. Keirin races featured up to nine riders. When the start gun fired, a designated pacer on the inside lane dashed ahead for contestants to draft. The pacer controlled the speed while increasing the tempo over a few laps to 30 mph before veering into the infield and letting everyone battle over the last lap and a half, about a half-mile, for cash prizes.

Keirin racing quickly caught on and steadily pumped money to revive Japan's economy. By the 1950s dozens of tracks proliferated up and down the crescent-shaped island nation. Audiences of fifty thousand packed velodrome stadiums. Would-be racers competed as intensely to gain acceptance into the two-week Japan Keirin School as American teens applying to Ivy League colleges. Crowds placed bets, watched riders bump shoulders and elbows for position, and cheered frenzied surges to the finish line at speeds topping 40 mph.

Today keirin races generate about $8 billion a year in bets. Keirin racers since the 1950s have been the best-paid cyclists. Some keirin stars compete into their fifties, longer than road racers.

• • •

The Lehigh County Velodrome became one of the first U.S. tracks to add keirin to its programs. Fans appreciated the keirin—like match sprints, two-rider Madison team events, tandem sprints, and other contests. "The Keirin Cup became a regular staple at the T-town track," Simes said.

The Japan Keirin Racing Association treated the UCI worlds as an audition for foreigners. Simes lined Hatton up for sponsorship from Fred Mengoni, USPRO's godfather, and entered him as America's representative in both the keirin and match sprint at the 1983 UCI worlds in Zürich, Switzerland. Winning a medal at the worlds was his only chance.

Zürich's Oerlikon Velodrome was an outdoor 333-meter concrete track, like in T-town, but with steeper banked turns. Hatton finished in the top three in a qualifier heat, advanced to the semifinal, and reached the final.

He lined up against eight headliners including Danny Clark, twice winner of the keirin worlds, defending world keirin champion Gordon Singleton of Canada, and Swiss ace Urs Freuler (rhymes with *oiler*), Swiss Sports Personality of the Year for winning six-days and Giro stages. "Freuler was quite cocky," Hatton said. "I was virtually unknown, a no-nonsense racer."

The start of the keirin final around the Oerlikon Velodrome was so aggressive that leaders crowded four abreast behind the motor-pacer (unlike the single bike racer used in Japanese keirin), the rest following tight. On the next faster lap riders streamlined to two parallel lines. At the end of the third lap, the motor-pacer steered into the infield as a brass bell clanged nonstop and Freuler attacked off the front into turn 1. Clark stuck to his rear wheel, followed by Hatton. Belgian ace

Michel Vaarten darted up on the inside to challenge Freuler. On turn 3, Vaarten fell and slid away.

"I was riding on the outside and missed going down," Hatton said. "We were pretty much going all out."

Freuler, legs spinning so fast they blurred, led Clark and Hatton over the line.

"At times a big race is like combat—the outcome determines if an athlete survives in his sport or retires," Hatton said. "When it comes down to that race, it takes a deep heart-felt passion to drive those wheels to success. What creates that passion? Very simple. You have to hate to lose in order to win. My bronze-medal ride got me the invitation to Japan. That allowed me to continue my career."

Hatton stepped up to the awards podium with Freuler and Clark before a big audience. "It was a fun race. I was in the right place. I was happy to be back to where I should have been."

In the match sprints, Hatton finished fifth, out of the medals yet still among the world's fastest sprinters.

His bronze medal at the 1983 worlds, Connie Carpenter's gold to the silver of her compatriot Cindy Olivarri in the women's individual pursuit, and Connie Paraskevin's gold in the women's match sprint raised America's medal tally to four, for third among a dozen medal-winning nations.

Nakano prevailed once more, scoring his seventh consecutive world match sprint title. He tied the record set by Belgium's Jef Scherens, world pro champion between 1932 and 1947.

• • •

In March 1984 Hatton jetted over the Pacific, the first American invited into the keirin circuit. "Everything was taken care of four months in advance by the Japanese Keirin Association—from my flight ticket down to death insurance. It was the first time in my career that I felt like a professional. I even received an agenda listing where I would be every day for ten weeks."

Aged twenty-eight, he began a new game, one of ten Westerners from eight countries attending the two-week Japan Keirin School. Classmates included Michael Vaarten. The Belgian's spill at the worlds prevented him from finishing, but keirin officials noted his determination, silky pedaling, and his silver medal in the kilometer at the Montreal Olympics and dozens of Belgian national track titles.

"Inviting foreigners from around Europe and me from the United States to race against their riders showcased their event to the world," Hatton said. "It was a pretty smart advertising ploy."

They lived in a country lodge with a kitchen and bedrooms. "We learned the protocol. Like at horse tracks, there's a new race every half-hour. Everything is very organized. You have to show up on time—not one minute late."

Only Japanese Keirin Association–approved brands of frames, pedals, and equipment were allowed, in an effort to avoid anyone gaming the system. "We had to submit the gear ratio on our bike a day in advance, and we weren't allowed to change it," Hatton said. "There were severe rules against cheating. Cheaters could get prison time or get banned for life."

For protection from falls, riders pulled on under-vests of lightweight hard plastic and donned nylon material featuring half-inch thick foam padding to cover the shoulders, backbone, and tailbone. Cyclists inserted thin forearm pads beneath long-sleeved jerseys and shoved their hands through long-fingered gloves. Thus padded, they looked like action heroes.

"Keirin is a fighting sport," Hatton said. "Japanese spectators go to see fighting, like samurai warriors. Nine guys racing on bikes are like nine boxers in the ring throwing punches."

Before each race, contestants received competitor numbers, from one to nine. Black numbers were displayed prominently on both arms of regulation jerseys, each a different primary color, and on the back for onlookers to spot easily. Cloth covers over hard-shell helmets matched numbers and jersey colors.

Hatton learned basic Japanese to discuss tactics with journalists. "Like horse tracks here, the bettors at keirin tracks get daily newspapers with the scoop on all racers—their background, their trainers."

Keirin races opened with a ceremony. Contestants inserted rear wheels into a row of metal track stands set up in lanes across the track.

Riders stood in numerical order, from number "1" on the inside lane. They bowed in unison, one beat to the waist, mounted bikes, and waited for the starter standing off to the side. Once the cyclists took off, track stands were pulled into the infield.

Hatton's class split up after graduation to travel for eight weeks among sixty keirin tracks. "There would be eighteen cyclists—nine in each race, made up of five foreigners like myself and four Japanese. We raced a preliminary heat, a semifinal, and the final. There was a point system scoring through the tournament. Winners earned nine points. The top point scorers rode a grand finale with a purse larger than the regular race. Lower-bracket cyclists rode a consolation race paying less. Bettors put their money on us in every race."

Most tracks measured 400 meters, some 500, others 333 meters. Keirin tournaments usually took place from Sunday to Tuesday. Cyclists competed three times daily, chiefly over two kilometers. Hatton discovered keirin racing required sustained end speed rather than explosive bursts of match sprints.

"Keirin sprints were pretty long, starting about 400 meters out. That means you're going all-out anaerobic for twenty seconds, which takes much more out of you than a ten-second 200-meter sprint."

Two-kilometer races took only three minutes, but winning tactics erupted in the last thirty seconds. In those final seconds at peak speed, tires sizzled. Audiences roared. Contestants kicked harder and harder, jockeyed for better position, and gave their best shot for a chunk of the day's purse—from $5,000 up to, in cases of major tournaments, as much as $250,000.

"A field of myself and eight other riders fit into my background, growing up in scratch racing for kids," Hatton said. "I tended to do well in those races. Going fast in keirin races, flying along at more than 40 mph, it's intense. It's exciting. It's dangerous. But not different from any bunch sprint on the track or the road. Elbow to elbow—that's the game of sprinting."

He picked up the finer aspects of keirin on the fly. "I learned by making mistakes, what not to do again. That way I improved my expertise." Mistakes were reaching top speed too soon or getting boxed in.

"You have to know yourself physically to gauge just how far out you can race at your top end. I survived by instinct. Instincts magically get you to where you need to go without thinking. Everybody's bunched up tight. You need a good eye to see a hole you can fit through. Not everybody has that kind of sight."

Hatton sized up which contenders went for victory from 400 meters out, those who took off at 300 meters, and cagey ones who blasted away in the final 100 meters, Hatton's favorite strategy. He pulled off a few victories. "Some of it is being in the right place at the right time and really digging deep, pushing yourself. Like deer hunting, you have only one shot to win."

By the time he said *sayonara* to Japan, he took home $50,000, worth $120,000 today. Earning his ticket to ride had required crossing two oceans and traveling halfway around the world. His travails paid off. The Japanese Keirin Association invited him to come back the following year, expenses paid.

• • •

Hatton reached T-town in May, before the Memorial Day weekend. He resumed coaching. "I have to teach kids that in cycling you're going to lose a lot," he said. "Once you swallow that pill, you can go on to become a winner."

He carried his sense of community from the international keirin circuit to the Lehigh County Velodrome. He fostered a family situation among cyclists, a group of peers rather than a hierarchy. Hatton has a low-key manner. When he sensed a pupil's anxiety, he made a strategic wisecrack to diffuse pressure or bolster confidence. He stood on the track infield during training sessions or races and yelled advice or encouragement through a raucous audience.

Hatton told journalists that coaching and riding with youngsters invigorated him. "I tell them that being successful in life comes in many forms. The smaller successes lead to bigger successes."

When he wasn't coaching, he competed in match sprints, kilometer time trials, two-rider Madison team races, and points races (pack races awarding points each third or fifth lap to the top four finishers to determine the winner).

The next spring he flew to Japan for another ten-week sojourn. He won a half-dozen more races and ranked among the top foreign money winners.

Back home, he kept his edge. He cleaned up in most track races he entered and claimed the 1985 USPRO match sprint title.

His 1986 keirin season was again profitable. He returned stateside and entered the keirin at the UCI worlds in Colorado Springs on the 7-Eleven Velodrome. "I didn't take well to high altitude," he said. "Colorado Springs wasn't my favorite place. Riding the worlds was a bittersweet experience."

Nakano liked Colorado Springs. He and two compatriots swept the world pro match sprint championship. He clinched an extraordinary tenth straight title, the most match sprint golds in cycling history, still unchallenged.

• • •

For eight years, Hatton flew over the Pacific for ten-week stints on the keirin circuit. He matched his talent, legs, and wits against the best speed merchants of his generation, including Nakano. He ate Japanese food, slept on tatami mats on the floor, and competed through all kinds of weather. "I raced often through the rain. Once I raced when there was snow on the infield."

Overseas excursions meant personal sacrifices. In 1988, he missed the birth of son Derrick. "He was a month old before I saw him for the first time." Hatton attended the birth of their second son, Joey.

For his efforts, Hatton earned more than $500,000, now worth $1.1 million. "I was doing the right thing for my family."

In 1991 Hatton said *sayonara* for the final time. "I rode 156 keirin races. The Japanese riders and officials treated myself and the other foreign riders fairly. I had my share of victories, usually three to five a year. In 1988 I had my best record—eight wins. Altogether I had thirty-five victories."

He retired from the pro ranks at age thirty-five, and took out an amateur license to keep racing. An *Allentown Morning Call* reporter told readers he fought more battles on tracks than Clint Eastwood in movies.

• • •

The Lehigh County Velodrome, over its first decade, took its turn as one of twenty-four tracks in nineteen states hosting national championships for pros, amateurs, and age-graded categories. About three thousand men and women of all ages took part in its Air Products development program. Yet none of its alumni had brought back a gold medal from the worlds or the Olympics.

Management shifted to developing a farm system, rebranded as the Air Products Youth Development Program. Pat McDonough, a California track specialist and a silver medalist at the LA Olympics in the 4,000-meter team pursuit, was hired to work with Hatton developing juniors. The velodrome attracted aspiring youngsters from around the Mid-Atlantic states. Jeanne Farrell of Herndon, Virginia, commuted for several years with her mother driving nearly two hundred miles each way, about four hours in moderate traffic, for track workouts and coaching. Farrell transformed into a leggy rocket and national junior champion—one of more than a hundred LCV alumni medaling at nationals. More included Bobby Lea of Easton, Maryland, and Jessica Grieco of Emerson, New Jersey.

In 1987 sixteen-year-old Marty Nothstein showed up at the track as atonement. He and his younger brother, Jay, were throwing rocks in their neighborhood to see who could throw the farthest when a rock hit the house of Heinz Walter, former cycling team manager at the 1984 LA Olympics and manager of a pro cycling team. The boys' mother ordered her sons to apologize. Walter advised they burn off energy pedaling around the velodrome.

At Emmaus High, Nothstein played football and baseball, and wrestled. A broad-shouldered six foot two, he expected to go on to play college sports. He'd never visited the velodrome, although he tried BMX (bicycle motocross) races on dirt tracks featuring jumps and rollers. He pedaled a BMX bike to the velodrome and hopped on a loaner track bike. He rode snaking up the twenty-eight degree banking and flying down to the twelve-degree straights.

"Looking back, I didn't want to be a cyclist," he told me. "Coming through the free development programs, I was hanging around riders who provided advice on riding and entertainment as well with their racing. I watched the riders and cheered them on. There was Mark "the Outlaw" Whitehead, Nelson "the Cheetah" Vails. These were colorful characters. They raced with speed, tactics, and danger. On the track they had rivalries. Their antics were like WWE wrestlers. I enjoyed that. The racing is what hooked me."

T-town's summer-long Friday night bike races were as popular a community phenomenon as Friday night football in West Texas. Sprinters inspired Nothstein. Aggressive, they grimaced in fierce elbow-to-elbow, head-down finishes. They won and lost by fractions of an inch. Sprinters drew fans to the track like opera tenors attract audiences to the theater.

Nothstein enrolled in the Bicycle Racing League for high schoolers, where he and Hatton connected. "He was Gibby the Bear. His persona was a rough-and-tumble tough man, but he was really easy going. We gravitated toward one another early on. He saw I was a hard worker, a tough kid. Throughout my career, he has been like an older brother, at times a father figure. In 1987, there was no internet. This was a sport available only through other people. Gil provided a lot of insight. He taught me how to put my handlebars in front of someone, lean on them."

As a novice Nothstein sometimes lost his balance and fell to the concrete. "I needed to gain balance and coordination. That comes only through practice, making mistakes, learning from them. As I got a little older and more comfortable bouncing around with him, I became one of the most feared guys. Then I could turn Gil's moves on him. Once I did that and he fell, he told me, 'Whoa! I don't have to teach *you* anymore!'"

Hatton's Japanese experiences impressed Nothstein. "He went to Los Angeles early in the year to live with his father and train for a month before flying to Japan to compete. I absorbed what he said like a sponge."

Nothstein, fifteen years younger, first struck Hatton as full of himself yet affable, eager to learn. "I liked Marty. I'd say, 'Come on, kid, let's go.' I'd give him some distance and chase him down. That's how the whole thing started."

• • •

Several teens were already outstanding, among them James (or "J-Me") and Jonas Carney of North Arlington, New Jersey. "Those guys had been coached by Gil," said Simes. "They were fast and had some endurance. They were fighters."

Andy Taus, a race commissaire, watched Nothstein's ascent. "When he was first coming up, he received a lot of advice from many people. He took in what coaches and mentors said. He became cocky, which is part of the mentality of sprinters. Sprinters get the audience to *ooh* and *ah* at their moves. When they battle to the line, sprinters get the audience to stand up and shout."

Nothstein's brashness came from pride about his great-grandfather Michael Nothstein—a high-wheel bike racer and bareknuckle boxer. Young Marty, the fourth of five children, came from a merchant-class family. His father owned a car dealership, Nothstein Motors.

By the tenth grade, he traded school sports for cycling and purchased his first track frame. He had a wide forehead, a narrow face, a look of innocence. In the heat of competition he occasionally grew frustrated and shouted, yet afterward told adversaries he forgot all about what had made him mad—a Jekyll and Hyde personality.

Hatton saw through his in-your-face attitude and detected mental toughness. He taught Nothstein about the oval track's zones to exploit and protect. Leading an opponent up the banking to the top can control him like a boxer backing a rival into a corner. Yet the leader must watch out for the blind spot behind and protect the area below to the sprinter's lane—keeping always ready to chase if the follower drops down to the prime real estate at the bottom.

On offense, Hatton schooled Nothstein to hold back and draft behind the leader, in what is called the surprise position, till the final turn and slingshot around the outside. Rather than just one signature move, the Bear gave pointers on how to lead and keep upping the pace to keep an opponent in check, and to spot narrow openings and dart under a rival to usurp the sprinter's lane, especially on the backstretch.

Nothstein won races by slicing through the pack and asserting his front wheel just a narrow margin ahead of rivals, always cutting it close. Razor-thin margins gained him the nickname: the Blade.

One of the velodrome's early stars, Paul "the Animal" Pearson, described standing on the track sideline, watching Nothstein make his move in a speeding pack of a dozen juniors. Pearson caught the look in his eyes: "You just knew he was not going to be beat."

Pat McDonough suggested road races for endurance. In 1988, his first full racing season, Nothstein captured the Keystone State junior championships in the match sprint and the seventy-five-mile road race. At the track nationals on the Alkek Velodrome in Houston, Texas, Nothstein took home his first stars-and-stripes jersey, winning the junior match sprint.

Nothstein's track bravado drew audiences. His race results made good copy in the *Allentown Morning Call*. He became a local hotshot and liked hanging out at the track with Hatton and sprinters in town, like Nelson Vails, the African American and former New York City bike messenger who took a silver medal in the LA Olympics match sprint.

"Marty was behind me in age and experience," Vails said. "He was the skinny kid who was going to be good someday. Marty had to race against me in the early rounds and get eliminated. I used to tell him what he did that was wrong and what he had to do to get better."

Another out-of-towner was the aptly named Paul Swift. Just under six feet tall and a taut 190 pounds, he was four years older than Nothstein. Swift had wrestled and played football in Kenosha, Wisconsin, till he felt the pull of its Washington Park Velodrome. "It was a popular place," Swift said. "People talked about legendary Olympians from Kenosha, Bobby Thomas and Bob Pfarr."

Swift had won the 1984 junior nationals match sprint and the kilometer time trial. He left Kenosha for Auburn University and earned a communications degree. Summers, he spent in T-town training and racing at the track. He rented a room from one of Nothstein's brothers.

In the summer of 1989 he and Nothstein, a recent graduate of Emmaus High, partnered in tandem sprints—Swift steered, the kid sat on the back. They packed the tandem and their track bikes to prospect for gold at the nationals on the Jerry Baker Velodrome in Redmond, Washington. Swift scored the bronze medal in the match sprint.

Nothstein claimed a rare double—one gold in the junior match sprint and another with Swift in the elite tandem sprint.

The USCF flew them on the national team to ride tandem sprints at the UCI worlds in Lyon, France. "We rode well together against other national teams in races," Swift said. "I saw Marty as a guy with talent. He was a first-year senior going to the worlds—a big deal. We went there with high expectations."

Tandem teams qualified with a flying 200-meter solo time trial. Teams had two laps to build speed high on the banking; on the third lap, they dived down to launch their race against the clock. Somehow Swift and Nothstein mixed up their lap count.

"On the third lap we crossed the line high on the track instead of low," Swift recalled. "We had the slowest qualifier time."

Jack Simes attended as a UCI board member and heard an official ring the bell twice—signaling their ride was over. "I looked at Marty. He had this dazed look on his face. His eyes were half-open. He was incredulous—he had traveled all that way to the worlds and his ride was over before he had even started."

The only USCF track rider to attain a medal was Janie Eickhoff of Long Beach, California, third in the elite women's points race.

In 1990 the Lehigh County Velodrome organized the nationals. Nothstein and Swift won their second national tandem title. Swift also won the keirin and took home a silver medal in the match sprint.

They went with the USCF team to the worlds in Maebashi, Japan. On their qualifier solo, they blasted around the track. They ultimately finished sixth.

• • •

Twenty-year-old Nothstein collected his third tandem national championship in 1991, with Erin "Erv" Hartwell in Redmond, Washington. Hartwell, twenty-two, kept his hair trimmed close. A 175-pound six-footer, he had competed in Indianapolis in track and field until he tore a groin muscle pole vaulting in high school. Cycling for rehab, he found the Major Taylor Velodrome. He shifted to riding the kilometer time trial, comparing it in speed and stamina to running 400 meters.

At the Redmond nationals, Nothstein finished fourth in the match sprint. Ken Carpenter, a six-foot-three Californian won his fourth championship at age thirty.

Nothstein and Hartwell joined the USCF national team climbing aboard an airliner to Havana, Cuba, for the 1991 Pan-Am Games. The games drew almost five thousand athletes from thirty-nine nations from Canada to Chile.

Nothstein entered match sprints expecting to uphold the winning streak begun by Nelson Vails in 1983 and defended four years later by Ken Carpenter. But sprinters from Canada, Cuba, and Colombia beat Nothstein. "I had lost a quarterfinal, so I didn't make it into the final four," he said.

Seven USCF men and women stepped up the podium steps for medals. Hartwell grabbed silver in the kilo. Kendra Kneeland, a University of California, Berkeley, grad, won the women's individual pursuit.

Nothstein flew home empty-handed. The velodrome in Havana served as his road to Damascus. "That was a turning point," he said in our interview. "I thought I was just as good as the others. I thought I had the talent to be one of the best in the sport." In a moment of introspection, he said natural talent took him only so far. "I had to work much harder to reach 100 percent of my capabilities."

After four years of racing and five national championships, he decided to get serious about reaching the top as a sprinter.

The Bear was blunt about the odds of reaching the top: "Only 2 percent of American racers win national championships. And only 2 percent of national champions win gold medals at the worlds or Olympics."

• • •

Nothstein intensified his regimen. Up to six hours daily, he pedaled speed workouts at the velodrome and rode for stamina on roads passing farms dotting hilly rural Lehigh County. He also hit the gym to crunch hundreds of sit-ups to bolster his core and lift free weights to strengthen muscles that propelled him on the bike. He did deep squats with weights. When he could shoulder the forty-five-pound York bar holding four forty-five-pound plates at each end—totaling more than four hundred pounds, double his body weight—the ends bowed as he dipped down; he stuck out his butt for balance, and stood up in a motion emulating a fiery sprint, as the plates clunked encouragement, rep after rep. His butt and quads grew so big he bought pants two or three sizes too large and wore a belt.

"I've always been a very strong kid—strong back and legs from hauling and chopping wood and working around my father's trucks and cars," he said. "Lifting heavy weight for me was natural."

By 1992 he bulked up to two hundred pounds, twenty more than in high school. Muscles flexed under tight-fitting spandex. "Sprinting had transformed since the 1970s," he said. "Sprinters have always had snappy legs and fast leg spin, but the way Jack Disney won his races wouldn't work today. Sprinters became more powerful, had more explosive power. Track cycling sprinters are big guys doing battle shoulder to shoulder. They're fearless."

Match races compress into seconds the decisive points that unfold over hours in criteriums and road races. Audiences seeing their first matches can be puzzled by seeing two riders start with an easy push from their handlers. Match races are chess games on wheels. After a lap or two of cat-and-mouse tactics, the tempo quickens until one contestant pops off the saddle, pumps his legs to 40 mph, as fast as a tiger runs, in just a few strokes, and goes for the line. The rider trailing can catch the leader's draft and then swing out—unless the leader surges again. Only the final 200 meters are timed.

"The outcome of match races, determining who wins, who loses, comes down to two or three strategic moves in five seconds," Nothstein told me.

Road pros measure careers on national championships won, how they placed in grand tours or one-day European classics. For track cyclists, the only thing comparable in worldwide media exposure is the Olympics.

"When I grew up, I wanted to be an Olympic gold medalist," Nothstein said. "When you win a world championship, that's great, but there's another worlds next year. Nothing compares with being an Olympic gold medalist. The Olympics come around only once every four years. Everybody knows the language of being an Olympic gold medalist. That's the beauty of the Games."

Nothstein trained harder than ever to earn a place on the U.S. team bound for the Barcelona, Spain, Olympics. Even though the keirin was not an Olympic event, he saw its aggressive pace and longer high-end finishes as a way to ramp up speed. He quizzed Hatton, America's premier keirin expert.

The Bear counseled assessing rivals and picking one to follow in the early laps. The next stage involved jockeying in position shuffles at faster tempo, requiring experience. There were times he had to insert his front wheel into an opening and hope to find daylight. The finale's all-out, high-end speed left no time to think. Even in the last 200 meters, he could see everyone fly by.

The USCF nationals in July on the 250-meter National Sports Center track in Blaine, Minnesota, doubled as the Olympic trials. Hatton predicted Nothstein could seriously challenge Carpenter for the lone Olympic sprinter berth. Hatton said his disciple had been practicing with Carpenter for a month, curtailed racing on the national circuit to travel less and concentrate more on training, and spent two weeks at altitude in the Colorado Rockies before going to the nationals. But even the best plans are vulnerable.

Nothstein's prospects seemed to soar when he edged Paul Swift to win the crowd-pleasing keirin exhibition race. Hours later, Nothstein blitzed the standing-start kilo time trial, four laps around North America's only wood-plank velodrome. He posted the fastest time—1 minute, 6.089 seconds—among thirty-seven of forty-nine entrants when rain fell that evening.

Officials cancelled the kilo due to precipitation and rescheduled it for the next morning. Under USCF rules, all contestants had to compete under the same conditions. Nothstein declined to try again, choosing instead to marshal his energy for the next afternoon's match sprint quarterfinals and semifinals.

Erv Hartwell had been waiting for his turn to ride the kilo before the rain. The next morning he darted around the track with the fastest time of forty-eight entrants. Although he clocked 0.012 of a second—one pedal revolution—slower than Nothstein's result the day before, Hartwell won his fourth straight kilo title and earned his flight to Barcelona.

In the match sprint semifinal, which determined who advanced to the final, Nothstein faced Paul Swift. Swift smoked Nothstein in two matches.

The final came down to Swift and Carpenter. Each won a match. The third match went to Carpenter. He aced his fifth consecutive match sprint championship to go to his second Olympics. Swift was an Olympic alternate.

Nothstein fought back in the repechage heat for third place. His consolation was winning his fourth tandem sprint championship, with Hartwell.

Hartwell brought home a bronze medal from Barcelona; Rebecca Twigg claimed a bronze in the individual pursuit.

Nothstein, an Olympic team alternate, had to wait four years for another chance of going to the Olympics.

"What kept me going was knowing I was almost there at the top," he said. "I showed I had what it took. I learned a tremendous amount from training with Ken Carpenter. Later that summer, I got invited to race in Paris in an international grand prix. I went after completing a great training block—I had been winning miss-and-outs [the last rider across the line drops out each lap] and Madisons. In Paris I was in the match sprints against top sprinters. I made it to the final against Jens Fiedler, gold medalist at the Barcelona Olympics. A light bulb went off in the mind when I realized I had jumped onto the world stage."

• • •

USCF leaders selected Nothstein for the 1993 national team. Committed to winning medals, generating media, and satisfying sponsors at the upcoming Atlanta Olympics, the USCF provided twenty men and thirteen women track and road racers with financial and technical support, underwritten by EDS, the Texas-based international information-technology corporation.

Members received plenty of team clothing for traveling, training, and racing: "When I put on the stars-and-stripes team jersey, I was definitely going into battle for my country," Nothstein said.

USCF sprint and kilo coach Andrzej Bek, bronze medalist in the tandem sprint at the Munich Olympics, became Nothstein's coach and start-line pusher. Bek had a decade of experience on the Polish national team, a force in cycling.

Nothstein and Hatton stayed in close touch. Hatton coached many juniors. Among them Jessica Grieco, a second-generation racer whose father, Alan Grieco, competed in the 1964 Tokyo Olympics match sprints with Jack Simes.

The 1993 nationals on the Major Taylor Velodrome in Indianapolis signaled Nothstein's breakthrough. He won the keirin, defeating two-time champion and USCF teammate Swift, and he won the match sprint title.

Nothstein flew with the USCF track squad to the UCI worlds in Hamar, Norway. The UCI had finally dropped the century-long tradition of separate categories for amateurs and pros to create an elite open competition. Nothstein took home the silver medal in the keirin and placed fourth in the match sprint.

"The keirin was a close race," he said. "Finishing fourth in the match sprint was very special to me. It was the first year in which amateurs and pros were combined, something overdue—the pro side was second rate compared with the amateurs. Fourth place meant there were only three other sprinters in the world ahead of me. At that point, things for me changed dramatically."

Rebecca Twigg won the women's individual pursuit while Janie Eickhoff took the bronze medal in that event; Jessica Grieco claimed bronze in the women's points race. The four medalists put the United States third among forty nations in the worlds program.

• • •

Nothstein and teammates looked to bring home medals in the 1994 worlds. That spring, however, he fell during a warm-up ride and fractured a heel bone. The injury proved painful and bothersome. After medical treatment, he put up with nagging aches that lasted months through spartan training and strenuous racing.

In August he joined the USCF squad flying to the track worlds in Palermo, on Italy's island of Sicily. Nothstein's contingent included women and professional support like Andrzej Bek and 1984 LA Olympics gold-medal sprinter Mark Gorski, the team coordinator.

Janie Eickhoff, a multi-time national champion, powered to a bronze medal in the women's individual pursuit. Erv Hartwell took the silver medal in the men's kilo. The four-man pursuit team of Mariano Friedick, Dirk Copeland, Carl Sundquist, and Adam Laurent took home a silver medal.

A gold medal eluded the team until Nothstein streaked through the keirin. He dethroned three-time world champion Michael Hübner of Germany. Nothstein became the first male American track rider to stand on the podium and pull on the rainbow jersey.

The program of eleven events culminated in match sprints, which drew thirty-seven contenders. Nothstein dispensed with opponents through preliminary heats to reach the semifinal. He lined up against Hübner, who was seeking to avenge his keirin loss to Nothstein. Twice world sprint champion, Hübner had held the world record for the flying 200 meters and gained the reputation of a cycling titan.

Nothstein's off-season weight workouts were paying dividends. Next to one another on bikes at the start line, he and the German, deep chested and muscular, looked like supermen. If they sauntered into a store and purchased something, cashiers would carefully give them correct change. Marketers could sell calendars featuring them striking poses. Nothstein, a smooth-faced twenty-three-year-old to Hübner's deep-lined visage at thirty-five, lost their first match before coming back to clinch the last two.

The final pitted Nothstein against Darryn Hill, who just turned twenty in Palermo. Hill was built straight up and down like a fire hydrant, five feet eight and 220 pounds. A former BMX racer in Perth, Australia, after victories he popped his front wheel up and cruised a lap on the rear wheel, like the Lone Ranger on his horse Silver rearing up on his back legs.

For the first match, Nothstein drew the pole. Bek pushed him away. Nothstein rolled easily, checking over his shoulder as Hill stalked him for the first two laps. When the bell rang, Hill jumped off the saddle, elbows out, and in ten pedal strokes bulleted ahead—tires whooshing as he picked up speed as fast as a car accelerating from the on-ramp to the highway. Nothstein shadowed him. They sat spinning, backs arched like fighting cats. Rounding the last turn Nothstein pulled even. They leaned against one another and poured onto the final straight. Nothstein on the outside surged to win by a length.

It was Hill's turn to lead the second match. He took it easy until the bell rang and he rushed outside up to the top rail, Nothstein in tow. On the back straight Hill dove down the banking. Nothstein tailed him before swerving sharply inside to claim the black pole line. They sped alongside one another in a drag race. With 200 meters left, Nothstein gained a length. Hill closed the gap and moved up on the outside. Head to head, both men threw their bicycles over the line. Nothstein won by inches.

On the warm-down lap, Nothstein yanked off his red helmet, tossed it into the infield, and shot his arms triumphantly in the air. Bek and Gorski, surrounded by officials and photographers, stepped from the infield onto the track at the finish line. Then Nothstein did something unexpected.

"I came across the line and I saw Bek and Gorski. It was the ten-year anniversary of Gorski's gold medal in the LA Olympics. I stopped at the finish and dismounted. Bek took my bike. Then I just kneeled down and kissed the finish line."

Hübner defeated compatriot Jens Fiedler in the race for third place.

For the awards ceremony in the center of the infield, Nothstein walked in sandals behind Hill and ahead of Hübner to the podium. They stood in national team jerseys and shorts. A gray-haired official in a blue blazer draped the medals, one by one, over the heads of the three men, then presented Nothstein with his second rainbow jersey of the week and helped him pull it on. Nothstein received a spray of flowers. The medalists stepped onto the podium, Nothstein on the top step. A hush fell over the stadium as the American flag was hoisted up the pole. Nothstein stood at attention, clasping the flowers, while "The Star-Spangled Banner" boomed over stadium speakers.

"It was like one year I was close to making the Olympic team," he recalled. "The next year I was close to the top of the world. The year afterward I was there—in three short years."

Nothstein had closed a circle that Frank Kramer as professional and his amateur counterpart Donald McDougall had left open when they won their match sprint championships at the 1912 worlds in Newark. Between the first official world sprint championship in 1893 in Chicago and 1912, five Americans—Arthur Zimmerman, George Banker, Major Taylor, Iver Lawson, and Marcus Hurley—won world sprint titles, raising the total to six.

Sixty-one years after Kramer and McDougall won their sprint titles, Sheila Young-Ochowicz captured her first of three UCI world match sprint championships for the United States. Sue Novara and Connie Paraskevin combined won six world sprint titles through 1990.

Nothstein's victory left the men three gold medals behind the women.

"There were a thousand guys who walked ahead of Marty with qualities to win," Jack Simes observed. "Maybe Kramer could have won more worlds, but he wasn't interested in all the travel. After him nobody in America seemed to give a damn about the worlds. With Heid and Disney, the talent was there, but we didn't have the tracks and development like today. Our style of racing was different. Heid had to go to Europe. I went to Europe. We brought back ideas. Improving was a gradual process."

Hatton put Nothstein's double victory in perspective. "Marty has a special internal makeup. What really shines is his ability to learn how to win."

At the Lehigh County Velodrome, Nothstein fans and the *Allentown Morning Call* heralded him as the kid who graduated from the Air Products Development Cycling Program and six years later won two world titles in one week.

That motivated raising $2.5 million for new grandstands erected to seat two thousand, along with upgraded restrooms for athletes and spectators, showers and lockers for competitors, and a concession stand serving food and beverages. In tribute to what Babe Ruth meant to attendance at Yankee Stadium, the track was called the House that Marty Built.

• • •

The 1995 Pan-Am Games in March in Mar del Plata, an Atlantic seaside resort in Argentina, showcased 5,144 athletes from forty-two nations in thirty-four sports. Cyclists competed in eight men's and six women's events on the track, road, and mountain biking in an Olympics prospects preview.

Nothstein flew with Hatton a week early to get extra time on the velodrome. Nothstein left girlfriend Christi, a cyclist, at home with their week-old son, Tyler.

Mar del Plata, Spanish for "Sea of the Silver Region," boasts Argentina's biggest seaside beach. But he never visited the sandy shore crowded with vacationers. He found the outdoor 250-meter track to his liking. He studied how to deal with gusty off-shore winds and meet his two goals: to set the Pan-Am Games record for the flying 200-meter time trial, which seeded the riders, and to win the match sprint gold medal.

When the games commenced, the USCF track team celebrated Kent Bostick winning the 4,000-meter individual pursuit. Forty-one-year-old Bostick, nicknamed Bostisaurus for his age, took home a gold medal. The pursuit team took another gold medal over the same distance.

Janie Eickhoff added two golds—in the 3,000-meter women's individual pursuit and the 3,000-meter points race.

Erv Hartwell claimed the silver in the kilo. Connie Paraskevin took home silver in the women's match sprint.

On the day of the men's match sprint 200-meter qualifier time trial, Nothstein sliced through blustery conditions and shaved one-tenth of a second from the record. He set the new mark: 10.5 seconds, 44 mph.

Sprint coach Bek on the start line pushed him on his way in qualifier matches. In the semifinal, Nothstein and Gil Cardovés of Cuba clashed. Cardovés, the kilo gold medalist, lost the first match to Nothstein. Halfway through the next match, Cardovés bumped him on the lower part of the oval into the blue infield border, possibly trying to knock him off balance.

USCF national coaching director Chris Carmichael told me that the greatest asset athletes have is attitude. He called Nothstein a fierce competitor, driven by anger: "When he's in a match sprint race, there's nothing anyone can do on a bike that he is afraid of, so he's going to handle it or crash."

Nothstein promptly swerved back onto the track. He used rising rage to dash away and crush Cardovés.

Nothstein advanced to the final against Marcelo Arrue, competing for Chile. Nothstein took his place on the start line held by Bek, alongside Arrue, supported by the coach of the Chilean national team, none other than Hatton.

Hatton's reputation extended into South America through Arrue. Born in Santiago, Chile, Arrue learned about cycling from his father, Willie Arrue, national sprint champion for a decade and a South American sports celeb. Marcelo was two years old in 1971 when his father moved the family to Fresno, California. He grew up holding dual citizenship in the United States and Chile. Arrue emerged as a national-class sprinter in his adopted country.

After Nothstein had won two world championships in Italy, Arrue approached Hatton to coach him, which Hatton agreed to do. Nothstein didn't mind. He and Arrue, two years older, knew each other. Nothstein didn't feel threatened. He told reporters he regarded Hatton as his best friend, a member of his family.

Arrue raced the Pan-Ams for his birth country. On the start line of the final, Hatton dutifully sent him on his way. Then Hatton stepped to the edge of the infield.

"After the rider is one foot away from the start line, there's nothing anybody else can do," he said. "Everything is up to the rider."

Through the matches, thousands of fans cheered. Hatton stood trackside in silence while his protégés battled for the championship of two continents. Nothstein outclassed Arrue.

As soon as an official at the awards ceremony draped the gold medal around Nothstein's neck and "The Star-Spangled Banner" filled the arena, he packed up and flew home. He had to help Christi feed three-week-old Tyler.

• • •

The USCF team concluded the Pan-Am track, road, and mountain bike races with fourteen gold, silver, and bronze medals, double the tally of both Canada and Cuba, tied for second. The medals bonanza served as an auspicious launch of USA Cycling Inc., incorporated on July 1 in Colorado as the not-for-profit national governing body overseeing all amateur and professional road, track, mountain bike, cyclocross, and BMX races and development.

Nothstein and the USAC national team jumped into a busy international and domestic schedule leading up to the 1996 Atlanta Olympics. Cyclists, coaches, and support staff traveled together like touring rock bands—flying in commercial jets, climbing into buses and taxis, and spending nights in a series of motels. Their destinations were velodromes, either on the UCI Track Cycling World Cup circuit—a six-city tournament on velodromes in cities spanning four continents—or USAC events around the country.

"Marty had really improved and became one of the guys I didn't want to race against because he was going to eliminate me," Vails said.

Nothstein had a philosophical outlook. "Spectators see the winner on the podium. They see an official put the ribbon with the gold medal over the winner's head; the winner receives a bouquet of flowers. People don't think of the general sacrifices that go into winning. I was racing not only for myself but also my country, then my region, and my hometown. When I was on the road two hundred days a year, so were the coaches and many support people. I thought that winning was for me and for them."

Sacrifices included recovering from accidents. In May at the UCI World Cup in Athens, Greece, Nothstein finished third in the match sprint. Then in the keirin, rounding the last turn, he wiped out at full speed. Another rider smashed into him lying on the hardwood track. Medics bundled Nothstein into an ambulance that rushed to a hospital. Doctors immediately removed splinters from his legs and treated him for coughing up blood from burst blood vessels in his lungs.

He was still recovering when he went to the USAC nationals that summer. He claimed second in the keirin and third in the match sprint. He was healthier by August and flew to the UCI World Cup in Manchester, England. He won the match sprint and finished second in the keirin.

In early September, on a training ride around his home velodrome, a wheel collapsed and slammed him to the concrete so hard he fractured his right kneecap, the patella bone. After emergency surgery came intense rehabilitation as he was determined to go to the UCI worlds in Bogotá, Colombia, in three weeks. He couldn't compete at his best. Yet the UCI had introduced a novel three-man team sprint, which appealed to him and sprint coach Andrzej Bek.

The USAC contingent flew to Bogotá. Erv Hartwell took the bronze medal in the kilo and set a new U.S. national record. The men's four-rider pursuit team of Mariano Friedick, Dirk Copeland, Zach Conrad, and Matt Hamon scored a bronze medal. Rebecca Twigg won the women's individual pursuit, USAC's only gold medal.

Nothstein joined Bill Clay, America's reigning match sprint champion, and Hartwell in the team sprint. Like the team pursuit, two teams start on opposite sides of the track and race against each other. At the end of the first lap, the leading sprinter in each team pulls up the banking to leave the second sprinter to lead for the next lap; at the end of that lap, the second sprinter does the same, leaving the third sprinter to complete the last lap alone. The team with the faster time wins. Nothstein, Clay, and Hartwell took home a bronze medal.

• • •

During the off-season Nothstein's patella healed. He stepped up training intensity and duration, under Hatton's guidance, tempered with what he had absorbed over the years from Hatton, Jack Simes, Pat McDonough, Andrzej Bek, Chris Carmichael, rivals Ken Carpenter and Bill Clay, and his pal Hartwell. The Olympics seemed months away, but Nothstein focused on developing his full potential to win a medal.

Hatton counseled he was competing against everybody in the world—adversaries he knew and those he didn't, living in different countries and overcoming harsh living conditions that drove them to train fiercely and race like their lives depended on winning.

When winter rain or snow confined him indoors, he fastened his bike on a stationary trainer. Nothstein increased his strength exercises. He shouldered more than 500 pounds in squats for explosive bursts. Heavier weights didn't interfere with pedaling a satin-smooth world-class 160 rpm. He gained more muscle mass and tipped the scales at 215 pounds, with body fat under 5 percent. He looked like a strong football fullback. His spandex shorts stretched over thirty-inch thighs, the waist size of Tour de France racers.

"Spending so many days away from my family made me angry," he said. "I put that anger into my cycling—training intensity and racing intensity."

He showed that intensity in the spring on the UCI World Cup circuit—three months of high-profile racing in five cities against other Olympic contenders. In April in Cali, Colombia, Nothstein won the keirin and match sprint. A week later in Havana, he again captured the keirin and match sprint. Only one USAC teammate medaled on the UCI World Cup circuit: Bill Clay won the match sprint in early June in Cottbus, Germany.

The UCI ranked Nothstein the world's top sprinter. He still had to earn a spot on the Olympic team for his dream to win an Olympic gold medal. USAC combined the national track championships and Olympic trials, set them for June, and awarded the program to the Lehigh Valley Velodrome.

Nothstein had lost national match sprint championships for the last two years. Just the year before he suffered a stinging upset. Wearing his world champion rainbow jersey in a semifinal against USAC team member Trey Gannon of Plano, Texas, Nothstein lost. Then Gannon was defeated in the final by Bill Clay. Nothstein salvaged third place.

He told ESPN that since he had reached international success, he underestimated the nationals. "It was tough for me to be world champion but not the national champion. That was kind of a kick in my face." He added: "That's never going to happen again. I'm going to take nationals seriously."

How seriously he proved in the flying 200-meter qualifier, which seeded more than thirty contestants. He rode warm-up laps at the top of the banking in front of hometown fans, his parents and siblings, and girlfriend Christi, holding their son Tyler. Nothstein plunged down the banking on the back straight into the sprinter's lane for his race against the clock—an anaerobic power burst.

Speeding at 44 mph, his solid carbon-fiber rear wheel whooshed against the concrete. Thousands hollered his name. He trounced the track record and set a new national best: 10.3 seconds.

Once again Hatton was pushing him from the start line. An early heat put Nothstein against 1994 sprint champion Jeff Solt, of Los Altos Hills, California. Solt sought to control the pace by leading. Nothstein trailed in the surprise position. Solt kept checking over his shoulder and steadily increased the tempo to a breakneck pace through the final turn. All went well for him until the last 100 meters. Nothstein passed him so fast on the outside that Solt abruptly lost five lengths and gave up trying. Nothstein had no trouble winning again.

Olympic trials can boost careers for winners and cause losers to retire. In the first match of the semifinal, thirty-year-old Paul Swift, a seasoned tactician, routed defending champion Bill Clay. Swift had five national titles, in the tandem sprint and keirin, but he most wanted to win the match sprint. He kept a collection of silver and bronze medals in a box. Vanquishing Clay put him one match closer to the match sprint championship and a gold medal.

Clay called Indianapolis's Major Taylor Velodrome his home track. His signature high-end speed earned him a nickname, the Razor. In his next match against Swift, he rode from the front; when Swift moved up to challenge, Clay accelerated to victory. In their deciding match, he outkicked Swift, who added a bronze medal to his collection in his last Olympic trials.

Nothstein and Clay squared off in the final. The contest had a David-versus-Goliath dimension. Nothstein outweighed his opponent by forty-five pounds and stood four inches taller. The Blade and the Razor matched pedal strokes around the velodrome, as close as boxers trading punches. Nothstein had honed a sharper edge and beat Clay in two straight. Nothstein finally seized his second national match sprint championship.

He and Clay were selected as sprinters and counted among the eleven men and women track cyclists representing the USAC the next month in Atlanta.

Hatton was hired as USAC assistant sprint coach, under Andrzej Bek. Hatton and Nothstein went together to their first Olympics.

• • •

The Atlanta Olympics opened July 19. Georgia's largest city launched media fanfare to let the world know it was presenting the Centenary Olympics. Over the next two weeks, 8.3 million tickets were sold—establishing an entry in the *Guinness Book of World Records* for the largest Olympics attendance. Another record: 10,300 men and women athletes from 197 nations competed in 271 events. More than fifteen thousand print and broadcast journalists reported in dozens of languages transmitted to more than a billion households, cafés, and bars around the planet. Popular American pastimes introduced for the first time as medal events included mountain biking and beach volleyball.

Some five hundred cyclists from sixty-eight countries competed. Road races took place in the city and neighboring suburbs for spectators to watch for free and cheer. Mountain biking was held in the Georgia International Horse Park. Track cycling went to the Stone Mountain Velodrome, twenty miles east of downtown.

Nothstein and teammates looked to claim at least as many medals as at the 1984 LA Olympics. USAC featured him on the cover of its 1996 Media Guide. *Sports Illustrated* picked him as a favorite to win the match sprint.

USAC men and women performed well in the road races and time trials, but Brits, Canadians, Danes, French, Italians, Russians, Spaniards, and Swiss did better. In mountain bike racing, only Susan DeMattei of Gunnison, Colorado, in the women's cross-country event, took home a bronze medal.

Eight men's and women's track events were held on an open-air 250-meter board saucer, crouched in the shadow of Stone Mountain, a quartz monzonite dome soaring 825 feet over an oak forest. Erv Hartwell snatched a silver medal in the kilo, a fraction of a second behind Florian Rousseau of France, who set an Olympic record.

Each time Nothstein rounded the track's last turn, he faced the gray mountain against the blue sky. He could have observed the massive bas-relief rock carving on one side of three Confederate leaders of the Civil War, President Jefferson Davis and Generals Stonewall Jackson and Robert E. Lee, on horseback. Nothstein went there to win a medal rather than see the sights. He even skipped the opening ceremony.

Instead, he took in the velodrome's steep banking, its board surface, and how to use them to his advantage. Nine years of pushing the limits of his body and mind culminated in the Olympics match sprints. He used the latest training techniques and equipment measuring heart rate, watts pedaled, and recovery time. He rode a prototype carbon-fiber bicycle worth as much as a Cadillac.

On a sweltering day under a roasting sun, more than sixty sprinters, one at a time, sped two and a half laps around the saucer for their timed 200-meter flying solo. Only the fastest twenty-four qualified for matches.

Nothstein, in a jazzy stars-and-stripes skinsuit, rode twice around the apex of the track before diving down, back arched, elbows pointed, legs churning to a near-blur. He clocked 10.176 seconds, 44 mph—a new Olympic record.

Fifteen minutes later, Gary Neiwand of Australia beat the record with 10.129 seconds. Canadian Curt Harnett bettered Nothstein's time by one-thousandth of a second for second seed. Jens Fiedler, the defending Olympic champion from Germany, qualified as fourth seed. Nothstein ended up third seed; his 200-meter time went on the USAC record books.

Five days of track racing filled the grandstand and seats on the backstretch, nearly seven thousand spectators—one of Nothstein's largest audiences. Most in the crowd were ordinarily obsessed with football and NASCAR.

Andrzej Bek pushed him off the line in matches. He breezed through his first three rounds and advanced to the quarterfinals against Darryn Hill, reigning world champion. Their matches came off as a rerun of two years before at the worlds in Palermo, Italy; Nothstein outkicked him from the front in their first go, then surged around after the final turn and hit the line half a length ahead.

Millions of Americans watching the Olympics television coverage were learning about Nothstein. The semifinal pitted him against Canadian champion Curt Harnett. Famous for holding the 200-meter world record, Harnett, a former hockey player from Thunder Bay, Ontario, had thirty-inch thighs. Unlike Nothstein who kept his brown hair in a no-nonsense buzz cut, Harnett wore his curly blond locks long and advertised shampoo products.

Nothstein and Harnett were ready for their morning matches when a rainstorm bucketed down. Four hours later, the sky cleared and the sun dried the track. The air turned oppressive by the time Nothstein led the first match. He took Harnett up and down the banking for two laps, steadily increasing speed. On the final lap, he hit too fast a clip for Harnett. Nothstein won by a half-length.

Harnett led the next match. Nothstein noticed his opponent's reflexes slowed and veered to the top of the banking. Harnett moved upward and pressed him against the railing, near seated spectators. The cyclists rode two slow laps, Harnett checking over his right shoulder. On the bell lap, Nothstein shot down the banking and opened a gap before Harnett reacted. The audience cheered his move. He bulleted along the sprinter's lane and won by two lengths.

Nothstein progressed to the final against defending Olympic sprint champion Jens Fiedler, who grew up in communist-controlled East Germany and apprenticed as an electrician (today he works for an electric power plant). The East German sports machine system developed his sprint talents till the fall of the Berlin Wall and Germany's reunification as a democratic country. Fiedler won the 1992 German national match sprint championship and the gold medal at the Barcelona Olympics. For five years he ruled as national champion.

On the Sunday morning of their matches, Nothstein told reporters, "Fiedler is going to have to have the best day of his life to beat me."

They lined up on the start line, Nothstein held by Andrzej Bek on the inside lane, next to Fiedler and his coach. The audience fell silent. Both riders looked ahead. Moments before the start-bell rang, Fiedler grabbed the drops of his handlebars, pulled his front wheel off the ground, snorted loud as a bull, and smacked the wheel down hard. Nothstein turned to look at him. Fiedler sat like nothing happened.

Both men were the same height, muscular, in their prime. Fiedler, twenty-six, was twelve months older. Nothstein had a fraction of a second quicker qualifying time. The two faster riders lost in knockout rounds. Fiedler and Nothstein were as closely paired as Muhammad Ali and Joe Frazier.

At the ring of the bell, Nothstein led the first lap. He headed to the top of the track to cut off Fiedler's line of attack. They pedaled two laps at a crawl through hot, soupy air. On the last lap, between the first two turns, Nothstein's front wheel trembled. He swiveled his head to regain balance.

Fiedler, familiar with how electricity flows in the path of least resistance, spotted his path. Off the saddle, legs pumping furiously, he dove below Nothstein and flew at 40 mph along the inside lane. Nothstein twisted his face in exertion and alarm as he fought to catch Fiedler's rear wheel. On the back straight he attempted to overtake Fiedler but failed and drafted through the last turns.

Whipping onto the final straight, Nothstein arced up on the outside. The partisan audience shouted a wall of sound. Fiedler kept highballing. He and Nothstein were spinning their legs into fuzzy shapes. They appeared even as they threw bikes in unison over the line.

They were so close that officials had to consult a photo. Silence descended on the track. The wait turned into a nail-biter. At last officials ruled for Fiedler—by a centimeter, about a third of an inch.

In the following match, Fiedler and Nothstein traded preliminary moves up the banking until midway through the second lap. Fiedler charged in full flight down to the pole lane and launched a long sprint. Riding at the front on a relatively small track, the German owned the shortest distance. Around the final turn, Nothstein tried to get around. But Fiedler was moving at the speed of light. He won by half a wheel, or fifteen inches.

Harnett defeated Neiwand for the bronze medal. He joined Nothstein and Fiedler on the awards podium for the medal ceremony.

Nothstein's silver medal added to Erv Hartwell's silver and Susan DeMattei's bronze to put the U.S. cyclists ninth of thirteen nations that medaled in Olympic cycling.

"Losing the gold medal was hard because I lost before my family, and friends, and sponsors," Nothstein told me. "Without a doubt, I felt I was the fastest, strongest guy there. But sprinting is a game of tactics. When you get a lot of riders close in speed and power, it comes down to tactics. I was beat by a formidable champion. I definitely took that loss hard."

• • •

Nothstein and many Olympic sprinters migrated the next month across the Atlantic to the track worlds in Manchester, England. Anger over losing the Olympic gold medal by less than an inch propelled him in the keirin. He rode flawlessly to victory, seizing his third world title.

Next, Nothstein entered the match sprints. Fiedler was absent—feted in Germany for spoiling the Olympic track gold medal sweep in seven other events by France and Italy. Nothstein stormed through qualifier heats to the final against a newcomer, Florian Rousseau, France's national sprint champion and the Olympic gold medalist in the kilo. The Frenchman was three years younger than Nothstein, a couple inches shorter, forty pounds lighter.

On the start line Rousseau pulled his face through a goofy series of expressions, which made his eyes bulge. Nothstein looked ahead, a visage of calm. In their matches, Rousseau lacked tactical slyness and avoided physical contact by riding in front. On the last lap he sped fast and deliberate as a heat-seeking missile. Nothstein tried in vain to move around him. Rousseau had little style, but he froze Nothstein out in two straight matches.

The Olympic and world silver medals around his neck felt like cold comfort.

The only other USAC medalist at the Manchester worlds was Jane Quigley of Long Beach, California, runner-up in the women's points race.

"Ninety-nine percent of the riders competing would be satisfied with a silver medal in the Olympics, winning the keirin at the worlds, and finishing second in the match sprint in the worlds," Nothstein said.

"But that wasn't good enough for me. When you lose the Olympic gold medal in a photo finish, you are one of the best. I decided to wipe the slate clean and start a new strength program. Training for the gold medal at the 2000 Sydney Olympics was to start the following day."

• • •

Nothstein revamped his diet, exercises, and weight training. He sought a modest-sounding half-percent performance improvement, pedaling a few more rpm, to put him over the top. Hatton suggested he consult John Graham of Allentown Sports Medicine & Human Performance Center for pointers on explosive strength, power, and agility. Nothstein joined the Lehigh Valley University football team running sprints on the infield, running with ankle weights, running with a parachute strapped to his back, box jumping, and clapping-hands push-ups.

"Marty was a more determined, driven athlete," Hatton said. "Nobody knew just how hard he worked to get on top and stay there."

In 1997 and 1998 Nothstein won a lion's share of keirin and match sprints on the UCI Track World Cup Classics circuit. From Cali, Colombia, to Fiorenzuola, Italy, from Trexlertown to Adelaide, Australia, he was flicking elbows and leaning through turns against the shoulders of the toughest sprinters—among them nemeses Jens Fiedler and Florian Rousseau.

At the 1997 worlds in Perth, Australia, Nothstein finished third in the keirin, the only USAC rider to take home a medal. In August 1998 on the National Sports Center Velodrome in Blaine, Minnesota, he set a new USAC 500-meter flying start record, 26.456 seconds.

USAC officials gave him a unique free rein in 1999 to train and race on his own as long as he kept winning. To support him and his family, he had sponsorship from Autotrader.com, an online market for buying and selling cars.

He continued to rely on Hatton's experience, no-nonsense approach, and understated humor. Hatton often drove a motorcycle to motorpace Nothstein. They often worked out together. In 1999 Hatton became his sounding board, mechanic, and general factotum taking care of loose ends.

"My role was more a corner man in boxing, or a caddy to a golfer,"

Hatton told me. "Marty knew how to win, how to ride his opponents. He didn't need coaching. In sprinting, you have to focus. Once you pin that number on, it's you versus the world. There's just a few things that an athlete wants to hear, to instill confidence."

Nothstein trusted Hatton to have his bike ready. "I was the mechanic taking care of his bike. I took his bike apart, packed it in the travel case. When we got to our destination, I unpacked his bike, put it together right so no nuts or bolts were going to come loose. I took his shoes and gloves and helmet to the track. That way, his mind was clear to think about how he was going to race."

The Bear had been competing in the masters division for the over-forty crowd, the USAC's fastest-growing category. Hatton's bear shape stuffed in a Lycra jersey baffled fitness buffs trying to drop him, only to watch him burst ahead once the finish came in sight.

He accompanied Nothstein to the 1999 Pan-Ams in late July in Winnipeg, Canada, as USAC assistant sprint coach to Andrzej Bek. This time, Hatton held Nothstein on his bike at the start line and pushed him off for match sprints. Nothstein dominated the qualifying heats. He reached the final against Marcelo Arrue, now a U.S. citizen and USAC teammate. Nothstein won in two straight.

The next day he won the keirin, new to the Pan-Ams, then joined Arrue and Johnny Barios, of Redlands, California, to beat Cubans in the new team sprint involving twenty nations. In two days, Nothstein claimed three gold medals, unprecedented in Pan-Am Games cycling.

Nothstein, Arrue, and Barios raised the USAC medal tally to eighteen that men and women took home from the track, road, and mountain bike events—double the medals won by host country Canada, tied with Cuba.

The USAC elite track nationals took place two weeks later at the Lehigh County Velodrome. On opening night of the five-day program fans flocked to watch the keirin championship. Hometown hero Nothstein, entitled to wear the stars-and-stripes jersey as defending champion, opted for his navy-and-yellow Autotrader.com jersey. The field of thirty included training partner Arrue and forty-three-year-old Hatton.

Nothstein blitzed through the qualifier heat and semifinal to reach the seven-rider keirin final. Arrue and Hatton also reached the final. After the motorcycle pulled away, Arrue forced the pace. On the last lap, Nothstein thrilled fans by surging ahead of Arrue for a decisive victory.

Hatton grabbed the bronze medal. "This is my last elite championship," he told reporters. "It was a pretty special race." He was the same age as when Jack Disney took the silver medal in his last nationals.

• • •

Arduous strength training and running drills with the Lehigh University football team changed Nothstein's muscular physique by the 2000 season. He reduced his body fat to below 4 percent and trimmed down to 210 pounds.

"Losing the gold was the best thing to happen in my career," he said. "It made me a lot hungrier, motivated, and disciplined for the next four years. I did not leave a rock unturned going into the Sydney Olympics."

USAC national team members and Olympic hopefuls from Canada, New Zealand, and Australia, led by Darryn Hill, went to T-town to workout with him as they sharpened for their Olympic trials and the Sydney Olympics.

Nothstein, now married to Christi, and father of a daughter, Devon, stayed home more than usual. In March his home track hosted an Olympic invitational. Audiences filled the stands to watch their local hero compete with panache against the best from the United States and abroad.

For Nothstein and some sixty other American men and women, the trip to the Sydney Olympics began at USAC Olympic cycling track trials in April on the Superdrome in Frisco, part of the Dallas-Fort Worth metroplex. Nobody automatically earned a berth five months before the Games, but results on the Superdrome and subsequent races figured in selection, set for July.

In the match sprints qualifier time trial, Nothstein laid down the law for more than thirty contenders. He blasted the fastest 200-meter qualifying time, 10.595 seconds. Only twelve men, all within one second, qualified. He also set a new record around the Superdome's 250-meter wood track, 13.419 seconds.

Former antagonist and 1994 national champion Jeff Solt qualified as second seed. Solt rode a winning streak through the qualifier heat, the quarterfinal, and semifinal. The Californian seemed ready to challenge Nothstein in the final. Nothstein shut him out in two straight.

Then Nothstein cruised through the keirin, a new Olympic event, defeating Marcelo Arrue in the final.

"Without a doubt, I sent a message today," Nothstein said in a press conference. "I've been training really hard, and this is a reward."

Nothstein curtailed travel to maintain a hard training routine and have evenings at home with his family. One exception was flying in May with Hatton to the UCI World Cup Classic in Cali, Colombia. Cali's track and the Dunc Gray Velodrome, where cycling track races were to be held in the Sydney Olympics, both were board ovals 250-meters around with similar banking. Riding in Cali gave him a preview against his competitors.

French sprinters flew to Cali. Nothstein reached the final for a showdown against two-time world champion Vincent Le Quellec. Nothstein nipped him twice. Joining them on the podium was bronze medalist Florian Rousseau. Nothstein showed his mettle to Rousseau and the track world.

In July the USAC announced Nothstein had been picked for the Olympic team along with Marcelo Arrue for the match sprint. Nothstein skipped domestic events until the five-day national track championships in August. He won the match sprint and the keirin, and joined Arrue, Jonas Carney, and Johnny Barios to win the team sprint.

Three new national championships raised Nothstein's total to twenty-two. That nudged him ahead of Frank Kramer's twenty national sprint titles—two amateur and eighteen pro, between 1899 and 1922. Nothstein's UCI World Cup victories and three world championships also compared with 1899 world champion Major Taylor's campaigns across Europe and Australia.

Yet Nothstein had little name recognition. Joe Lindsey wrote a feature in *Bicycling* magazine: "Marty the Obscure." Lindsey called him one of the world's elite sprinters in a niche nesting like a Russian doll in the niched sport of cycling. Lindsey touted Nothstein as a favorite to win a gold medal in Sydney.

• • •

Sydney's 2000 Olympics commenced on September 15 to the biggest numbers yet. Although fewer tickets were sold—6.7 million compared with Atlanta's 8.3 million—the Harbour City hosted a record 199 nations, 10,651 athletes, three hundred events, and twenty-eight sports.

Almost five hundred track, road, and mountain-bike cyclists from fifty-five countries competed. Mari Holden of Ventura, California, snatched the silver medal in the road race time trial. She was the only USAC medalist on the road. Mountain bikers came up empty-handed.

Nothstein and the track squad went to the Dunc Gray Velodrome. It was named for Edgar "Dunc" Gray, the first Aussie cyclist to win an Olympic gold medal—in the 1932 LA Games track cycling kilometer, after a bronze medal in the 1928 Amsterdam Olympics kilo.

Accompanying Nothstein to Sydney were wife, Christi, five-year-old, Tyler, and two-year-old, Devon. Tyler, a towhead like his mother, skipped kindergarten classes. He collected souvenir Olympic pins to show classmates.

"Marty was spectacular," said Jack Simes. "Going with him was Gil Hatton. When Hatton held Marty as his pusher, it was like when Muhammad Ali had Angelo Dundee in his corner."

Nothstein in Lycra looked as big and muscular as Arnold Schwarzenegger in *The Terminator*. "Marty was focused as a red laser beam," Hatton said. "The four-letter word *fear*, as in fear of losing, was not in his mind. What Marty did in training taught his mind to overcome fear and accept the challenge."

Once again Nothstein ignored the opening ceremonies. While his family visited the Botanic Gardens and dined in a restaurant within view of the landmark Sydney Opera House, he trained on the velodrome. Hatton told him often in a soft, firm voice that he was the strongest and fastest sprinter in the world.

On Monday, September 18, the match sprint qualification round began for more than fifty riders. They took turns on timed flying 200-meter solos; only the fastest eighteen went to the first-round matches. Nothstein, twenty-nine, pedaled the fastest: 10.166 seconds.

Frenchmen Laurent Gané and Florian Rousseau, both world champions, were second and third fastest. Jens Fiedler was fourth. All were within one-tenth of a second behind Nothstein. Arrue made the cut, eighteenth place.

Next came the knockout rounds before six thousand rowdy spectators in the indoor arena. Nothstein squared off against Arrue and won to reach the next round. Also winning to advance were Gané, Rousseau, and Fiedler. Another round that day saw the same winners progress to the eighth-finals. Both Frenchmen were turning in similar 200-meter times to Nothstein.

On Tuesday in the quarterfinals, the same four prevailed for the semifinals a day later.

Nothstein faced his nemesis Fiedler. Reminiscent of their duel in Atlanta, Fiedler took the lead. But this time, off the final turn when Fielder was flying, the Blade arced around, pulled next to Fiedler, and won by a few inches. Nothstein finally pushed away four years of soul-searching to redeem himself.

In their second match, he won even more decisively.

After a short break, on the start line of the best-of-three final Hatton held Nothstein, sitting up straight on his bike, hands on hips, next to Rousseau and his trainer. As the Frenchman went through his facial tics, Nothstein stared ahead and appeared bored. He took deep breaths, rolled his shoulders. He waited till Rousseau, a five-time world champion, reached down and gripped the handlebars. Nothstein counted backward from ten before he grabbed the drops. He turned toward Rousseau with cold eyes.

The official blew a whistle. Rousseau led on the sprinter's lane. Nothstein trailed by a length. One easy lap. Another. The bell rang. Rousseau stood on his pedals and jumped the speed to 40 mph.

On the back straight Nothstein surged in three pedal strokes from behind to alongside Rousseau. Another three pedal revolutions put Nothstein a half-wheel ahead, prodding the Frenchman to go faster.

The audience yelled a wall of sound watching the two men as they flew through the last turns, Rousseau ahead. Around the final turn, Nothstein went wide up the home straight. He blew past Rousseau and won going away.

In their next match, Rousseau led around the final turn like a rocket. Nothstein moved around up the final straight and surged ahead. With fifty meters left, halfway between the last turn and the finish line, he looked back over his shoulder—shooting an icy look of revenge, a dish best served cold.

Jack Simes, the Frank Sinatra of American cycling, mused that what made a difference for Nothstein in Sydney was Hatton holding him on the start line. "Gil is like Angelo Dundee—he knew what to say and when. As they got to the final against Florian Rousseau, Gil spotted Rousseau sitting down on a chair in the infield. Rousseau looked tired. Gil turned to Marty and said: 'That Rousseau, he's blown.' Marty won it then, in his head, before they rode the final."

Nothstein stopped at the finish line, in front of Christi holding Devon, Tyler sitting alert, on the front row of seats. Nothstein lifted his bike over his head and roared as the audience cheered—an image beamed worldwide.

Fiedler defeated Gané in the match for the bronze medal. He joined Nothstein and Rousseau on the podium. Nothstein wore the gold medal around his neck and held a spray of flowers while "The Star-Spangled Banner" played. He won the USAC's only gold medal.

Then he headed to the track for a lap of honor. On impulse, he scooped up Tyler from the audience and took him for a victory lap. Tyler hugged his father's neck and took in the audience cheering.

"That was a handful too," Nothstein said. "I had the gold medal around my neck. I was holding a victory bouquet. It was an incredible feeling of accomplishment. But I realized, too, that I was holding my son, which I had never done before on the bike with the flowers, and I might fall. I briefly worried about that. Yet it worked out. My shoulders felt so much lighter."

23

A Mother, Three Olympics, Three Gold Medals

If everything seems under control,
you're not going fast enough.
—MARIO ANDRETTI

Evie Stevens confirmed her world-hour-record fitness bump in April 2016 in Belgium at La Flèche Wallonne Féminine. After eighty miles the field of 140 starters had shredded to seven leaders, including her and compatriot and Boels-Dolman teammate Megan Guarnier when defending champion Anna van der Breggen attacked at the base of the classic's beastly steep Mur de Huy. Only Stevens could go with her.

"Anna didn't mess around with that attack," Stevens told *Cyclingnews*. "Even anticipating the move, it wasn't easy to follow her." She and Van der Breggen, an Olympic prospect from the Netherlands, dueled to the hilltop finish.

Van der Breggen's round face and cherubic smile gave no hint of her fierce competitiveness. She came from a cycling family and began racing at age seven. Off the bike, she let her long blonde hair tumble below her shoulders; before she strapped on her helmet, she pulled her locks back in a braid. She developed into a powerful climber and explosive sprinter. At the 2015 worlds in Richmond, Virginia, she narrowly lost the road race. Sportswriters in the Netherlands named her best Dutch woman cyclist of the year.

She and Stevens appeared evenly matched up the Mur, twenty seconds in front of a chase group. Both were Flèche Wallonne Féminine winners and the same size—they could switch bikes without altering the height of the saddle or handlebars. Like Stevens, Van der Breggen was a college grad, with a nursing degree from Windesheim University, including an internship in Ghana. One difference was that Van der Breggen, twenty-six, was defending champion and seven years younger.

Midway up the pitiless ascent and through the S-shaped curve rising to a muscle-burning 26 percent pitch, Van der Breggen gained several bike lengths. Stevens powered back up to her rear wheel. The Dutch rider storm-surged ahead. Once more, Stevens caught her. Another Van der Breggen burst opened a gap, but Stevens bridged to her wheel. A hundred meters from the finish, Van der Breggen gutted out one more jump and finally soloed ahead to win by eight seconds.

Megan Guarnier followed fourteen seconds later, in third.

Guarnier held an advantage over Stevens. At the 2015 worlds road race in Richmond, Guarnier's bronze medal automatically secured her berth on the USAC team going to the Rio de Janeiro Olympics. The USAC Olympic selection committee was choosing twenty-one men and women for the road, track, mountain bike, and BMX events based on a series of results rather than one-day national championships.

After losing La Flèche Wallonne Féminine, Stevens told journalists that if she had won, she believed she would have earned a spot on the USAC team. She faced pressure to make the squad when she went in late May to the Amgen Women's Tour of California, a four-day 195-mile competition, from South Lake Tahoe to Sacramento. It served as the de facto USAC Olympic trials for the women's four road-racing slots and two time-trial openings. California's event was on the UCI's Women's WorldTour calendar.

Guarnier won the Women's Tour of California, seventeen seconds ahead of Kristin Armstrong, and twenty-eight seconds up on Stevens in third. Mara Abbott of Boulder won the Queen of the Mountains jersey as best climber.

In June the USAC announced those four women were selected for the Olympic road race; Armstrong, gold medalist in the previous two Olympic time trials, and Stevens were also picked for the time trial. By contrast, only two men were named for the road and time trial races:

Taylor Phinney and Brent Bookwalter of Ashville, North Carolina, and a graduate of Lees-McRae College.

Guarnier, Stevens, and Abbott traveled to Gaiarine, Italy, for the Giro d'Italia Femminile, a ten-day, 533-mile trek across Italy's mountainous north. Over twenty-seven years, many high-profile women's multiday tours had come and gone, including the women's Tour de France. Italy's annual elite event had endured through rebranding as the Giro Donne, the Giro Rosa, and the Giro d'Italia Femminile. The longstanding men's Giro rated as the second grand tour, but the Femminile emerged as the premier women's grand tour. It was part of the UCI Women's WorldTour and drew twenty-three teams of six riders each, representing three continents.

The Giro d'Italia Femminile opened July 1 with a 1.2-mile prologue in Gaiarine, thirty miles north of Venice. Leah Kirchmann of Canada triumphed by one second over Dutch women Thalita de Jong and defending champion Van der Breggen. Guarnier came in fourth, three seconds down; Stevens scored tenth, trailing by six seconds. Kirchmann donned the race leader's *maglia rosa*, the "pink jersey."

Stage 1's sixty-five-mile run from Gaiarine to San Fior went to Giorgia Bronzini of Italy, edging Guarnier as Stevens and Abbott finished in the top ten. Guarnier rose to first overall, usurping the *maglia rosa*. Stevens jumped to fifth. Abbott, on the British Wiggle-High5 Pro Cycling Team, held tenth.

On stage 2, a sixty-nine-mile leg, Stevens won in a breakaway with Abbott and two others. Stevens gained twenty-four seconds over Guarnier to take over as the leader in the *maglia rosa*. Guarnier held third, eighteen seconds behind Stevens; Abbott claimed sixth.

Stevens wore the pink jersey for two days before losing it to Abbott, winner of stage 5 in the mountains, featuring a scenic but strenuous hour-long uphill grind. Guarnier, fourth and thirty-seven seconds down that day, moved up to second overall; Stevens lost two minutes, in ninth, and fell to sixth overall.

Abbott, age thirty, flew up mountains like an eagle. In 2009 she had won the event's green jersey as Queen of the Mountains. The next year she became the first U.S. woman to win overall. She was to the women's

Giro what Andy Hampsten had been to the men's Giro—Americans who beat Italians on their own turf.

Stage 6 went the longest distance, seventy-four miles, from Andora to the Madonna della Guardia hill summit above Alassio. Stevens attacked in the closing miles and won, six seconds up on Guarnier; Van der Breggen took third, nineteen seconds later. Abbott crossed the line fifty-three seconds down for fifth. The day concluded with Guarnier as overall leader, wresting back the *maglia rosa*. Stevens stood second overall, Abbott in third—giving U.S. women the top three spots.

Stevens won stage 7's exhausting individual time trial over a hilly and twisting 13.6 miles. She finished four seconds faster than runner-up Van der Breggen and twenty-nine seconds quicker than Guarnier, fourth. Guarnier still held the *maglia rosa* by thirty-four seconds over Stevens, second overall.

The two compatriots clashed like Dartmouth versus Middlebury. Some scribes questioned Stevens's tactics in stages 2 and 6 for attacking her Boels-Dolman teammate Guarnier on the road. All the while, Van der Breggen nipped at their heels in third place overall, with Abbott fourth.

Even though Guarnier and Stevens had lost two teammates—one crashed out, the other withdrew due to illness—their remaining two teammates helped keep them in the top two spots. The final day in Verbania, at the top of Italy's boot shape, noisy fans created a deafening roar as the women sped around the stage 9 circuit race of sixty-five miles. Guarnier and Stevens cruised in the pack and clinched their one-two general classification finish.

The podium held La Flèche Wallonne Féminine déjà vu. This time, Guarnier won, Stevens locked second place, and Van der Breggen took third. Guarnier stood grinning in the *maglia rosa*, gripped a spray of flowers, and shot her arms up in victory.

Abbott claimed fifth; Canadian Leah Kirchmann finished eighth.

The U.S. women's road team was primed for the Rio Olympics.

• • •

Rio de Janeiro, on Brazil's Atlantic coast, gave the world swinging bossa nova music and rhythmic samba dance steps. The Rio Olympics opened on August 5, the first Games held in South America. A total of 205 nations sent more than eleven thousand athletes to compete in 306 events in twenty-eight sports—among them eighteen cycling events contested by riders from 80 nations.

The road race circuit featured seashore-flat stretches and inland hills so steep the course ranked as the toughest in Olympic cycling history. The route featured a mile-long section of cobblestones bumpy enough to knock chains off sprockets and cause more mechanical mischief.

Megan Guarnier as team captain, Stevens, and Kristin Armstrong agreed the road race favored their climbing specialist, Mara Abbott, five foot five and 115 pounds. Guarnier, Stevens, and Armstrong would sacrifice themselves for Abbott.

On Sunday, August 7, the women's eighty-eight-mile road race took off outside Fort Copacabana and sped along the crescent of iconic Copacabana Beach. They rode a shorter version of the men's course the previous day, when Brent Bookwalter finished sixteenth and Taylor Phinney pulled out to save his legs for the individual time trial three days later.

Guarnier, Stevens, and Armstrong raced more than three hours to protect Abbott—chasing down breakaway attempts, including the formidable Marianne Vos of the Netherlands, and shielding Abbott from the wind while keeping her near the head of the pack. The unrelenting speed and hills decimated the field of sixty-eight starters to a front group of ten.

At twelve miles to go, the leaders heaved up the final steep climb. Armstrong abandoned to focus on the individual time trial. Guarnier and Stevens guided Abbott at the front. Near the summit, Abbott and Dutch rider Annemiek van Vleuten, a national time trial champion in her second Olympics, dashed over the top and charged downhill as rain began to splash on the pavement.

Abbott and Van Vleuten vanished from sight around a curve. In the final seven miles Van Vleuten exploited a precipitous descent on slick pavement cutting through a forest. Her derring-do forced Abbott to back off, sitting up, letting the wind blunt her pace.

The tires of a car carrying officials preceding Van Vleuten screeched around a sharp bend. She owned the road. Negotiating the bend, she slammed at 50 mph against a concrete curb. She catapulted off the bike and landed face down on the pavement, her body as motionless as the trees at her feet.

Abbott dashed past and hoped her fallen rival would soon recover. Van Vleuten remained unmoving as a half-dozen road guards on motorcycles arrived. They spread along the road and yelled to caution the approaching riders.

Van Vleuten regained consciousness as paramedics put her on a gurney and lifted it into the ambulance. It roared away, lights flashing, siren blaring. (A month after back surgery for three broken vertebrae, she resumed racing.)

Abbott, a role model for Americans fighting anorexia, time trialed for all she was worth on the coastal road back to the Fort Copacabana finish. Crowds grew deeper and louder in each closing mile.

Less than a minute behind, Van Vleuten's teammate Anna van der Breggen, along with Emma Johansson of Sweden and Elisa Longo Borghini of Italy formed a chase group pursuing the lone Abbott.

Abbott gutted her way through the miles, never considering she could win—until she streaked past the 200-meter sign, in sight of the finish banner. "I thought, 'Oh my God, this is going to happen,'" she told an NBC reporter.

But the chasing trio caught her at 150 meters. Nearly four hours of racing came down to a four-way sprint for three medals. The contestants rose from their saddles, throwing their bikes back and forth under them with each ferocious down stroke. Abbott watched helplessly as the podium finishers pulled ahead.

In the final fifty meters, Van der Breggen led Johansson, tucked on her rear wheel, followed by Longo Borghini. Van der Breggen beat Johansson to the line and thrust her arms overhead as Johansson grabbed her bars and slumped.

Abbott finished fourth, haggard and heartbroken, but proud of her performance. Guarnier followed in eleventh; Stevens twelfth.

• • •

The last chance for Team USA to score a medal on the road rested in the time trials on Wednesday, August 10—a rainy, windy day. The circuit of 29.8 kilometers (18.5 miles) traversed rolling and twisting roads and two difficult climbs, but no cobblestones. In the absence of flat or straight sections, the course translated in cycling vernacular as technical—stressing bike-handling skills over physical strength.

It was ladies first as the women's time trial began in the morning. Rain had washed oil residue from the pavement but wet and windy conditions prevailed. The media buzzed about race favorite Van der Breggen on the brink of a possible road-race-and-time-trial historic double gold.

Another favorite was hour-record-holder Stevens. "It's a wild course," she said. "It's got everything."

Kristin Armstrong, despite gold medals in the time trial at Beijing and London, was widely overlooked. The mother of a five-year-old son worked full time in communications for a Boise, Idaho, hospital, which limited international travel. At the Richmond worlds, she had finished fifth in the time trial. Now she was racing the day before her forty-third birthday. Yet she felt confident.

"I want a third gold medal," she told Caley Fretz of *VeloNews*. "I really like this course. I like the undulations. I like the challenges. I like the variability."

Stevens's risk-averse nature through the gauntlet of curves and wind gusts, compounded by struggling up a climb, cost her valuable seconds. The elements differed radically from her world hour record in controlled conditions.

Armstrong could read the course's geometry—spotting tangents to shave time and exploiting ups and downs. Pushing her body to its physical edge, her nose started to bleed. She felt motivated by Abbott's courage and pedaled as hard as she could until she crossed the finish line. Exhausted, she gingerly dismounted and set her bike down before sitting like a folding yardstick on the wet pavement, chest heaving. Paramedics rushed to her.

"Did I win?" she asked. Upon hearing she indeed had, she burst into tears.

She won by five seconds, less than fifty yards, over a Russian, eleven seconds faster than Van der Breggen, and a minute and a half quicker than Stevens, tenth place.

Armstrong made U.S. Olympic history as the first woman to claim three Olympic gold medals in the same event.

When medical attendants pronounced she was all right, her son, Lucas, toddled over. They hugged each other tight.

In the men's time trial that afternoon Phinney, in his third Olympics, looked to improve on his fourth place in London. More than wanting to medal for the United States, he sought to earn a podium finish like his parents.

Taylor Phinney and Bookwalter time trialed two laps on the same course as the women. Phinney and Bookwalter finished twenty-second and twenty-third.

Connor Fields of Plano, Texas, won the gold medal in the men's BMX race, the first U.S. rider to win the BMX Olympics gold, and the only male cyclist to take home a medal from Rio. Alise "the Beast" Post of St. Cloud, Minnesota, attained a silver medal in the women's BMX race.

On the track, Californian Sarah Hammer scored a silver medal in the women's omnium—four short races, including a time trial. She won another silver in the team pursuit with Chloé Dygert, Jennifer Valente, and Kelly Catlin.

The two gold and three silver medals put the United States in third place of twenty-one nations that won medals in Olympic cycling.

• • •

In August Stevens announced she would retire from racing at the end of the season and resume a career in finance. She qualified to represent the United States in the elite women's road race and team time trial at the UCI worlds in October in Doha, the capital of Qatar, on the coast of the Persian Gulf. She chose the team time trial with her Boels-Dolmans sisters for her final race.

Eight women's professional teams of six riders opened the week-long program. Flat roads sliced through desert sand. Daytime temperatures pushed past 100 degrees. The route began at the Lusail National Sports Complex, surrounded by modern residential and commercial skyscrapers like a pumped-up Manhattan, and finished in the city's outskirts, on an artificial island, Pearl-Qatar.

Several teams fell apart as a result of combatting crosswinds and heat. Anna van der Breggen's Rabo-Liv team finished last after a teammate clipped a metal barrier and crashed, throwing the squad into disarray.

Stevens was the only U.S. rider on the Boels-Dolmans team, in orange-and-yellow colors, with two Dutch women, a Canadian, a Brit, and one from Luxembourg. They rode a flawless rotation, each taking her turn for just a few seconds at the front before pulling to the side and dropping neatly to the rear. They averaged a swift 30 mph and needed less than forty-nine minutes to win by almost a minute. Stevens claimed her fourth gold medal in the women's team time trial at UCI road worlds.

Phinney on the BMC Racing Team with Joey Rosskopf of Decatur, Georgia, and teammates from three other countries took home a silver medal in the team time trial.

In the women's individual time trial, Amber Neben won the gold medal.

Stevens retired from racing at the top of her game. "I rode for the best teams, with the best women, and the best equipment," she told Bonnie D. Ford of ESPN in an interview looking back over her seven-year career. "I didn't accomplish all of my goals, but I got the chance to go after them."

The queen of the oval hour retired from the sport with her world hour record intact to challenge the next generation.

24

The Summing Up

Everything changes and nothing remains still.

—PLATO, *Cratylus*

American cycling, like painting, has gone through many periods. My interviews with more than a thousand cyclists, embracing careers stretching back to 1908, in Alf Goullet's case, through the 2016 Rio Olympics, impressed me that James Armando had been correct in his biting complaints that my heroes in the early 1960s didn't know real bicycle racing.

We were part of the sport's phoenix-like resurgence. Our premier events were downtown fifty-mile criteriums, from the Tour of Somerville in New Jersey to the Nevada City Classic in California. Crits mixed speed, stamina, and bike-handling skills in a speeding pack trying to beat two hours, an average of 25 mph.

On Memorial Day in 1964, Hans Wolf won the Tour of Somerville and broke two hours, 1:59:43, an unofficial record (only times on tracks are official). Like others in the loose-knit cycling community, I learned about this from another rider, who may or may not have been there, but, if he wasn't, heard from someone else and shared the news. We relied on word of mouth. Wolf's time meant as much to us as when English runner Roger Bannister broke the mythical four-minute-mile barrier.

Wolf, a German-born naturalized U.S. citizen living in New York, wore the black-and-white colors of the German Bicycle Club. He inspired us.

His unofficial record didn't last long. Jack Simes II won the 1967 Tour of Somerville with a time of 1:56:14. Californian Ron Skarin, a three-time Olympian and Pan-Am Games track gold medalist, shattered it in the 1974 Tour of Somerville: 1:54:01.

A decade later I sat in the James Madison Memorial Building of the Library of Congress, turning the squeaky handle advancing a reluctant spool of microfilm on a balky gray metal machine. I read Damon Runyon's articles in the *New York American* of 1920s six-days in Madison Square Garden. A thunderbolt seemed to strike. Runyon, one of the most influential scribes in gray fedoras punching index fingers on manual typewriter keys, reported cyclists cruised under 2 hours for the first fifty miles—and they had 142 more hours to go.

A *Newark Evening News* booklet of American cycling records published in 1930 listed Goullet's fifty-mile record set on the Newark Velodrome: 1:49:08. The date was August 19, 1920. He would have gained an incredible ten-minute margin over Wolf—at least four miles. How could Goullet and his brothers on wheels go so fast? Why didn't we know about it?

Goullet was carrying on a tradition going back to the first national cycling championships on Memorial Day in 1880 in Newport, Rhode Island. Every year riders rode faster and lowered records until the 1930s Great Depression. The golden days of American track cycling disappeared like biplanes, player pianos, running boards from cars, gloves for women, and hats for men.

In 1985 I asked Goullet about the fifty-mile record he'd set. He relaxed with a chilled can of beer, sitting in a comfortable chair in his living room. He looked preppy in a white button-down shirt and slacks with a sharp crease.

"Fifty miles was an unusual distance," he said. Promoter John M. Chapman favored shorter, faster events to keep audiences engaged. To offer something different, he devised a program featuring a fifty-miler that promised a world record. Up for grabs was a purse of $1,000—worth $13,000 today—paying $500 to the winner, when factory workers earned $6 a week.

The August sun glowed as an orange ball on the western horizon at the start of the 300-lap battle, contested by more than a dozen pros. The infield band belted out lively tunes like "Alexander's Ragtime Band" and "I Wish I Could Shimmy Like My Sister Kate." Onlookers pulled out wallets and donated folding money for lap primes that kept an official ringing the bell for another lap prime—cash to the rider who put his front wheel first over the line.

"They kept the pace high," Goullet said. "On the last lap, I won the sprint. I set the record."

The so-called world record was showbiz to sell tickets. But it was set on a track certified at six laps to the mile. In the 1976 Tour of Somerville, Dave Boll of Stanford, California, won in 1:47:18 to finally better Goullet's mark.

Faster speeds continued to punctuate American cycling—assisted by lighter equipment, better training methods, corporate sponsorships, and greater resources from USA Cycling.

Armando had disparaged the state of American racing in the 1960s. Cycling's historic past is a long succession of overlapping wheels. The great George M. Hendee racked up five straight national titles in the early 1880s on high-wheelers. Arthur Zimmerman shifted to modern safety bicycles. He beat countrymen and foreigners for the sprint title at the inaugural worlds in 1893 in Chicago, which launched today's UCI worlds. George Banker accompanied Zim to France. In 1898 Banker became the first American to win the world pro sprint title, in Vienna, Austria. A year later, in Montreal, Major Taylor succeeded Banker as world champion. Iver Lawson and Marcus Hurley won the pro and amateur titles in 1904 in London. Frank Kramer won the 1912 worlds in Newark.

More than half a century passed before Audrey McElmury spun through the rain in Brno, Czechoslovakia, to claim the 1969 world women's road racing championship. Michigan track sprinters Sheila Young-Ochowicz, Sue Novara, and Connie Paraskevin-Young won closets of rainbow jerseys before Greg LeMond triumphed in the 1983 worlds road race in Altenrhein, Switzerland—followed by winning the Tour de France three years later.

From one generation to the next, riders are connected like legs to their torsos. All that separates cyclists today from those of the past is a series of overlapped wheels.

American cycling emerged from its doldrums to internationally competitive levels through generations of men and women building on what they inherited. If Armando could watch from the sidelines today, he would likely nod with begrudging appreciation and announce: it took long enough!

ACKNOWLEDGMENTS

Writing this history of American cycling was like assembling a giant puzzle, yielding a rich load of Americana and stories of struggle, agony, and triumph that kept me going. I am indebted to countless men and women riders, family members, coaches, announcers, and officials who over several decades generously shared personal experiences. They deepened my understanding of the sport, its players competing in plain sight or toiling in the background, and its unique allure.

Special thanks to Jack Simes III, Anne Samplonius, Dan Lee, Louise Blum, Ray Cipollini, Vince Menci, Mark and Danielle Typinski, Bobby Walthour, Davis and Connie Carpenter Phinney, Pieter Dehaan, Brodie Hamilton, George Mount, Wayne Stetina, Tom Schuler, Jeff Groman, Bob Bowen, William Brunner, Bruce Donaghy, Bill and Carol McGann, John Meyer, Manny Carbahal, Seth Wolins, Oscar Wastyn Jr., Andy Taus, Debbie Schiff, Richard Olken, John Hess, John Howard, Neal Sandler, Sue Novara, Lorne Shields, Andy Hampsten, Gil Hatton, Nelson Vails, John Eustice, Oscar Swan, and unwavering friends Bob and Janis Keough, Gerry Ives, and Clint and Dar Webb Page.

Many people read drafts and commented, including my Marine Corps sharpshooter friend Lawrence Herman, Pete "Swanee" Swan, John and Owen Mulholland, Mel Pinto, Matt Koschara, M. G. Lord, Joseph Esposito, and Bob Plumb. Bob Keough proofread the manuscript and brought his deep American history knowledge to the task. I feel fortunate to have had John Wilcockson, the dean of English-speaking cycling journalists and authors, as copyeditor and for sharing nuances, insights, and historic material gained from his decades of global reportage. And thank you to my good friend for the index.

This second edition owes its existence to Rob Taylor and Courtney Ochsner at the University of Nebraska Press, and builds on the 1988 edition published under the editorial guidance of Mary Cunnane at W. W. Norton.

I want to express gratitude to the Library of Congress for preserving newspapers on microfilm and stacks of bound volumes of magazines that captured so much of what has taken place so that we can look back and learn.

Finally, I thank my son, Trevor, and wife, Valerie, for kindness, patience, and understanding.

BIBLIOGRAPHY

Abt, Samuel. *Breakaway: On the Road with the Tour de France.* New York: Random House, 1985.

Armstrong Kelly, Linda. *No Mountain High Enough: Raising Lance, Raising Me.* With Joni Rodgers. New York: Crown Archetype, 2005.

Arnold, Peter. *History of Boxing.* Secaucus NJ: Chartwell Books, 1985.

Balf, Todd. *Major: A Black Athlete, a White Era, and the Fight to Be the World's Fastest Human Being.* New York: Three Rivers Press, 2009.

Bardgett, Walter. "The Bicycle Racing Stars of the Nineteenth Century Assn. Reverently Honor the Memory of 'Major' Taylor." *American Bicyclist and Motorcyclist*, July 1948, p. 32.

Bassons, Christophe. *A Clean Break: My Story.* With Benoît Hopquin. New York: Bloomsbury Sport, 2015.

Borysewicz, Edward. *Bicycle Road Racing: Complete Program for Training and Competition.* Brattleboro VT: Velo-News, 1986.

Brady, William A. *The Fighting Man.* Indianapolis: Bobbs-Merrill, 1916.

———. *Showman.* New York: E. P. Dutton, 1937.

Breyer, Victor. "Arthur Zimmerman—Greatest Pedaller of All Time." *Cycling Weekly* (London), April 30, 1947, pp. 336–37.

———. "The Great Parade." *American Bicyclist and Motorcyclist*, December 1955, p. 117.

"Champion on Wheels: Harlem Youth Is Star Cyclist after Only Four Years' Racing." *Ebony Magazine*, September 1967, pp. 108–13.

Chany, Pierre. *La Fabuleuse Histoire du Cyclisme: 1. Des Origines à 1955.* Paris: Nathan, 1988.

Coffey, Steve. "Crashes, but Fine Racing!" *Cyclist*, September 25, 1971, pp. 2–3.

Connor, Dick. "F. Don Miller: The Colonel Leaves a Legacy." *Olympian Magazine*, February 1985, pp. 4–7.

Dempsey, Jack. *Dempsey.* With Barbara Piattelli. New York: Harper & Row, 1977.

de Visé, Daniel. *The Comeback: Greg LeMond, the True King of American Cycling, and a Legendary Tour de France.* New York: Atlantic Monthly Press, 2018.

Dickow, Ray. "Round and Round and Roundsteak." *Butcher Workman*, May 1957, pp. 6–8.

Durso, Joseph. *Madison Square Garden: 100 Years of History*. New York: Simon and Schuster, 1979.

Eisele, Otto, ed. *Cycling Almanac*. New York: 1950.

———, ed. *Cycling Almanac*. New York, 1951.

———, ed. *Cycling Almanac*. New York, 1952.

———, ed. *Cycling Almanac*. New York, 1953.

———, ed. *Cycling Almanac*. New York, 1954.

———. "A History of the Amateur Bicycle League of America, Inc." In *Review of Cycling*, edited by Watson N. Nordquist, 18–25. 1943.

Finison, Lorenz J. *Boston's Cycling Craze, 1880–1900: A Story of Race, Sport, and Society*. Amherst: University of Massachusetts Press, 2014.

Fitzpatrick, Jim. *Major Taylor in Australia*. Karana Downs, Queensland, Australia: Star Hill Studio, 2011.

Gabriele, Michael C. *The Golden Age of Bicycle Racing in New Jersey*. Charleston SC: History Press, 2011.

Gilles, Roger. *Women on the Move: The Forgotten Era of Women's Bicycle Racing*. Lincoln: University of Nebraska Press, 2018.

Goddard, Stephen B. *Colonel Albert Pope and His American Dream Machines: The Life and Times of a Bicycle Tycoon Turned Automotive Pioneer*. Jefferson NC: McFarland, 2008.

Goullet, Alfred T., and Charles J. McGuirk. "The Infernal Grind." *Saturday Evening Post*, May 29, 1926, pp. 18–19, 181.

Held, John, Jr. *The Most of John Held Jr.* Foreword by Marc Connelly. Introduction by Carl J. Weinhardt. Brattleboro VT: Stephen Greene Press, 1972.

———. *Outlines of Sport*. New York: E. P. Dutton, 1930.

Hemingway, Ernest. *A Moveable Feast*. New York: Scribner, 1973.

Herlihy, David V. *Bicycle: The History*. New Haven CT: Yale University Press, 2006.

Hincapie, George, and Craig Hummer. *The Loyal Lieutenant: My Story, Leading Out Lance and Pushing through Pain on the Rocky Road to Paris*. New York: William Morrow, 2014.

Homan, Andrew M. *Life in the Slipstream: The Legend of Bobby Walthour Sr.* Washington DC: Potomac Books, 2011.

Hovis, Joe. "Disney, Neiman, and Metzler, National Champions." *Staten Island Transcript*, September 20, 1957, p. 1.

Hurne, Ralph. *The Yellow Jersey*. New York: Breakaway Books, 1996.

Karr, Mary. *The Art of Memoir*. New York: Harper, 2015.

Keene, Judy. "Marshall Taylor—Bike Champ from Indianapolis." *Indianapolis Magazine*, May 1977, pp. 41–54.

Kiernan, John. *The American Sporting Scene*. New York: Macmillan, 1941.

Kimmage, Paul. *Rough Ride: Behind the Wheel with a Pro Cyclist*. New York: Yellow Jersey Press, 2007.

Krabbé, Tim. *The Rider*. New York: Bloomsbury, 2003.

Kranish, Michael. *The World's Fastest Man: The Extraordinary Life of Cyclist Major Taylor, America's First Black Sports Hero*. New York: Scribner, 2019.

Lacy, Robert. *Ford: The Men and the Machine*. Boston: Little, Brown, 1986.
LaMarre, Thomas S. "One Piece at a Time: The Cars of C.H. Metz." *Automobile Quarterly* 32, (November 3, 1994): 4–19.
Lee, Dan. *The Belgian Hammer: Forging Young Americans into Professional Cyclists*. New York: Breakaway Books, 2011.
Levine, Peter. *A.G. Spalding and the Rise of Baseball: The Promise of American Sport*. New York: Oxford University Press, 1985.
Liebling, A. J. *The Sweet Science*. New York: North Point Press, 2004.
Litsky, Frank. "Avery Brundage of Olympics Dies." *New York Times*, May 9, 1975, p. 1.
Lucas, Robert. "The World's Fastest Bicycle Racer." *Negro Digest*, May 1948, pp. 10–13.
L'Union Cycliste Internationale. *Cinquantenaire de L'Union Cycliste Internationale, 1900–1950*. Paris: L'Union Cycliste Internationale.
Macur, Juliet. *Cycle of Lies: The Fall of Lance Armstrong*. New York: HarperCollins, 2014.
McCullagh, James C., ed. *American Bicycle Racing*. Emmaus PA: Rodale, 1976.
McCullough, David. *The Wright Brothers*. New York: Simon & Schuster, 2015.
McKay, Feargal. "Revolutionary Times—The Birth of the Women's Hour Record." Podium Café, September 11, 2018.
Mendel, Harry. "Frank Kramer's Life Story. How Kramer Entered the Professional Ranks. What Taylor's 'Roll' Did," *Motorcycle Illustrated*, January 6, 1916, pp. 49–50.
Morand, Paul. *Open All Night*. New York: Thomas Seltzer, 1923.
Murphy, Charles M. *A Story of the Railroad and a Bicycle: When "A Mile a Minute" Was Born*. New York: Jamaica Law Printing, 1936.
Neiman Baranet, Nancy. *The Turned Down Bar*. Philadelphia: Dorrance, 1964.
Ottum, Bob. "Lure of the Wild White Noise." *Sports Illustrated*, September 14, 1964, pp. 22–25.
Pavelka, Ed. *Ten Years of Championship Bicycle Racing, 1972–1981*. Brattleboro VT: Velo-News, 1983.
Phinney, Davis, and Austin Murphy. *The Happiness of Pursuit: A Father's Courage, a Son's Love and Life's Steepest Climb*. New York: Houghton Mifflin Harcourt, 2011.
Rickard, Maxine Hodges. *Everything Happened to Him: The Story of Tex Rickard*. With Arch Oboler. New York: Frederick A. Stokes, 1936.
Ritchie, Andrew. *Flying Yankee: The International Cycling Career of Arthur Augustus Zimmerman*. Cheltenham, UK: John Pinkerton Memorial Publishing, 2009.
———. *Major Taylor: The Extraordinary Career of a Champion Bicycle Racer*. San Francisco: Bicycle Books, 1988.
Samuels, Charles. *The Magnificent Rube: The Life and Gaudy Times of Tex Rickard*. New York: McGraw-Hill, 1957.
Sinsabaugh, Chris. *Who, Me? Forty Years of Automobile History*. Detroit: Arnold-Powers, 1940.
Taylor, Marshall W. "Major." *The Fastest Bicycle Rider in the World*. Worcester MA: Wormley Publishing, 1928.
Walsh, David. *Seven Deadly Sins: My Pursuit of Lance Armstrong*. New York: Atria Books, 2015.

Wheatcroft, Geoffrey. *Le Tour: A History of the Tour de France*. London: Pocket Books, 2007.
Wilcockson, John. *Lance: The Making of the World's Greatest Athlete*. Boston: Da Capo Press, 2009.
Williams, G. Grant. "Marshall Walter Taylor: The World Famous Bicycle Rider." *Colored American Magazine*, September 1902, pp. 336–45.
Woodland, Les. *The Crooked Path to Victory: Drugs and Cheating in Professional Bicycle Racing*. San Francisco: Van der Plas, 2003.
Zimmerman, A. A., and John M. Erwin. *Zimmerman Abroad and Points on Training*. Chicago: Blakely Printing, 1895.
Zimmerman, Arthur Augustus. *Zimmerman on Training: Points for Cyclists*. Leicester, UK, 1893.

INDEX

Italicized figure numbers refer to illustrations following page 244.